Ex Libris

Randy Manning

Law and Resistance

Law and Resistance

American Attitudes Toward Authority

Edited by
Laurence Veysey

◆ *HARPER TORCHBOOKS*
Harper & Row, Publishers
New York, Evanston, and London

First HARPER TORCHBOOKS edition published 1970

Library of Congress Catalog Card Number: 74–114618

For Sheila and John

Contents

PART ONE.   ARGUMENT OVER
THE NATURE AND LIMITS OF AUTHORITY

Three Classic Traditions

Perspectives on Freedom During the Period
of Industrialization

PART TWO. PATTERNS OF CONFRONTATION OUTSIDE THE LAW

Extralegal Majorities

Extralegal Resistance

PART THREE. THE POLICE AS CONTEMPORARY SYMBOL OF AUTHORITY

Preface

America is moving through a disturbing period in its history. Violent social protest has flared to unusual levels. On all sides emotions are running high. A strong mood of reaction in the name of "law and order" has recently taken shape, dominating the mind of the majority. Yet this demand has in turn provoked new arguments—for instance, over the legitimate scope of civil disobedience on the one side and the legitimate role of the police in urban neighborhoods on the other. The police, the draft, and the tactics of protesters have caused a great many Americans to ponder in fundamental terms the individual's relation to the state.

"Law and order" has been rather unthinkingly promoted as a popular slogan, and its significance as a concept may indeed be challenged (see the Introduction). But the basic issue to which it refers—that of the subject's duty to obey, or political obligation—is a central and time-honored one both in political sociology and in the history of political thought. As the entire American social system comes to be challenged by increasingly militant minority groups, bedrock matters of legitimacy and loyalty are bound to come to the fore in persons' imaginations.

Of course such questions never arise in isolation. They are always closely tied to substantive attitudes, prejudices, and conflicts, and to competing ethical codes. Therefore, though the present volume focuses upon the issue of obedience to law, it does not define this in a narrow fashion. It seeks also to illuminate the deeper attitudes and the more specific cleavages in modern America which have brought this theme into prominence.

The book opens with an introduction and a speculative essay of my own about American patterns of thinking and behavior on freedom and lawlessness—asking especially how these patterns managed to jell so markedly during the early period of our history. The first part of the volume consists of selected philosophical arguments on these topics, written over the last century and a third by a highly varied group of Americans, many of them well known, others undeservedly obscure. What this amounts to is an extended debate between a number of so-called conservatives, liberals, and radicals on the role of the individual in relation to authority. The next section of the book contains a group of first-hand documents which describe actual episodes of lawlessness in American history, intended to illustrate the practical consequences of disobedience in different social circumstances. The final readings focus on the controversial role of the police in recent years, giving space both to police spokesmen and their critics.

I have not aimed at systematic coverage in the text. Almost any reader glancing at the table of contents will immediately be able to think of major aspects of American life which are neglected. The extralegal qualities of the Southern caste system and of the Northern big-city racket, the struggle for liberty among astrologers, faith healers, and enthusiasts for erotic liberation, the behavior of soldiers in wartime, delinquent gangs, and drug users—all these topics suggest further ways in which one might approach attitudes toward law and authority in this society.

Nor have I spent much time in trying to define such basic terms as "freedom," "authority," "liberalism," or "radicalism." I am aware that I have often employed them in a free-and-easy fashion. But these words constitute a series of well-scarred academic battlefields over which I have felt it best to tread lightly, avoiding temptations to enter the semantic debates which are the staple of political science. I have sought instead to glean what appeared to be the most striking patterns of evidence, with the aim of putting together a variegated but reasonably balanced collage.

Yet I also hope this book may be considered a very modest part of an effort—now visible in many quarters—to rethink the meaning of American history, both in the direction of more contemporary relevance and greater clearheadedness. Younger historians are becoming aware of the extent to which nationalistic assumptions have unconsciously affected the judgment of even the most alert and "liberal" professional scholars in viewing every phase of the American past.[1] There is a growing belief that nationalistic and racialistic emotions and goals should be explicitly indicated as major factors in producing many of our recent troubles, rather than allowing these motives to be tacitly (or even beneficently) assumed. An important trend is under way which may gradually result in the rewriting of American history so that it more closely resembles that of the Roman Empire. What this means is that we are achieving a critical distance from ourselves which the historians of few other countries have ever approached. And we are at the same time arriving at a historical vision which, despite its bleakness, may be deeply relevant to an understanding of the contemporary national and global situation.

Thus, ironically, the study of history sometimes gains its relevance by sparking a sense of genuine liberation from the past. The very act of reading in detail what men formerly said and did may help to free us from an unthinking acceptance of those earlier ideas and values. It may make us realize how much we would like to separate ourselves from previous generations by giving us a vivid awareness of the many mistakes we wish we could avoid repeating. Historical study can therefore on occasion be subversive of established traditions, just as in other contexts it can help to conserve them.

Of course these effects, whether in the direction of binding us to the past or of liberating us from it, are the result of the particular forms of moral commitment we bring to our reading of history; they do not flow in automatic fashion from history itself. Here is an important limitation on the contemporary relevance of history which should also be kept in mind. History can profitably connect with an ethical point of view, but it can never serve as a substitute for one, because a moral standpoint is something each person must work out for himself afresh. Historical study can greatly broaden and deepen the perspective of an already committed person; but it cannot, from scratch, tell men whether they should fight in a given war or whether they should remain loyal to their national traditions. If history could really do such things as these, men would have no right to think of themselves as free

1. See, for example, the brilliant article by a Stanford graduate student, John S. Rosenberg, "Toward a New Civil War Revisionism," *American Scholar*, XXXVIII (1969), 250–72.

moral agents. On an ultimate level, therefore, we must never expect too much from history, no matter how exciting and fruitful the current attempt at rewriting it may appear.

But these strictures are less important than many historians and social scientists used to think. It is far more urgent to move ahead in the task of looking clearly and unsentimentally at the American past, taking advantage of the new sense of distance we think we have gained. Beliefs about law, freedom, and authority are obviously central to any such reappraisal, and by pointing to the great variety of what Americans have actually said and done in these respects, I hope this book of readings will help break a little new ground.

I want to thank Peter Euben of the University of California, Santa Cruz; Fred and Jean Matthews of York University; and Richard Frost of Colgate University, all of whom gave me good ideas which are reflected in the contents. A faculty research grant from the University of California at Santa Cruz in 1967 enabled me to make initial contact with some of these materials, especially in the Labadie Collection at the University of Michigan Library, Ann Arbor.

Santa Cruz, California
Cambridge, Massachusetts

Law and Resistance

Introduction: What Does the Theme
of "Law and Order" Mean?

As the question of recurring lawlessness and violence in America
has come to prominence, many have begun to wonder whether
"law and order" is in some sense a peculiarly American problem.
Contradictory generalizations are often put forth—that Americans
are fundamentally peaceful and law-abiding; that on the other hand
they have always been anarchically suspicious of external restraints; that they rarely question the legitimacy of their constitutional system; that, on the contrary, they have debated the rights
and wrongs of coercive legal authority more energetically than
most other peoples.

Has this been a nation of gun-slinging wild men and in-
dividualists? Or one of self-restrained, pragmatic conformists? How
do political and racial violence relate to either of these images?
Americans are no longer sure of their collective identity in these
terms. The historical record is beginning to be re-examined with
this kind of query in mind.[1]

Naturally there are no simple answers which stand up to serious
analysis. The problem of American responses to law and authority
is a complex one which necessarily leads in many directions. It is
entangled, at the very outset, with the still larger issue of national
character as such. Whether certain character traits can confidently
be ascribed to entire societies, particularly over long periods of
time, remains a matter on which historians and social scientists
have profoundly disagreed during the past several decades.[2] The

1. See especially Hugh Davis Graham and Ted Robert Gurr, *Violence
in America: Historical and Comparative Perspectives* (New York: Bantam
Books, 1969), which contains much indispensable and hitherto unavailable
factual information.

2. See, for example, David M. Potter, *People of Plenty* (Chicago: University of Chicago Press, 1954), for a discussion of this theme. There
seems to be a more general willingness to use the concept now than there
was a decade or two ago.

1

existence of this debate should caution us at the start to avoid defining American traditions too casually or sweepingly. But, even if we decide that such arguments ought not to detain us— partly because lawlessness should be a relatively easy character trait to identify—still the question of American attitudes toward law, violence, and extralegal resistance remains a difficult one.

It involves, for instance, the basic notion of continuity in American history. What is the relevance of frontier violence, Indian warfare, or even rural vigilantism, to the tensions and upheavals facing an urban, industrialized America in the latter part of the twentieth century? If it is misleading, as most historians now think, to explain Hitler's rise to power on the basis of German conditions a century or two ago, then is it not equally absurd to emphasize connections between the pre-industrial "anarchy" of the Wild West and the militance, say, of Eldridge Cleaver or LeRoi Jones? A respectable school of sociological opinion states that the process of industrialization creates a new kind of personality, so-called industrial man.[3] According to this line of reasoning, violence and civil disobedience are the products of a given socioeconomic system—its internal strains and conflicts—and not primarily of a cultural heritage. The proper topic of inquiry therefore should be lawlessness in the entire Western industrial world at a given moment in its structural growth.

But if the United States is presently the world's leading example of a modern, industrial, or "mass" society, the course of its development has long been recognized, by Karl Marx among many others, as in major respects quite an exceptional one, and one in which the continuity between pre-industrial and more recent patterns has been pronounced. As early as the pre-Civil War generation, American ways of thinking and acting are apt to seem strikingly familiar to us. One already finds among most Americans of that time a characteristically paradoxical combination of openness, fluidity, and egalitarianism, along with exploitativeness, soaring patriotism, and a persistent harshness toward outsiders, especially nonwhites. This portrait commonly remains our own.

3. Alex Inkeles, "Industrial Man," *American Journal of Sociology*, LXVI (1960), 1–31. In a very different and apocalyptic way the writings of Erich Fromm and Herbert Marcuse also make this assumption, which is really that of the Marxist tradition in general.

Thinking back to the history of slavery, we realize that long before industrialization, many Americans had got thoroughly used to treating at least some men as if they were things. They had early become accustomed to thinking of their environment as a set of building blocks for constant private manipulation rather than as a predetermined structure into which each man must passively fit. Of immediate relevance, by the 1840's Americans had also conceived, at least in outline, of just about the entire range of responses to questions of "law and order" which they would display from then on. In view of these continuities, one can hardly deny that the cultural heritage looms large in explaining present-day American realities.[4]

The picture is greatly complicated, however, by the fact that by the 1840's American attitudes in many fundamental areas had already divided into well-defined majority and minority viewpoints. Thereafter, throughout the course of American history, the parallel existence of widely differing, self-aware subsectors of the American population severely limits the overall generalizations one can make about American beliefs. Much confusion about the history of violence, lawlessness, and protest in America—as well as about the concept of national character itself—could be dispelled if it were clearly recognized that America has long been divided between a dominant majority, with its own internal ambivalences but also with great resilience and staying power, and a series of minorities, both ethnic and intellectual, who have been unable or unwilling to assimilate themselves into the majority. This very fact is actually one of the great continuities of our national experience. It means that, for any given problem in the realm of American values, there exist not one but at least two, and perhaps several, quite separate tasks of historical explanation. Questions of law and order, for instance, have seemed so utterly different to men and women on opposite sides of these fundamental dividing lines within our society that there is little point in talking about a single "history" of American attitudes in this area.

4. A recent worldwide comparative study, though rather crudely constructed, shows that the amount of civil turmoil in each country correlates much more highly with that nation's cultural heritage than with either its economic conditions or its political system. Graham and Gurr, *op. cit.*, p. 616.

Just a few years ago it was possible for historians and social scientists to bypass this whole problem of multiple definitions, by the device of simply ignoring every viewpoint other than that of the dominant majority. It was this simplification which enabled the so-called consensus school of American history to flourish in the 1950's.[5] The liberal, pragmatic majority was seen to stand effectively for the entire nation, both in terms of numbers and power. Blacks, working-class radicals, and all kinds of intellectuals were left out, dismissed as unrepresentative and therefore as unimportant.

By focusing so exclusively on the American majority, consensus-oriented historians greatly advanced our understanding of that majority. They taught us that fundamental conflict did not usually exist at the center of the political spectrum, that there was little difference between the two major parties during most periods of our history, and that leading politicians, like leading businessmen, might often appear to fight each other while actually accepting identical underlying goals. They taught us that radicalism could not succeed in America because, lacking a feudal heritage, American society had always been bland and fluid enough to co-opt its potential internal opponents. But they assumed that because large-scale success for a variety of minority viewpoints was impossible, these viewpoints were intrinsically unimportant. Thereby, such historians sought unconsciously to reduce American intellectual and cultural life to the generally monotonous and predictable level of American political life. Further, with the exception of Louis Hartz, these historians tended to minimize the less wholesome aspects of the majority's state of mind, especially its racial harshness.[6]

The inner restraint which seemed such a characteristic American trait to academic commentators in the 1950's (despite the presence of McCarthyism) lost much of its credibility as the 1960's un-

5. The basic expositions of this viewpoint remain Daniel J. Boorstin, *The Genius of American Politics* (Chicago: Universty of Chicago Press, 1953); Louis Hartz, *The Liberal Tradition in America* (New York: Harcourt, Brace, 1955); and Daniel Bell, *The End of Ideology* (Glencoe, Ill.: Free Press of Glencoe, 1959).

6. Hartz brilliantly integrated a recognition of this harshness into his larger model of Lockean consensus in America; see the introduction to Louis Hartz, *et al.*, *The Founding of New Societies* (New York: Harcourt, Brace, 1963), where he traces it to the Calvinist religious tradition.

rolled. Confrontations, assassinations, and the many varieties of resurgent radicalism—black, white, nonpolitical, and highly politicized—made it impossible any longer to write an American history with the inconvenient minorities left out. Some of these minorities—it was again remembered—had led an articulate existence for a century and a half, and some of them had long questioned the fundamentals of obedience to the nation-state or else had deeply challenged accepted moral and economic standards. In certain earlier decades, such as the 1880's and 1890's, the verbal outpouring of these minority groups had reached loud proportions, and episodes of violent protest attributed to them had sent spasms of fear running through the mind of the majority. Despite the fact that even now all such radicals remain a fairly small numerical minority within the total population, their apparently waxing strength, their special appeal to highly intelligent youth, and their powerful vision of a basic desired change in human relationships combine to make them an unmistakably important cultural force in America.

Thus we have come to realize that we are living in a deeply fragmented society, not in one that is blandly homogeneous. Increasingly, we perceive, the divisions are cultural—that is, based on differing world views and moral systems—as well as ethnic and economic. Indeed, perhaps the most fundamental rift between Americans is no longer that running between white and black, but instead the one running between those who believe in planning, large-scale organization, a conventional work and family life, and the rights of private property, and those who believe in decentralization, separatism, spontaneous expressiveness, and the prime value of survival as such. Put in these terms (which are themselves far too simple, of course), the contrast between majority and minority is no doubt even less bridgeable than when it is viewed racially. But this is merely to emphasize the variegated quality of the dividing lines which transect America at present. Attitudes toward "law and order," resistance or obedience to authority are inextricably intertwined with the substantive attitudes and prejudices of the majority and of each of these significant minorities. "Consensus" history failed because it did not prepare us to appreciate this complexity.

Yet, as all the wildness and bitter conflict in our national past are rediscovered, sometimes an equally sweeping claim is made to the effect that Americans as a whole have been an unusually violent people, consistently prone to unlawful excesses. If the historians of consensus offered us a version of American history minus blacks, radicals, and intellectuals, the nascent countervailing myth of an anarchic society results in an American history without New England patricians, clever mainstream politicians, or, most important of all, managerial bureaucrats.[7]

Perhaps neither moderation nor murder has ever really been *the* American norm. The corrective to all these overly simple formulas, once again, lies in a due appreciation of the complicated, often symbiotic relationship between the majority and the series of minorities in American history. It also lies in a willingness to accept the fact that neither the majority nor most of the minorities have been unambiguous in their attitudes toward going outside the law in an effort to achieve certain kinds of social or private purposes. Order and disorder, legalism and illegality, have thrived in America, often simultaneously—for instance, on different levels of the same person's mind. The man who easily accepts law as a noble abstract ideal may just as easily flout it in certain areas of his daily existence. And social order can mean many specific things in people's imaginations besides sheer tranquillity or absence of overt conflict. Both in the realm of practical moral conduct and in that of abstract definition, Americans—whether politically moderate or radical, whether socially conservative or revolutionary —would display few throughgoing consistencies in this area of their thinking. Indeed, it is only a rare (and rather tedious) kind of person who, from some inner compulsion, constantly displays a slavishly obedient attitude toward each and every law and regulation which comes his way. The man who craves submission to authority in this totally consistent sense we are apt to term rather sick.[8]

The readings in intellectual history which make up the first

7. A variant to this alternative, that of thinking of Americans as violent and unrestrained but in a moral, heroic fashion, has long led an important "underground" existence, both among Saturday moviegoers and, on a different plane, among radical admirers of Samuel Adams, John Brown, and Big Bill Haywood.

8. Although the modern bureaucrat—whether Adolph Eichmann or the rule-conscious university administrator—frequently leans in this direction.

part of this volume, therefore, are designed to illustrate ambiguities and paradoxes, rather than pointing to any simple conclusions about the nature of American thinking. Although I believe I can discern at the outset three "classic" positions which were already current in the 1840's, one may easily dispute how distinct and how exhaustive these statements are, as well as argue over the way in which each of them should be interpreted. Moving forward into the industrial period of the past century, where we must confront the thinking of the entire spectrum from conservatives to moderates to anarchists, there is even less hope of finding tidy agreement. What I do think can be found in this material, besides the definition of majority and minority standpoints, are arresting individual angles of vision, striking areas of similarity or conflict between unlikely people, and an unsuspected richness of rhetoric and viewpoint both within and outside the social group now termed the "Establishment." Meaning, I believe, is more apt to reveal itself in such an intricate counterpoint of evidence than in a few crashing tonic chords.

Abstract statements about ideals should never be examined in isolation, and least of all in American history, where a vast gap has so often been suspected between formal verbiage and everyday behavior. One must juxtapose the rhetoric against the record of what Americans have actually done in extralegal situations. One must gain a sense of how they have gone about defying each other and repressing each other, and what the practical consequences have been of civil disobedience or deliberate outlawry. Thus a series of episodes have been chosen which reveal some of the concrete possibilities of nonconformity and repression in American life. These vignettes are entirely in the words of first-hand eyewitnesses, because even here the verbal flavor is often important. In time and locale, they range from the Montana frontier of a century ago to the present-day American city. They should permit a fresh discussion of historical continuities and changes on the basis of highly specific evidence.

The large urban police department becomes the final focus in this volume because in our own time the police have emerged as the most central and controversial symbol of everyday authority in the minds of nearly all Americans. Here the major aim is to observe how the police see themselves (and the surrounding society) and the radical differences between this perspective and that of certain other minority groups. The absence of mutual comprehension confirms, in a violence-laden context, the depth of the cultural split in twentieth-century America; it again shows how many arguments seemingly about "law and order" are actually expressions of this cultural dividedness. In the present day, just as in previous decades of debate on the topic, the issue of obedience to authority tends to crumble into the prejudices (and the conflicting moral visions) of the various social groups which seize upon it. In literal terms, the police are only one such group, and a rather special one, but they also are supposed to embody the aims and wishes of the majority which entrusts them with physical power. The police may thus epitomize, in a direct sense, the ambiguity of majority-minority relationships which haunts this entire problem.

How much viability the issue of "law and order" possesses apart from mere group prejudices must be left to each reader to decide. It may be that "law and order," far from being a single, constantly identifiable theme in American history, is instead a phrase which only masks a series of particular social conflicts, some of them subtle, some overt. Similarly, it may be that no individual can hope to approach the topic of "law and order" without subconsciously identifying himself, from the very start, either with the role of law enforcer or of lawbreaker. On the other hand, many social scientists assume—and believe they can verify—that the craving for social order is a deep constant in the history of human societies, and that efforts to defy such an order predictably engage the emotions in a profound and very distinct manner, regardless of the specific character of the groups involved in the conflict. Those who have been moved by *King Lear* will no doubt tend to agree.

Quite aside from the question of the intrinsic continuity of such concepts as freedom and authority, in my own view their study in America has frequently been hampered by too great a degree of intellectual formalism. Historians examining these ideas have largely stayed within the framework of constitutional philosophy and legal or political argument. Thus, for instance, they have emphasized the importance of Jeffersonian distrust toward central authority; they have traced the shifting role of the Supreme Court with respect to civil liberties and civil rights; or they have re-capitulated the debate between individualist and collectivist forms of economic liberalism which flourished at the turn of the twentieth century. These approaches to questions of law and freedom assume a universal acceptance of the underlying system. They do not inquire into the psychology of that acceptance. They frequently overestimate the power of reason and the duration of calm, quasi-parliamentary reflection in the human mind. That is, they are largely the products of an unconscious but pervasive liberal bias.

The minds of most men are deeper and more complicated than these formalistic approaches will allow. The emotional magnetism of group conflict and the deflective force of background and self-interest demand proper recognition in analyzing any line of argument.[9] Besides following the course of political and constitutional debate, one must quite simply ask how various Americans—intellectuals, frontiersmen, government officials, policemen, and black people—have reacted to "the system" of law and authority itself, especially at moments of real or imagined crisis. Here the question is one which consensus historians had too easily answered in affirmative terms—namely, whether most Americans have accepted the basic system as an automatically "given" element in their lives and whether they have actually lived by the terms of that acceptance. Deeds and emotions, as well as words, form the material of an answer.

Of course it is true that one may reduce all political and philosophical issues rather too easily to mere questions of sociological conflict or of personal psychology. "Authority," for instance, may be glibly equated with the figure of "the father" in Freudian language, as if that were a sufficient explanation of how various people have reacted to it. Or again, all interest groups—policemen

9. There is some empirical evidence to show that among Americans, immediate situation has counted for more than abstract moral or philosophical beliefs in determining the position on concrete issues (such as civil disobedience) of moral philosophers themselves. This, at least, is the conclusion of Edward H. Madden, *Civil Disobedience and Moral Law in Nineteenth-Century American Philosophy* (Seattle, Wash.: University of Washington Press, 1968), who finds no direct correlation between overall moral belief and concrete moral stand but does find a very high correlation between such matters as family outlook, personal position, regional background, and so on, and one's concrete stand.

and blacks—may be falsely placed on a par simply because they are interest groups. If earlier historians took constitutional argument somewhat too seriously on its own terms, present-day seekers for a ready explanation of "violence on our streets" may far too easily neglect the role of ideas (including extremely simple ones like justice). It is actually self-defeating to draw rigid lines between cognitive thought, or social philosophy, on the one hand, and social psychology on the other. The very borderland between these regions in the mind is often the richest and most revealing source of evidence. A constant mixture of ideological posture, moral vision, and barely controlled emotion most closely resembles the flow of life itself, and it is as the embodiment of such a mixture that all these documents should be read.

As a help toward rethinking American history, we need to look more closely at the extremes of argument and behavior (both liberated and repressive) which have occurred during the course of this society's development. Rather than confining our historical net to the mainstream, it is important to seek out the furthest and most diverse limits of the American potential. This is one of the major aims of the selections given here. And it is especially important to study in detail the reactions of the American majority to the most uncompromising and apparently obnoxious "outsider" minorities. These reactions are so very significant because it is, after all, the stable majority that defines the character of American life as it is generally perceived. One highly revealing aspect of "the American character," as the majority determines it, must surely be our degree of willingness to respect diversity and tolerate dissent. It is hardly necessary to argue, after the experience of Nazi Germany, that the extreme limits of the treatment accorded to internal groups of "outsiders" provide an important measure of the quality of any civilization. The awareness of these limits as reflected in the behavior of powerful majorities may well be what the phrase "law and order" should most centrally refer to, even though it has more often been used in an opposite sense by the majority seeking to curb minority protests. In any event, this anthology tries to explore the extreme and often lawless limits of majority and minority imagination, both in the realm of words and in that of action.

Freedom and Disorder in American History:
An Interpretation

American history may seem rudely unfamiliar when it is viewed from outside certain highly traditional assumptions about what it means to be a free individual. These assumptions, which were held by nearly all Americans until the mid-nineteenth century and still are by a great majority today, limit the domain of freedom to a number of public and conventional activities. For instance, freedom means the right to participate in politics by voting and holding office; the right to earn and to spend money with minimal interference; the right to worship at the church of one's choice; and the right to move about and to speak without being molested.

Anyone would agree that these are important freedoms. But it is now clear to us that many other possible conceptions of freedom exist as well, and that some American minorities, beginning at least by the 1840's, have moved to embrace them. There is freedom to daydream, freedom to create what one calls art, freedom to taunt authority symbols, and freedom simply to go barefoot. Minority redefinitions of freedom along such lines as these have sometimes amounted to a proposal for a radically new collective ethic.

On the other hand, it is now equally clear that the dominant American majority has long prized still different kinds of freedom, which it has not so often talked about. These are, above all else, freedom to indulge in temporary but violent binges or sprees and freedom to take almost any measures against "undesirable" persons in one's community (defining undesirability not only in terms of political and moral beliefs but also in those of unkempt appearance and skin color). These hallowed majoritarian freedoms have greatly conditioned American attitudes toward legal authority.

The history of American freedom in this broad, or mixed, sense clearly needs to be examined anew, even though the tools for

11

such an inquiry are not yet fully at hand and some of the main outlines, to say nothing of details, remain more speculative and uncertain than one would like.

The story may well begin with the fears of the earliest American colonists, stranded on a wild continent distant from everything that was reassuring and familiar, that unless they guarded themselves carefully they might turn into savages. One way in which they perhaps maintained their civilized self-conception against environmental pressures was, paradoxically, to oppress the "savage" figure of the black man—by literally beating him in order to beat out the impulses toward savagery and abandon within their own minds. Such at least is the highly suggestive thesis in Winthrop Jordan's recent study of early American racism.[1] The wilderness may thus have implanted a yearning for unrestrained freedom which was hastily covered up in a series of compensating maneuvers.

If something like this process occurred, it was soon obscured by the easy, confident public picture which the colonists presented nearly everywhere. Steady, successful exploitation of the environment, not fear and rigidity over the unfamiliar, became the norm by the beginning of the eighteenth century. (A Freudian in Jordan's vein might go on to insist that harshness toward the black man permitted this nonchalant release of energy in all other areas of life.) Set loose among abundant resources, Americans seemed rapidly and matter-of-factly to master their circumstances. For quite a long time they continued to identify freedom with disciplined self-direction rather than with any truly wild forms of inner release.

There were, to be sure, important regional and ethnic variations in the pattern of life that emerged. New Englanders wove a high degree of self-control into the fabric of their existence while at the same time keeping alive the seeds of a pronounced moral and intellectual individualism. The sermon, the town meeting, and later the revival provided substitutes for excessive legalism of an explicit kind. New England sternness sat heavily upon antinomian impulses without ever quite extinguishing them; simultaneously it

1. Winthrop Jordan, *White Over Black* (Baltimore: Penguin Books, 1969), p. 543. The argument invites firmer documentation, but see note 12 below. It would perhaps also apply to treatment of the Indian.

permitted a steady deflection of energy into the quest for worldly profit. Meanwhile, by way of contrast, the Pennsylvania Scotch-Irish, another group which would contribute much to the tone of nineteenth-century America, began leading a kind of life in the wilderness which owed little to any sense of inner restraint. By all accounts, these migrants freely indulged in every form of recklessness. Their unashamed eagerness to murder Indians is especially well known, as is the quarrelsome and disorderly pattern of their own lives. Even their religion eventually acquired a highly emotional form, producing scenes of ecstatic physical abandon at mass camp meetings on the transappalachian frontier.

Important as the Scotch-Irish life style was as an alternative, the more self-disciplined patterns of the New Englander, the seaboard merchant, and the Southern planter remained dominant in American society by the time of the Revolution.[2] The proof of this was that America endured seven years of internal military conflict, followed by eight years of extremely weak government, without any evidence that the society was fundamentally falling apart. Instead, beneath the level of political infighting, the impression was one of continued stability, mastery, and confidence in the future. That is why the American Revolution, touch-and-go as it might have been in military and diplomatic terms, has come more and more to be seen as basically conservative and self-protective. The questioning of the mother country's authority did not lead to an anarchic undermining of all authority within the society, and this would have been true even if the anti-Federalists of 1788 had won. Despite all the concern over "liberty" and "tyranny," the Revolution posed remarkably few challenges to the deeper notion of a self-restrained and orderly society.

In this period and the decades that followed, obstacles to achievement were still primarily physical ones, not those stemming from a profound dividedness in men's minds. Even over the issue of slavery, Southern planters only paused and hesitated for about two decades before they began once again—around 1800—de-

2. John Hope Franklin has argued that the entire Southern pattern was strongly violent; see *The Militant South* (Cambridge, Mass.: Harvard University Press, 1956). Much violence was built into the very necessities of maintaining the system of slavery. But when the Scotch-Irish are compared with the Virginia planter aristocracy of the 1770's, it is obvious that the differences far outweigh any similarities.

cisively to bolster the institution. Individuals, except for a highly unusual John Woolman, did not noticeably set themselves against social groups on grounds of principle. The quarrel between Patrick Henry and James Madison over the Constitution, for instance, was one between a greater Virginia and a greater America, not one between a sensitive moral conscience and a political establishment. And on most issues Thomas Jefferson's position was no more dramatic than that of a moderate. (As a middle-of-the-roader, he accepted the Constitution with reservations.) In the twentieth century the Bill of Rights would be celebrated as the traditional foundation for guarantees to free individual self-expression; but the eighteenth century hardly would have known what the concept "self-expression" was supposed to mean.[3]

Political contests, and occasionally questions of civil liberties, occupied the attention of large numbers of Americans during the Jeffersonian and Jacksonian periods. But individual fortune seeking busied people far more of the time. Political issues themselves frequently concerned matters of economic development. Thus the entire conflict between the ideas that have been termed "mercantilism" and "laissez faire"[4] was a quarrel over the division of the economic pie, and a quarrel in which neither side was desperately starving. The blacks and the Southern poor whites sat through this quarrel between large and small business, decade after decade, as passive or unwilling bystanders. From some points of view, therefore, early American history was rather a monotone, whose variations simply were not profound enough to disturb a dominant impression of agreement over fundamentals. Most Americans were speculators or would-be speculators, either in land or in paper; they defined the good life in material terms, as an expanding "stake" for themselves, their families and descendants. The freedom they cherished was the freedom to move upward, not inward. In leading such a visibly dynamic and aggressive kind of life, religion and patriotism (whether national or Southern) were very likely

3. Looking back, we can perceive "self-expression" of a familiar kind in Benjamin Franklin, masked as highly moral self-discipline. Yet even Franklin's expressiveness was largely lacking in introspective qualities, and in any event we tend to seize upon his case precisely because he seems so atypically "modern" from this point of view.

4. See William Appleman Williams, *The Contours of American History* (Cleveland, Ohio: World Publishing Co., 1961).

indispensable comforts. The American sense of mission legitimized a great many forms of military and economic acquisitiveness as the nineteenth century wore on.[5]

In all this, American responses to abstract questions about law and order were anything but clear-cut. Indeed, as compared with the later industrial period, these questions were still rarely posed or pondered. Exploitation of the environment, not the task of defining legitimate social authority, occupied men's minds. Nonetheless, one may approach the problem by asking what separate functions law served and how Americans reacted to each of them.

In early nineteenth-century America, law probably fulfilled three main social functions.[6] First of all, it was a means of enforcing community standards in a basic and quite ordinary sense. The moral standpoint of the community was of course much more definite in many areas of life than it has since become, and toleration of diversity, for instance in sexual practices, was far more limited. The horrified reaction to Mormon polygamy, as late as the 1890's, is well known, and the physical remoteness of the Mormons on the frontier did not affect the severity of the judgment. In this fundamental respect, early Americans were strong believers in a conventional social order, and in law as an appropriate vehicle for establishing the permissible limits of behavior. Any propensity to see an easygoing anarchism among the pioneers must take this into account. In other words, most Americans of that day, like most peoples, adopted a far less than "anything goes" attitude toward many central aspects of their existence.

A second major function of law, especially in the South but to some extent throughout the country, was as a direct instrument of social oppression. Without laws to establish it and maintain it, the institution of slavery would have been impossible. This of course remains true even though many particular laws regulating its conditions were violated freely by white masters. Until the abolition

5. For a deeply suggestive evocation of how the themes of religious zeal and economic canniness could intermingle in the mind of a nineteenth-century Ohio farmer, see the story "Godliness" in Sherwood Anderson, *Winesburg, Ohio* (New York: B. W. Huebsch, 1919).

6. The analysis that follows does not, I believe, contradict the basic argument in the extremely fertile and authoritative study by James Willard Hurst, *Law and the Conditions of Freedom in the Nineteenth-Century United States* (Madison, Wisc.: The University of Wisconsin Press, 1956).

movement and more especially the Fugitive Slave Act of 1850, the necessity for these laws was rarely questioned either in the North or in the South, however often some of the details might be argued or ignored. Here again, most early Americans emerge as firm advocates of law and order.

Finally, law also served as a device continually affecting people in the scramble for private economic rewards which occupied so much of their attention. Law determined the price of frontier land; it defined fraud; it established (or frequently failed to establish) rules for banking and currency. In this role it could create opportunities and then shut some people effectively out of them. Therefore, many Americans were genuinely ambivalent about this third and final function of law in their lives. If it helped them personally, they might well be for it; if not, they might become staunch advocates of laissez faire. This indecisiveness explains much about American popular thought in the nineteenth century. It was this same widespread vacillation about whether to accept legal restraints that were personally hurtful in the race for success which Mugwumps, Progressives, and their later descendants would rather belatedly try to resolve in favor of a consistent legalism. But at the beginning of the nineteenth century, when lawyers by all accounts were held in low public esteem, much of the grudging attitude toward legal interference no doubt centered precisely in this third and final social function of law. The man with a glint of hope in his eye does not appreciate being suddenly tricked by an unfamiliar expert, usually hired in behalf of someone else's selfish interest.

The majority of the American public thus probably grew to embrace a firm adherence to standards of "law and order" in two major senses but a sometimes wishful, sometimes resentful dislike of law in a third. Meanwhile, several different kinds of domestic violence (and otherwise lawless behavior) had also come into existence in America, somewhat paralleling the functions of law itself. There was, first of all, a certain amount of conventional criminal activity, of kinds which are liable to occur in almost any society and which need not detain us. Secondly, there was lawlessness (only occasionally expressing itself in actual violence) connected with the struggles between rival economic interests; this would greatly increase in the post-Civil War period, during the age of railroad wars. There was, thirdly, violent subjection of slaves and a certain degree of violent resistance to the slave system on the part of its victims; in this way a constant "background noise" of brutality was injected into the American system over a very long period of time. Finally, on the frontier a distinctive pattern of uncontrolled behavior also developed, expressing itself in the cycle of the spree and eventually sometimes producing the type of personality known as the outlaw.

Nearly all these separate forms of lawlessness in pre-industrial America seem relevant to American predilections during our own century. But the legacy of frontier violence for later generations is a particularly subtle one, requiring careful attention.[7]

The first question one wants to ask about the Wild West is how it initially got started. For, as a distinctive social environment it really came into existence only in the early nineteenth century, and in the transappalachian region rather than in the very earliest wilderness forests encountered by the colonists. In other words, there was nothing at all inevitable about the eventual identification of the frontier with outlawry or with extreme individualism as a way of life, even though a certain amount of Indian warfare (hence violence) had of course taken place there from the outset. The mythic overtones of the West, as the locale of a peculiar sort of restless individual assertiveness, are the product of the Jefferson and, more especially, the Jackson periods. The fascinating question as to why the kind of West we are all acquainted with, the West of semianarchic legend, takes shape at such a late date is one on which surprisingly little may be found either in Frederick Jackson Turner or Henry Nash Smith.[8]

7. The other kinds of lawlessness may be explained more straightforwardly. Violent conflicts over property are understandable in a society which places high value on entrepreneurship, and indeed the interesting question may be why such conflicts (and such extralegal interests and syndicates) did not become even more powerful than they did. Again, the violence of racial subjection does not require elaborate explanation, once one assumes that, for whatever reasons, some human beings are seeking to control the bodily movements of others; the important question is not the cause of this violence but the reason why it was so limited in extent for such a long time.

8. Henry Nash Smith, *Virgin Land* (Cambridge, Mass.: Harvard University Press, 1951) is of course an enormously fruitful work in terms of explaining and analyzing these myths and legends. On p. 81 he briefly credits the rise of an anarchic view of the West in the 1830's to the

The vast size and greater isolation of the transappalachian environment, making it a poorer locale than the earlier seaboard frontier in terms of basic mental health, may have been relevant. There was also the fact that Scotch-Irish life styles (and, if one is to be quite honest, those of many Indians) intensified the trend toward certain kinds of emotional abandon. A temporary weakening of social institutions thus occured over a much larger area than ever before—though it should be noted that this situation might conceivably have fostered the spread of "democracy" without leading to any idealization of the outlaw. Finally, a neglected factor to which I shall later return: the existence at this very time of the Romantic movement in Europe with its new tendency to link the idea of individual freedom to states of emotional abandon.

Once the West began to take on the character of an explicitly wild and wide-open place, in the early part of the nineteenth century, the growing sanction of lawlessness collided with the continuing and more basic instinct of support for social order, and the result was the peculiarly persistent phenomenon known as vigilantism.[9] During the nineteenth century several hundred separately recorded vigilante movements came into existence, widely scattered over the entire nation west of the Appalachians. The essence of vigilantism is that men take the law into their own hands, ostensibly in the name of a higher, unwritten need for social control. Most vigilante movements indulged in lynchings of outlaws or pariah figures. In some cases they functioned out of what they thought was sheer necessity during an effective legal vacuum. In others, they became high-handed, tinged with partisanship and overt criminality. Instances of the first sort are usually distinguishable by the general support of the local community for the actions of the vigilantes; these movements directly embodied the will of the majority and exercised it without heeding custom-

---

actual growth of the Rocky Mountain fur trade in that period. Of course this avoids asking why Kit Carson rapidly became such a major literary prototype. On p. 52 Smith alludes in passing to a Byronic influence on Francis Parkman.

9. For a thorough factual study of vigilantism in nineteenth-century America, see Richard Maxwell Brown, "The American Vigilante Tradition," in Hugh Davis Graham and Ted Robert Gurr, *Violence in America*, pp. 154–226. See also John W. Caughey, *Their Majesties the Mob* (Chicago: University of Chicago Press, 1960), pp. 1–25.

ary legal forms. Such legal authorities as did exist tended in these cases to cooperate with the vigilantes. (An example of this style of frontier vigilantism is provided in "The Hanging of 'Captain' Slade," in this volume.)

Vigilantism of this kind has usually been regarded favorably, both by leading American public figures and by later historians. It is generally seen as "socially constructive" in that it genuinely displaces anarchy with social order.[10] Yet, in its unrestrained and lawless application of majority will, it became the direct ancestor of anti-radical "neo-vigilantism" conducted at the local and federal levels in the twentieth century by A. Mitchell Palmer (also represented in the readings below), Joseph McCarthy, and many others. Nor is it really distinguishable from the thousands of lynchings of Negroes which have occurred in the South and the West since the Civil War, except that these occasions were even less formally organized.[11]

The second form of vigilantism, by contrast, was divisive and factional in the immediate response it drew and tended to be universally condemned by later observers. It bore many of the marks of the rebellion or the private army. Its leaders were often self-seeking and unconcerned with or hostile to community norms. It was a rather naked excuse for outlawry.

A word should also be said about public attitudes toward lynching itself. Lynching of Negroes was openly defended by many— if not most—Southern whites. Lynching comprised the truly civilized form of response to rape, wrote a Marylander in 1918 who held a Ph.D. degree, because "our civilization teaches that one should hold certain personal rights and considerations even more dear than life itself. To have in mind such ideas [of honor] and live up to them measures our reach above lower peoples."[12]

These gradations of extralegal behavior (and justifications for

10. Graham and Gurr, op. cit., pp. 183–185. Caughey sought to counter this judgment.

11. For some statistics on lynching, see p. 194 below.

12. Winfield H. Collins, A.M., Ph.D., The Truth About Lynching and the Negro in the South (New York: The Neale Publishing Company, 1918), pp. 55–56. The argument of course assumes a society based on status hierarchy rather than on equality and thus differs greatly from the grounds on which Western vigilantism was defended. Collins' words, however, do incidentally provide some tardy evidence in favor of Winthrop Jordan's thesis on the meaning of subjugation (n. 1, above).

it) in the American West and South further confirm the ambiguity of American attitudes toward law and order during the earlier period of our history. The ambiguity was then given a greater dimension in more recent decades, as fictionalized accounts of frontier episodes began entering deeply into the mass imagination. No less than three heroic models emerged—the outlaw as extra-legal individualist; the law officer as the purveyor of justice; and, most interesting of all, the "constructive" vigilante, midway between the two, exemplifying at one and the same time a deep craving for social order and an impatience with the pedestrian qualities of the legal system. (The Lone Ranger, Superman, the Shadow, and Humphrey Bogart's major roles, among many others, all conform to this pattern of the "constructive" vigilante.)[13] Since in actual life the same frontier hero might move among all three roles, the ambiguity was often immediately biographical as well as far-reaching in its mythological implications. The defender of the community might at the same time be the breaker of some of its laws. And the lawbreaker might be regarded with secret or open admiration by the very people, then or later, who also would demand social control in the abstract.[14]

The frontier gunfighter was glorified in a way that never proved true of other kinds of violent men in nineteenth-century America. The slave overseer, for example, was greatly looked down upon even by his employer, and lynching mobs, though widely defended, were scarcely made into symbols of romance. Nor were ordinary policemen or Pinkerton detectives given the status of major heroes, either at the time or later on.[15] American blood-lust must cer-

13. They all ferret out and often proceed to punish criminals personally, well in advance of the slothful police. On the other hand, it is interesting that most of these twentieth-century vigilante characterizations involve a strong element of loneliness and secret disguise which was not present in genuine frontier vigilantism.

14. To permit their later use, outlaw legends sometimes had to be unconsciously prettified. For instance, the James brothers were mistakenly believed never to plan hold-ups which involved the taking of human life. Legendary outlaws were credited with an innate sense of honor imposing certain limits on their violence (e.g., not shooting men from behind) and frequently were twisted into Robin Hoods.

15. It is true that in a pronounced mood of conservative reaction following the Haymarket bombing of 1886, Chicago citizens the next year erected a ten-foot bronze statue in honor of the policemen killed by the bomb. The statue served thereafter as a scene of annual commemorative

tainly not be exaggerated. It was, after all, but one theme among others in the majority imagination.

No doubt far more pervasive was the peaceful myth of the virtuous pioneer, the yeoman farmer, again linked specifically to the West, but a figure seen as a "child of nature" in a much more innocent sense—far removed from the coercion of established institutions, including law itself, yet self-reliant rather than self-indulgent. The pioneer, as a stereotype, is neither violent nor erratic, despite all his imagined loneliness. Above all he displays a serene (though highly active and practical) quality of inner direction.

The ordinary frontiersman—whether in myth or in reality—in no sense really deserves the label of an anarchist. For at the deepest level, not even his degree of individualism was conducive to the disruption of the established social order. Instead the pioneer was constantly re-creating that order, albeit with some egalitarian modifications. Despite the temporary excesses of the Scotch-Irish and certain other groups, on the whole few settlers gave way to anything like savagery.[16] Nor, on the other hand, despite numerous utopian experiments, did the pioneer ever create a genuinely novel social order on an important scale in the United States.[17] Legislative government, the property system, and the family remained at the core of American civilization; these fundamental institutions scarcely differed from those in the English society that was left behind. Early Americans may have been hostile to external legal restraints, especially when arbitrarily altered by a distant mother country, but they themselves automatically worked to create a civilization which contained new bonds and limits of its own, especially in those central areas of life whose patterns most people then took completely for granted.

Thus individualism and a sense of community could usually go

---

rallies led, however, by the police department itself and not by outside citizens. This statue was destroyed by some carefully placed dynamite on October 6, 1969.

16. Appalachia continued to be something of an exception; see the very fine social history of the region in Harry M. Caudill, *Night Comes to the Cumberlands* (Boston: Little, Brown, 1963).

17. The Mormons came closest, but within half a century their viewpoints and secular institutions became almost indistinguishable from those of the American majority.

hand in hand, rather than conflicting with each other, in early-day America. This happy conjunction might seemingly have been what a later socialist or anarchist would most highly regard. But in nineteenth-century America the union of individual aspiration with community sentiment was of a very particular kind. It was forged in a context of private economic aggrandizement and exploitation. And the individualism of the day was, as we have seen, practical and manipulative, not inward-turning or aesthetic. The frontier hero—especially the outlaw, sheriff, or vigilante leader—embodied a kind of *machismo* which, though highly romantic, remained thoroughly physical and nonintrospective. Meanwhile, the yeoman farmer "expressed" himself by the simple act of increasing his yields.

The narrowness of spirit in much of early nineteenth-century America, both North and South, disturbed such acute commentators as Alexis de Tocqueville at the time. There were many symptoms of intolerance, social climbing, extreme racial prejudice, and unconcern for genuine social or intellectual diversity.[18] And it was in this very period that one could note rising in the popular mind an ambiguous but very real fascination with certain heroic forms of violence and extralegal activity.[19] The American majority, with all its characteristic uncertainties of mind and its limited understanding of individual liberty, had now come fully into its own.

What was to become the majority frame of mind gradually matured during the closing decades of the colonial period and the opening ones of the American nation. The course of its evolution was slow and unforced. In contrast, several important American minorities began noticeably to take shape in a far more sudden

18. See, for example, Leon F. Litwack, *North of Slavery* (Chicago: University of Chicago Press, 1961); and Francis J. Grund, *Aristocracy in America* (London: R. Bentley, 1839).

19. Andrew Jackson no doubt served as an important transition symbol in this respect, helping to shift the revolutionary tradition of legitimate violence into the locale of the West (the Battle of New Orleans being both anti-British and far from the Atlantic seaboard). Since in his Florida campaigns Jackson conspicuously went beyond his legal instructions, he may indeed provide a vital link in the gradual apotheosis of the outlaw. See John W. Ward, *Andrew Jackson: Symbol for an Age* (New York: Oxford University Press, 1962), esp. Chap. 1.

manner during the 1820's and 1830's.[20] Though later histories of these minorities were often complicated, in some respects their own continuities—from the abolitionism and Transcendentalism of the 1830's down to the black demands for freedom and the revived Asian mysticism of the 1960's—appear in turn altogether remarkable, as if American majorities and minorities were somehow fated to go on repeating the same mutual tug of war century after century.

Among the diverse minorities which became important in these early-nineteenth-century decades, such groups as the Transcendentalists and abolitionists played a distinctive role, one that would have the largest impact on the later history of American radicalism and upon the history of American attitudes toward freedom and authority.[21] It was the special contribution of Thoreau's generation, deeply influenced by the European Romantic movement, to define a new kind of introspective individualism—indeed, to create a markedly new definition of the self—which would thereafter provide a continuing radical counterthrust to majority points of view.

Before this, as we saw, Americans scarcely conceived of the idea of "self-expression." They had assumed that one's public life in the community—political, religious, economic—together with one's family life constituted the whole of life. (Even religion was largely a public matter, involving church membership and constant social participation.) This was the heart of what the Transcendentalists rejected. It is probably not going too far to say that they were responsible for introducing privacy as an important minority ideal and taste into the United States. And this, with all its implications—architectural, philosophical, psychological—may

20. Antecedents of all of them could be found in earlier decades, to be sure. Perry Miller strenuously (but also rather forcedly) argues the continuity of New England thought from Edwards to Emerson in *Errand into the Wilderness* (Cambridge, Mass.: Harvard University Press, 1956). But Edwards was an isolated figure, whereas Emerson was part of a recognizable movement—and that is precisely the difference that matters in the present context.

21. Another well-known minority, the white Southern planter class, was more important in political terms at the time but far less distinctive intellectually, since, with only rare exceptions, its members agreed with the American majority in its basic assumptions about the nature of freedom and disagreed only on certain matters of application.

have been the single most important intellectual revolution ever to occur in our society, especially if it is defined to include the privacy of small groups as well as that of the single person. Of course one must immediately add that it was not a real revolution, in the classic definition of the term, because it never fully succeeded; it never converted a majority of the American population to its new outlook. Instead it launched into being a perpetually restless, dissatisfied intellectual minority, the minority responsible for most of America's subsequent artistic and literary breakthroughs and, on another side, the minority whose descendants comprise many of the "hip" and disaffected of the present moment.

The Transcendentalists, like the European Romantics from whom they sprang, were the first to put forward a definition of the self which strongly emphasized inner depth and mystery. They placed an infinitely high value on the individual human mind, in a way that went beyond either the purely rationalistic humanitarianism of the enlightenment or the sin-ridden individualism of Christianity. They also encouraged the individual not so much to defy the state as to ignore it. The individual could make direct contact with the moving forces of the universe, through nature and through introspective meditation. There was no real need for intermediaries. Social institutions, while not always explicitly rejected, were reduced to a plane of relative insignificance. They counted among the externals, whereas the heart of a man's life properly lay in self-development.

Unfriendly critics of this intellectual revolution would eventually accuse it of fostering a tone of narcissism. The self was endlessly, legitimately, exhilaratingly interesting. One was by no means ashamed to spend long periods of time watching it, taking notes about it, communing with it. Nor was one ashamed to be caught thinking abstractly—passionately, expansively, but nonetheless abstractly—about everything that seemed most important in life. (The solipsism and the abstract quality are well captured in Margaret Fuller's famous pronouncement: "I accept the universe.") Together the tendencies toward introspection and toward extreme generality enabled the ordinary realm of social relations to be largely bypassed—thereby fostering a style of social criticism which struck many contemporaries either as too harshly logical or else as too far-fetched. An altogether new pattern of living and thinking had been created, with political as well as aesthetic implications.

It is impossible to exaggerate the importance of this shift in consciousness, even though it occurred to relatively few people in America during the 1830's and 1840's.[22] Only the modern concept of the self, produced in this fashion by the Romantic movement, gave full definition to future debates over the individual's relations to external authority. Not until the coming of Transcendentalism (and the utopian socialism that was contemporary with it) did even a few Americans begin to conceive what it might be like to exile themselves from the usual norms of the community and instead lead a life that was as self-directed as possible—a goal that was both fundamentally noneconomic and non-Christian. Here lay the source of a deeper and far more troublesome variety of individualism than any that had entered into the minds of the Founding Fathers.[23] Little had those men dreamed, when they worked to deliver men from certain oppressive social institutions (monarchical governments and the like), that within another half century some Americans would come to view nearly all forms of customary social and political attachment as irrelevant to their highest inward aspirations.

The gulf between the liberalism of the Bill of Rights and the

22. Yet it has been greatly downplayed (or at most, as with Stanley Elkins, recognized and deplored) because of the pervasive anti-Romantic bias among academics, including historians. A well-known textbook history of American thought devotes three pages to Transcendentalism out of nearly 900.

23. The idea of the sanctity of the individual conscience was not new, of course; it had been prominent in the Quaker, and to a degree the Puritan, traditions. What was novel and important was its claim to authority on the basis of a much more largely self-sufficient human psychology, de-emphasizing any need for correspondence to established Christian modes of thought. Conscience could now be linked with an ideal of "liberation" (see below), rather than with conformity to "higher" traditions temporarily being violated by particular governments, etc. Individual freedom could thus be defined in ways that were far more free-wheeling and diverse than, for instance, was possible within the highly stylized Quaker tradition. Since a secular (or at any rate non-Christian) conception of individual human liberation is basic to modern radical thought, the shift brought about by the Transcendentalists is a crucial one. It must be admitted that Christian perfectionism, contemporary with Transcendentalism, carried some of these same implications; it was also deeply contrary to the spirit of traditional Christianity.

world view of the Transcendental minority was thus a profound one. Leonard Levy has argued that civil liberties questions assumed their modern definition in the United States by the year 1800.[24] This may be true so far as formal legal arguments are concerned, but the point effectively conceals an enormous transformation in the underlying rationale for many forms of minority protest thereafter. This change clearly separates the civil libertarianism of Jefferson from the civil disobedience (and indeed the entire pattern of thinking and living) of Henry David Thoreau.

Jefferson, whose ringing rhetoric and frequent compromises make him the fit progenitor of the liberal tradition in American politics, was far more often concerned with states' rights than with the rights of individuals. More important, Jefferson, perhaps because he was such a major architect of religious and educational freedom, lacked the imagination to conceive of a life in which neither newspaper reading, politicking, nor any form of public religious observance would occupy a very large place. He was a stranger, that is, to the new world of privacy and inward intensity which Romanticism, for better or worse, would introduce.

One should not, of course, in the least belittle the importance of the conventional struggle for civil liberties in America, either in 1800 or in the mid-twentieth century. But the aim of providing equal justice to all under the Constitution is not fully attuned to the quality of psychological revolt from established authority which has increasingly involved certain kinds of people in the modern age. It is a "liberal" rather than a "radical" aim, in that a "reasonable" conception of social order still underlies the civil libertarian plea for maximum variety and tolerance. Today, for example, the Jeffersonian supports the right of young men to grow long hair because of its seeming harmlessness, not for the opposite reason that an increasing acceptance of unisex fashions may help subvert existing moral inhibitions.

The Romantic movement, because it legitimized so many forms of the irrational, effectively created the ideal of "liberation," both individual and social. It is this conception which fundamentally underlies the modern spirit of revolt in both culture and politics. "Liberation," as an image, mingles elements of joy and harsh-

24. Leonard W. Levy, *Jefferson and Civil Liberties: The Darker Side* (Cambridge, Mass.: Harvard University Press, 1963), p. 175.

ness, projecting them upon a single future moment of triumphant release from social bondage. Though it has precedents in certain extreme or heretical versions of Christianity, it is uniquely present as a central element in nineteenth- and twentieth-century revolutionary ideology. By focusing on a climactic, almost ecstatic instant when man loses his alienation and discovers his true potential, both Marxism and anarchism revealed their debt not only to the Enlightenment but also to the apocalyptic modes of thinking that were more immediately contemporaneous to them.

The new spirit of the 1830's and 1840's is the one which is still commonly with us today in radical circles. To be sure, the current conception of a "deep," mysterious, and infinitely valuable human self derives more directly from Freud and Jung than from Emerson; but this is a less important distinction than at first it seems, for (despite his brave posturings as a scientist) we now know how greatly Freud's own efforts to explore the unconscious during the 1890's were affected by the neo-Romantic revival in Europe at that time, and we are further beginning to appreciate how closely the initial promotion of Freudian ideas in the United States was linked to American philosophical idealism.[25] Beneath all these finer distinctions, the fundamental point remains: the legitimization of serious (but non-Christian) inward self-exploration, often linked with a contemptuous attitude toward existing social institutions, has taken root as a strikingly recurrent minority pattern in American thought over the past hundred and forty or so years. Much of the conflict between the majority and radical minorities during this long period, for instance on questions of law and freedom, has actually amounted to a running battle between two world views: the pragmatic (matter-of-fact, acquisitive, manipulative) and the transcendental (self-absorbed, cosmic). The question of marijuana is not the least case in point.

One final irony about the impact of Romanticism on the American imagination needs to be noted. There is a further and quite separate dimension to the decisive change which occurred in the

25. A forthcoming book by Nathan Hale, Jr., on the reception of Freudian ideas in America will greatly elucidate this latter subject. The major difference, of course, between the earlier Romantic and the later Freudian conceptions of the self is the open acceptance of its sexual basis. Yet even here the contrast (for instance between Walt Whitman and Abbie Hoffman) is far from absolute.

early nineteenth century. For without doubt Romanticism also greatly affected the popular, or majority, level of American thinking, giving it a new and distinctive conception of emotional "liberation" as well. The emergence of the bold frontier figure, with overtones of lawlessness, as a characteristic American hero has already been discussed. It is at least an interesting coincidence that the Western hero should gain so much leverage upon the American imagination in an age dominated by hero-worship in European thought. Even in this, their apparently most indigenous form of mythology, Americans may have been responding quite unconsciously to changing intellectual climates overseas.

Therefore, at the broadest level, Romanticism may have produced both the self-expressive revolutionary leader, ultimately defying the Chicago police in the name of orgasmic liberation in 1968, and the virile vigilante leader (or police chief) who, in the name of law and order, would move against the revolutionary with the enthusiastic assent of a Western-fed majority of the population.

In a curious sense, both the gun-slinging sheriff and the anarchistic rebel are therefore very specific, and perhaps somewhat parallel, creations of the early nineteenth century. Both lead lives alien to the rationalism of the Founding Fathers. That earlier spirit of rationalism, as embodied in our Constitutional and civil libertarian traditions, continues to define the moderate center of American politics. But the influences, both direct and indirect, of the Romantic movement may well have given crucial sustenance to what later became the American left and right wings. If this analysis is plausible, then the American majority reveals a basic right-of-center predilection, for over the decades it has vacillated between sober Constitutionalism on the one hand and admiration for the romantic vigilante figure on the other—never (after 1848) between Constitutionalism and admiration for the romantic left-wing revolutionary.

But any possible parallel between the sources of right-wing and left-wing imagery, or between the roles of law enforcer and deliberate lawbreaker, should not be carried too far. The differences between "liberation" as defined on the main street of a Wild Western town and the same concept in the mind of a Greenwich Village socialist are, after all, quite enormous, far outweighing any remote similarities of origin. If the Romantic

movement created both versions of the ideal, it did so by crystal-
lizing tendencies which were already separate and distinct. For
most Americans, the change in the early nineteenth century was
merely one from an unthinking pragmatic activism to a conscious
admiration for a more heroic and sometimes violent expression
of those same qualities. For the Transcendental and socialist
minorities, however, the basic change was toward a new habit of
questioning fundamentals, and this was a trait which remained
highly uncharacteristic and deeply suspect in the larger society.[26]
A contrast in style between Americans was thus created at a very
central level, one which would continue powerfully to affect all
future arguments over questions of political legitimacy and obedience.

If much attention has been paid to the early nineteenth century in this essay, it is for two reasons—because so many current
American patterns seem to have jelled at that time, and because
the documents (and the series of introductory essays to them)
which follow will carry many of these themes of discussion forward into the more recent period. Here one might make a few
broad observations about the fate of these issues in modern times.

Although American society continued to be dominated by such
traditional institutions as legislative government, private property,
and the monogamous family, in the post-Civil War period the new
ecology of the city and of a closely knit national empire changed
the basic quality of experience both for the majority and for the
minorities. By the time of the First World War, and more especially the Second, government had become far more powerful in
scope and in technological capacity. The American majority—
gradually absorbing a flow of new immigrant groups—continued
to identify itself with goals of personal economic success (or
security) and with the vicarious satisfactions of national prestige;
it continued, only somewhat less openly, to attach great moral
importance to physical appearance and to skin color. Among the
intellectual minorities, the anonymity of the city whetted an appetite both for personal privacy and for a social revolution. Yet
at the same time urban drabness, poverty, and harsh working
conditions intensified an awareness of obstacles to be overcome

26. Discussion of this point is continued in the headnotes to documents
below, pp. 196–197.

before any basic change was likely to occur. Black people, as they moved into Northern cities and became more articulate and unafraid, began to make up another embittered and potent source of discontent. Meanwhile, as the decades wore on, the United States became the most powerful nation in the world.

During this industrial and imperial period of American history, episodes of domestic violence and lawlessness continued to be widespread. It is difficult, however, to equate varying rates of lawlessness with distinct stages of industrial growth. Civil disorders and major crimes of violence, both of which were frequent in the late nineteenth century, seem to have reached an even higher peak around the time of the First World War and the 1920's, declining greatly in the 1930's and 1940's, only to begin rising again in the 1960's.[27] The meaning of such variations over time is almost impossible to discern, since they correlate in precise fashion neither with economic cycles nor with wartime crises.

Disregarding these somewhat mysterious short-term changes, one may say that domestic violence has occurred at substantial levels throughout the whole industrial era. But what is the meaning of such a fact? Comparisons between the United States and other countries on this score might be expected to furnish a helpful yardstick, but in turn they produce no really dramatic results— unless one limits the contrast to an unusually law-abiding society such as England's.[28] Thus, for instance, a recent study of the entire world from this point of view ranks the United States twenty-fourth among all the nations in amount of civil strife during the years 1963 to 1968.[29] This places it at the outer edge of the

27. Graham and Gurr, *op. cit.*, pp. 90, 490.
28. Despite the notorious unreliability of crime statistics, Americans in the early twentieth century were indisputably far more lawless than Englishmen. The rate of premeditated murders in the population from 1914 to 1918 was something like one-twelfth as great in London as it was in Chicago, and in 1919 Cleveland reported thirty-one robberies for every one committed in Liverpool. Discrepancies in reporting, and the effects of the First World War, can hardly account for so enormous a disparity. Furthermore, crime rates among old-stock white Americans were much higher than among Englishmen. Raymond B. Fosdick, *American Police Systems* (New York: The Century Co., 1920), pp. 15–19. But why should England, in isolation, be taken as an important standard of comparison?
29. Graham and Gurr, *op. cit.*, p. 575; see also pp. 808–809 for a balanced overall summary. Elaborate efforts were made in this study to codify newspaper reports of such occurrences with reasonable objectivity, but of

normal range among highly developed Western democracies. American violence appears high as compared with Britain, Canada, Germany, Scandinavia, and the like, but low as compared with most (but not all) Asian, African, and Latin American states.

Again, what do these comparisons mean? A certain amount of collective violence is simply normal and to be expected, the sociologist Charles Tilly reminds us. At least this has been true throughout the recorded course of Western civilization.[30] America has had its share of labor violence and class conflict. Its frontier heritage and its racial antagonisms have somewhat intensified these tendencies. But one may be tempted to ask, so what? The statistical picture, if we are to have any faith in it, is altogether unremarkable.

It would, however, be far too arbitrary to dismiss the issue of American lawlessness on this basis. In the first place, these same comparative studies do reveal something important about the *kind* of civil strife that took place in America, as distinct from many other nations, during the 1960's. The figures show that an unusually large proportion of violent domestic conflict in America took the form of relatively unorganized turmoil, rather than conspiratorial or revolutionary movements. In other words, a very large share of American violence, in riots or demonstrations, involves persons and groups who have no thought of seeking consciously to overthrow the entire political system. Instead, most protest still concerns particular, limited grievances (for instance, over foreign policy or instances of police brutality).[31] Though groups with these limited grievances may go outside the law in seeking publicity for their causes, or because they are emotionally distraught, there is a major difference between such use of illegal or semilegal tactics and the stirring up of strife in order deliberately to bring the entire political system into a state of collapse. A certain number of self-conscious revolutionaries have

course any such cross-cultural study which is dependent upon the press is bound to be somewhat suspect. All one can say is that it is the best study yet done on a fascinating topic.

30. *Ibid.,* pp. 4–5.

31. This leaves aside the important question as to whether a major share of violence has actually been caused by the police, due to over-eager responses in crowds.

indeed appeared in America during the 1960's, but these statistics remind us that they are few and far between as compared with the same phenomenon in the non-Western world.

And here, in turn, one may find a clue as to how questions of obedience to authority have indeed functioned as a genuine issue in American history, despite the rather undramatic character of the statistics on violence. The statistics reveal nothing of the peculiar character of group conflict in America, which only partly (and decreasingly) involves social classes, and which very largely concerns intellectual and ethnic minorities such as have already been discussed. It is a mistake—as the statistical evidence confirms—to conceive of violence or revolution as unusual problems in our society at the level of practical deeds. Instead, "political" lawlessness, and threat of revolution itself whenever it does occur, are to be understood as moral and intellectual challenges to the existing majority—attempts, that is, to dramatize one side of an argument, or a minority world view. One may safely and appropriately conceive of all threats to the existing system in this fashion precisely because, in any extreme form, they have no chance whatever of success.[32]

In other words, it is the arena of debate that matters, not the arena of physical struggle, because we know the outcome of all such struggles in advance. (Physical deeds, it is true, have sometimes functioned to help keep debate flourishing, but that is an altogether different point.) The realm of debate, on the other hand, is always filled with surprises. Debate tends to unmask underlying attitudes and bring them into the open. Analysis of these attitudes is far more important than a counting of physical weapons.

It is the total qualitative vision of life implied by majority and minority viewpoints which one wants to try to understand, if one is to assess contemporary American society. The debate on law and authority, because it reveals a great deal about these larger visions, serves as a peculiarly important bellwether of American civilization. What, for instance, are the implications of an ethic that is closely attuned to suppression, as compared with one that is attuned to quiescence or to liberation? (Or, how does a policeman's world view compare with that of a moderate or a revolutionary?) Is "liberation" a viable concept or a self-deceptive one?

32. This assertion is elaborated at greater length on pp. 281–282.

How can it be defined more concretely? These are the kinds of questions we should be asking, and they have little to do with the statistical incidence of gunfighting.

But debate on questions of freedom and authority has been conducted in direct terms only at the outermost margins of the society. Minorities which question the deferential character of individual relationships to authority have remained extremely small in size. The socialist movement, relatively strong in the opening years of the twentieth century, moved in 1912 decisively toward moderatism, even before the party began its slow decline. Communism, though it temporarily attracted some restless spirits in the 1930's, always had far less influence, and it lacked the intellectual independence which would have made its contributions to a debate on political authority at all novel or stimulating. Furthermore, the Marxist tradition developed until very recently along centralist and statist lines which greatly lessened its radicalism in this particular respect. Therefore, from the radical side, the burden of lively agitation about questions of governmental authority long fell upon truly tiny groups of pacifists, anarchists, and right-wing and left-wing believers in a policy of economic decentralization.

Meanwhile, the majority has usually discussed the issue of obedience only obliquely. Exceptions to this have occurred during particular seasons of panic over real or assumed subversive threats (1917–1920, 1950–1954, 1965–   ), when explicit talk of a need for "law and order" would reach wide proportions.[33] More often, however, majority opinion would retain the ambiguity and evasiveness which it inherited from the nineteenth century. It is frequently puzzled, unsure of itself, and indecisive. Impulses toward vigilantism have often reappeared in a modern, urban setting, directed against labor groups, radicals, immigrants, and black people. But these outbursts have alternated with periods of quiet faith in Constitutional processes.

The majority has remained inconsistent on the level of theory as well as on that of emotional response. Neither twentieth-century

33. Those who consistently—year in and year out—talked about the need for more repressive authority constituted another kind of radical minority, expressing majority attitudes but in a far more intense fashion. Sometimes this was due to the rationale of certain occupations (such as police work itself), sometimes conceivably to psychological disorder.

liberalism nor conservatism—the two loose and ill-defined sub-
varieties of moderatism—achieved a clear-cut posture toward the
question of so-called big government and the free individual.
Liberals favored a strong role for government in matters of economic control and public welfare but a weak role so far as regulation of personal moral conduct and self-expression were concerned. Conservatives precisely reversed these two tendencies.
Both conservatives and liberals, at least after 1941, agreed on a
strong role for government in the area of warfare and national
defense, in order to give the United States a major position in
determining the outcome of events throughout the world. Thus
the rise of the so-called military-industrial complex and even the
existence (for most of its history) of the military draft were
noncontroversial within the entire political mainstream. All this
added up to a complicated patchwork of attitudes toward freedom,
both on the moderate left and right. The general tendency of the
American majority may perhaps be described as an acceptance
of an ever larger role for governmental authority in the lives of
individuals, but with various rather myopic and strenuously argued
qualifications.

Broader intellectual changes have further affected debate about
individual freedom over the last several decades. Most importantly,
twentieth-century social science has emphasized the extent to which
the individual is patterned or conditioned by his environment—
whether by parents, peers, or the larger surrounding culture.
"Science" has thus cast doubt upon the whole concept of individual
autonomy and just possibly made the very idea of individualism
meaningless. No man could live as a recognizable human being
without simultaneously being part of a social group, anthropologists are always reminding us, pointing by way of proof to the
sad fate of feral children. Indeed, the very concept of the self
arises tardily in infancy, as Mead and Cooley discovered long
ago, and it comes as the result of reasoning back to our own
existence from the already perceived existence of others. Perhaps,
therefore, what we used to call individuality amounts either to some
sort of mental wound—mild or severe—or else (in a more positive sense) merely to playing out a given cultural role with a
certain flair and relish.[34]

34. This point of view is, for instance, attractively presented in Dorothy
Lee, *Freedom and Culture* (Englewood Cliffs, N.J.: Prentice-Hall, 1959).

This version of social science, with its deterministic implications, seemingly clashed with the resurgent Romanticism of the younger radicals. But in fact the radicals were themselves highly ambivalent in their view of individual freedom—for on the one hand they emphasized such values as "autonomy" and self-expression while on the other they elevated the idea of the "tribe" or communal group even more passionately than did the earlier anthropologists. The fashionable rhetoric of existentialism did not really smooth over this disparity. Individualism, in any event, clearly no longer meant isolation to the degree that it had in Thoreau's time or in the mythology of the "lonely" frontier. Privacy was still very much sought after, in the mountains or in the city, but it was the privacy of the minority group, seeking a collective sense of protection and freedom from the potentially repressive majority.

In a broader sense, the heritage of the Romantic movement remains extremely powerful in setting the tone of utopian thinking today. It permeates the writings of Erich Fromm, Herbert Marcuse, and Norman O. Brown. It essentially shapes the alternative vision of a "deep" yet spontaneous relationship among human beings—although an image of what the early Christians are thought to have been like also contributes to this view. Contemporary radicals do indeed have a positive conception of the good society; it is still the primitivistic, handicraft-oriented, Gemeinschaft ideal first formulated by nineteenth-century critics of the Industrial Revolution and now, despite its apparent implausibility, made far more attractive by the realities of mid-twentieth-century technology, bureaucracy, and warfare.[35]

It should be remembered, of course, that not all radicals embraced the heavily introspective style of neo-Transcendentalism, just as, conversely, many believers in individual psychological "depth" were by no means radical—or even much concerned with politics. Indeed, it was fortunate that two such major polarities in American society—between the politically moderate and radical and between the temperamentally "deep" and the matter-of-fact—did not consistently reinforce each other, just as neither of them neatly coincided with that third major polarity, between

35. The quest for a new cultural identity among younger blacks is not dissimilar to this ideal, although it is the civilizations of ancient Africa (not its primitiveness) which attract them.

the white and the black. America continued to be marked by diverse minorities rather than by a single subject population, clearly identifiable in one swoop. This variety silently helped to make American society more bearable—it was never quite possible to conclude that all political radicals, all psychoanalysts, or all white people were truly alike, and therefore in everyday encounters to treat them in accord with one's often harsh stereotypes.

But, even if the American majority was frequently indecisive and ambivalent, and even if several overlapping minorities continued to exist side by side, softening the impact of any single one, it would be wrong to minimize the very real sense of insecurity and anxiety among the middle class, on the one hand, and the equally real pursuit of an alternative social vision by a series of smaller groups on the other. (Certainly no such innocuous phrase as "pluralism" sufficed to convey the actual flavor of this kind of social situation.) And even if fear of violence, by every available statistical indication, had been greatly exaggerated, an undue sense of alarm in itself constitutes an important symptom of mutual distrust.

Such distrust may very well continue, so long as the conflict remains one between deeply held and yet sharply contrasting moral codes (hip and square, absolutistic and instrumental, black nationalist and white moderate). But, with the outcome of violence so readily predictable, both in terms of power and of human pain, it is only to be hoped that even fundamental ethical viewpoints may be put forward by means of calm words, controlled emotions, and quiet personal and communal experiments.

Is it impossibly old-fashioned to wish for a return to debate, no matter on how intense a level? Frank debate may, after all, spur action, not necessarily deflect men from what they must ultimately do. The readings which follow furnish the materials for a new round in such a debate; all sides are represented, and there has been no effort at toning anyone down. Perhaps it is not yet too late to arrive at one's convictions about the American future calmly and reflectively.

Part One

Argument over the
Nature and Limits
of Authority

We are frequently told that the range of serious political discussion in America has been quite narrow, as compared with the spectrum of viewpoints to be found in most other countries. No monarchists and few determined aristocrats could be found among us, nor could many theoretical anarchists. In a worldwide context, nearly all Americans are often defined simply as middle-of-the-roaders, or perhaps as mild conservatives.

But American argument over questions of political authority has in fact been richer and more diverse than such a gross interpretation will allow. Even leaving aside the figure of John C. Calhoun, whose oft-noted defense of minorities is probably best relegated, when all is said and done, to the category of special pleading, by the early nineteenth century one could find in America political viewpoints that were both markedly to the left and to the right of the Lockean mainstream—in one direction, toward making the individual into the final judge of the state; in the other, toward a Burkean organicist conservatism. One could thus find the role of the state being both boldly minimized and explicitly glorified, as well as being casually harmonized with notions of freedom, individualism, and social progress.

As time passed, these three positions continued to be voiced, sometimes with greater force and sometimes with a subtler intricacy. Though industrialism failed to produce either as much radical militance or as deep a backward-looking, anti-modernist reaction as it did in European countries, both these tendencies have certainly appeared here in the twentieth century, sometimes drawing sustenance from the anti-statist tradition in nineteenth-century American thought. Just as importantly, growing variations of tone manifested themselves within the central liberal school of thinking. It made some difference, after all, whether one's liberalism was the product of a scientific or a humanistic vision of reality, whether it was grounded on legalistic, historical, biological, or psychological arguments, and whether it sprang from a populistic or a tacitly elitist frame of reference. It also mattered in what direction this liberal tradition was being manipulated in each given case—toward sanctioning certain kinds of permissiveness and not others, for instance. For in these nuances lay much of the actual history of freedom as an idea in America.

There are those who will argue that American political discussion is as bland and uniform as any well-thumbed book whose pages lack further mystery. But American writers of the past century have in fact displayed nothing like the monotony of, let us say, the Chinese during the long neo-Confucian centuries after A.D. 1300, nor the sterility of other highly traditional and static intellectual systems one might easily name. Instead Americans have actively participated in the movement toward lively self-analysis which has occurred recently throughout Western thought. To that larger arena of twentieth-century speculation they have brought a special—if often too narrowly defined—concern for human freedom. As individuals, therefore, and not merely as representatives of "Lockeanism" or liberalism, quite a few Americans who have written on these subjects are worth listening to, no matter how critical one may be of what they sometimes have to say.

We should not, in other words, feel intimidated by the existence of an American mainstream. To comprehend the variety of what has been said in America about questions of freedom and obedience is to realize, by virtue of the very disagreements, that one has every right to reach conclusions of one's own. Knowing this, we need have no fear of being numbed by the actual process of reading what was written in the past.

Three Classic Traditions

It is always pleasant to approach nineteenth-century America by the easy device of reading Henry David Thoreau. His paragraphs have much the same simple majesty as Lincoln's. His thinking can appeal to us in a sense that seems almost timeless. He is, moreover, a highly fashionable source of inspiration at the present moment.

Unfortunately, however, one should read Thoreau last rather than first, because he has not been representative of American thinking on questions of law and authority—and had little direct influence in his own day. To understand the full spectrum of American attitudes about relations between the individual and the state, we must begin with what has been the majority viewpoint— both then and now. Further, the early appearance of a minority viewpoint opposite to Thoreau's must not be neglected. Only this triple perspective, at the very least, can serve as an adequate introduction to the scope of American thinking in this area.

1. Primacy of the Majority

An ideal of democratic unity gained increasingly wide acceptance in the United States during the half century after independence. As resistance to such mildly levelling tendencies on the part of conservative New Englanders melted, and as the franchise was extended in every state to include all adult white males, this viewpoint emerged as the dominant American answer to questions of liberty and authority. Deviant groups and individuals might sometimes be tolerated, as in the experimental communities which flourished briefly in New England and on the frontier, or they might more often be persecuted, as in the case of mob attacks on early abolitionists. But, in theory, obedience to law and custom was justified in terms of majority rule.

Eccentric individuals certainly abounded in pre-Civil War America, often enjoying great practical freedom, but spokesmen for the rising tide of democracy seldom explicitly celebrated them. Instead, their language was that of the community, the nation. In their rhetoric they encouraged Americans to think of themselves as "the people" in a general sense, often seeing no contradiction between this form of political collectivism and the advocacy of economic laissez faire. (Indeed, perhaps economic individualism could thrive only when sustained by a reassuring patriotic focus at another level of the imagination.) Politically, Americans in this period gained the sense of unity and purpose which, perhaps more than anything else, would paradoxically enable them to sustain a prolonged Civil War on both sides.[1]

It requires an effort of the imagination in our own day to re-call how readily nationalism and political liberalism could once be combined as ideals, not only in the United States but among advanced thinkers in Western Europe. The growing collective patriotic consciousness did not then appear to contradict progres-sive social hopes and expectations. Society, civilization, humanity would all advance in step with the nation. Although Americans had already in fact demonstrated a deep division on the subject of recent French upheavals, many liberal nationalists long after-ward found it easy to assume that the cause of revolution could be linked with that of the majority in the United States.

The liberal mentality, parading its own recent liberation, thus adopted a majoritarian outlook in a generous, confident spirit. Ancient and far-removed enemies, such as monarchy and aristoc-racy, could still be attacked in extravagant terms, providing a wel-come sense of reassurance. In an opposite direction, the socialist ethos, then in its utopian phase, could usually be regarded as a beneficent extension of liberal principles rather than as a genuine threat from below.

One might never gather that beneath such expansiveness of tone could be found political instincts fully geared to the realities of partisan infighting—that is, to the very real existence of persistent, unconvinced, and deeply passionate minorities within the nation. Lawless disobedience to George III was still a wonderful memory;

1. For much evidence concerning this mood, see the early chapters of Merle Curti, *The Roots of American Loyalty* (New York: Columbia Uni-versity Press, 1946). See also Daniel J. Boorstin, *The Americans: The National Experience* (New York: Vintage Books, 1965), pp. 337–390; and Arthur A. Ekirch, Jr., *The Decline of American Liberalism* (New York: Atheneum, 1967), pp. 93–94.

only when the question suddenly became one of disobedience to Abraham Lincoln did Northern majoritarians fully realize that their developing philosophy of liberal consensus had turned them into defenders of an established continental empire, with its own dignity and territorial boundaries to protect. And only much later on did the repressive possibilities of this patriotic collective consciousness begin to exhibit themselves against men with a more modern dream of revolutionary disruption.

George Bancroft (1800–1891) perfectly embodied the rising exhilaration of this liberal mood when it was still young. His lyrical writings, steeped in the florid romanticism of the day, provide a window onto the optimistic faith of large numbers of ordinary Americans, both then and more recently. As an historian of the War for Independence, Bancroft directly helped to promote the spread of this spirit, by inculcating a view of the past which reconciled the legacy of revolutionary sympathies with a sense of national pride and solidarity. In his further role as a Jacksonian politician, he sought to carry his ideas into the practical realm of action.

Yet one should realize that Bancroft's rhetoric was far more assured than his personal situation. The product of a New England ministerial family whose politics remained conservative, he was a rather lonely figure in the context of his immediate environment in Massachusetts. As a Harvard tutor and schoolmaster, he had been something of a failure. In politics, he acquired a reputation for shiftiness, and he expressed a partisan emotionalism out of keeping with the buoyantly inclusive spirit of his writings. His embrace of the cause of the common man came only after an initial hesitation, during which he was capable of describing the crowd at one of Andrew Jackson's receptions as "the vilest promiscuous medley, that ever was congregated in a decent house . . . all the refuse that Washington could turn forth from its workshops and stables."[2]

It was perhaps no internal contradiction, but rather an inherent difficulty of his liberal nationalist philosophy, which led him, as Secretary of the Navy and acting Secretary of War under James K. Polk, to express publicly the hope that "war is permanently out of fashion in the civilized world," while in the same role he willingly signed the order that launched American troops into ter-

2. Mark DeWolfe Howe, ed., *The Life and Letters of George Bancroft* (New York: Charles Scribner's Sons, 1908), Vol. I, p. 196.

ritory disputed with Mexico and thereby aggressively fulfilled American dreams of expansion. There was in him none of the fastidiousness which would have led him seriously to weigh the claims of humane idealism against those of patriotic emotion. The most that can be said is that he appears to have been a shade less bellicose than other members of Polk's cabinet. It was entirely consistent with his earlier thinking, therefore, that in 1861 he proceeded to attack Southern secession as "the doctrine of individualism, pushed to its extremist limit; it would have dissolved the country, society itself, into atoms as lifeless and unconnected as the particles of sound; it would have left no room for the love of country."

Again one must remember how seldom the liberal nationalist mind could perceive contradictions between those aspects of its faith which seem in the twentieth century to march awkwardly together. For Bancroft, faith in progress (which made each new historical development seem good in its place) allowed him simultaneously to praise revolution and order, peace and patriotism, material strength and moral force. If confronted by the choice between individual and society, it seems clear that he would consciously have chosen to support the claims of society. Yet this is to place him in a dilemma uncongenial not only to him but to his age. When he affirms that "individuals are of limited sagacity" and again says that truth does not acknowledge "the solitary mind," he might appear to be replying to a Thoreau (though of the actual Thoreau, incidentally, he seems never to have taken particular notice). But in such statements he was really announcing more of an inclination than a decision. For, after all, he also claimed to be a generous respecter of individual differences, even those of "the brutal Hottentot." Here surely is no easy case for Louis Hartz, claiming that American liberal consensus was always firmly etched by racism at its outer boundary. Perhaps, indeed, it was somewhat easier for a man of Bancroft's stripe to say yes to a Hottentot or to an Indian than to a nearby Margaret Fuller.

Thus Bancroft, with his generous version of the philosophy of majority rule, seems to stand as the ancestor of more than one later American position on matters of liberty and obedience. Not promoting an extreme individualism, he nonetheless fostered the liberal ideal of individual as well as collective human worth; not rhetorically authoritarian, he made practical concessions which look forward to a toleration for the garrison state. In all these respects, as in his very tendency toward easy inconsistency, he becomes the smooth-minded spokesman for the American main-stream.

George Bancroft, "The Office of the People in Art, Government, and Religion"

I

The material world does not change in its masses or in its powers. The stars shine with no more lustre than when they first sang together in the glory of their birth. The flowers that gemmed the fields and the forests, before America was discovered, now bloom around us in their season. The sun that shone on Homer shines on us in unchanging lustre. The bow that beamed on the patriarch still glitters in the clouds. Nature is the same. For her no new forces are generated; no new capacities are discovered. The earth turns on its axis, and perfects its revolutions, and renews its seasons, without increase or advancement.

But a like passive destiny does not attach to the inhabitants of the earth. For them the expectations of social improvement are no delusion; the hopes of philanthropy are more than a dream. The five senses do not constitute the whole inventory of our sources of knowledge. They are the organs by which thought connects itself with the external universe; but the power of thought is not merged in the exercise of its instruments. We have functions which connect us with heaven, as well as organs which set us in relation with earth. We have not merely the senses opening to us the external world, but an internal sense, which places us in connexion with the world of intelligence and the decrees of God.

There is a *spirit in man:* not in the privileged few; not in those of us only who by the favor of Providence have been nursed in

An oration delivered before the Adelphi Society of Williamstown College, 1835. From George Bancroft, *Literary and Historical Miscellanies* (New York: Harper & Brothers, 1855), pp. 408–417, 418–419, 421–427, 430–431, 433–435.

public schools: IT IS IN MAN: it is the attribute of the race. The spirit, which is the guide to truth, is the gracious gift to each member of the human family.

Reason exists within every breast. I mean not that faculty which deduces inferences from the experience of the senses, but that higher faculty, which from the infinite treasures of its own consciousness, originates truth, and assents to it by the force of intuitive evidence; that faculty which raises us beyond the control of time and space, and gives us faith in things eternal and invisible. There is not the difference between one mind and another, which the pride of philosophers might conceive. To them no faculty is conceded, which does not belong to the meanest of their countrymen. In them there can not spring up a truth, which does not equally have its germ in every mind. They have not the power of creation; they can but reveal what God has implanted in every breast.

The intellectual functions, by which relations are perceived, are the common endowments of the race. The differences are apparent, not real. The eye in one person may be dull, in another quick, in one distorted, and in another tranquil and clear; yet the relation of the eye to light is in all men the same. Just so judgment may be liable in individual minds to the bias of passion, and yet its relation to truth is immutable, and is universal.

In questions of practical duty, conscience is God's umpire, whose light illumines every heart. There is nothing in books, which had not first, and has not still its life within us. Religion itself is a dead letter, wherever its truths are not renewed in the soul. Individual conscience may be corrupted by interest, or debauched by pride, yet the rule of morality is distinctly marked; its harmonies are to the mind like music to the ear; and the moral judgment, when carefully analyzed and referred to its principles, is always founded in right. The eastern superstition, which bids its victims prostrate themselves before the advancing car of their idols, springs from a noble root, and is but a melancholy perversion of that self-devotion, which enables the Christian to bear the cross, and subject his personal passions to the will of God. Immorality of itself never won to its support the inward voice; conscience, if questioned, never forgets to curse the guilty with the memory of sin, to cheer the upright with the meek tranquillity of approval. And this admirable power, which is the instinct of Deity, is the attribute of every man; it knocks at the palace gate, it dwells in the meanest hovel. Duty, like death, enters every abode, and delivers its message. Conscience, like reason and judgment, is universal.

That the moral affections are planted every where, needs only to be asserted to be received. The savage mother loves her offspring with all the fondness that a mother can know. Beneath the odorous shade of the boundless forests of Chili, the native youth repeats the story of love as sincerely as it was ever chanted in the valley of Vaucluse. The affections of family are not the growth of civilization. The charities of life are scattered every where; enamelling the vales of human being, as the flowers paint the meadows. They are not the fruit of study, nor the privilege of refinement, but a natural instinct.

Our age has seen a revolution in works of imagination. The poet has sought his theme in common life. Never is the genius of Scott more pathetic, than when, as in the Antiquary, he delineates the sorrows of a poor fisherman, or as in the Heart of Mid Lothian, he takes his heroine from a cottage. And even Wordsworth, the purest and most original poet of the day, in spite of the inveterate character of his political predilections, has thrown the light of genius on the walks of commonest life; he finds a lesson in every grave of the village churchyard; he discloses the boundless treasures of feeling in the peasant, the laborer and the artisan; the strolling peddler becomes, through his genius, a teacher of the sublimest morality; and the solitary wagoner, the lonely shepherd, even the feeble mother of an idiot boy, furnishes lessons in the reverence for Humanity.

If from things relating to truth, justice, and affection, we turn to those relating to the beautiful, we may here still further assert, that the sentiment for the beautiful resides in every breast. The lovely forms of the external world delight us from their adaptation to our powers.

> Yea, what were mighty Nature's self?
> Her features could they win us,
> Unhelped by the poetic voice
> That hourly speaks within us?

The Indian mother, on the borders of Hudson's Bay, decorates her manufactures with ingenious devices and lovely colors, prompted by the same instinct which guided the pencil and mixed the colors of Raphael. The inhabitant of Nootka Sound tattoos his body with the method of harmonious Arabesques. Every form, to which the hands of the artist have ever given birth, sprung first into being as a conception of his mind, from a natural faculty, which belongs not to the artist exclusively, but to man. Beauty, like truth and justice, lives within us; like virtue and like moral law, it is a companion of the soul. The power which leads to the production of beautiful forms, or to the perception of them in the works which God has made, is an attribute of Humanity.

But I am asked if I despise learning? Shall one who has spent much of his life in schools and universities plead the equality of uneducated nature? Is there no difference between the man of refinement and the savage?

"I am a man," said Black Hawk nobly to the chief of the first republic in the world; "I am a man," said the barbarous chieftain, "and you are another."

I speak for the universal diffusion of human powers, not of human attainments; for the capacity for progress, not for the perfection of undisciplined instincts. The fellowship which we should cherish with the race, receives the Comanche warrior and the Caffre within the pale of equality. Their functions may not have been exercised, but they exist. Immure a person in a dungeon; as he comes to the light of day, his vision seems incapable of performing its office. Does that destroy your conviction in the relation between the eye and light? The rioter over his cups resolves to eat and drink and be merry; he forgets his spiritual nature in his obedience to the senses; but does that destroy the relation between conscience and eternity? "What ransom shall we give?" exclaimed the senators of Rome to the savage Attila. "Give," said the barbarian, "all your gold and jewels, your costly furniture and treasures, and set free every slave." "Ah," replied the degenerate Romans, "what then will be left to us?" "I leave you your souls," replied the unlettered invader from the steppes of Asia, who had learnt in the wilderness to value the immortal mind, and to despise the servile herd, that esteemed only their fortunes, and had no true respect for themselves. You cannot discover a tribe of men, but you also find the charities of life, and the proofs of spiritual existence. Behold the ignorant Algonquin deposit a bow and quiver by the side of the departed warrior; and recognise his faith in immortality. See the Comanche chieftain, in the heart of our continent, inflict on himself severest penance; and reverence his confession of the needed atonement for sin. The Barbarian who roams our western prairies has like passions and like endowments with ourselves. He bears within him the instinct of Deity; the consciousness of a spiritual nature; the love of beauty; the rule of morality.

And shall we reverence the dark-skinned Caffre? Shall we respect the brutal Hottentot? You may read the right answer written on every heart. It bids me not despise the sable hunter, that gathers a livelihood in the forests of Southern Africa. All are men. When we know the Hottentot better, we shall despise him less.

II

If it be true, that the gifts of mind and heart are universally diffused, if the sentiment of truth, justice, love, and beauty exists in every one, then it follows, as a necessary consequence, that the common judgment in taste, politics, and religion, is the highest authority on earth, and the nearest possible approach to an infallible decision. From the consideration of individual powers I turn to the action of the human mind in masses.

If reason is a universal faculty, the universal decision is the nearest criterion of truth. The common mind winnows opinions; it is the sieve which separates error from certainty. The exercise by many of the same faculty on the same subject would naturally lead to the same conclusions. But if not, the very differences of opinion that arise prove the supreme judgment of the general mind. Truth is one. It never contradicts itself. One truth cannot contradict another truth. Hence truth is a bond of union. But error not only contradicts truth, but may contradict itself; so that there may be many errors, and each at variance with the rest. Truth is therefore of necessity an element of harmony; error as necessarily an element of discord. Thus there can be no continuing universal judgment but a right one. Men cannot agree in an absurdity; neither can they agree in a falsehood.

If wrong opinions have often been cherished by the masses, the cause always lies in the complexity of the ideas presented. Error finds its way into the soul of a nation, only through the channel of truth. It is to a truth that men listen; and if they accept error also, it is only because the error is for the time so closely interwoven with truth, that the one cannot readily be separated from the other.

Unmixed error can have no existence in the public mind. Wherever you see men clustering together to form a party, you may be sure that however much error may be there, truth is there also. Apply this principle boldly; for it contains a lesson of candor, and a voice of encouragement. There never was a school of philosophy, nor a clan in the realm of opinion, but carried along with it some important truth. And therefore every sect that has ever flourished has benefited Humanity; for the errors of a sect pass away and are forgotten; its truths are received into the common inheritance. To know the seminal thought of every prophet and leader of a sect, is to gather all the wisdom of mankind.

> "By heaven! there should not be a seer, who left
> The world one doctrine, but I'd task his lore,
> And commune with his spirit. All the truth
> Of all the tongues of earth, I'd have them all,
> Had I the powerful spell to raise their ghosts."

The sentiment of beauty, as it exists in the human mind, is the criterion in works of art, inspires the conceptions of genius, and exercises a final judgment on its productions. For who are the best judges in matters of taste? Do you think the cultivated individual? Undoubtedly not; but the collective mind. The public is wiser than the wisest critic. In Athens, the arts were carried to perfection, when "the fierce democracie" was in the ascendant; the temple of Minerva and the works of Phidias were planned and perfected to please the common people. When Greece yielded to tyrants, her genius for excellence in art expired; or rather, the purity of taste disappeared; because the artist then endeavored to gratify a patron, and therefore, humored his caprice; while before he had endeavored to delight the race. . . .

If with us the arts are destined to a brilliant career, the inspiration must spring from the vigor of the people. Genius will not create, to flatter patrons or decorate saloons. It yearns for larger influences; it feeds on wider sympathies; and its perfect display can never exist, except in an appeal to the general sentiment for the beautiful. . . .

III

In like manner the best government rests on the people and not on the few, on persons and not on property, on the free development of public opinion and not on authority; because the munificent Author of our being has conferred the gifts of mind upon every member of the human race without distinction of outward circumstances. Whatever of other possessions may be engrossed, mind asserts its own independence. Lands, estates, the produce of mines, the prolific abundance of the seas, may be usurped by a privileged class. Avarice, assuming the form of ambitious power, may grasp realm after realm, subdue continents, compass the earth in its schemes of aggrandizement, and sigh after other worlds; but mind eludes the power of appropriation; it exists only in its own individuality; it is a property which cannot be confiscated and cannot be torn away; it laughs at chains; it bursts from imprisonment; it defies monopoly. A government of equal rights must, therefore, rest upon mind; not wealth, not brute force, the sum of the moral intelligence of the community should rule the State. Prescription can no more assume to be a valid plea for political injustice; society studies to eradicate established abuses, and to bring social institutions and laws into harmony with moral right; not dismayed by the natural and necessary imperfections of all human effort, and not giving way to despair, because every hope does not at once ripen into fruit.

The public happiness is the true object of legislation, and can be secured only by the masses of mankind themselves awakening to the knowledge and the care of their own interests. Our free institutions have reversed the false and ignoble distinctions between men; and refusing to gratify the pride of caste, have acknowledged the common mind to be the true material for a commonwealth. Every thing has hitherto been done for the happy few. It is not possible to endow an aristocracy with greater benefits than they have already enjoyed; there is no room to hope that individuals will be more highly gifted or more fully developed than the greatest sages of past times. The world can advance only through the culture of the moral and intellectual powers of the people. To accomplish this end by means of the people themselves, is the highest purpose of government. If it be the duty of the individual to strive after a perfection like the perfection of God, how much more ought a nation to be the image of Deity. The common mind is the true Parian marble, fit to be wrought into likeness to a God. The duty of America is to secure the culture and the happiness of the masses by their reliance on themselves.

The absence of the prejudices of the old world leaves us here the opportunity of consulting independent truth; and man is left to apply the instinct of freedom to every social relation and public interest. We have approached so near to nature, that we can hear her gentlest whispers; we have made Humanity our lawgiver and our oracle; and, therefore, the nation receives, vivifies and applies principles, which in Europe the wisest accept with distrust. Freedom of mind and of conscience, freedom of the seas, freedom of industry, equality of franchises, each great truth is firmly grasped, comprehended and enforced; for the multitude is neither rash nor fickle. In truth, it is less fickle than those who profess to be its guides. Its natural dialectics surpass the logic of the schools. Political action has never been so consistent and so unwavering, as when it results from a feeling or a principle, diffused through society. The people is firm and tranquil in its movements, and necessarily acts with moderation, because it becomes but slowly impregnated with new ideas; and effects no changes, except in harmony with the knowledge which it has acquired. Besides, where it is permanently possessed of power, there exists neither the occasion nor the desire for frequent change. It is not the parent of tumult; sedition is bred in the lap of luxury, and its chosen emissaries are the beggared spendthrift and the impoverished libertine. The government by the people is in very truth the strongest government in the world. Discarding the implements of terror, it dares to rule by moral force, and has its citadel in the heart.

Such is the political system which rests on reason, reflection, and the free expression of deliberate choice. There may be those who scoff at the suggestion, that the decision of the whole is to be preferred to the judgment of the enlightened few. They say in their hearts that the masses are ignorant; that farmers know nothing of legislation; that mechanics should not quit their workshops to join in forming public opinion. But true political science does indeed venerate the masses. It maintains, not as has been perversely asserted, that "the people can make right," but that the people can DISCERN right. Individuals are but shadows, too often engrossed by the pursuit of shadows; the race is immortal: individuals are of limited sagacity; the common mind is infinite in its experience: individuals are languid and blind; the many are ever wakeful: individuals are corrupt; the race has been redeemed: individuals are time-serving; the masses are fearless: individuals may be false, the masses are ingenuous and sincere: individuals claim the divine sanction of truth for the deceitful conceptions of their own fancies; the Spirit of God breathes through the combined intelligence of the people. Truth is not to be ascertained by the impulses of an individual; it emerges from the contradictions of personal opinions; it raises itself in majestic serenity above the strifes of parties and the conflict of sects; it acknowledges neither the solitary mind, nor the separate faction as its oracle; but owns as its only faithful interpreter the dictates of pure reason itself, proclaimed by the general voice of mankind. The decrees of the universal conscience are the nearest approach to the presence of God in the soul of man.

Thus the opinion which we respect is, indeed, not the opinion of one or of a few, but the sagacity of the many. It is hard for the pride of cultivated philosophy to put its ear to the ground, and listen reverently to the voice of lowly humanity; yet the people collectively are wiser than the most gifted individual, for all his wisdom constitutes but a part of theirs. When the great sculptor of Greece was endeavoring to fashion the perfect model of beauty, he did not passively imitate the form of the loveliest woman of his age; but he gleaned the several lineaments of his faultless work from the many. And so it is, that a perfect judgment is the result of comparison, when error eliminates error, and truth is established by concurring witnesses. The organ of truth is the invisible decision of the unbiased world; she pleads before no tribunal but public opinion; she owns no safe interpreter but the common mind; she knows no court of appeals but the soul of humanity. It is when the multitude give counsel, that right purposes find safety; theirs is the fixedness that cannot be shaken; theirs is the understanding which exceeds in wisdom; theirs is the heart, of which the largeness is as the sand on the sea-shore.

It is not by vast armies, by immense natural resources, by accumulations of treasure, that the greatest results in modern civilization have been accomplished. The traces of the career of conquest pass away, hardly leaving a scar on the national intelligence. The famous battle grounds of victory are, most of them, comparatively indifferent to the human race; barren fields of blood, the scourges of their times, but affecting the social condition as little as the raging of a pestilence. Not one benevolent institution, not one ameliorating principle in the Roman state, was a voluntary concession of the aristocracy; each useful element was borrowed from the Democracies of Greece, or was a reluctant concession to the demands of the people. The same is true in modern political life. It is the confession of an enemy to Democracy, that "ALL THE GREAT AND NOBLE INSTITUTIONS OF THE WORLD HAVE COME FROM POPULAR EFFORTS."

It is the uniform tendency of the popular element to elevate and bless Humanity. The exact measure of the progress of civilization is the degree in which the intelligence of the common mind has prevailed over wealth and brute force; in other words, the measure of the progress of civilization is the progress of the people. . . .

It is alone by infusing great principles into the common mind, that revolutions in human society are brought about. They never have been, they never can be, effected by superior individual excellence. . . .

Yes, reforms in society are only effected through the masses of the people, and through them have continually taken place. New truths have been successively developed, and, becoming the common property of the human family, have improved its condition. This progress is advanced by every sect, precisely because each sect, to obtain vitality, does of necessity embody a truth; by every political party, for the conflicts of party are the war of ideas; by every nationality, for a nation cannot exist as such, till humanity makes it a special trustee of some part of its wealth for the ultimate benefit of all. The irresistible tendency of the human race is therefore to advancement, for absolute power has never succeeded, and can never succeed, in suppressing a single truth. An idea once revealed may find its admission into every living breast and live there. Like God it becomes immortal and omnipresent. The movement of the species is upward, irresistibly upward. The individual is often lost; Providence never disowns the race. No principle once promulgated, has ever been forgotten. No "timely tramp" of a despot's foot ever trod out one idea. The world cannot retrograde; the dark ages cannot return. Dynasties perish; cities are buried; nations have been victims to error, or martyrs for right; Humanity has always been on the advance; gaining maturity, universality, and power.

Yes, truth is immortal; it cannot be destroyed; it is invincible, it cannot long be resisted. Not every great principle has yet been generated; but when once proclaimed and diffused, it lives without end, in the safe custody of the race. States may pass away; every just principle of legislation which has been once established will endure. Philosophy has sometimes forgotten God; a great people never did. The skepticism of the last century could not uproot Christianity, because it lived in the hearts of the millions. Do you think that infidelity is spreading? Christianity never lived in the hearts of so many millions as at this moment. The forms under which it is professed may decay, for they, like all that is the work of man's hands, are subject to the changes and chances of mortal being; but the spirit of truth is incorruptible; it may be developed, illustrated, and applied; it never can die; it never can decline.

No truth can perish; no truth can pass away. The flame is undying, though generations disappear. Wherever moral truth has started into being, Humanity claims and guards the bequest. Each generation gathers together the imperishable children of the past, and increases them by new sons of light, alike radiant with immortality.

2. Primacy of the State

Eighty years after the American Revolution, not all men agreed with Bancroft that its memory was a safe one to invoke. In 1856 a Massachusetts lawyer and politician, Rufus Choate, wrote a famous letter in which he referred with distaste to the "glittering and sounding generalities of natural right which make up the Declaration of Independence." Choate was articulating a frankly conservative philosophy which, though somewhat unusual in its own day, looks not only backward to the Federalists but also ahead to the pronounced defense of law and order among moderate and right-wing Americans in the twentieth century.

Choate recognized the logical difficulty that men like Bancroft slid over so easily—that a revolutionary tradition was an uncertain source of internal stability for an established government. Thus he argued, as so few Americans were then willing to do, that the state (or each of the American states) was its own eternal end. Law would not be venerated or reverenced, he declared, if it were based merely on majority rule, for majorities may rapidly change and continuity is the only source of strength. Law should instead be viewed as "the absolute justice of the State, enlightened by the perfect reason of the State." Although he sometimes claimed to accept much of the tradition of natural rights, Choate perceived that if the state were viewed merely as a voluntary association, the promoters of undesirably rapid social change would be given too much encouragement. Above all, he attacked the spirit that said we can "be and do just what we please" at any given moment. Old forms, especially the American Constitution, should be revered simply because of their age.

Thus it would not be amiss to consider Choate an early exponent of Burkean ideas in America, long before they became fashionable among the so-called New Conservatives of the 1950's. It is worth reading Choate to recall the existence of a persistent undercurrent of statist thinking in America, perhaps ultimately as powerful as the one in the opposite direction represented by Thoreau.

True, Choate made certain concessions to the spirit of reform. All political systems, he said, have two aspects—liberty and order, progression and conservatism. Particular changes might be salutary from time to time; it was the basic organic form of government which must at all costs be conserved. But in the American Constitution he found an instrument which was already more or less perfect. Thus, while some other nations might still require drastic overhauls, this was certainly not true of the United States. Our basic reforms had been accomplished by the year 1789. The "people" had then ceded their power forever to duly elected officers under the Constitution. Any talk of further revolution in this country was illegitimate and dangerous. For this very reason, however, public policy should be moderate and conciliatory in any given context; thus the brand-new Republican Party of 1856 was ominously provocative in an anti-Southern direction, and Choate, a former Whig, refused to support it.

Choate's beliefs were closely tied to his pride, as a lawyer, in the developing legal profession in the United States. They are particularly interesting for this reason. In seeing the lawyer as above all else the servant of the state, Choate was laying the foundation for the close identification of law with forces of social and political conservatism. This kind of argument would eventually become the main basis for bitter opposition to the Warren Court in the mid-twentieth century. In his address to the graduates of the Harvard Law School in 1845, portions of which appear below, Choate exhorts future lawyers to think of themselves as the guardians of stability against all threats posed by disrespect for authority, whether advanced by individuals, small groups, or even numerical majorities.

The speech, besides being so striking in terms of substance, is also a rather marvellous example of nineteenth-century American oratory, more vivid and extreme in this respect than Bancroft's. Choate, whose original inclination to study law was sparked by hearing one of Daniel Webster's great speeches, was by all accounts a highly magnetic public figure—tall, graceful, and dignified in his physical presence, and strongly persuasive in the courtroom. An eminent leader of the state bar, he also served in both houses of Congress. In these roles he became known as a staunch defender of business interests, associating himself closely with Webster. Culturally he was less plebeian; he loved Greek and Latin literature, which he would memorize and recite at great length. His rather exquisite social urbanity was relieved by a great sense of humor.

The American legal profession, at the time when Choate was seeking to lead it in these conservative directions, was still in an uncertain and fluid state. A few leading lawyers, such as Choate, had become powerful figures, usually in conjunction with politics. On the other hand, low standards generally prevailed for admission to the bar, and a strong (but sometimes exaggerated) current of public opinion was hostile to the whole profession. Lawyers were distrusted as experts and sophisticates. Justice was believed to flow directly from a perception of the natural order, not from learned and complicated historical precedents. Yet this attitude, which Thoreau would embody and which always retained a certain degree of currency in American thought, was noticeably ebbing even by the 1840's. More and more widespread was the belief that law and democracy were reconcilable.[1] This growing acceptance of lawyers did not necessarily lead to Rufus Choate's exact position, of course, but it does give Choate the right to be regarded as every bit as forward-looking a figure as Thoreau. From opposite

1. See Perry Miller, *The Life of the Mind in America* (New York: Harcourt, Brace, 1965), p. 115. For a more general and extended discussion of popular attitudes toward law in this period, see above, pp. 15–16.

ends of the spectrum, Choate and Thoreau were tugging in contrary directions. Though each man's general position would have
its followers in the twentieth century, one suspects that a great
many latter-day Americans unconsciously embrace Rufus Choate
during moments of crisis, while exclaiming harmlessly over the
beauty of Thoreau's prose when they read casually at bedtime.

Rufus Choate, "The Position and Functions of the American Bar, as an Element of Conservatism in the State"

. . . There are reasons without number why we should love and
honor our noble profession, and should be grateful for the necessity or felicity or accident which called us to its service.

But of these there is one, I think, which, rightly apprehended,
ought to be uppermost in every lawyer's mind, on which he cannot dwell too thoughtfully and too anxiously; to which he should
resort always to expand and erect his spirit and to keep himself
up, if I may say so, to the height of his calling; from which he
has a right to derive, in every moment of weariness or distaste
or despondency,—not an occasion of pride, but,—ceaseless ad-
monitions to duty and incentives to hope. And that reason is,
that better than any other, or as well as any other position or
business in the whole subordination of life, his profession enables
him to *serve the State*. As well as any other, better than any other
profession or business or sphere, more directly, more palpably,
it enables and commands him to perform certain grand and difficult and indispensable duties of patriotism,—certain grand, difficult and indispensable duties to our endeared and common native
land.

Turning for the present then, from other aspects of the profession, survey it under this. Certainly it presents no nobler aspect.
It presents none so well adapted—I do not say, to make us vain

An address delivered before the Harvard Law School in 1845. From
Samuel Gilman Brown, ed., *The Works of Rufus Choate, with a
Memoir of His Life* (Boston: Little, Brown, 1862), Vol. I, pp. 415–
422, 423–426, 427–428, 430, 431–432, 432–433.

of it, but—to make us fit for it, to make us equal to it, to put us on turning it to its utmost account, and working out its whole vast and various and highest utilities. It raises it from a mere calling by which bread, fame, and social place may be earned, to a function by which the republic may be served. It raises it from a dexterous art and a subtle and flexible science,—from a cunning logic, a gilded rhetoric, and an ambitious learning, wearing the purple robe of the sophists, and letting itself to hire,—to the dignity of almost a department of government,—an instrumentality of the State for the well-being and conservation of the State. Consider then the position and functions of the American Bar in the Commonwealth.

I make haste to say that it is not at all because the legal profession may be thought to be peculiarly adapted to fit a man for what is technically called "public life," and to afford him a ready, too ready an introduction to it,—it is not on any such reason as this that I shall attempt to maintain the sentiment which I have advanced. It is not by enabling its members to leave it and become the members of a distinct profession,—it is not thus that in the view which I could wish to exhibit, it serves the State. It is not the jurist turned statesman whom I mean to hold up to you as useful to the republic,—although jurists turned statesmen have illustrated every page, every year of our annals, and have taught how admirably the school of the law can train the mind and heart for the service of constitutional liberty and the achievement of civil honor. It is not the jurist turned statesman; it is the jurist as jurist; it is the jurist remaining jurist; it is the bench, the magistracy, the bar,—the profession as a profession, and in its professional character,—a class, a body, of which I mean exclusively to speak; and my position is, that as such it holds, or may aspire to hold, a place, and performs a function of peculiar and vast usefulness in the American Commonwealth.

Let me premise, too, that instead of diffusing myself in a display of all the modes by which the profession of the law may claim to serve the State, I shall consider but a single one, and that is its agency as an element of conservation. The position and functions of the American Bar, then, as an element of conservation in the State,—this precisely and singly is the topic to which I invite your attention.

And is not the profession such an element of conservation? Is not this its characteristical office and its appropriate praise? Is it not so that in its nature, in its functions, in the intellectual and practical habits which it forms, in the opinions to which it conducts, in all its tendencies and influences of speculation and action, it is and ought to be professionally and peculiarly such an element and such an agent,—that it contributes, or ought to be held to contribute, more than all things else, or as much as anything else, to preserve our organic forms, our civil and social order, our public and private justice, our constitutions of government,— even the Union itself? In these crises through which our liberty is to pass, may not, must not, this function of conservatism become more and more developed, and more and more operative? May it not one day be written, for the praise of the American Bar, that it helped to keep the true idea of the State alive and germinant in the American mind; that it helped to keep alive the sacred sentiments of obedience and reverence and justice, of the supremacy of the calm and grand reason of the law over the fitful will of the individual and the crowd; that it helped to withstand the pernicious sophism that the successive generations, as they come to life, are but as so many successive flights of summer flies, without relations to the past or duties to the future, and taught instead that all—all the dead, the living, the unborn—were one moral person,—one for action, one for suffering, one for responsibility,—that the engagements of one age may bind the conscience of another; the glory or the shame of a day may brighten or stain the current of a thousand years of continuous national being? Consider the profession of the law, then, as an element of conservation in the American State. I think it is naturally such, so to speak: but I am sure it is our duty to make and to keep it such.

It may be said, I think with some truth, of the profession of the Bar, that in all political systems and in all times it has seemed to possess a twofold nature; that it has seemed to be fired by the spirit of liberty, and yet to hold fast the sentiments of order and reverence, and the duty of subordination; that it has resisted despotism and yet taught obedience; that it has recognized and vindicated the rights of man, and yet has reckoned it always among the most sacred and most precious of those rights, to be shielded and led by the divine nature and immortal reason of law; that it appreciates social progression and contributes to it, and ranks in the classes and with the agents of progression, yet evermore counsels and courts permanence and conservatism and rest; that it loves light better than darkness, and yet like the eccentric or wise man in the old historian, has a habit of looking away as the night wanes to the western sky, to detect there the first streaks of returning dawn. . . .

It is certain, on the one hand, that the sympathies of the lawyer in our system are with the people and with liberty. They are with the greatest number of the people; they are with what you call the masses; he springs from them; they are his patrons; their favor gives him bread; it gives him consideration; it raises him, as Curran so gracefully said of himself, "the child of a peasant to the table of his prince." The prosperity of the people employs and enriches him.

It does not fall within my immediate object to dwell longer on this aspect of the twofold nature of the profession of the Bar, —its tendencies and leanings to the people and to liberty. It might not be uninstructive to sustain and qualify the view by a glance at a few remarkable periods of its history, under a few widely discriminated political systems of ancient States and times,—the Roman Bar, for example, before and under the earliest times of the Empire; the French Bar at the Revolution; the American Bar from the planting of the colonies. But I must hasten to my principal purpose in this address,—an exhibition of the other aspect of the profession, its function of conservatism.

In proceeding to this, I think I may take for granted that conservatism is, in the actual circumstances of this country, the one grand and comprehensive duty of a thoughtful patriotism. I speak in the general, of course, not pausing upon little or inevitable qualifications here and there,—not meaning anything so absurd as to say that this law, or that usage, or that judgment, or that custom or condition, might not be corrected or expunged,—not meaning still less to invade the domains of moral and philanthropic reform, true or false. I speak of our general political system; our organic forms; our written constitutions; the great body and the general administration of our jurisprudence; the general way in which liberty is blended with order, and the principle of progression with the securities of permanence; the relation of the States and the functions of the Union,—and I say of it in a mass, that conservation is the chief end, the largest duty, and the truest glory of American statesmanship.

There are nations, I make no question, whose history, condition, and dangers, call them to a different work. There are those whom everything in their history, condition, and dangers admonishes to reform fundamentally, if they would be saved. With them the whole political and social order is to be rearranged. The stern claim of labor is to be provided for. Its long antagonism with capital is to be reconciled. Property is all to be parcelled out in some nearer conformity to a parental law of nature. Conventional discriminations of precedence and right are to be swept away. Old forms from which the life is gone are to drop as leaves in autumn. Frowning towers nodding to their fall are to be taken down. Small freeholds must dot over and cut up imperial parks. A large infusion of liberty must be poured along these emptied veins and throb in that great heart. With those, the past must be resigned; the present must be convulsed, that "an immeasurable future," as Carlyle has said, "may be filled with fruitfulness and a verdant shade."

But with us the age of this mode and this degree of reform is over; its work is done. The passage of the sea, the occupation and culture of a new world, the conquest of independence,—these were our eras, these our agency, of reform. In our jurisprudence of liberty, which guards our person from violence and our goods from plunder, and which forbids the whole power of the State itself to take the ewe lamb, or to trample on a blade of the grass of the humblest citizen without adequate remuneration; which makes every dwelling large enough to shelter a human life its owner's castle which winds and rain may enter but which the government cannot,—in our written constitutions, whereby the people, exercising an act of sublime self-restraint, have intended to put it out of their own power forever, to be passionate, tumultuous, unwise, unjust; whereby they have intended, by means of a system of representation; by means of the distribution of government into departments, independent, coordinate for checks and balances; by a double chamber of legislation; by the establishment of a fundamental and paramount organic law; by the organization of a judiciary whose function, whose loftiest function it is to test the legislation of the day by this standard for all time,—constitutions, whereby by all these means they have intended to secure a government of laws, not of men; of reason, not of will; of justice, not of fraud,—in that grand dogma of equality,—equality of right, of burthens, of duty, of privileges, and of chances, which is the very mystery of our social being—to the Jews, a stumbling block; to the Greeks, foolishness—our strength, our glory,—in that liberty which we value not solely because it is a natural right of man; not solely because it is a principle of individual energy and a guaranty of national renown; not at all because it attracts a procession and lights a bonfire, but because when blended with order, attended by law, tempered by virtue, graced by culture, it is a great practical good; because in her right hand are riches, and honor, and peace; because she has come down from her golden and purple cloud to walk in brightness by the weary ploughman's side, and whisper in his ear as he casts the seed with tears, that the harvest which frost and mildew and canker-worm shall spare, the government shall spare also; in our distribution into separate and kindred States, not wholly independent, not quite identical, in "the wide arch of the ranged empire" above,—these are they in which the fruits of our age and our agency of reform are embodied; and these are they by which, if we are wise,—if we understand the things that belong to our peace,—they may be perpetuated. It is for this that I say the fields of reform, the aims of reform, the uses of reform here, therefore, are wholly unlike the fields, uses, and aims of reform elsewhere. Foreign examples, foreign counsel,—well or ill meant, —the advice of the first foreign understandings, the example of the wisest foreign nations, are worse than useless for us. Even the teachings of history are to be cautiously consulted, or the guide of human life will lead us astray. We need reform enough, Heaven knows; but it is the reformation of our individual selves, the bettering of our personal natures; it is a more intellectual industry; it is a more diffused, profound, and graceful, popular, and higher culture; it is a wider development of the love and discernment of the beautiful in form, in color, in speech, and in the soul of man,—this is what we need,—personal, moral, mental reform —not civil—not political! No, no! Government, substantially as it is; jurisprudence, substantially as it is; the general arrangements of liberty, substantially as they are; the Constitution and the Union, exactly as they are,—this is to be wise, according to the wisdom of America.

To the conservation, then, of this general order of things, I think the profession of the Bar may be said to be assigned, for this reason, among others—the only one which I shall seek to develop—that its studies and employments tend to form in it and fit it to diffuse and impress on the popular mind a class of opinions—one class of opinions—which are indispensable to conservation. Its studies and offices train and arm it to counteract exactly that specific system of opinions by which our liberty must die, and to diffuse and impress those by which it may be kept alive.

By what means a State with just that quantity of liberty in its constitution which belongs to the States of America, with just those organizations into which our polity is moulded, with just those proportions of the elements of law and order and restraint on the one hand, and the passionate love of freedom, and quick and high sense of personal independence on the other,—by what means such a State may be preserved through a full life-time of enjoyment and glory, what kind of death it shall die, by what diagnostics the approach of that death may be known, by what conjuration it is for a space to be charmed away, through what succession of decay and decadence it shall at length go down to the tomb of the nations,—these questions are the largest, pertaining to the things of this world, that can be pondered by the mind of man. More than all others, too, they confound the wisdom of man. But some things we know. A nation, a national existence, a national history, is nothing but a production, nothing but an exponent, of a national mind. At the foundation of all splendid and remarkable national distinction there lie at last a few simple and energetic traits: a proud heart, a resolute will, sagacious thoughts, reverence, veneration, the ancient prudence, sound maxims, true wisdom; and so the dying of a nation begins in the heart. There are sentiments concerning the true idea of the State, concerning law, concerning liberty, concerning justice, so active, so mortal, that if they pervade and taint the general mind, and transpire in practical politics, the commonwealth is lost already. . . .

And now, what are these sentiments and opinions from which the public mind of America is in danger, and which the studies and offices of our profession have fitted us and impose on us the duty to encounter and correct?

In the first place, it has been supposed that there might be detected, not yet in the general mind, but in what may grow to be the general mind, a singularly inadequate idea of the State as an unchangeable, indestructible, and, speaking after the manner of men, an immortal thing. I do not refer at this moment exclusively to the temper in which the Federal Union is regarded, though that is a startling illustration of the more general and deeper sentiment, but I refer in a larger view to what some have thought the popular or common idea of the civil State itself, its sacredness, its permanence, its ends,—in the lofty phrase of Cicero, its eternity. The tendency appears to be, to regard the whole concern as an association altogether at will, and at the will of everybody. Its boundary lines, its constituent numbers, its physical, social, and constitutional identity, its polity, its law, its continuance for ages, its dissolution,—all these seem to be held in the nature of so many open questions. Whether *our country*—words so simple, so expressive, so sacred; which, like father, child, wife, should present an image familiar, endeared, definite to the heart—whether our country shall, in the course of the next six months extend to the Pacific Ocean and the Gulf, or be confined to the parochial limits of the State where we live, or have no existence at all for us; where its centre of power shall be; whose statues shall be borne in its processions; whose names, what days, what incidents of glory commemorated in its anniversaries, and what symbols blaze on its flag,—in all this there is getting to be a rather growing habit of politic non-committalism. Having learned from Rousseau and Locke, and our own revolutionary age, its theories and its acts, that the State is nothing but a contract, rests in contract, springs from contract; that government is a contrivance of human wisdom for human wants; that the civil life, like the Sabbath, is made for man, not man for either; having only about seventy years ago laid hold of an arbitrary fragment of the British empire, and appropriated it to ourselves, which is all the country we ever had; having gone on enlarging, doubling, trebling, changing all this since, as a garment or a house; accustomed to encounter every day, at the polls, in the market, at the miscellaneous banquet of our Liberty everywhere, crowds of persons whom we never saw before, strangers in the country, yet just as good citizens as ourselves; with a whole continent before us, or half a one, to choose a home in; teased and made peevish by all manner of small, local

jealousies; tormented by the stimulations of a revolutionary philanthropy; enterprising, speculative, itinerant, improving, "studious
of change, and pleased with novelty" beyond the general habit of
desultory man;—it might almost seem to be growing to be our
national humor to hold ourselves free at every instant, to be and
do just what we please, go where we please, stay as long as we
please and no longer; and that the State itself were held to be
no more than an encampment of tents on the great prairie, pitched
at sun-down, and struck to the sharp crack of the rifle next
morning, instead of a structure, stately and eternal, in which the
generations may come, one after another, to the great gift of this
social life.

On such sentiments as these, how can a towering and durable
fabric be set up? To use the metaphor of Bacon, on such soil how
can "greatness be sown"? How unlike the lessons of the masters,
at whose feet you are bred! The studies of our profession have
taught us that the State is framed for a duration without end,—
without end—till the earth and the heavens be no more. *Sic con-
stituta civitas ut eterna!* In the eye and contemplation of law, its
masses may die; its own corporate being can never die. If we inspect the language of its fundamental ordinance, every word expects, assumes, foretells a perpetuity, lasting as "the great globe
itself, and all which it inherit." If we go out of that record and
inquire for the designs and the hopes of its founders *ab extra,*
we know that they constructed it, and bequeathed it, for the
latest posterity. If we reverently rise to a conjecture of the purposes for which the Ruler of the world permitted and decreed
it to be instituted, in order to discern how soon it will have performed its office and may be laid aside, we see that they reach
down to the last hour of the life of the last man that shall live
upon the earth; that it was designed by the Infinite Wisdom, to
enable the generation who framed it, and all the generations, to
perfect their social, moral, and religious nature; to do and to be
good; to pursue happiness; to be fitted, by the various discipline
of the social life, by obedience, by worship, for the life to come.
When these ends are all answered, the State shall die! . . .

In the next place, it has been thought that there was developing itself in the general sentiment, and in the practical politics of
the time, a tendency towards one of those great changes by which

free States have oftenest perished,—a tendency to push to excess the distinctive and characteristic principles of our system, whereby, as Aristotle has said, governments usually perish,—a tendency towards transition from the republican to the democratical era, of the history and epochs of liberty.

Essentially and generally, it would be pronounced by those who discern it, a tendency to erect the actual majority of the day into the *de jure* and actual government of the day. It is a tendency to regard the actual will of that majority as the law of the State. It is a tendency to regard the shortest and simplest way of collecting that will, and the promptest and most irresistible execution of it, as the true polity of liberty. It is a tendency which, pressed to its last development, would, if considerations of mere convenience or inconvenience did not hinder, do exactly this: it would assemble the whole people in a vast mass, as once they used to assemble beneath the sun of Athens; and there, when the eloquent had spoken and the wise and the foolish had counselled, would commit the transcendent questions of war, peace, taxation, and treaties; the disposition of the fortunes and honor of the citizen and statesman; death, banishment, or the crown of gold; the making, interpreting, and administration of the law; and all the warm, precious, and multifarious interests of the social life, to the madness or the jest of the hour.

I have not time to present what have been thought to be the proofs of the existence of this tendency; and it is needless to do so. It would be presumptuous, too, to speculate, if it has existence, on its causes and its issues. I desire to advert to certain particulars in which it may be analyzed, and through which it displays itself, for the purpose of showing that the studies, employments, and, so to say, professional politics, of the bar are essentially, perhaps availably, antagonistical to it, or moderative of it.

It is said, then, that you may remark this tendency, first, in an inclination to depreciate the uses and usurp the functions of those organic forms in which the regular, definite, and legally recognized powers of the State are embodied,—to depreciate the uses and usurp the function of written constitutions, limitations on the legislature, the distribution of government into departments, the independence of the judiciary, the forms of orderly proceeding, and all the elaborate and costly apparatus of checks and balances, by which, as I have said, we seek to secure a government of laws and not of men. . . .

And now am I misled by the influence of vocation, when I venture to suppose that the profession of the Bar may do somewhat—should be required to do somewhat—to preserve the true proportion of liberty to organization,—to moderate and to disarm that eternal antagonism?

These "organic forms" of our system—are they not in some just sense committed to your professional charge and care? In this sense, and to this extent, does not your profession approach to, and blend itself with, one, and that not the least in dignity and usefulness, of the departments of statesmanship? Are you not thus statesmen while you are lawyers, and because you are lawyers? These constitutions of government by which a free people have had the virtue and the sense to restrain themselves,—these devices of profound wisdom and a deep study of man, and of the past, by which they have meant to secure the ascendency of the just, lofty, and wise, over the fraudulent, low, and insane, in the long run of our practical politics,—these temperaments by which justice is promoted, and by which liberty is made possible and may be made immortal,—and this *jus publicum,* this great written code of public law,—are they not a part, in the strictest and narrowest sense, of the appropriate science of your profession? More than for any other class or calling in the community, is it not for you to study their sense, comprehend their great uses, and explore their historical origin and illustrations,—to so hold them up as shields, that no act of legislature, no judgment of court, no executive proclamation, no order of any functionary of any description, shall transcend or misconceive them—to so hold them up before your clients and the public, as to keep them at all times living, intelligible, and appreciated in the universal mind? . . .

It has been thought, in the next place, that you may remark this unfavorable tendency in a certain false and pernicious *idea of law,* which to some extent possesses the popular mind,—law, its source, its nature, its titles to reverence. Consider it a moment, and contrast it with our idea of law.

It is one of the distemperatures to which an unreasoning liberty may grow, no doubt, to regard *law* as no more nor less than just the will—the actual and present will—of the actual majority of the nation. The majority govern. What the majority pleases, it may ordain. What it ordains is law. So much for the source of law, and so much for the nature of law. But, then, as law is nothing but the will of a major number, as that will differs from the will of yesterday, and will differ from that of to-morrow, and as all law is a restraint on natural right and personal independence, how can it gain a moment's hold on the reverential sentiments of the heart, and the profounder convictions of the judgment? How can it impress a filial awe; how can it conciliate a filial love; how can it sustain a sentiment of veneration; how can it command a rational and animated defence? Such sentiments are not the stuff from which the immortality of a nation is to be woven! Oppose now ιo this, the loftier philosophy which we have learned. In the language of our system, the law is not the transient and arbitrary creation of the major will, nor of any will. It is not the offspring of will at all. It is the absolute justice of the State, enlightened by the perfect reason of the State. That is law. Enlightened justice assisting the social nature to perfect itself by the social life. It is ordained, doubtless, that is, it is chosen, and is ascertained by the wisdom of man. But, then, it is the master-work of man. . . .

By the costly and elaborate contrivances of our constitutions we have sought to attain the transcendent result of extracting and excluding haste, injustice, revenge, and folly from the place and function of giving the law, and of introducing alone the reason and justice of the wisest and the best. By the aid of time,—time which changes and tries all things; tries them, and works them pure,—we subject the law, after it is given, to the tests of old experience, to the reason and justice of successive ages and generations, to the best thoughts of the wisest and safest of reformers. And then and thus we pronounce it good. Then and thus we cannot choose but reverence, obey, and enforce it. We would grave it deep into the heart of the undying State. We would strengthen it by opinion, by manners, by private virtue, by habit, by the awful hoar of innumerable ages. All that attracts us to life, all that is charming in the perfected and adorned social nature, we wisely think or we wisely dream, we owe to the all-encircling presence of the law. Not even extravagant do we think it to hold, that the Divine approval may sanction it as not unworthy of the reason which we derive from His own nature. Not extravagant do we hold it to say, that there is thus a voice of the people which is the voice of God.

Doubtless the known historical origin of the law contributes to this opinion of it. Consider for a moment—what that law really is, what the vast body of that law is, to the study and administration of which the lawyer gives his whole life, by which he has trained his mind, established his fortune, won his fame, the theatre of all his triumphs, the means of all his usefulness, the theme of a thousand earnest panegyrics,—what is that law? Mainly, a body of digested rules and processes and forms, bequeathed by what is for us the old and past time, not of one age, but all the ages of the past,—a vast and multifarious aggregate, some of which you trace above the pyramids, above the flood, the inspired wisdom of the primeval East; some to the scarcely yet historical era of Pythagoras, and to Solon and Socrates; more of it to the robust, practical sense and justice of Rome, the lawgiver of the nations; more still to the teeming birthtime of the modern mind and life; all of it to some epoch; some of it to every epoch of the past of which history keeps the date. In the way in which it comes down to us, it seems one mighty and continuous stream of experience and reason, accumulated, ancestral, widening and deepening and washing itself clearer as it runs on, the grand agent of civilization, the builder of a thousand cities, the guardian angel of a hundred generations, our own hereditary laws. To revere such a system, would be natural and professional, if it were no more. But it is reasonable, too. There is a deep presumption in favor of that which has endured so long. To say of anything, that it is old, and to leave the matter there,—an opinion, a polity, a code, a possession, a book,—is to say nothing of praise or blame. But to have lived for ages; to be alive to-day,—in a real sense alive,—alive in the hearts, in the reason of to-day; to have lived through ages, not swathed in gums and spices and enshrined in chambers of pyramids, but through ages of unceasing contact and sharp trial with the passions, interests, and affairs of the great world; to have lived through the drums and tramplings of conquests, through revolution, reform, through cycles of opinion running their round; to have lived under many diverse systems of policy, and have survived the many transmigrations from one to another; to have attended the general progress of the race, and shared in its successive ameliorations,

—thus to have gathered upon itself the approbation or the sentiments and reason of all civilization and all humanity,—that is,
per se, a *prima-facie* title to intelligent regard. . . .

It is certain that in the American theory, the free theory of
government, it is right of the people, at any moment of its representation in the legislature, to make all the law, and by its representatives in conventions, to make the Constitution anew. It is
their right to do so so peaceably and according to existing forms,
and to do it by revolution against all forms. This is the theory. But
I do not know that any wise man would desire to have this theory
every day, or ever, acted upon up to its whole extent, or to have
it eternally pressed, promulgated, panegyrized as the grand peculi-
arity and chief privilege of our condition. Acting upon this theory,
we have made our constitutions, founded our policy, written the
great body of our law, set our whole government going. It worked
well. It works to a charm. I do not know that any man displays
wisdom or common sense, by all the while haranguing and stimulating the people to change it. I do not appreciate the sense or humanity of all the while bawling: true, your systems are all good;
life, character, property, all safe,—but you have the undoubted
right to rub all out and begin again. If I see a man quietly eating
his dinner, I do not know why I should tell him that there is a
first-rate, extreme medicine, prussic acid, aquafortis, or what not,
which he has a perfectly good right to use in any quantity he
pleases! If a man is living happily with his wife, I don't know why
I should go and say: yes, I see; beautiful and virtuous; I con-
gratulate you,—but let me say, you can get a perfectly legal
divorce by going to Vermont, New Jersey, or Pennsylvania. True
wisdom would seem to advise the culture of dispositions of rest,
contentment, conservation. True wisdom would advise to lock up
the extreme medicine till the attack of the alarming malady. True
wisdom would advise to place the power of revolution, overturning
all to begin anew, rather in the background, to throw over it a
politic, well-wrought veil, to reserve it for crises, exigencies, the
rare and distant days of great historical epochs. These great, transcendental rights should be preserved, must be, will be. But perhaps
you would place them away, reverentially, in the profoundest recesses of the chambers of the dead, down in deep vaults of black
marble, lighted by a single silver lamp,—as in that version of the

Gothic king,—to which wise and brave men may go down, in the hour of extremity, to evoke the tremendous divinities of change from their sleep of ages.

3. Primacy of the Individual Conscience

The third position toward law and authority which developed in the early nineteenth century has become exceedingly familiar to us through the name attached to it. Thoreau has of course exerted a major influence upon a number of forms of radicalism in recent times. Yet it should be remembered that Thoreau's writings typically sold only in the hundreds of copies when they first appeared (a single essay, "Slavery in Massachusetts," was indeed printed in the *New York Tribune*). If one is to argue that Thoreau's extreme suspicion of government was widely shared among his contemporaries, the argument cannot depend on any direct measurable reaction during his own lifetime to what he placed in print. Moreover, Thoreau's centrality cannot be "proved" by reference to the earlier Jeffersonian tradition in America, despite its own considerable distrust of state power. The many and profound differences between the outlooks of Jefferson and Thoreau have been discussed elsewhere.[1] Moreover, as Jeffersonianism became Jacksonianism it lost much of its earlier anti-nationalist thrust, especially in noneconomic respects. (Jackson's reaction to nullification in South Carolina was the visible sign of this trend.) Meanwhile, on a popular level, distrust of law and lawyers was evidently beginning to decline, as we have already seen. It seems undeniable that in the 1840's men like George Bancroft, celebrating the will of the nationalistic majority, also spoke for the wishes of the majority.

It is true that an important faction located in New England and in a few abolitionist outposts in the West did move at this time to a position on governmental authority roughly similar to Thoreau's, and Thoreau may be seen as the most eloquent spokesman for this significant minority, even if few people seem to have been aware of him at the time. Thoreau certainly did not act to

1. See above, pp. 25–26.

defy the state all by himself. At Oberlin, for instance, civil disobedience on slavery issues was constantly being practiced between 1835 and 1860. Bronson Alcott went to jail for his conscience before Thoreau did. Yet, even when Thoreau is compared with these others who most closely resembled him, in many respects he stands completely alone. He shared none of the abolitionists' passion for evangelical Christianity. Further, it should be recalled that most Transcendentalists were fervent nationalists, whose rhetoric blended easily with the tone of Fourth of July orations. This above all is what set Thoreau sharply apart.[2]

Thoreau's view of government has been clouded by a flurry of debate as to its meaning. Such issues as whether he deserves to be called an anarchist and whether he belongs in the natural law tradition of political theory have been hotly argued.[3] As is usual in such quarrels, positions have been taken which largely reflect the writers' own biases. Thus, for instance, Thoreau's "anarchism" has been denied by those who like Thoreau but don't like anarchistic ideas. Meanwhile, Quakers and others have tried incorrectly to bend Thoreau into an advocate of their own style of passive, nonviolent resistance to the state.

What was Thoreau's actual position on law and government? In his view, government was not always wrong or useless, but officially established institutions of any kind were usually lacking in fundamental morality. Governments might on occasion become the vehicles for moral actions, as the American government temporarily did during the Revolution of 1776, and as local governments might do when they supplied such necessary services as roadways and schools. When governments did fulfill morality, he said he would be willing to fight in their behalf rather than against them. But much more often, he believed, laws and governments operated contrary to morality. It was the ordinary nature of institutions to be "dirty," to come into being during "a lull of truth." One should therefore approach government in a mood of ingrained distrust, but with a willingness to recognize particular instances when it functioned beneficently. It might be "a last resort," as he called

2. See Edward H. Madden, *Civil Disobedience and Moral Law in Nineteenth-Century American Philosophy,* pp. 79, 95–97.

3. For instance see the essays in Owen Thomas, ed., *Henry David Thoreau: Walden and Civil Disobedience* (New York: Norton, 1966), among which that of Richard Drinnon, pp. 410–422, is an especially good example of helpful insights and special pleading.

it in one unpublished manuscript; but it might also serve as one of man's "tools and utensils," especially when approached with caution.[4]

It is true, as one scholar has elaborately shown, that in many places in Thoreau's writings, especially in his early college essays, he casually accepts a positive role for government in remedying various concrete situations.[5] But this finding is placed in proper perspective by a portion of a single well-known sentence from "Civil Disobedience": "I quietly declare war with the State . . . though I will still make what use and get what advantage of her I can. . . ."

At moments Thoreau did flirt with thoroughgoing anarchism. At one point in the same essay he stated that he might look forward to the eventual prospect of having no government at all. But it is dangerous to make too much of some of Thoreau's isolated sentences when taken out of context. This passage may be regarded as no more than a heightened rhetorical dramatization of his more frequent point that the authority of the state should be granted only a grudging tolerance based upon a careful weighing of the particular good and evil it promoted at any given moment. Likewise, the somewhat opposite passage at the very end of "Civil Disobedience," where he briefly offers a vision of an ideal, or perfectly just state, may be seen not so much to express a genuine hope as to provide a wistful rhetorical flourish. And when, yet again in "Civil Disobedience," he once implies that he would really like to conform to the expectations of others and to give the state the benefit of the doubt, it is frankly hard to take him seriously.

One is best advised to discount such occasional statements because in most of this essay, as in his other political writings, what stands out is neither a utopian anarchism nor an underlying desire after all to be "helpful," but rather a sour and suspicious realism concerning the consequences of organized human relationships. More than anything else, Thoreau offers an attitude of mind which defiantly asserts the right of the individual (aided by conscience) to be his own judge. From the viewpoint of the state, it is an attitude of calculated insubordination. From Thoreau's own viewpoint, it could be termed one of zealous independence.

4. Quoted in Sherman Paul, *The Shores of America: Thoreau's Inward Exploration* (Urbana, Ill.: University of Illinois Press, 1958), p. 249, which remains an unusually fine investigation into Thoreau's thought.

5. John C. Broderick, "Thoreau's Proposals for Legislation," *American Quarterly*, VII (1955), 285–290.

Rather than providing a well-thought-out political philosophy in any formal sense, Thoreau really sought to mount an attack upon the psychology of automatic obedience to external authority. And it is on this level that he genuinely confronts a man like Rufus Choate. Choate was seeking to instill a reverence for established authority, and especially for the institutions that visibly symbolized it. Thoreau was trying with all his skill to disperse that very aura of sacredness which hovered about forms of government, politics, and the law. This is what remains so modern (or timeless) about their disagreement. For Thoreau's primary goal has also been revived by many radicals of the 1960's, even if this has often been obscured beneath particular concrete issues or sets of demands.[6]

In undertaking this assault, Thoreau practiced a whole range of tactics. Uncompromising in his moral intensity, he was nonetheless highly flexible in his strategy. One's entire life, he believed, should "be a counter-friction to stop the machine," but within the context of this overall commitment the technique of resistance might greatly vary. Thus at the time of the Mexican War (the very war that Bancroft had helped us enter), Thoreau felt it proper to refuse to pay taxes and to go to jail in a passive protest. At the time of John Brown's raid (and on other occasions) he was receptive to the idea of thoroughly violent gestures. Elsewhere he urged boycotts. In 1860, despite his usual disdain for ordinary political acts such as voting and petitioning, he wrote a letter to his senator. Again he might sometimes feel moved merely to speak out. His essays and addresses on political themes, occurring at infrequent intervals, were thus yet another among a varied arsenal of weapons for getting men to re-examine their habit of deferential obedience.

Within his writings themselves, Thoreau's tactics were also resourcefully chosen. It was no accident, for instance, that he went out of his way periodically to call the Constitution—and the Bible —into question. These, for most Americans, were the prime symbols of authority in matters secular and religious, and he must directly attack their sacred quality, for here lay the very root of unthinking acquiescence. Similarly, he must challenge the concept

6. The psychological desanctification of official authority must be distinguished from actual revolution as a goal; earlier (p. 31) it was pointed out that relatively few current radicals are seeking to promote the latter. Indeed, it is far more radical to question all authority simply because it is authority than to conspire to substitute one political or social system (in the familiar sense) for another.

of American patriotism (despite the undoubted fact that he retained an affirmative vision of the American future on another
level of his mind). We are men first and Americans second, he
would say; or again, he would insist that national survival was
less important than firm adherence to moral principles. Naturally
he also had to attack the growing enshrinement of majority rule.

In making use of these targets, Thoreau constantly sought to
undercut or reverse the reader's normal expectations. Again and
again he poured scorn upon those things which he knew Americans viewed with respect: parties, presidents, governors, law
courts, and the will of the public itself. Common to these negative
forays is the theme of cutting down to size all awesome and pre-
tentious public figures, all hallowed popular shibboleths. By
brazenly addressing them as equals, he would strip these objects
of their special dignity. Thoreau's knife-thrust was directed at
what Robert Bellah would eventually term America's "civil religion"—the sum total of the rituals, institutions, and symbols
which operated to command respectful deference from the people
and which might be said to form the sensitive nerve endings of
the body politic.[7]

Because Thoreau so consistently sought to undermine authority
in this fashion, he was as deeply subversive as it is possible to be.
This is true despite those rare passages in which he appears to
warn himself against the dangers of mere obstinacy for its own
sake. Obstinacy was the very essence of what he expressed; it
was the attitude that gave him his cutting edge as a social critic.
He completely saw through "the system," insistently refused to
acknowledge any automatic loyalty to it, and urged his fellow
Americans to do likewise. There is an enormous difference between accepting the role of government in a hesitant and skeptical
spirit for the achievement of limited welfare benefits and giving
government one's deep and unthinking respect. That is why it
does not really matter whether Thoreau was a formal anarchist.
His psychology was far more devastating than if he had advocated
some specific form of social revolution.

Thoreau's underlying attitude of irreverence toward symbols of
authority was far more consistent, too, than his rather haphazard
and contradictory attempts to specify the exact source of the inner
moral authority he upheld as superior to the external authority of
civil government. Thus, to argue whether Thoreau accepted the

7. See Robert N. Bellah, "Civil Religion in America," *Daedalus,* XCVI
(1967), 1–21.

idea of natural law is again largely beside the point. In various places in his essays we may find him referring to such yardsticks as world opinion, "higher law," a God-given internal moral constitution, "the seasonable experience and effectual complaints of the people" (a passage that is both pragmatic and, for once, populistic), "the light within you," nature (implicitly interpreted in a vitalistic sense), conscience, absolute goodness, the superior wisdom of minorities, and the greater political virtue of the countryside as opposed to the city. There is no common denominator which runs through all these diverse substitutes for conventional authority as a source of judgment. Thoreau, like many later radicals, displayed far more power in his negative criticisms than in his affirmative answers. In his own case, this may well have been because at the deepest level of his being he was simply not political at all.

All one may say, after reviewing the cumbersome and rather ambiguous list of what Thoreau on occasion positively believed in, is that his fundamental alternative to the blind acceptance of external authority centered in the individual conscience. It is unfair to press him further than this: for instance, as to whether conscience is variable and subjective or whether it flows in some automatic fashion from universal reason. This is an improper question just as it was for George Bancroft, because nineteenth-century thinkers hardly ever perceived any conflict between the individual and the universal. Bancroft pictured the individual, the national, the universal, and the morally absolute as all harmoniously flowing together in a single undifferentiated progressive stream. Thoreau, aside from denying the inevitability of progress, differed only in deleting the national (or societal) level and presuming a normal state of opposition between it and the other three. Because of the power of nationalist sentiment, growing steadily from Napoleon's day to ours, Thoreau's single exception was sufficient to brand him as among the most extreme radicals in the modern world. But one should not forget that his easy conjunction of the individual, the universal, and the absolute imprisoned much of his thinking in the naïveté of an earlier generation.

Thus in the final paragraph of "Civil Disobedience," Thoreau could even parallel Bancroft, for a brief sentence or two, in pointing to the rise of democracy in the modern world. The difference, and it was a crucial one, was that for Bancroft democracy—with its majoritarian connotations—was the highest stage of human history, whereas for Thoreau it was at most the highest but one.

Thoreau dreamed that it might be superseded some day by a society in which there was "true respect for the individual" as a "higher" power than the state and independent of it. In this society "a few" people would "live aloof" from all contact with government and remain unmolested. There—at bottom skeptical of its fulfillment—Thoreau let matters rest. This was his basically nonpolitical utopia.

It was this very kind of concession to "a few" which the United States, and most other modern nations, would be unwilling to grant as time wore on. But for "the few," replenishing themselves over the generations and feeling equally frustrated by majority attitudes toward war and social justice, Thoreau would one day become almost the only nineteenth-century American name they could remember.

Henry David Thoreau, "Civil Disobedience"

I heartily accept the motto, "That government is best which governs least"; and I should like to see it acted up to more rapidly and systematically. Carried out, it finally amounts to this, which also I believe: "That government is best which governs not at all"; and when men are prepared for it, that will be the kind of government which they will have. Government is at best but an expedient; but most governments are usually, and all governments are sometimes, inexpedient. The objections which have been brought against a standing army—and they are many and weighty, and deserve to prevail—may also at last be brought against a standing government. The standing army is only an arm of the standing government. The government itself, which is only the mode which the people have chosen to execute their will, is equally liable to be abused and perverted before the people can act through it. Witness the present Mexican war, the work of comparatively a few individuals using the standing government as their

---

Written in 1849; first published in full in *A Yankee in Canada, With Anti-Slavery and Reform Papers* (Boston: Ticknor and Fields, 1866). Printed here in its entirety.

tool; for, in the outset, the people would not have consented to this measure.

This American government—what is it but a tradition, though a recent one, endeavoring to transmit itself unimpaired to posterity, but each instant losing some of its integrity? It has not the vitality and force of a single living man; for a single man can bend it to his will. It is a sort of wooden gun to the people themselves. But it is not the less necessary for this; for the people must have some complicated machinery or other, and hear its din, to satisfy that idea of government which they have. Governments show thus how successfully men can be imposed on, even impose on themselves, for their own advantage. It is excellent, we must all allow. Yet this government never of itself furthered any enterprise, but by the alacrity with which it got out of its way. It does not keep the country free. It does not settle the West. It does not educate. The character inherent in the American people has done all that has been accomplished; and it would have done somewhat more if the government had not sometimes got in its way. For government is an expedient by which men would fain succeed in letting one another alone; and, as has been said, when it is most expedient, the governed are most let alone by it. Trade and commerce, if they were not made of india rubber, would never manage to bounce over the obstacles which legislators are continually putting in their way; and, if one were to judge these men wholly by the effects of their actions and not partly by their intentions, they would deserve to be classed and punished with those mischievous persons who put obstructions on the railroads.

But to speak practically and as a citizen, unlike those who call themselves no-government men, I ask for, not at once no government, but at once a better government. Let every man make known what kind of government would command his respect, and that will be one step toward obtaining it.

After all, the practical reason why, when the power is once in the hands of the people, a majority are permitted, and for a long period continue, to rule is not because they are most likely to be in the right, nor because this seems fairest to the minority, but because they are physically the strongest. But a government in which the majority rule in all cases cannot be based on justice, even as far as men understand it. Can there not be a government in which majorities do not virtually decide right and wrong, but conscience?—in which majorities decide only those questions to which the rule of expediency is applicable? Must the citizen ever for a moment, or in the least degree, resign his conscience to the legislator? Why has every man a conscience, then? I think that we should be men first, and subjects afterward. It is not desirable to cultivate a respect for the law, so much as for the right. The only obligation which I have a right to assume is to do at any time what I think right. It is truly enough said that a corporation has no conscience; but a corporation of conscientious men is a corporation with a conscience. Law never made men a whit more just; and, by means of their respect for it, even the well disposed are daily made the agents of injustice. A common and natural result of an undue respect for law is that you may see a file of soldiers—colonel, captain, corporal, privates, powder monkeys, and all—marching in admirable order over hill and dale to the wars, against their wills, ay, against their common sense and consciences, which makes it very steep marching indeed, and produces a palpitation of the heart. They have no doubt that it is a damnable business in which they are concerned; they are all peaceably inclined. Now, what are they? Men at all? or small movable forts and magazines, at the service of some unscrupulous man in power? Visit the navy yard, and behold a marine, such a man as an American government can make, or such as it can make a man with its black arts—a mere shadow and reminiscence of humanity, a man laid out alive and standing, and already, as one may say, buried under arms with funeral accompaniments, though it may be:

> Not a drum was heard, not a funeral note,
>   As his corse to the rampart we hurried:
> Not a soldier discharged his farewell shot
>   O'er the grave where our hero we buried.

The mass of men serve the state thus, not as men mainly, but as machines, with their bodies. They are the standing army, and the militia, jailers, constables, posse comitatus, etc. In most cases there is no free exercise whatever of the judgment or of the moral sense; but they put themselves on a level with wood and earth and stones; and wooden men can perhaps be manufactured that will serve the purpose as well. Such command no more respect than men of straw or a lump of dirt. They have the same sort of worth only as horses and dogs. Yet such as these even are commonly esteemed good citizens. Others—as most legislators, politicians, lawyers, ministers, and officeholders—serve the state chiefly with their heads; and, as they rarely make any moral distinctions, they are as likely to serve the devil, without intending it, as God. A very few—as heroes, patriots, martyrs, reformers in the great sense, and men—serve the state with their consciences also, and so necessarily resist it for the most part; and they are commonly treated as enemies by it. A wise man will only be useful as a man, and will not submit to be "clay," and "stop a hole to keep the wind away," but leave that office to his dust at least:

> I am too high-born to be propertied,
> To be a secondary at control,
> Or useful serving man and instrument
> To any sovereign state throughout the world.

He who gives himself entirely to his fellow men appears to them useless and selfish; but he who gives himself partially to them is pronounced a benefactor and philanthropist.

How does it become a man to behave toward this American government today? I answer that he cannot without disgrace be associated with it. I cannot for an instant recognize that political organization as my government which is the slave's government also.

All men recognize the right of revolution; that is, the right to refuse allegiance to, and to resist, the government when its tyranny or its inefficiency are great and unendurable. But almost all say that such is not the case now. But such was the case, they think, in the Revolution of '75. If one were to tell me that this was a bad government because it taxed certain foreign commodities brought to its ports, it is most probable that I should not make an ado about it, for I can do without them. All machines have their friction; and possibly this does enough good to counterbalance the evil. At any rate, it is a great evil to make a stir about it. But when the friction comes to have its machine, and oppression and robbery are organized, I say, let us not have such a machine any longer. In other words, when a sixth of the population of a nation which has undertaken to be the refuge of liberty are slaves, and a whole country is unjustly overrun and conquered by a foreign army and subjected to military law, I think that it is not too soon for honest men to rebel and revolutionize. What makes this duty the more urgent is the fact that the country so overrun is not our own, but ours is the invading army.

Paley, a common authority with many on moral questions, in his chapter on the "Duty of Submission to Civil Government," resolves all civil obligation into expediency; and he proceeds to say that "so long as the interest of the whole society requires it, that is, so long as the established government cannot be resisted or changed without public inconveniency, it is the will of God . . . that the established government be obeyed—and no longer. This principle being admitted, the justice of every particular case of resistance is reduced to a computation of the quantity of the danger and grievance on the one side, and of the probability and expense of redressing it on the other." Of this, he says, every man shall judge for himself. But Paley appears never to have contemplated those cases to which the rule of expediency does not apply, in which a people, as well as an individual, must do justice, cost what it may. If I have unjustly wrested a plank from a drowning man, I must restore it to him though I drown myself. This, according to Paley, would be inconvenient. But he that would save his life, in such a case, shall lose it. This people must cease to hold slaves, and to make war on Mexico, though it cost them their existence as a people.

In their practice, nations agree with Paley; but does any one think that Massachusetts does exactly what is right at the present crisis?

> A drab of state, a cloth-o'-silver slut,
> To have her train borne up, and her soul trail in the dirt.

Practically speaking, the opponents to a reform in Massachusetts are not a hundred thousand politicians at the South, but a hundred thousand merchants and farmers here, who are more interested in commerce and agriculture than they are in humanity, and are not prepared to do justice to the slave and to Mexico, cost what it may. I quarrel not with far-off foes, but with those who, near at home, cooperate with, and do the bidding of, those far away, and without whom the latter would be harmless. We are accustomed to say that the mass of men are unprepared; but improvement is slow because the few are not materially wiser or better than the many. It is not so important that many should be as good as you, as that there be some absolute goodness somewhere; for that will leaven the whole lump. There are thousands who are in opinion opposed to slavery and to the war, who yet in effect do nothing to put an end to them; who, esteeming themselves children of Washington and Franklin, sit down with their hands in their pockets and say that they know what to do, and do nothing; who even postpone the question of freedom to the question of free trade, and quietly read the prices-current along with the latest advices from Mexico, after dinner, and, it may be, fall asleep over them both. What is the price-current of an honest man and patriot today? They hesitate, and they regret, and sometimes they petition; but they do nothing in earnest and with effect. They will wait, well disposed, for others to remedy the evil, that they may no longer have it to regret. At most, they give only a cheap vote and a feeble countenance and Godspeed to the right as it goes by them. There are nine hundred and ninety-nine patrons of virtue to one virtuous man. But it is easier to deal with the real possessor of a thing than with the temporary guardian of it.

All voting is a sort of gaming, like checkers or backgammon, with a slight moral tinge to it, a playing with right and wrong, with moral questions; and betting naturally accompanies it. The character of the voters is not staked. I cast my vote, perchance, as I think right; but I am not vitally concerned that that right should prevail. I am willing to leave it to the majority. Its obligation, therefore, never exceeds that of expediency. Even voting for the right is doing nothing for it. It is only expressing to men feebly your desire that it should prevail. A wise man will not leave the right to the mercy of chance, nor wish it to prevail through the power of the majority. There is but little virtue in the action of masses of men. When the majority shall at length vote for the abolition of slavery, it will be because they are indifferent to slavery, or because there is but little slavery left to be abolished by their vote. They will then be the only slaves. Only his vote can hasten the abolition of slavery who asserts his own freedom by his vote.

I hear of a convention to be held at Baltimore, or elsewhere, for the selection of a candidate for the Presidency, made up chiefly of editors and men who are politicians by profession; but I think, what is it to any independent, intelligent, and respectable man what decision they may come to? Shall we not have the advantage of his wisdom and honesty, nevertheless? Can we not count upon some independent votes? Are there not many individuals in the country who do not attend conventions? But no: I find that the respectable man, so called, has immediately drifted from his position, and despairs of his country, when his country has more reason to despair of him. He forthwith adopts one of the candidates thus selected as the only available one, thus proving that he is himself available for any purposes of the demagogue. His vote is of no more worth than that of any unprincipled foreigner or hireling native who may have been bought. O for a man who is a man, and, as my neighbor says, has a bone in his back which you cannot pass your hand through! Our statistics are at fault: the population has been returned too large. How many men are there to a square thousand miles in this country? Hardly one. Does not America offer any inducement for men to settle here? The American has dwindled into an Odd Fellow—one who may be known by the development of his organ of gregariousness, and a manifest lack of intellect and cheerful self-reliance; whose first and chief concern, on coming into the world, is to see that the almshouses are in good repair; and, before yet he has lawfully donned the virile garb, to collect a fund for the support of the widows and orphans that may be; who, in short, ventures to live only by the aid of the Mutual Insurance company, which has promised to bury him decently.

It is not a man's duty, as a matter of course, to devote himself to the eradication of any, even the most enormous, wrong; he may still properly have other concerns to engage him; but it is his duty, at least, to wash his hands of it, and, if he gives it no thought longer, not to give it practically his support. If I devote myself to other pursuits and contemplations, I must first see, at least, that I do not pursue them sitting upon another man's shoulders. I must get off him first, that he may pursue his contemplations, too. See what gross inconsistency is tolerated. I have heard some of my townsmen say, "I should like to have them order me out to help put down an insurrection of the slaves, or to march to Mexico—see if I would go." And yet these very men have each, directly by their allegiance, and so indirectly, at least, by their money, furnished a substitute. The soldier is applauded who refuses to serve in an unjust war by those who do not refuse to sustain the unjust government which makes the war; is applauded by those whose own act and authority he disregards and sets at naught; as if the state were penitent to that degree that it hired one to scourge it while it sinned, but not to that degree that it left off sinning for a moment. Thus, under the name of Order and Civil Government, we are all made at last to pay homage to and support our own meanness. After the first blush of sin comes its indifference; and from immoral it becomes, as it were, unmoral, and not quite necessary to that life which we have made.

The broadest and most prevalent error requires the most disinterested virtue to sustain it. The slight reproach to which the virtue of patriotism is commonly liable, the noble are most likely to incur. Those who, while they disapprove of the character and measures of a government, yield to it their allegiance and support are undoubtedly its most conscientious supporters, and so frequently the most serious obstacles to reform. Some are petitioning the State to dissolve the Union, to disregard the requisitions of the President. Why do they not dissolve it themselves—the union between themselves and the State—and refuse to pay their quota into its treasury? Do not they stand in the same relation to the State that the State does to the Union? And have not the same reasons prevented the State from resisting the Union which have prevented them from resisting the State?

How can a man be satisfied to entertain an opinion merely, and enjoy it? Is there any enjoyment in it if his opinion is that he is aggrieved? If you are cheated out of a single dollar by your neighbor, you do not rest satisfied with knowing that you are cheated, or with saying that you are cheated, or even with petitioning him to pay you your due; but you take effectual steps at once to obtain the full amount, and see that you are never cheated again. Action from principle, the perception and the performance of right, changes things and relations; it is essentially revolutionary, and does not consist wholly with anything which was. It not only divides States and churches, it divides families; ay, it divides the individual, separating the diabolical in him from the divine.

Unjust laws exist: shall we be content to obey them, or shall we endeavor to amend them, and obey them until we have succeeded, or shall we transgress them at once? Men generally, under such a government as this, think that they ought to wait until they have persuaded the majority to alter them. They think that, if they should resist, the remedy would be worse than the evil. But it is the fault of the government itself that the remedy is worse than the evil. It makes it worse. Why is it not more apt to anticipate and provide for reform? Why does it not cherish its wise minority? Why does it cry and resist before it is hurt? Why does it not encourage its citizens to be on the alert to point out its faults, and do better than it would have them? Why does it always crucify Christ, and excommunicate Copernicus and Luther, and pronounce Washington and Franklin rebels?

One would think that a deliberate and practical denial of its authority was the only offense never contemplated by government; else, why has it not assigned its definite, its suitable and proportionate, penalty? If a man who has no property refuses but once to earn nine shillings for the State, he is put in prison for a period unlimited by any law that I know, and determined only by the discretion of those who placed him there; but if he should steal ninety times nine shillings from the State, he is soon permitted to go at large again.

If the injustice is part of the necessary friction of the machine of government, let it go, let it go: perchance it will wear smooth —certainly the machine will wear out. If the injustice has a spring, or a pulley, or a rope, or a crank, exclusively for itself, then perhaps you may consider whether the remedy will not be worse than the evil; but if it is of such a nature that it requires you to be the agent of injustice to another, then, I say, break the law. Let your life be a counterfriction to stop the machine. What I have to do is to see, at any rate, that I do not lend myself to the wrong which I condemn.

As for adopting the ways which the State has provided for remedying the evil, I know not of such ways. They take too much time, and a man's life will be gone. I have other affairs to attend to. I came into this world, not chiefly to make this a good place to live in, but to live in it, be it good or bad. A man has not everything to do, but something; and because he cannot do everything, it is not necessary that he should do something wrong. It is not my business to be petitioning the Governor or the Legislature any more than it is theirs to petition me; and if they should not hear my petition, what should I do then? But in this case the State has provided no way: its very Constitution is the evil. This may seem to be harsh and stubborn and unconciliatory; but it is to treat with the utmost kindness and consideration the only spirit that can appreciate or deserves it. So is all change for the better, like birth and death, which convulse the body.

I do not hesitate to say that those who call themselves Abolitionists should at once effectually withdraw their support, both in person and property, from the government of Massachusetts, and not wait till they constitute a majority of one before they suffer the right to prevail through them. I think that it is enough if they have God on their side, without waiting for that other one. Moreover, any man more right than his neighbors constitutes a majority of one already.

I meet this American government, or its representative, the State government, directly, and face to face, once a year—no more—in the person of its tax gatherer. This is the only mode in which a man situated as I am necessarily meets it; and it then says distinctly, Recognize me; and the simplest, the most effectual, and, in the present posture of affairs, the indispensablest mode of treating with it on this head, of expressing your little satisfaction with and love for it, is to deny it then. My civil neighbor, the tax gatherer, is the very man I have to deal with—for it is, after all, with men and not with parchment that I quarrel—and he has voluntarily chosen to be an agent of the government. How shall he ever know well what he is and does as an officer of the government, or as a man, until he is obliged to consider whether he shall treat me, his neighbor, for whom he has respect, as a neighbor and well-disposed man, or as a maniac and disturber of the peace, and see if he can get over this obstruction to his neighborliness without a ruder and more impetuous thought or speech corresponding with his action. I know this well, that if one thousand, if one hundred, if ten men whom I could name— if ten *honest* men only—ay, if *one* HONEST man, in this State of Massachusetts, *ceasing to hold slaves,* were actually to withdraw from this copartnership, and be locked up in the county jail therefor, it would be the abolition of slavery in America. For it matters not how small the beginning may seem to be: what is once well done is done forever. But we love better to talk about it: that we say is our mission. Reform keeps many scores of newspapers in its service, but not one man. If my esteemed neighbor, the State's ambassador, who will devote his days to the settlement of the question of human rights in the council chamber, instead of being threatened with the prisons of Carolina, were to sit down the prisoner of Massachusetts, that State which is so anxious to foist the sin of slavery upon her sister—though at present she can discover only an act of inhospitality to be the ground of a quarrel with her—the Legislature would not wholly waive the subject the following winter.

Under a government which imprisons any unjustly, the true place for a just man is also a prison. The proper place today, the only place which Massachusetts has provided for her freer and less desponding spirits, is in her prisons, to be put out and locked out of the State by her own act, as they have already put themselves out by their principles. It is there that the fugitive slave and the Mexican prisoner on parole and the Indian come to plead the wrongs of his race should find them; on that separate, but more free and honorable, ground where the State places those who are not *with* her but *against* her—the only house in a slave State in which a free man can abide with honor. If any think that their influence would be lost there and their voices no longer afflict the ear of the State, that they would not be as an enemy within its wall, they do not know by how much truth is stronger than error, nor how much more eloquently and effectively he can combat injustice who has experienced a little in his own person. Cast your whole vote, not a strip of paper merely, but your whole influence. A minority is powerless while it conforms to the majority; it is not even a minority then; but it is irresistible when it clogs by its whole weight. If the alternative is to keep all just men in prison, or give up war and slavery, the State will not hesitate which to choose. If a thousand men were not to pay their tax bills this year, that would not be a violent and bloody measure, as it would be to shed innocent blood. This is, in fact, the definition of a peaceable revolution, if any such is possible. If the tax gatherer, or any other public officer, asks me, as one has done, "But what shall I do?" my answer is, "If you really wish to do anything, resign your office." When the subject has refused allegiance, and the officer has resigned his office, then the revolution is accomplished. But even suppose blood should flow. Is there not a sort of blood shed when the conscience is wounded? Through this wound a man's real manhood and immortality flow out, and he bleeds to an everlasting death. I see this blood flowing now.

I have contemplated the imprisonment of the offender, rather than the seizure of his goods—though both will serve the same purpose—because they who assert the purest right, and consequently are most dangerous to a corrupt State, commonly have not spent much time in accumulating property. To such the State renders comparatively small service, and a slight is wont to appear exorbitant, particularly if they are obliged to earn it by special labor with their hands. If there were one who lived wholly without the use of money, the State itself would hesitate to demand it of him. But the rich man—not to make any invidious comparison—is always sold to the institution which makes him rich. Absolutely speaking, the more money, the less virtue; for money comes between a man and his objects, and obtains them for him; and it was certainly no great virtue to obtain it. It puts to rest many questions which he would otherwise be taxed to answer; while the only new question which it puts is the hard but superfluous one, how to spend it. Thus his moral ground is taken from under his feet. The opportunities of living are diminished in proportion as what are called the "means" are increased. The best thing a man can do for his culture when he is rich is to endeavor to carry out those schemes which he entertained when he was poor. Christ answered the Herodians according to their condition. "Show me the tribute money," said he—and one took a penny out of his pocket; if you use money which has the image of Caesar on it, and which he has made current and valuable, that is, *if you are men of the State,* and gladly enjoy the advantages of Caesar's government, then pay him back some of his own when he demands it. "Render therefore to Caesar that which is Caesar's, and to God those things which are God's"—leaving them no wiser than before as to which was which; for they did not wish to know.

When I converse with the freest of my neighbors, I perceive that, whatever they may say about the magnitude and seriousness of the question and their regard for the public tranquillity, the long and the short of the matter is that they cannot spare the protection of the existing government, and they dread the consequences to their property and families of disobedience to it. For my own part, I should not like to think that I ever rely on the protection of the State. But, if I deny the authority of the State when it presents its tax bill, it will soon take and waste all my property, and so harass me and my children without end. This is hard. This makes it impossible for a man to live honestly, and at the same time comfortably, in outward respects. It will not be worth the while to accumulate property; that would be sure to go again. You must hire or squat somewhere, and raise but a small crop, and eat that soon. You must live within yourself, and depend upon yourself always tucked up and ready for a start, and not have many affairs. A man may grow rich in Turkey even, if he will be in all respects a good subject of the Turkish government. Confucius said: "If a state is governed by the principles of reason, poverty and misery are subjects of shame; if a state is not governed by the principles of reason, riches and honors are the subjects of shame." No: until I want the protection of Massachusetts to be extended to me in some distant Southern port, where my liberty is endangered, or until I am bent solely on building up an estate at home by peaceful enterprise, I can afford to refuse allegiance to Massachusetts, and her right to my property and life. It costs me less in every sense to incur the penalty of disobedience to the State than it would to obey. I should feel as if I were worth less in that case.

Some years ago the State met me in behalf of the Church, and commanded me to pay a certain sum toward the support of a clergyman whose preaching my father attended, but never I myself. "Pay," it said, "or be locked up in the jail." I declined to pay. But, unfortunately, another man saw fit to pay it. I did not see why the schoolmaster should be taxed to support the priest, and not the priest the schoolmaster; for I was not the State's schoolmaster, but I supported myself by voluntary subscription. I did not see why the lyceum should not present its tax bill, and have the State to back its demand, as well as the Church. However, at the request of the selectmen, I condescended to make some such statement as this in writing: "Know all men by these presents, that I, Henry Thoreau, do not wish to be regarded as a member of any incorporated society which I have not joined." This I gave to the town clerk; and he has it. The State, having thus learned that I did not wish to be regarded as a member of that church, has never made a like demand on me since; though it said that it must adhere to its original presumption that time. If I had known how to name them, I should then have signed off in detail from all the societies which I never signed on to; but I did not know where to find a complete list.

I have paid no poll tax for six years. I was put into a jail once on this account, for one night; and, as I stood considering the walls of solid stone, two or three feet thick, the door of wood and iron, a foot thick, and the iron grating which strained the light, I could not help being struck with the foolishness of that institution which treated me as if I were mere flesh and blood and bones, to be locked up. I wondered that it should have concluded at length that this was the best use it could put me to, and had never thought to avail itself of my services in some way. I saw that, if there was a wall of stone between me and my townsmen, there was a still more difficult one to climb or break through before they could get to be as free as I was. I did not for a moment feel confined, and the walls seemed a great waste of stone and mortar. I felt as if I alone of all my townsmen had paid my tax. They plainly did not know how to treat me, but behaved like persons who are underbred. In every threat and in every compliment there was a blunder; for they thought that my chief desire was to stand the other side of that stone wall. I could not but smile to see how industriously they locked the door on my meditations, which followed them out again without let or hindrance, and they were really all that was dangerous. As they could not reach me, they had resolved to punish my body; just as boys, if they cannot come at some person against whom they have a spite, will abuse his dog. I saw that the State was half-witted, that it was timid as a lone woman with her silver spoons, and that it did not know its friends from its foes, and I lost all my remaining respect for it, and pitied it.

Thus the State never intentionally confronts a man's sense,

intellectual or moral, but only his body, his senses. It is not armed with superior wit or honesty, but with superior physical strength. I was not born to be forced. I will breathe after my own fashion. Let us see who is the strongest. What force has a multitude? They only can force me who obey a higher law than I. They force me to become like themselves. I do not hear of men being forced to live this way or that by masses of men. What sort of life were that to live? When I meet a government which says to me, "Your money or your life," why should I be in haste to give it my money? It may be in a great strait, and not know what to do: I cannot help that. It must help itself; do as I do. It is not worth the while to snivel about it. I am not responsible for the successful working of the machinery of society. I am not the son of the engineer. I perceive that, when an acorn and a chestnut fall side by side, the one does not remain inert to make way for the other, but both obey their own laws, and spring and grow and flourish as best they can, till one, perchance, overshadows and destroys the other. If a plant cannot live according to its nature, it dies; and so a man.

The night in prison was novel and interesting enough. The prisoners in their shirt sleeves were enjoying a chat and the evening air in the doorway when I entered. But the jailer said, "Come, boys, it is time to lock up"; and so they dispersed, and I heard the sound of their steps returning into the hollow apartments. My roommate was introduced to me by the jailer as "a first-rate fellow and a clever man." When the door was locked, he showed me where to hang my hat, and how he managed matters there. The rooms were whitewashed once a month; and this one, at least, was the whitest, most simply furnished, and probably the neatest apartment in the town. He naturally wanted to know where I came from, and what brought me there; and when I had told him, I asked him in my turn how he came there, presuming him to be an honest man, of course; and, as the world goes, I believe he was. "Why," said he, "they accuse me of burning a barn; but I never did it." As near as I could discover, he had probably gone to bed in a barn when drunk, and smoked his pipe there; and so a barn was burned. He had the reputation of being a clever man, had been there some three months waiting for his trial to come on, and would have to wait as much longer; but he was quite domesticated and contented, since he got his board for nothing, and thought that he was well treated.

He occupied one window, and I the other; and I saw that if one stayed there long, his principal business would be to look out the window. I had soon read all the tracts that were left there, and examined where former prisoners had broken out, and where a grate had been sawed off, and heard the history of the various occupants of that room; for I found that even here there was a history and a gossip which never circulated beyond the walls of the jail. Probably this is the only house in the town where verses are composed, which are afterward printed in a circular form, but not published. I was shown quite a long list of verses which were composed by some young men who had been detected in an attempt to escape, who avenged themselves by singing them.

I pumped my fellow prisoner as dry as I could, for fear I should never see him again; but at length he showed me which was my bed, and left me to blow out the lamp.

It was like traveling into a far country, such as I had never expected to behold, to lie there for one night. It seemed to me that I never had heard the town clock strike before, nor the evening sounds of the village; for we slept with the windows open, which were inside the grating. It was to see my native village in the light of the Middle Ages, and our Concord was turned into a Rhine stream, and visions of knights and castles passed before me. They were the voices of old burghers that I heard in the streets. I was an involuntary spectator and auditor of whatever was done and said in the kitchen of the adjacent village inn—a wholly new and rare experience to me. It was a closer view of my native town. I was fairly inside of it. I never had seen its institutions before. This is one of its peculiar institutions; for it is a shire town. I began to comprehend what its inhabitants were about.

In the morning our breakfasts were put through the hole in the door, in small oblong-square tin pans, made to fit, and holding a pint of chocolate, with brown bread, and an iron spoon. When they called for the vessels again, I was green enough to return what bread I had left; but my comrade seized it, and said that I should lay that up for lunch or dinner. Soon after he was let to work at haying in a neighboring field, whither he went every day, and would not be back till noon; so he bade me good day, saying that he doubted if he should see me again.

When I came out of prison—for some one interfered, and paid that tax—I did not perceive that great changes had taken place on the common, such as he observed who went in a youth and emerged a tottering and gray-headed man; and yet a change had to my eyes come over the scene—the town, and State, and country—greater than any that mere time could effect. I saw yet more distinctly the State in which I lived. I saw to what extent the people among whom I lived could be trusted as good neighbors and friends; that their friendship was for summer weather only; that they did not greatly propose to do right; that they were a distinct race from me by their prejudices and superstitions, as the Chinamen and Malays are; that in their sacrifices to humanity they ran no risks, not even to their property; that after all they were not so noble but they treated the thief as he had treated them, and hoped, by a certain outward observance and a few prayers, and by walking in a particular straight though useless path from time to time, to save their souls. This may be to judge my neighbors harshly; for I believe that many of them are not aware that they have such an institution as the jail in their village.

It was formerly the custom in our village, when a poor debtor came out of jail, for his acquaintances to salute him, looking through their fingers, which were crossed to represent the grating of a jail window, "How do you do?" My neighbors did not thus salute me, but first looked at me, and then at one another, as if I had returned from a long journey. I was put into jail as I was going to the shoemaker's to get a shoe which was mended. When I was let out the next morning, I proceeded to finish my errand, and, having put on my mended shoe, joined a huckleberry party, who were impatient to put themselves under my conduct; and in half an hour—for the horse was soon tackled—was in the midst of a huckleberry field, on one of our highest hills, two miles off, and then the State was nowhere to be seen.

This is the whole history of "My Prisons."

I have never declined paying the highway tax, because I am as desirous of being a good neighbor as I am of being a bad subject; and as for supporting schools, I am doing my part to educate my fellow countrymen now. It is for no particular item in the tax bill that I refuse to pay it. I simply wish to refuse allegiance to the State, to withdraw and stand aloof from it effectually. I do not care to trace the course of my dollar, if I could, till it buys a man or a musket to shoot one with—the dollar is innocent—but I am concerned to trace the effects of my allegiance. In fact, I quietly declare war with the State, after my fashion, though I will still make what use and get what advantage of her I can, as is usual in such cases.

If others pay the tax which is demanded of me, from a sympathy with the State, they do but what they have already done in their own case, or rather they abet injustice to a greater extent than the State requires. If they pay the tax from a mistaken interest in the individual taxed, to save his property or prevent his going to jail, it is because they have not considered wisely how far they let their private feelings interfere with the public good.

This, then, is my position at present. But one cannot be too much on his guard in such a case, lest his action be biased by obstinacy or an undue regard for the opinions of men. Let him see that he does only what belongs to himself and to the hour.

I think sometimes, Why, this people mean well, they are only ignorant; they would do better if they knew how: why give your neighbors this pain to treat you as they are not inclined to? But I think again, This is no reason why I should do as they do, or permit others to suffer much greater pain of a different kind. Again, I sometimes say to myself, When many millions of men, without heat, without ill will, without personal feeling of any kind, demand of you a few shillings only, without the possibility, such is their constitution, of retracting or altering their present demand, and without the possibility, on your side, of appeal to any other millions, why expose yourself to this overwhelming brute force? You do not resist cold and hunger, the winds and the waves, thus obstinately; you quietly submit to a thousand similar necessities. You do not put your head into the fire. But just in proportion as I regard this as not wholly a brute force, but partly a human force, and consider that I have relations to those millions as to so many millions of men, and not of mere brute or inanimate things, I see that appeal is possible, first and instantaneously, from them to the Maker of them, and, secondly, from them to themselves. But if I put my head deliberately into the fire, there is no appeal to fire or to the Maker of fire, and I have only myself to blame. If I could convince myself that I have any right to be satisfied with men as they are, and to treat them accordingly, and not according, in some respects, to my requisitions and expectations of what they and I ought to be, then, like a good Mussulman and fatalist, I should endeavor to be satisfied with things as they are, and say it is the will of God. And, above all, there is this difference between resisting this and a purely brute or natural force, that I can resist this with some effect; but I cannot expect, like Orpheus, to change the nature of the rocks and trees and beasts.

I do not wish to quarrel with any man or nation. I do not wish to split hairs, to make fine distinctions, or set myself up as better than my neighbors. I seek rather, I may say, even an excuse for conforming to the laws of the land. I am but too ready to conform to them. Indeed, I have reason to suspect myself on this head; and each year, as the tax gatherer comes round, I find myself disposed to review the acts and position of the general and State governments, and the spirit of the people, to discover a pretext for conformity.

> We must affect our country as our parents,
> And if at any time we alienate
> Our love or industry from doing it honor,
> We must respect effects and teach the soul
> Matter of conscience and religion,
> And not desire of rule or benefit.

I believe that the State will soon be able to take all my work of this sort out of my hands, and then I shall be no better a patriot than my fellow countrymen. Seen from a lower point of view, the Constitution, with all its faults, is very good; the law and the courts are very respectable; even this State and this American government are, in many respects, very admirable, and rare things, to be thankful for, such as a great many have described them; but seen from a point of view a little higher, they are what I have described them; seen from a higher still, and the highest, who shall say what they are, or that they are worth looking at or thinking of at all?

However, the government does not concern me much, and I

shall bestow the fewest possible thoughts on it. It is not many moments that I live under a government, even in this world. If a man is thought-free, fancy-free, imagination-free, that which *is not* never for a long time appearing *to be* to him, unwise rulers or reformers cannot fatally interrupt him.

I know that most men think differently from myself; but those whose lives are by profession devoted to the study of these or kindred subjects content me as little as any. Statesmen and legislators, standing so completely within the institution, never distinctly and nakedly behold it. They speak of moving society, but have no resting place without it. They may be men of a certain experience and discrimination, and have no doubt invented ingenious and even useful systems, for which we sincerely thank them; but all their wit and usefulness lie within certain not very wide limits. They are wont to forget that the world is not governed by policy and expediency. Webster never goes behind government, and so cannot speak with authority about it. His words are wisdom to those legislators who contemplate no essential reform in the existing government; but for thinkers, and those who legislate for all time, he never once glances at the subject. I know of those whose serene and wise speculations on this theme would soon reveal the limits of his mind's range and hospitality. Yet, compared with the cheap professions of most reformers, and the still cheaper wisdom and eloquence of politicians in general, his are almost the only sensible and valuable words, and we thank Heaven for him. Comparatively, he is always strong, original, and, above all, practical. Still, his quality is not wisdom, but prudence. The lawyer's truth is not Truth, but consistency or a consistent expediency. Truth is always in harmony with herself, and is not concerned chiefly to reveal the justice that may consist with wrongdoing. He well deserves to be called, as he has been called, the Defender of the Constitution. There are really no blows to be given by him but defensive ones. He is not a leader, but a follower. His leaders are the men of '87. "I have never made an effort," he says, "and never propose to make an effort; I have never countenanced an effort, and never mean to countenance an effort, to disturb the arrangement as originally made, by which the various States came into the Union." Still thinking of the sanction which the Constitution gives to slavery, he says, "Because it was a part of the original compact—let it stand." Notwithstanding his special acuteness and ability, he is unable to take a fact out of its merely political relations, and behold it as it lies absolutely to be disposed of by the intellect—what, for instance, it behooves a man to do here in America today with regard to slavery—but ventures, or is driven, to make some such desperate answer as the following, while professing to speak absolutely, and as a private man—from which, what new and singular code of social duties might be inferred? "The manner," says he, "in which the governments of those States where slavery exists are to regulate it is for their own consideration, under their responsibility to their constituents, to the general laws of propriety, humanity, and justice, and to God. Associations formed elsewhere, springing from a feeling of humanity, or any other cause, have nothing whatever to do with it. They have never received any encouragement from me, and they never will."

They who know of no purer sources of truth, who have traced up its stream no higher, stand, and wisely stand, by the Bible and the Constitution, and drink at it there with reverence and humility; but they who behold where it comes trickling into this lake or that pool, gird up their loins once more, and continue their pilgrimage toward its fountainhead.

No man with a genius for legislation has appeared in America. They are rare in the history of the world. There are orators, politicians, and eloquent men by the thousand; but the speaker has not yet opened his mouth to speak who is capable of settling the much-vexed questions of the day. We love eloquence for its own sake, and not for any truth which it may utter or any heroism it may inspire. Our legislators have not yet learned the comparative value of free trade and of freedom, of union, and of rectitude, to a nation. They have no genius or talent for comparatively humble questions of taxation and finance, commerce and manufactures and agriculture. If we were left solely to the wordy wit of legislators in Congress for our guidance, uncorrected by the seasonable experience and the effectual complaints of the people, America would not long retain her rank among the nations. For eighteen hundred years, though perchance I have no right to say it, the New Testament has been written; yet where is the legislator who has wisdom and practical talent enough to avail himself of the light which it sheds on the science of legislation?

The authority of government, even such as I am willing to submit to—for I will cheerfully obey those who know and can do better than I, and in many things even those who neither know nor can do so well—is still an impure one: to be strictly just, it must have the sanction and consent of the governed. It can have no pure right over my person and property but what I concede to it. The progress from an absolute to a limited monarchy, from a limited monarchy to a democracy, is a progress toward a true respect for the individual. Even the Chinese philosopher was wise enough to regard the individual as the basis of the empire. Is a democracy, such as we know it, the last improvement possible in government? Is it not possible to take a step further towards recognizing and organizing the rights of man? There will never be a really free and enlightened State until the State comes to recognize the individual as a higher and independent power, from which all its own power and authority are derived, and treats him accordingly. I please myself with imagining a State at last which can afford to be just to all men, and to treat the individual with respect as a neighbor; which even would not think it inconsistent with its own repose if a few were to live aloof from it, not meddling with it, nor embraced by it, who fulfilled all the duties of neighbors and fellow men. A State which bore this kind of fruit, and suffered it to drop off as fast as it ripened, would prepare the way for a still more perfect and glorious State, which also I have imagined, but not yet anywhere seen.

Perspectives on Freedom During the Period of Industrialization

An industrializing society, as it has often been pointed out, requires the creation on a large scale of a certain kind of personality—oriented toward work, punctuality, saving, the postponement of gratifications, and, above all else, a sense of self-discipline. Both among manual workers and the middle class, these are the qualities that permit human energy to be harnessed efficiently in the drive to raise productive output. The absence of these qualities among peasants and other traditional peoples is often seen as a major reason why modernization of their societies is so difficult.

But it would be too simple to suggest, in line with this analysis, that a society as it undergoes a major period of industrialization will automatically de-emphasize personal freedom and instead solely promote the naked subordination of the individual to centrally determined productive goals. This happened, to be sure, in the Soviet Union during the Stalin period, and in a less consistent form in certain of the emerging nations more recently. However, those societies which industrialized at an earlier time, particularly England and the United States, did so in a context which interestingly combined the values of liberty and social responsibility, voluntarism and discipline. The element of compulsion was far less obvious or pervasive than it has since become. The norms of productivity were more internalized and self-generating; indeed, especially in America, freedom itself could easily be identified with the achievement of productive success. Long before the Industrial Revolution, Americans were commonly pushing in these directions in their innermost thought processes. Benjamin Franklin urged the kind of planning and control, on a purely personal scale, which would much later seem appropriate in a large steel mill or university.

Thus, when industrial development began in the United States, in the period around the Civil War, the fact of economic transformation did not in itself settle previous debates over the meaning of obedience to authority. Instead, each of the older positions exemplified by Bancroft, Choate, and Thoreau could still thrive, even if in a somewhat altered context.

More important than the direct impact of industrialization on the debate over these ideas was the growing diversity of American society. New immigrant groups, sometimes with an important sprinkling of radicals, came to our shores. Black people eventually left the obscurity of the South and placed themselves centrally on stage in our largest cities. Universities were founded and became a major force in American intellectual life, giving many discussions about order and freedom a formal and scholarly quality. And in some subtler and more diffuse sense, an urban civilization permitted greater variety and sophistication to infuse such arguments. There was an enriching of perspectives on all sides, which should not be confused with a change in most of the fundamental issues.[1] Perhaps the most interesting aspect of modern American life has been the way in which great cultural and educational diversity could flower and yet at the same time leave fundamental lines of division in the society—and fundamental attitudes reflective of them—very little touched. It is this paradox which surrounds the debate over obedience to authority during the last hundred years in the United States.

4. A Call for More Discipline

In the late nineteenth century, economic freedom was accompanied by little sense of legal restraint. Since discipline was internalized (hence invisible), even the most disciplined pursuit of profits could seem almost anarchic to outside beholders. For a time, as Americans gorged themselves on success, even the compensating pull toward patriotic political feeling seemed less important than it had in the pre-Civil War period. Each rational, efficient, calculating man was out for himself.

For these reasons the moralists of the age, including men like the Yale sociologist William Graham Sumner, may be accused

1. Except perhaps so far as the rise of a deterministic social science threatened to make the concept of human freedom meaningless; on this, see the lengthier discussion of changing intellectual climates in recent decades, pp. 34–36.

of urging an attitude of stern self-control while at the same time condoning the flagrant indulgence of uninhibited laissez faire. Indeed, Sumner in several respects had a difficult row to walk. Not only did he have to face a possible contradiction between his moralism and his scientific determinism (which would explain away all behavior as the product of the natural evolution of folk habits), but he had to reconcile a materialistic view of life with a deep-seated concern for responsibility and restraint. He was capable of asserting that "in my philosophy of life, the accumulation of wealth is the first step to everything 'higher.' "[1] Yet he also passionately attacked what he called the "spurious liberty of doing as we please." Was not wealth-seeking precisely the form of pleasure that pleased Americans most?

For all his desire to be outspoken in an arresting way, Sumner was thus a philosopher whose thinking depended on a careful sense of balance. Liberty must be judiciously matched by social obligation and responsibility. Without law, life would be impossible, and yet law could sometimes smother legitimate individual aspirations. Believing strongly in free enterprise, which was a rapid and unsettling force in American life, Sumner also placed a high value on the survival of slowly developing social institutions, closely echoing Burke and Choate. There was, it is true, more emphasis in Sumner's thinking on the evolution of these basic institutions—on their susceptibility to change, as befitted a Darwinian—yet his truly conservative instincts did not allow him to argue for the likelihood of such change beyond a certain point.

The moral sense of the community evolves, but it does so only very gradually, and individuals must hold themselves back from the temptation to help push it along. Voluntary agreements, indeed the whole philosophy of natural rights, are too dangerously unstable as the basis of change; Sumner paralleled Choate in rejecting the fundamental viewpoint of John Locke while on occasion inconsistently slipping back into its vocabulary. Law must be positive; it cannot depend merely upon the shifting will of majorities. Law must nonetheless conform to the pattern of "right living."

On the role of the state as such, Sumner was both more balanced and more ambiguous than Choate. His belief in laissez faire did not permit him to reverence government, yet he could be found emphasizing the continuity of what he called "state

1. Sumner to C. W. Squires, May 20, 1874, Sumner Papers, Yale University Library.

burdens" as a constant factor in human life since the Middle Ages, and of course he detested anarchism. The major functions of the state were to protect private property and to enforce community moral standards (here Choate would hardly have disagreed). Sumner's willingness to employ legal coercion toward these ends, but not toward humane reforms, announced what would become a characteristic compromise on the role of government among conservatives from then on. In effect, law-breaking corporations would be regarded more tolerantly than law-revising reformers.

In the context of late nineteenth-century industrialism, still more suggestive is the theme of psychological self-restraint which permeates Sumner's thought. His emphasis on the need for inner discipline helps bring his otherwise somewhat tangled views on law and the state into better focus.

A call for discipline and obedience runs through Sumner's writings on many levels. For instance, he said that these qualities lay "at the very root" of the meaning of education, whether at the primary school or the university. The same built-in attitude of restraint was supposed to inhibit reformers from tampering with the established order; Sumner may indeed have displayed so much hostility to reformers because they symbolized for him a loss of the important capacity to endure life with Stoic dignity. Certain details of Sumner's personal life seem to support such an interpretation of his frame of mind. In childhood he was remembered as stiff, reserved, and overly serious, once priggishly reprimanding his own parents for making spectacles of themselves by sledding joyously down a hill![2] As a Yale undergraduate, he was standoffish and abnormally diligent; though he thawed considerably later on, he retained such indicative traits as a reputation for being an extremely careful dresser. Thus he seems to have lived, to a marked degree, the kind of nonimpulsive life which he commended to others as the basic source of social control in civilization.

Discipline, work, study—these habits, deeply imbedded in the popular psyche, could largely (though never entirely) replace the need for governmental compulsion, even in a modern industrial setting. Law always remains necessary in the background, to deal with occasional anarchists and troublemakers, but a very large degree of freedom can exist so long as this personal discipline is maintained. Emphasis on the need for an accommodative indus-

2. Harris E. Starr, *William Graham Sumner* (New York: Henry Holt and Company, 1925), p. 21.

trial personality thus enabled Sumner to minimize the role of state intervention while at the same time decrying lawlessness and anarchy. Reading Sumner with this in mind, perhaps it is not hard to grasp why "hip" people of the 1960's appeared to threaten many of their elders so deeply; here was a group basing its entire life style on rejection of precisely those personality traits which Sumner perceived were most functional for modern industrialism.

Although Sumner combined a belief in discipline with a belief in liberty in a fairly intricate way, one is tempted to conclude that the theme of restraint, obedience, and obligation was more fundamental to his thought. If so, he should not be remembered primarily as the promoter of a nearly anarchic philosophy of laissez faire; on the contrary, he should be viewed as a powerful articulator of an anti-libertarian ethic. This ethic was highly suitable to an age of large-scale organization, even if in America, by the year 1888, there was already a certain superfluousness about explicit exhortations in this direction.

William Graham Sumner, "Liberty and Responsibility"

Sir Robert Filmer defined freedom to be "liberty of every one to do as he lists, to live as he please, and not to be tied by any laws"; on this definition he based a philosophical treatise on absolutism in government, affirming its natural necessity and political propriety. He was perfectly right, for that definition of liberty is the one which would lead to despotism. At the same time, it is the anarchistic definition. There is no contradiction in this. Sir Robert meant by his definition to lay a basis from which to affirm that liberty is impossible, absurd, irrational; the anarchists affirm the same definition, and take it to be rational, real, and true. Around this issue all the great controversies in political science of the last two hundred years have raged, and around this issue they must revolve without solution so long as the metaphysical notion of liberty is accepted.

The liberty to do what one lists can never be complete, unless

---

Written in 1888. From William Graham Sumner, *Earth-Hunger and Other Essays* (New Haven, Conn.: Yale University Press, 1913), pp. 161–171.

it is supplemented by the further liberty not to do anything. A man who had this liberty might, therefore, be in the society but not of it, living upon it and enjoying a privilege to exert his energies in any way, no matter how harmful to other men. The notions of social rights, social duties, and liberty are, therefore, all born together, and correct definitions of them all will be consistent and coherent. The notion of liberty which we have been criticizing, however, is hostile to all notions of rights and duties; the man who had that liberty would have no duties, nor any rights, properly speaking, because he would have privileges. Rights and duties, in a combination consistent with liberty, constitute the social bond. Such rights, duties, and liberty are the elements of political institutions which give them their form and value.

We who live in the midst of a modern civilized state, with high security of persons and property, with well-defined rights, with no burdensome duties, with no privileges secured to some at the expense of others, easily assume that this all comes of itself, that it is the natural order of things, and that any departure from it would have to be forced by injustice. We believe that men have easily made up their minds that they would have it in this way, and that, by adopting proper resolutions at the right moment, they have brought it about. We therefore suppose that all we have is secured to us by the most stable and unquestionable reality, that we run no risk of losing it, that we can afford to find fault with it, throw it away, despise it, and break it in pieces.

The facts are far otherwise. The peace, order, security, and freedom from care of modern civilized life are not the product of human resolutions; they are due at last to economic forces, which, by expanding the conditions of human existence during the last three hundred years, have made all which we possess possible. Our history has been written on politics almost entirely; and, without joining in the current easy abuse of it on that account, we may fairly say that people have not learned at all to understand the extent to which political resolutions are controlled by economic conditions, or the extent to which political and social institutions are conditioned in economic facts. It is not too much to say that economic facts are always present and controlling in the apparently arbitrary acts of constitution-makers and legislators. Our whole history must be reconstructed with a view to this fact. If that is once done, we shall understand better the narrow range within which the law-givers, philosophers, constitution-makers, and legislators can work.

It is the opening of the new continents and the great discoveries and inventions which have made this modern age; they account for the power of man, and they have, by their form, conditioned the mode in which that power might be used. It has been wasted and abused to such an extent that man has never enjoyed more than a small percentage of the real power which was at his disposal for the enhancement of his earthly existence; and the modes in which it has been wasted have been chiefly those of social policy and political device. The ignorance, folly, and wickedness of statesmen, together with the incompetence of the social philosophers, seem great enough to have brought the world to universal penury, if the discoveries of science and the inventions of art had not been rapid and strong enough to bear all the losses and leave a surplus, by virtue of which mankind could gain something. The chief source of new power, however, has been the simplest of all, that is, an extension of population over new land. If a half-million proletarians in Europe should inherit each an estate, no one would think it any mystery that they were not proletarians any more; why, then, should it be a mystery that they are not proletarians when they have inherited an estate in America or Australia by going to it? To this we append, in passing, another useful reflection. If the statesmen and philosophers of the past made such mistakes, which are now visible to us, how do we know we are not making equally gross mistakes, which somebody will expose a century hence? We do not know it. We should hold this ever in mind. It is exactly the reason for distrusting our wisdom and for "letting things alone."

The political and civil liberty which we enjoy has issued out of all the stumbling and blundering of the past. The errors have been cured, to some extent, by bitter experience. The institutions which are strong and sound have only grown up through long correction, and have been purified of the stubborn folly of men only after long and bitter suffering. They are not stable; they are not founded in immovable facts; they are delicate products of care and study and labor. They could be easily lost and they require high good sense and self-control for their maintenance. Civil liberty is in the highest degree unstable. If we should fill libraries with written constitutions we could never guarantee liberty. Terms change their meaning, ideas move through a development of their own; nothing stands still here more than elsewhere. Intelligent conscience and educated reason are the only things which can maintain liberty, for they will constantly be needed for new cases and new problems. We could not make a greater mistake than to suppose that we could throw down all social institutions and guarantees, and still keep all the peace, order, security, and freedom from political anxiety, which we now enjoy. Time and again in history men have sacrificed liberty rather than incur anarchy. When anarchy comes and every one tries to realize the liberty to do as he likes, the man who has anything knows that he will not be able to do as he likes, because it will take all his energies and more to protect his property. He knows that some of the other people who will be doing as they like will be sure to rob him. The man who is too young or too old, or physically weak, and the women, know that they will not do as they like, because somebody else will make them do as he likes. These will all flee to any protection which can save them from plunder and abuse, because liberty and anarchy are totally inconsistent with each other, no matter what the definition we give to liberty. Filmer was right when he held that, if liberty meant license to do as you list, it made despotism the only rational and possible form of civil government.

There is, therefore, no liberty but liberty under law. Law does not restrict liberty; it creates the only real liberty there is—for liberty in any real sense belongs only to civilized life and to educated men. The sphere of it is not in the beast-like non-reflection of savages; it is in the highest self-determination of fully educated and responsible men. It belongs to defined rights, regulated interests, specified duties, all determined in advance, before passions are excited and selfishness engaged, prescribed in solemn documents, and guaranteed by institutions which work impersonally without fear or favor. Such are the institutions under which we live. Their integrity is worth more to us than anything else in the domain of politics; their improvement, that they may perform their functions better, is the highest political task of our civilization. That is why liberty in its true sense is worth more than the suppression of intemperance, or the restriction of trusts, or the limitation of corporations, or any other pet reform. Liberty which consists in the equilibrium of rights and duties for all members of the state under the same prescriptions, liberty which secures each man, in and under the laws and constitution, the use of all his own powers for his own welfare, has not therefore the slightest kinship with the spurious liberty of doing as we please, but is the prime condition of happy life in human society. The thing to which it has generally been sacrificed in the past has been "the reason of state"; that is, some other object than the happiness of men, an object selected and imposed upon the society by some arbitrary political authority. There is a modern abuse which is exactly parallel to this, and which consists in using the law to impose pet social aims on society, which use up the time and energy of the citizens in other aims than those chosen by themselves for their own happiness. Thus the most difficult problem in respect to liberty under law is now what it has always been, to prevent the law from overgrowing and smothering liberty.

The proposition that "every man should be free to do as he likes, without encroaching on the similar liberty of every other man," is commonly used as if it were a simple and final definition of social and civil liberty. It is not so, however. It is only one of those formulas which we get into the habit of using because they save us the trouble of thinking, not because they are real solutions. Evidently any two men might easily disagree as to the limits set by this formula to their respective spheres of right and liberty—if so they would quarrel and fight. Law, peace, and order would not therefore be guaranteed; that is to say, the problem would not be solved.

Civil liberty must therefore be an affair of positive law, of institutions, and of history. It varies from time to time, for the notion of rights is constantly in flux. The limiting line between the rights and duties of each man, up to which each may go without trenching on the same rights and liberty of others, must be defined at any moment of time by the constitution, laws, and institutions of the community. People often deny this, and revolt at it, because they say that one's notions of rights and liberty are not set for him by the laws of the state. The first man you meet will undoubtedly tell you that there are a number of laws now in force in the United States which he does not think are consistent with liberty and (natural) rights—I who write this would say so of laws restricting immigration, laying protective taxes, etc. But it is to be observed that behind the positive law existing at any time, there is the moral reflection of the community which is at work all the time. This is the field of study, debate, and reflection, on which moral convictions are constantly being formed; and when they are formed, they find their way into laws, constitutions, and institutions, provided that the political institutions are free, so as to allow this to take place. If not, there is opened a gap between the positive law and the moral convictions of the people, and social convulsions ensue. It is a constant phenomenon of all exaggerated philosophers of the state, that they obscure this distinction between public morals and positive law. The older abuse was to suppress public morals in the name of positive law; the later abuse is to introduce public morals into positive law directly and immaturely.

If now we turn to individual liberty, still it is true that all liberty is under law. The whole life of man is under law—it is impossible to conceive of it otherwise. It is impossible to understand society except we think of it as held and governed by forces which maintain equilibrium in it, just as we have learned to conceive of nature. The objections which are made to this notion are exactly parallel to those which were formerly brought against the same conception of physics, and it is impossible to argue against them, because, if they were true, there would be no thinking or arguing possible. If social science deals only with matters of expediency, then there is no social science. It is a question of expediency whether there shall be two Houses in the Legislature or one; whether the Cabinet ministers shall have seats in Congress; whether men shall work ten hours a day or eight; whether we should use more or less paper money inside the requirement of the country; whether university education should be based on Greek; whether women should have the suffrage; and so on. If all the questions of social science are of this nature, there is no social science; there is nothing to find out. All that can be said is: "Go on and try it"; and the people who have "views" may be listened to if they show what they think to be the advantages of one or another arrangement.

In truth, however, the field of expediency is very circumscribed. It is surrounded by the domain of forces, so that when we seem most free to adopt such plans as we please, we find ourselves actually controlled by facts in the nature of man and of the earth, and we find that it is the sum of our wisdom to find out those facts and to range ourselves under them and in obedience to them. Then our science and our art have their proper places and fall into due relation to each other.

Thus we come to this: that there is no liberty for the intelligent man as an individual, or in voluntary co-operation with others, except in intelligent obedience to the laws of right living. His first task is to know the world in which he finds himself. He must work and he must study. He is not turned out to riot in self-indulgence because he is free; he must conform to the conditions in which he finds himself. He must obey. When he has broken all the bonds of old institutions, of superstition and human tyranny, he wakes to find that he can have no liberty unless he subdues himself; labor and self-control are the conditions of welfare. He must not cry out that liberty is only a delusion and a juggle; he must understand that what liberty properly means for the individual, is intelligent acceptance of the conditions of earthly life, conformity to them, and manful effort to make life a success under them.

Not to follow this line of thought into the domain of private morals, I turn back to the relation of individual liberty to civil liberty. Civil and political liberty cannot release a man from state burdens. It is interesting and instructive to notice that free yeomen in the United States have to take up, of their own accord, many of those burdens which, in the Middle Ages, were regarded as the heaviest feudal obligations. The farmers in a New England township have to maintain roads and bridges, do police duty, and maintain all public institutions as much as if they lived upon a manor. A farmer who works out his taxes on a road does not know how near he comes to reproducing a mediæval villain. The burdens are there, because society is there; and they must be borne. If the state does them on a larger scale than the township, then they must be paid for; and when we see men eager to work them out if they can, we must infer that the burden is increased, not lessened, by being turned into taxes.

When the peasant obtains freedom, therefore, and sets up a

democratic republic, he finds that that means only that he must turn about and do again voluntarily, as an intelligent citizen, what he did before under human compulsion. When he gets self-government, he finds that it still means government; only that now it is turned into personal discipline instead of being governmental compulsion. If he gets his personal liberty, then civil liberty is nothing but a guarantee that, in doing his best to learn the laws of right living and to obey them, to the end that his life may be a success, no one else shall be allowed to interfere with him or to demand a share in the product of his efforts. That is what the function of the state is; and if it does more or less it fails of its function.

Discipline, therefore, is the great need of our time. It should be the first object of education. By it we mean something much more than the mental training about which we used to hear so much. We mean training of thought, feeling, and emotions, so as to apprehend and appreciate all things correctly; and habits of self-control so as to hold one's self within the limits which enable free men in a free society to live in harmony and pursue their ends successfully without encroaching on each other. Our children need it. Their freedom and fearlessness give them spirit and courage; but they lack form and training—they would not be any less free if they were considerably chastened. We need it as parents; we should discharge our responsibilities in that relationship much better if we were schooled to more patience and to more rational methods of exercising authority or instruction. We need it in social relations, because it is only by virtue of discipline that men can co-operate with each other. The notion that co-operation is a power which can take the place of the intelligence of well-trained men, is itself a product and proof of undisciplined thinking. Men increase their power indefinitely by co-operation and organization; but in order to co-operate they must make concessions. The prime condition is concord, and it is only disciplined men who are capable of attaining to that. It has often been said that men have to surrender their liberty in order to organize; but it is better stated that they gain new power consistently with liberty by organizing. We need better discipline in science, at least in social science. There is a great luxuriance in the production of "views" and notions in this field; and the greatest need is of a set of guarantees and criteria by which this exuberance could be trimmed down. There is one set of persons whose liberty would certainly gain by the production of such tests and guarantees, *viz.,* those who are now likely to have to pay the expense of all the social speculation which is on foot, if any of it should be put to experiment. We need more discipline in public affairs. Our freedom would lose nothing if it were more sober, and if a great many abuses which the law cannot reach were more under the ban of public opinion.

Thus liberty in a free state, and for intelligent men, is limited, first by responsibility, and second by discipline.

5. Rejection of Nonconformist Individualism

If Sumner sought to convey a rather predictable message about the need for a stronger disciplinary harness in America, Woodrow Wilson launched an attack upon the spirit of doing what one pleased which was couched in personal, psychological (and therefore more modern) terms. Wilson's words thus provide an answer to Thoreau on a deeper and quite powerful level. At the very time when such now respected academic philosophers as George Herbert Mead and Charles Horton Cooley were challenging the viability of the concept of an isolated self, Wilson was setting forth a closely parallel insight in more popular language. Perhaps the parallelism partly reflected the general upsurge of holistic concern for society and "social efficiency" which was so marked among thinkers with a progressive orientation at the turn of the century. But it is also noteworthy that Wilson's context for asserting the primacy of social claims upon the individual was more one of business careerism than of democratic reform. In this respect Wilson was not yet—and would not become until some years later—a full-blown progressive. It is his use of psychological arguments, not his social views as such, which makes Wilson's essay of 1901 seem unusually suggestive.

A strong thread of anti-individualist sentiment runs through the whole of Wilson's life. This has not been fully appreciated because in economic terms Wilson's "New Freedom," like Sumner's defense of laissez faire, appears to promote individualism of

a sort. Many are therefore surprised, or have felt a sense of be-
trayal, at Wilson's wartime record of 1917–18, during which his
administration played a repressive role toward dissenters as part
of its campaign for unflagging national unity of purpose. But Wilson's highly emotional war patriotism and his considerable intolerance of opposition were in fact perfectly consistent extensions
of his earlier views on the proper relationship between individual
aspiration and social conformity.

That this is so can be clearly seen when one reads his essay,
"When a Man Comes to Himself." This piece sets forth in model
terms the case for accepting an establishmentarian frame of thinking in modern America. It completely conforms to the mentality
of managerialism. In it Wilson deliberately seeks to combat the
"once fashionable" view that organized society is merely "a necessary evil, an irritating but inevitable restriction upon the 'natural'
sovereignty and entire self-government of the individual." Such
an attitude reflects egotism, crankishness, and mere eccentricity.
Invoking the now familiar concept of the life cycle, Wilson equates
the process of maturation with a growing awareness of one's place
inside the large network of existing social relationships. He then
links this awareness with a mental state that is "thoroughly sane
and healthy." His use of the word "adjustment" to describe this
result places him in the forefront of the popular psychologists of
the succeeding two generations. Any urge toward individual isolation is dismissed in the vocabulary of sickness, or of infantilism,
as well as in the more usual nineteenth-century terminology of
moral reproof.

Of course one must not discount the persistence of ethical and
perhaps religious elements in Wilson's perspective, and his brief
explorations into the psychology of adolescence and young manhood should not be confused with the far bolder probing of early
childhood by George Herbert Mead. But what is interesting is the
no doubt unconscious willingness of Wilson, whose mind was so
often old-fashioned, to incorporate this newer approach to the
problem of individualism into his perspective in such a definite
way. When Wilson says, "A man *is* the part he plays among his
fellows," he is not far from the more recent formulation, "Man
is the sum of his roles." As an educator, Wilson always remained
contemptuous of the "younger" social sciences, and he probably
did not gain his insight from any deliberate study of them; but
he and the social scientists were at least sharing in a common
effort to combat the older and, as they saw it, naïve conception
of individualism in American thought.

It would be maliciously unfair, in another direction, to detect more than the faintest whiff of Bruce Barton in this essay of Wilson's, even though both men linked Christianity with business success. Wilson's advice on the psychology of how to make one's way in the world was actually far sounder, far more in tune with the realities of life at or near the top, than Barton's shallow recipe of salesmanship would be in the 1920's. Wilson fully grasped that the potential leader, whether in business or politics, must spend most of his time sensitively attuning himself to his social environment, through a careful process of listening, observing, and responding to subtle cues, rather than advertising himself in a brash fashion. It is tempting to add, incidentally, that for both Wilson and Barton Christianity appears a mere embellishment in a message at bottom almost wholly secular; if anything, its extraneousness is more obvious in Wilson's essay, where religion is introduced as a kind of coda in the final paragraph.

Wilson's difficult state of mind, his troubling internal contradictions, are often emphasized by those who study him. There is indeed considerable evidence in "When a Man Comes to Himself" that Wilson is speaking *to* himself, as well as to the *Century* audience. When he says that we sometimes talk "with distaste and uneasiness, of men who 'have no sense of humor,' who take themselves too seriously, who are intense, self-absorbed, over-confident in matters of opinion," we immediately realize that these are adjectives frequently applied to Wilson by later observers. Wilson was capable of astute self-analysis concerning these traits, as for instance when he confided to a friend in 1897 that "I often feel foolish when I realize how very seriously I am taking myself."[1] It seems undeniable that a major aim of Wilson's in writing this essay was to set forth the rules he himself must try to live by if he was to seek a position of greater prominence—in other words, self-admonition. It is surely no accident that he finds it entirely natural for men to be "in love with power and greatness" because such prominence "affords them so pleasurable an expansion of faculty." In this context, Wilson's warning against undiluted "moral enthusiasm" as a guide to action is highly significant. In urging men to obtain a realistic knowledge of the network of interests they will inevitably disturb by their activities, Wilson seems not merely to be expressing caution about the reform spirit but also to be counselling himself against too strident a personal expression of evangelism.

1. Wilson to Mrs. H. F. Reid, October 3, 1897, Woodrow Wilson Papers, Library of Congress.

Many American presidents grow gradually into their office. In Wilson's case the reverse seems almost to have been true. He was giving much extremely sound advice in 1901 to anyone who might covet such a high position; yet once in the White House he often displayed the very kinds of excesses he had cautioned against. To read his earlier words, therefore, is to discover an added dimension to his tragedy—that of self-knowledge.[2] Intellectually he was consistent in his dislike of individual assertiveness and willful dissent from the common spirit of the moment; emotionally, he could not follow his own prescription of adapting in mature fashion to the practical needs of his social context. Praising Samuel Gompers in the speech he gave to the A. F. of L. during late 1917, other parts of which are printed below, Wilson significantly confessed: "I like to lay my mind alongside of a mind that knows how to pull in harness. The horses that kick over the traces will have to be put in corral."

During the war, Wilson's posture on matters of conformity and dissent became shocking to many members of the American liberal community. Wilson's curiously mild words on this subject need to be balanced against the record of his administration. His one-time fervent admirer Frederic C. Howe, who was in a position to observe the conduct of daily affairs as Commissioner of Immigration at Ellis Island, voiced an indictment which has come to be accepted as the standard judgment of the Wilson administration: "Things that were done forced one almost to despair of mind, to distrust the political state. Shreds were left of our courage, our reverence. The Department of Justice, the Department of Labor, and Congress not only failed to protest against hysteria, they encouraged these excesses; the state not only abandoned the liberty which it should have protected, it lent itself to the stamping out of individualism and freedom." Howe cited the use of the agent provocateur, the turning over to private detective agencies of the task of uncovering "sedition," and the creation of much of the atmosphere of the police state.[3]

Wilson's actions—especially his tolerance of overzealous sub-

2. He seems to have changed by 1909, when, in a speech at a teachers' conference in New Jersey, he said: "The crying need of modern society is the man who will fight for what is right without stopping to count the cost and consequence to loved ones." Quoted in Henry W. Bragdon, *Woodrow Wilson: The Academic Years* (Cambridge, Mass.: Harvard University Press, 1967), p. 367.

3. Frederic C. Howe, *The Confessions of a Reformer* (New York: Charles Scribner's Sons, 1925), p. 276.

ordinates such as A. Mitchell Palmer[4]—revealed the depth of his commitment to a concept of community loyalty and, by contrast, the relative lack of concern he felt for the right of personal expression. If he had been unable to accept the psychological justification for individual assertiveness against the claims of society in 1901, in 1917 he certainly was not going to give comfort to dissident elements during a war.

In the course of that conflict, he spoke out only twice on the subject of lawlessness, once at the conclusion of a speech to the A. F. of L. of which the main brunt had been to put pressure on labor unions not to disrupt the nation's productive effort; and once again in 1918 when he issued a statement deploring lynchings, on one of the very few occasions when he responded to pressure from the N.A.A.C.P. Even in the A. F. of L. speech, his criticisms of lawlessness were carefully balanced by an appeal to let nothing stand in the way of a vigorous prosecution of the war.

Despite his academic background in political science, Wilson defined the claims of society not primarily in legal terms but on the basis of a series of policy goals which sprang from his emotions and to which he clung with a tenacity which knew few bounds. Wilson thus was not merely a curiously perceptive commentator on the conformitarian state of mind, as he demonstrates in his early essay; he was also, notwithstanding his occasional nods in the direction of legalism, a principal saboteur of American traditions of individual dissent (such as they had been) during a profound turning point in the history of the nation.

Woodrow Wilson, "When a Man Comes to Himself"

It is a very wholesome and regenerating change which a man undergoes when he "comes to himself." It is not only after periods of recklessness or infatuation, when he has played the spendthrift or the fool, that a man comes to himself. He comes to himself after experiences of which he alone may be aware: when he has left off being wholly preoccupied with his own powers and interests and with every petty plan that centers in himself; when

4. See pp. 234–245.

The Century Illustrated Monthly Magazine, LXII (June 1901), 268–273.

he has cleared his eyes to see the world as it is, and his own true place and function in it.

It is a process of disillusionment. The scales have fallen away. He sees himself soberly, and knows under what conditions his powers must act, as well as what his powers are. He has got rid of earlier prepossessions about the world of men and affairs, both those which were too favorable and those which were too unfavorable—both those of the nursery and those of a young man's reading. He has learned his own paces, or, at any rate, is in a fair way to learn them; has found his footing and the true nature of the "going" he must look for in the world; over what sorts of roads he must expect to make his running, and at what expenditure of effort; whither his goal lies, and what cheer he may expect by the way. It is a process of disillusionment, but it disheartens no soundly made man. It brings him into a light which guides instead of deceiving him; a light which does not make the way look cold to any man whose eyes are fit for use in the open, but which shines wholesomely, rather, upon the obvious path, like the honest rays of the frank sun, and makes traveling both safe and cheerful.

There is no fixed time in a man's life at which he comes to himself, and some men never come to themselves at all. It is a change reserved for the thoroughly sane and healthy, and for those who can detach themselves from tasks and drudgery long and often enough to get, at any rate once and again, view of the proportions of life and of the stage and plot of its action. We speak often with amusement, sometimes with distaste and uneasiness, of men who "have no sense of humor," who take themselves too seriously, who are intense, self-absorbed, over-confident in matters of opinion, or else go plumed with conceit, proud of we cannot tell what, enjoying, appreciating, thinking of nothing so much as themselves. These are men who have not suffered that wholesome change. They have not come to themselves. If they be serious men, and real forces in the world, we may conclude that they have been too much and too long absorbed; that their tasks and responsibilities long ago rose about them like a flood, and have kept them swimming with sturdy stroke the years through, their eyes level with the troubled surface—no horizon in sight, no passing fleets, no comrades but those who struggled in the flood like themselves. If they be frivolous, light-headed, men without purpose or achievement, we may conjecture, if we do not know, that they were born so, or spoiled by fortune, or befuddled by self-indulgence. It is no great matter what we think of them.

It is enough to know that there are some laws which govern a man's awakening to know himself and the right part to play. A man *is* the part he plays among his fellows. He is not isolated; he cannot be. His life is made up of the relations he bears to others—is made or marred by those relations, guided by them, judged by them, expressed in them. There is nothing else upon which he can spend his spirit—nothing else that we can see. It is by these he gets his spiritual growth; it is by these we see his character revealed, his purpose, and his gifts. Some play with a certain natural passion, an unstudied directness, without grace, without modulation, with no study of the masters or conscious-ness of the pervading spirit of the plot; others give all their thought to their costume and think only of the audience; a few act as those who have mastered the secrets of a serious art, with deliberate subordination of themselves to the great end and motive of the play, spending themselves like good servants, indulging no wilfulness, obtruding no eccentricity, lending heart and tone and gesture to the perfect progress of the action. These have "found themselves," and have all the ease of a perfect adjustment.

Adjustment is exactly what a man gains when he comes to him-self. Some men gain it late, some early; some get it all at once, as if by one distinct act of deliberate accommodation; others get it by degrees and quite imperceptibly. No doubt to most men it comes by the slow processes of experience—at each stage of life a little. A college man feels the first shock of it at graduation, when the boy's life has been lived out and the man's life sud-denly begins. He has measured himself with boys; he knows their code and feels the spur of their ideals of achievement. But what the world expects of him he has yet to find out, and it works, when he has discovered it, a veritable revolution in his ways both of thought and of action. He finds a new sort of fitness demanded of him, executive, thoroughgoing, careful of details, full of drudgery and obedience to orders. Everybody is ahead of him. Just now he was a senior, at the top of a world he knew and reigned in, a finished product and pattern of good form. Of a sudden he is a novice again, as green as in his first school year, studying a thing that seems to have no rules—at sea amid cross-winds, and a bit seasick withal. Presently, if he be made of stuff that will shake into shape and fitness, he settles to his tasks and is comfortable. He has come to himself: understands what capacity is, and what it is meant for; sees that his training was not for ornament or personal gratification, but to teach him how to use himself and develop faculties worth using. Henceforth there is a zest in action, and he loves to see his strokes tell.

The same thing happens to the lad come from the farm into the city, a big and novel field, where crowds rush and jostle, and a rustic boy must stand puzzled for a little how to use his placid and unjaded strength. It happens, too, though in a deeper and more subtle way, to the man who marries for love, if the love be true and fit for foul weather. Mr. Bagehot used to say that a bachelor was "an amateur in life," and wit and wisdom are married in the jest. A man who lives only for himself has not begun to live—has yet to learn his use, and his real pleasure too, in the world. It is not necessary he should marry to find himself out, but it is necessary he should love. Men have come to themselves serving their mothers with an unselfish devotion, or their sisters, or a cause for whose sake they forsook ease and left off thinking of themselves. It is unselfish action, growing slowly into the high habit of devotion, and at last, it may be, into a sort of consecration, that teaches a man the wide meaning of his life, and makes of him a steady professional in living, if the motive be not necessity, but love. Necessity may make a mere drudge of a man, and no mere drudge ever made a professional of himself; that demands a higher spirit and a finer incentive than his.

Surely a man has come to himself only when he has found the best that is in him, and has satisfied his heart with the highest achievement he is fit for. It is only then that he knows of what he is capable and what his heart demands. And, assuredly, no thoughtful man ever came to the end of his life, and had time and a little space of calm from which to look back upon it, who did not know and acknowledge that it was what he had done unselfishly and for others, and nothing else, that satisfied him in the retrospect, and made him feel that he had played the man. That alone seems to him the real measure of himself, the real standard of his manhood. And so men grow by having responsibility laid upon them, the burden of other people's business. Their powers are put out at interest, and they get usury in kind. They are like men multiplied. Each counts manifold. Men who live with an eye only upon what is their own are dwarfed beside them—seem fractions while they are integers. The trustworthiness of men trusted seems often to grow with the trust.

It is for this reason that men are in love with power and greatness: it affords them so pleasurable an expansion of faculty, so large a run for their minds, an exercise of spirit so various and refreshing; they have the freedom of so wide a tract of the world of affairs. But if they use power only for their own ends, if there be no unselfish service in it, if its object be only their personal aggrandizement, their love to see other men tools in their hands, they go out of the world small, disquieted, beggared, no enlargement of soul vouchsafed them, no usury of satisfaction. They have added nothing to themselves. Mental and physical powers alike grow by use, as every one knows; but labor for one's self alone is like exercise in a gymnasium. No healthy man can remain satisfied with it, or regard it as anything but a preparation for tasks in the open, amid the affairs of the world,—not sport, but business,—where there is no orderly apparatus, and every man must devise the means by which he is to make the most of himself. To make the most of himself means the multiplication of his activities, and he must turn away from himself for that. He looks about him, studies the face of business or of affairs, catches some intimation of their larger objects, is guided by the intimation, and presently finds himself part of the motive force of communities or of nations. It makes no difference how small a part, how insignificant, how unnoticed. When his powers begin to play outward, and he loves the task at hand not because it gains him a livelihood but because it makes him a life, he has come to himself.

Necessity is no mother to enthusiasm. Necessity carries a whip. Its method is compulsion, not love. It has no thought to make itself attractive; it is content to drive. Enthusiasm comes with the revelation of true and satisfying objects of devotion; and it is enthusiasm that sets the powers free. It is a sort of enlightenment. It shines straight upon ideals, and for those who see it the race and struggle are henceforth toward these. An instance will point the meaning. One of the most distinguished and most justly honored of our great philanthropists spent the major part of his life absolutely absorbed in the making of money—so it seemed to those who did not know him. In fact, he had very early passed the stage at which he looked upon his business as a means of support or of material comfort. Business had become for him an intellectual pursuit, a study in enterprise and increment. The field of commerce lay before him like a chess-board; the moves interested him like the manœuvers of a game. More money was more power, a greater advantage in the game, the means of shaping men and events and markets to his own ends and uses. It was his will that set fleets afloat and determined the havens they were bound for; it was his foresight that brought goods to market at the right time; it was his suggestion that made the industry of unthinking men efficacious; his sagacity saw itself justified at home not only, but at the ends of the earth. And as the money poured in, his government and mastery increased, and his mind was the more satisfied. It is so that men make little kingdoms for themselves, and an international power undarkened by diplomacy, undirected by parliaments.

It is a mistake to suppose that the great captains of industry, the great organizers and directors of manufacture and commerce and monetary exchange, are engrossed in a vulgar pursuit of wealth. Too often they suffer the vulgarity of wealth to display itself in the idleness and ostentation of their wives and children, who "devote themselves," it may be, "to expense regardless of pleasure"; but we ought not to misunderstand even that, or condemn it unjustly. The masters of industry are often too busy with their own sober and momentous calling to have time or spare thought enough to govern their own households. A king may be too faithful a statesman to be a watchful father. These men are not fascinated by the glitter of gold: the appetite for power has got hold upon them. They are in love with the exercise of their faculties upon a great scale; they are organizing and overseeing a great part of the life of the world. No wonder they are captivated. Business is more interesting than pleasure, as Mr. Bagehot said, and when once the mind has caught its zest, there's no disengaging it. The world has reason to be grateful for the fact. . . .

This is the positive side of a man's discovery of the way in which his faculties are to be made to fit into the world's affairs, and released for effort in a way that will bring real satisfaction. There is a negative side also. Men come to themselves by discovering their limitations no less than by discovering their deeper endowments and the mastery that will make them happy. It is the discovery of what they can *not* do, and ought not to attempt, that transforms reformers into statesmen; and great should be the joy of the world over every reformer who comes to himself. The spectacle is not rare; the method is not hidden. The practicability of every reform is determined absolutely and always by "the circumstances of the case," and only those who put themselves into the midst of affairs, either by action or by observation, can know what those circumstances are or perceive what they signify. No statesman dreams of doing whatever he pleases; he knows that it does not follow that because a point of morals or of policy is obvious to him it will be obvious to the nation, or even to his own friends; and it is the strength of a democratic polity that there are so many minds to be consulted and brought to agreement, and that nothing can be wisely done for which the thought, and a good deal more than the thought, of the country, its sentiment and its purpose, have not been prepared. Social reform is a matter of coöperation, and, if it be of a novel kind, requires an infinite deal of converting to bring the efficient majority to believe in it and support it. Without their agreement and support it is impossible.

It is this that the more imaginative and impatient reformers find out when they come to themselves, if that calming change ever comes to them. Oftentimes the most immediate and drastic means of bringing them to themselves is to elect them to legislative or executive office. That will reduce over-sanguine persons to their simplest terms. Not because they find their fellow legislators or officials incapable of high purpose or indifferent to the betterment of the communities which they represent. Only cynics hold that to be the chief reason why we approach the millennium so slowly, and cynics are usually very ill-informed persons. Nor is it because under our modern democratic arrangements we so subdivide power and balance parts in government that no one man can tell for much or turn affairs to his will. One of the most instructive studies a politician could undertake would be a study of the infinite limitations laid upon the power of the Russian Czar, notwithstanding the despotic theory of the Russian constitution—limitations of social habit, of official prejudice, of race jealousies, of religious predilections, of administrative machinery even, and the inconvenience of being himself only one man, and that a very young one, over-sensitive and touched with melancholy. He can do only what can be done with the Russian people. He can no more make them quick, enlightened, and of the modern world of the West than he can change their tastes in eating. He is simply the leader of Russians.

An English or American statesman is better off. He leads a thinking nation, not a race of peasants topped by a class of revolutionists and a caste of nobles and officials. He can explain new things to men able to understand, persuade men willing and accustomed to make independent and intelligent choices of their own. An English statesman has an even better opportunity to lead than an American statesman, because in England executive power and legislative initiative are both intrusted to the same grand committee, the ministry of the day. The ministers both propose what shall be made law and determine how it shall be enforced when enacted. And yet English reformers, like American, have found office a veritable cold-water bath for their ardor for change. Many a man who has made his place in affairs as the spokesman of those who see abuses and demand their reformation has passed from denunciation to calm and moderate advice when he got into Parliament, and has turned veritable conservative when made a minister of the crown. . . .

It is not that such men lose courage when they find themselves charged with the actual direction of the affairs concerning which they have held and uttered such strong, unhesitating, drastic opinions. They have only learned discretion. For the first time they see in its entirety what it was that they were attempting. They are at last at close quarters with the world. Men of every interest and variety crowd about them; new impressions throng them; in the midst of affairs the former special objects of their zeal fall into new environments, a better and truer perspective; seem no longer so susceptible to separate and radical change. The real nature of the complex stuff of life they were seeking to work in is revealed to them,—its intricate and delicate fiber, and the subtle, secret interrelationship of its parts,—and they work circumspectly, lest they should mar more than they mend. Moral enthusiasm is not, uninstructed and of itself, a suitable guide to practicable and lasting reformation; and if the reform sought be the reformation of others as well as of himself the reformer should look to it that he knows the true relation of his will to the wills of those he would change and guide. When he has discovered that relation he has come to himself: has discovered his real use and planning part in the general world of men; has come to the full command and satisfying employment of his faculties. Otherwise he is doomed to live forever in a fools' paradise, and can be said to have come to himself only on the supposition that he is a fool.

Every man—if I may adopt and paraphrase a passage from Dr. South—every man hath both an absolute and a relative capacity: an absolute in that he hath been endued with such a nature and such parts and faculties; and a relative in that he is part of the universal community of men, and so stands in such a relation to the whole. When we say that a man has come to himself, it is not of his absolute capacity that we are thinking, but of his relative. He has begun to realize that he is part of a whole, and to know *what* part, suitable for what service and achievement.

It was once fashionable—and that not a very long time ago—to speak of political society with a certain distaste, as a necessary evil, an irritating but inevitable restriction upon the "natural" sovereignty and entire self-government of the individual. That was the dream of the egotist. It was a theory in which men were seen to strut in the proud consciousness of their several and "absolute" capacities. It would be as instructive as it would be difficult to count the errors it has bred in political thinking. As a matter of fact, men have never dreamed of wishing to do without the "trammels" of organized society, for the very good reason that those trammels are in reality no trammels at all, but indispensable aids and spurs to the attainment of the highest and most enjoyable things man is capable of. Political society, the life of men in states, is an abiding natural relationship. It is neither a mere convenience nor a mere necessity. It is not a mere voluntary association, not a mere corporation. It is nothing deliberate or artificial, devised for a special purpose. It is in real truth the eternal and natural expression and embodiment of a form of life higher than that of the individual—that common life of mutual helpfulness, stimulation, and contest which gives leave and opportunity to the individual life, makes it possible, makes it full and complete.

It is in such a scene that man looks about to discover his own place and force. In the midst of men organized, infinitely cross-related, bound by ties of interest, hope, affection, subject to authorities, to opinion, to passion, to visions and desires which no man can reckon, he casts eagerly about to find where he may enter in with the rest and be a man among his fellows. In making his place he finds, if he seek intelligently and with eyes that see, more than ease of spirit and scope for his mind. He finds himself—as if mists had cleared away about him and he knew at last his neighborhood among men and tasks.

What every man seeks is satisfaction. He deceives himself so long as he imagines it to lie in self-indulgence, so long as he deems himself the center and object of effort. His mind is spent in vain upon itself. Not in action itself, not in "pleasure," shall it find its desires satisfied, but in consciousness of right, of powers greatly and nobly spent. It comes to know itself in the motives which satisfy it, in the zest and power of rectitude. Christianity has liberated the world, not as a system of ethics, not as a philosophy of altruism, but by its revelation of the power of pure and unselfish love. Its vital principle is not its code, but its motive. Love, clear-sighted, loyal, personal, is its breath and immortality. Christ came, not to save himself, assuredly, but to save the world. His motive, his example, are every man's key to his own gifts and happiness. The ethical code he taught may no doubt be matched, here a piece and there a piece, out of other religions, other teachings and philosophies. Every thoughtful man born with a conscience must know a code of right and of pity to which he ought to conform; but without the motive of Christianity, without love, he may be the purest altruist and yet be as sad and as unsatisfied as Marcus Aurelius.

Christianity gave us, in the fullness of time, the perfect image of right living, the secret of social and of individual well-being; for the two are not separable, and the man who receives and verifies that secret in his own living has discovered not only the best and only way to serve the world, but also the one happy way to satisfy himself. Then, indeed, has he come to himself. Henceforth he knows what his powers mean, what spiritual air they breathe, what ardors of service clear them of lethargy, relieve them of all sense of effort, put them at their best. After this fretfulness passes away, experience mellows and strengthens and makes more fit, and old age brings, not senility, not satiety, not regret, but higher hope and serene maturity.

"Self-Control in Wartime"

. . . If we are true friends of freedom, our own or anybody else's, we will see that the power of this country and the productivity of this country are raised to their absolute maximum, and that absolutely nobody is allowed to stand in the way of it. When I say that nobody is allowed to stand in the way I do not mean that he shall be prevented by the power of the Government, but by the power of the American spirit. Our duty, if we are to do this great thing and show America to be what we believe her to be— the greatest hope and energy of the world—is to stand together night and day until the job is finished. . . .

Now, to stand together means that nobody must interrupt the processes of our energy if the interruption can possibly be avoided without the absolute invasion of freedom. To put it concretely, that means this: Nobody has a right to stop the processes of labor until all the methods of conciliation and settlement have been exhausted. . . .

. . . We are all of the same clay and spirit, and we can get together if we desire to get together. Therefore, my counsel to you is this: Let us show ourselves Americans by showing that we do not want to go off in separate camps or groups by ourselves, but that we want to coöperate with all other classes and all other groups in the common enterprise which is to release the spirits of the world from bondage. I would be willing to set that up

---

This title has been given to some concluding parts of Wilson's speech to the American Federation of Labor at Buffalo, November 12, 1917, in Ray Stannard Baker and William E. Dodd, eds., *War and Peace: Presidential Messages, Addresses, and Public Papers (1917–1924)* (New York: Harper & Brothers, 1927), Vol. I, pp. 120–121, 122–123, 124.

as the final test of an American. That is the meaning of democracy. I have been very much distressed, my fellow citizens, by some of the things that have happened recently. The mob spirit is displaying itself here and there in this country. I have no sympathy with what some men are saying, but I have no sympathy with the men who take their punishment into their own hands; and I want to say to every man who does join such a mob that I do not recognize him as worthy of the free institutions of the United States. There are some organizations in this country whose object is anarchy and the destruction of law, but I would not meet their efforts by making myself partner in destroying the law. I despise and hate their purposes as much as any man, but I respect the ancient processes of justice; and I would be too proud not to see them done justice, however wrong they are.

So I want to utter my earnest protest against any manifestation of the spirit of lawlessness anywhere or in any cause. Why, gentlemen, look what it means. We claim to be the greatest democratic people in the world, and democracy means first of all that we can govern ourselves. If our men have not self-control, then they are not capable of that great thing which we call democratic government. A man who takes the law into his own hands is not the right man to cooperate in any formation or development of law and institutions, and some of the processes by which the struggle between capital and labor is carried on are processes that come very near to taking the law into your own hands. I do not mean for a moment to compare them with what I have just been speaking of, but I want you to see that they are mere gradations in this manifestation of the unwillingness to cooperate, and that the fundamental lesson of the whole situation is that we must not only take common counsel, but that we must yield to and obey common counsel. . . .

So, my fellow citizens, the reason I came away from Washington is that I sometimes get lonely down there. So many people come to Washington who know things that are not so, and so few people who know anything about what the people of the United States are thinking about. I have to come away and get reminded of the rest of the country. I have to come away and talk to men who are up against the real thing, and say to them, "I am with you if you are with me." And the only test of being with me is not to think about me personally at all, but merely to think of me as the expression for the time being of the power and dignity and hope of the United States.

6. Law as an Evolving Collective Tool

Woodrow Wilson's approach to the problem of social obligation was highly personal. But in the early twentieth century a large body of liberals wrestled with the problem of law and of its relationship to social justice in a still more concrete fashion. They pursued this inquiry within the context of a highly practical problem: the judicial system was upholding the rights of private property to such a degree that nearly all effective reform legislation found itself blocked. The Constitution, as the courts were then interpreting it, threatened to become a millstone around the necks of the majority who advocated progressive social goals. In actual fact, not until the Supreme Court, under unusual pressure, decisively changed its mind in 1937 about the constitutionality of most New Deal measures did the legal system appear once again to be in line with social needs.

For several decades, therefore, liberals tended to feel almost as much frustration about the state of the law in America as did the few radicals who were being openly repressed. But the liberal answer was not a direct attack upon law; rather, it was a redefinition of it in the context of social science. By means of their writings, liberal intellectuals hoped to convert public opinion to an acceptance of their viewpoint that law was not intended as something static or absolute, but rather should operate as a flexible, ever-shifting reflection of community will. Law, when looked at historically or anthropologically, had exhibited enormous variations over time and space. Why should it not continue to alter, especially in the direction of providing guarantees for collective social welfare? Why should it not safeguard the poor as well as the rich? But the liberals of course continued to agitate for change from within the established system. Though their mood was often urgent, their writings nonetheless revealed a serene quality which reflected their confident faith that science was on their side and that they were bound to win out in the long run.

The central spokesman for American liberalism in this period was John Dewey. Although Dewey's tortuous prose repels most present-day readers, his underlying faith—in scientific expertise bringing about social welfare in complete harmony with democratic sentiment—was simple enough to win him wide influence. For instance, Oliver Wendell Holmes, Jr., whose temperament was far more skeptical and in many ways old-fashioned, once confessed about Dewey that "his view of the universe came home to me closer than any other that I know."[1]

While Dewey gave great rhetorical obeisance to the concept of individual freedom, the central direction of his thought was always toward an ideally defined collective whole. Existing definitions of collectivity he attacked for their rigid formalism and conservatism. But his liberal superego nonetheless prevented him from accepting any notion of individual liberation simply for its own sake. To sanction a mood of wild self-expression was deeply alien to his cast of thinking. Instead, his viewpoint looked toward sober state planning along the lines of revisionist socialism, or perhaps toward the dispassionate and rather middle-aged utopia of B. F. Skinner.[2] Legitimate personal satisfaction, John Dewey once argued, was to be found "neither in the getting of a lot of pleasures through the satisfaction of desires just as they happen to rise, nor in obedience to law simply because it is law. It is found in satisfaction of desires according to law." The satisfaction of a desire "requires that it be fitted" into the "entire and continuous activity" of collective social evolution.[3]

For liberals like Dewey, a humanitarian and utilitarian conception of science offered a way of transcending the classic dichotomy between the individual and society, even as psychologists were attacking the older formulation at its roots by pointing to the decisive role of socialization among infants. But, one might ask, was the dichotomy truly transcended? Was the older idea of individualism decisively made obsolete, or was this pattern of liberal thinking merely another and subtler form of the attack upon truly libertarian arguments? In other words, these liberals, despite their receptivity to social change, may have ended up providing nothing more than still another variant to the anti-individualist arguments of moral conservatives. On certain important levels of their minds, they seemed to echo Sumner's call for a greater

1. Holmes to Sir Frederick Pollock, July 26, 1930, in Mark DeWolfe Howe, ed., *Holmes-Pollock Letters* (Cambridge, Mass.: Harvard University Press, 1941), Vol. II, p. 272.

2. B. F. Skinner, *Walden Two* (New York: Macmillan, 1948).

3. John Dewey, *Outlines of a Critical Theory of Ethics* (Ann Arbor, Mich.: Register Publishing Co., 1891), pp. 95–96.

discipline, albeit directed toward a different kind of social creation, and they even seemed not too far removed from Wilson's
disdain for "adolescent" self-gratification.

Oliver Wendell Holmes, Jr., the distinguished jurist, is a good
touchstone for the exploration of this mentality, for the very
reason that in personal terms he was far less consistent, predictable, or serene than Dewey. His intermittent skepticism and
mulishness mark him as possessing some of the tendencies toward
uninhibited self-assertion that might almost befit an anarchist with
a very small "a." Yet Holmes's independence of mind was actually
tied to his aristocratic position in Boston, and it produced a stance
that can best be described as erratically middle-of-the-road.[4]

Holmes's essay, "Law in Science and Science in Law," has rarely
been anthologized because much of it consists of a series of digres-
sions into specific legal examples. But the central line of argument
is refreshingly clear-cut and constitutes an important statement of
the presuppositions which underlay liberal thinking about the
meaning of law in America during his generation.[5] Indeed, despite
some occasional hedging and backtracking, it reveals Holmes as a
surprisingly docile spokesman for English utilitarianism (he was,
incidentally, a great admirer of Sir Leslie Stephen). Facts, he
asserts, are potentially precise and can be measured; if they appear ambiguous, it is nonetheless the judge's task to sort them
out as finely as possible. Legal conflict measures the competing
interests within any society at any given moment; the real aim
of law is thus to help "bring about a social end which we desire."
These desires can also be measured, by the very yardstick of their
success or failure in influencing given judicial decisions. Science
remains the ideal toward which we should strive as lawyers, even
if it is never possible fully to reach it. To be sure, Holmes calls
at one point for "an inspirational combined with a logical method"
in legal study, but then he corrects himself to insist upon a clarity

4. Irving Bernstein, "Patrician Conservatism: Mr. Justice Holmes," in
Cushing Strout, ed., *Intellectual History in America* (New York: Harper &
Row, 1968), Vol. II, pp. 83–97, elaborately tries to show that Holmes was
a conservative rather than a liberal. Though much of his evidence is appropriate and revealing, he claims that Holmes believed there were "few,
if any, scientific criteria for measuring legislation" (p. 93), an interpretation directly contradicted by the essay printed below. Bernstein emphasizes Holmes's cynical moods, whereas, in fact, he vacillated between them
and some degree of liberal belief.

5. The long examples have been eliminated from the essay as it appears
in this volume; without them, the basic arguments remain unaffected.

of aim entirely consistent with the pragmatist's call for "social intelligence." Rights are never absolute; one is always weighing and
balancing particular situations. Therefore legal interpretations
should be loose and flexible, so as to foster a constant process of
rethinking as social conditions change. Juries are suspect because
of their lack of scientific expertise, though they are justifiable in
the sense that they accurately embody shifting community standards.

It is true that Holmes gives a larger place to social conflict,
and to law as the mirror of such conflict, than would have been
congenial to John Dewey. Liberals have usually wished to minimize the persistence of irreconcilable interests, especially within a
country such as America. (Their own battles against vested com-
binations they perceive as final steps toward the creation of a
just community.) In this respect, Holmes's realism is admittedly
closer to that of Darwinians like William Graham Sumner. And
there is also in Holmes's essay just a touch of the reverence for
established procedures and institutions which both Choate and
Sumner embodied. But he is fully aware that such historical
precedents can easily be invoked on both sides of most social
conflicts, and that it is the reality of the conflict that finally matters,
not a slavish attitude toward antecedents. There is less guarantee
in Holmes than in other liberals that the humanitarian side will
emerge the victor in running social struggles; but his openness to
change is never in real doubt, and this, together with his admiration of scientific method and his evolutionary view of morality,
provides a decisive indication of his posture. Science, it is equally
important to note, was for him a manageable tool, not the grim
and inevitable force that it was for Sumner. Holmes pictures
lawyers as social engineers, duly estimating the "proportions" between "different social ends," not as bystanders (or blind agents)
in the struggle for existence. The distinction is a crucial one.

Having gone so far in establishing Holmes's credentials as a
liberal, one is still left wondering whether, in more basic terms,
"liberals" have differed very much from "conservatives" over the
matter of respect for existing authority in America. From some
points of view, Sumner, Woodrow Wilson, and Holmes present no
more than three interesting variants on a common theme of celebrating the claims of society upon the individual. None of these
men was at all close to the perspective of Thoreau. And even if
the social sciences were now declaring man to be the inexorable
product of his relationships with others, thus attempting to rule

Thoreau's mode of thinking obsolete, it was an undeniable fact that many twentieth-century Americans continued to feel imposed upon by what they believed to be the conformitarian demands of the social environment. To these people, neither the liberal nor conservative versions of the social ethic seemed convincing or attractive. Liberalism, indeed, might if anything be more suspect, especially after exposure to Woodrow Wilson's practice of it, because it so often made tantalizing promises of a fundamental change in human existence, yet only within the context of what proved to be a renewed and intensified appeal to social authority. (In this respect, liberalism was astonishingly similar to communism.) Holmes, at least, by shunning grandiose promises managed to let few people down.

Oliver Wendell Holmes, Jr.,
"Law in Science and Science in Law"

The law of fashion is a law of life. The crest of the wave of human interest is always moving, and it is enough to know that the depth was greatest in respect of a certain feature or style in literature or music or painting a hundred years ago to be sure that at that point it no longer is so profound. I should draw the conclusion that artists and poets, instead of troubling themselves about the eternal, had better be satisfied if they can stir the feelings of a generation, but that is not my theme. It is more to my point to mention that what I have said about art is true within the limits of the possible in matters of the intellect. What do we mean when we talk about explaining a thing? A hundred years ago men explained any part of the universe by showing its fitness for certain ends, and demonstrating what they conceived to be its final cause according to a providential scheme. In our less theological and more scientific day, we explain an object by tracing the

An address delivered before the New York State Bar Association, January 17, 1899. Published in *Harvard Law Review,* XII, 443, and reprinted in Oliver Wendell Holmes, *Collected Legal Papers* (New York: Harcourt, Brace and Howe, Inc., 1920), pp. 210–211, 212–214, 224–226, 231, 232–233, 235–237, 237–239, 241–243.

order and process of its growth and development from a starting point assumed as given.

This process of historical explanation has been applied to the matter of our profession, especially of recent years, with great success, and with so much eagerness, and with such a feeling that when you had the true historic dogma you had the last word not only in the present but for the immediate future, that I have felt warranted heretofore in throwing out the caution that continuity with the past is only a necessity and not a duty. As soon as a legislature is able to imagine abolishing the requirement of a consideration for a simple contract, it is at perfect liberty to abolish it, if it thinks it wise to do so, without the slightest regard to continuity with the past. That continuity simply limits the possibilities of our imagination, and settles the terms in which we shall be compelled to think. . . .

. . . It is perfectly proper to regard and study the law simply as a great anthropological document. It is proper to resort to it to discover what ideals of society have been strong enough to reach that final form of expression, or what have been the changes in dominant ideals from century to century. It is proper to study it as an exercise in the morphology and transformation of human ideas. The study pursued for such ends becomes science in the strictest sense. Who could fail to be interested in the transition through the priest's test of truth,[1] the miracle of the ordeal, and the soldier's, the battle of the duel, to the democratic verdict of the jury! Perhaps I might add, in view of the great increase of jury-waived cases, a later transition yet—to the commercial and rational test of the judgment of a man trained to decide.

It is still only the minority who recognize how the change of emphasis which I have called the law of fashion has prevailed even in the realm of morals. The other day I was looking over Bradford's history—the book which Mr. Bayard brought as a gift from Lambeth to the Massachusetts State House—and I was struck to see recounted the execution of a man with horrible solemnities for an offence which still, to be sure, stands on the statute book as a serious crime, but which no longer is often heard of in court, which many would regard as best punished simply by the disgust of normal men, and which a few think of only

1. I do not forget that the church abolished the ordeal.

as a physiological aberration, of interest mainly to the pathologist. I found in the same volume the ministers consulted as the final expounders of the law, and learnedly demonstrating that what now we should consider as needing no other repression than a doctor's advice, was a crime punishable with death and to be ferreted out by searching the conscience of the accused, although after discussion it was thought that torture should be reserved for state occasions.

To take a less odious as well as less violent contrast, when we read in the old books that it is the duty of one exercising a common calling to do his work upon demand and to do it with reasonable skill, we see that the gentleman is in the saddle and means to have the common people kept up to the mark for his convenience. We recognize the imperative tone which in our day has changed sides, and is oftener to be heard from the hotel clerk than from the guest. . . .

. . . The main ends of the subject [of law] are practical, and from a practical point of view, history, with which I have been dealing thus far, is only a means, and one of the least of the means, of mastering a tool. From a practical point of view, as I have illustrated upon another occasion, its use is mainly negative and skeptical. It may help us to know the true limit of a doctrine, but its chief good is to burst inflated explanations. Every one instinctively recognizes that in these days the justification of a law for us cannot be found in the fact that our fathers always have followed it. It must be found in some help which the law brings toward reaching a social end which the governing power of the community has made up its mind that it wants. And when a lawyer sees a rule of law in force he is very apt to invent, if he does not find, some ground of policy for its base. But in fact some rules are mere survivals. Many might as well be different, and history is the means by which we measure the power which the past has had to govern the present in spite of ourselves, so to speak, by imposing traditions which no longer meet their original end. History sets us free and enables us to make up our minds dispassionately whether the survival which we are enforcing answers any new purpose when it has ceased to answer the old. Notwithstanding the contrasts which I have been making, the practical study of the law ought also to be scientific. The true science of the law does not consist mainly in a theological working out of dogma or a logical development as in mathematics, or only in a study of it as an anthropological document from the outside; an even more important part consists in the establishment of its postulates from within upon accurately measured social desires instead of tradition. . . .

The growth of education is an increase in the knowledge of measure. To use words familiar to logic and to science, it is a substitution of quantitative for qualitative judgments. The difference between the criticism of a work of art by a man of perception without technical training and that by a critic of the studio will illustrate what I mean. The first, on seeing a statue, will say, "It is grotesque," a judgment of quality merely; the second will say, "That statue is so many heads high, instead of the normal so many heads." His judgment is one of quantity. On hearing a passage of Beethoven's Ninth Symphony the first will say, "What a gorgeous sudden outburst of sunshine!" the second, "Yes, great idea to bring in his major third just there, wasn't it?" Well, in the law we only occasionally can reach an absolutely final and quantitative determination, because the worth of the competing social ends which respectively solicit a judgment for the plaintiff or the defendant cannot be reduced to number and accurately fixed. The worth, that is, the intensity of the competing desires, varies with the varying ideals of the time, and, if the desires were constant, we could not get beyond a relative decision that one was greater and one was less. But it is of the essence of improvement that we should be as accurate as we can. . . .

In our approach towards exactness we constantly tend to work out definite lines or equators to mark distinctions which we first notice as a difference of poles. It is evident in the beginning that there must be differences in the legal position of infants and adults. In the end we establish twenty-one as the dividing point. There is a difference manifest at the outset between night and day. The statutes of Massachusetts fix the dividing points at one hour after sunset and one hour before sunrise, ascertained according to mean time. When he has discovered that a difference is a difference of degree, that distinguished extremes have between them a penumbra in which one gradually shades into the other, a tyro thinks to puzzle you by asking where you are going to draw the line, and an advocate of more experience will show the arbitrariness of the line proposed by putting cases very near to it on one side or the other. But the theory of the law is that such lines exist, because the theory of the law as to any possible conduct is that it is either lawful or unlawful. As that difference has no gradation about it, when applied to shades of conduct that are very near each other it has an arbitrary look. We like to disguise the arbitrariness, we like to save ourselves the trouble of nice and doubtful discriminations. In some regions of conduct of a special sort we have to be informed of facts which we do not know before we can draw our lines intelligently, and so, as we get near the dividing point, we call in the jury. From saying that we will leave a question to the jury to saying that it is a question of fact is but a step, and the result is that at this day it has come to be a widespread doctrine that negligence not only is a question for the jury but is a question of fact. I have heard it urged with great vehemence by counsel, and calmly maintained by professors that, in addition to their wrongs to labor, courts were encroaching upon the province of the jury when they directed a verdict in a negligence case, even in the unobtrusive form of a ruling that there was no evidence of neglect. . . .

When we rule on evidence of negligence we are ruling on a standard of conduct, a standard which we hold the parties bound to know beforehand, and which in theory is always the same upon the same facts and not a matter dependent upon the whim of the particular jury or the eloquence of the particular advocate. And I may be permitted to observe that, referring once more to history, similar questions originally were, and to some extent still are, dealt with as questions of law. It was and is so on the question of probable cause in malicious prosecution. It was so on the question of necessaries for an infant. It was so in questions of what is reasonable, as—a reasonable fine, convenient time, seasonable time, reasonable time, reasonable notice of dishonor. It is so in regard to the remoteness of damage in an action of contract. Originally in malicious prosecution, probable cause, instead of being negatived in the declaration, was pleaded by the defendant, and the court passed upon the sufficiency of the cause alleged. In the famous case of Weaver v. Ward, the same course was suggested as proper for negligence. I quote: "as if the defendent had said that the plaintiff ran across his piece when it was discharging, or had set forth the case with the circumstances, so as it had appeared to the court that it had been inevitable, and that the defendant had committed no negligence to give occasion to the hurt." But about the middle of the last century, when the rule of conduct was complicated with practical details the court began to leave some of these questions to the jury. Nevertheless, Mr. Starkie, a man of intellect, who was not imposed upon by phrases, very nearly saw the ground upon which it was done, and puts it on the purely practical distinction that when the circumstances are too special and complicated for a general rule to be laid down the jury may be called in. But it is obvious that a standard of conduct does not cease to be law because the facts to which that standard applies are not likely often to be repeated.

I do not believe that the jury have any historic or *a priori* right to decide any standard of conduct. I think that the logic of the contrary view would be that every decision upon such a question by the court is an invasion of their province, and that all the law properly is in their breasts. . . . I confess that in my experience I have not found juries specially inspired for the discovery of truth. I have not noticed that they could see further into things or form a saner judgment than a sensible and well trained judge. I have not found them freer from prejudice than an ordinary judge would be. Indeed one reason why I believe in our practice of leaving questions of negligence to them is what is precisely one of their gravest defects from the point of view of their theoretical function: that they will introduce into their verdict a certain amount—a very large amount, so far as I have observed—of popular prejudice, and thus keep the administration of the law in accord with the wishes and feelings of the community. Possibly such a justification is a little like that which an eminent English barrister gave me many years ago for the distinction between barristers and solicitors. It was in substance that if law was to be practised somebody had to be damned, and he preferred that it should be somebody else.

My object is not so much to point out what seem to me to be fallacies in particular cases as to enforce by various examples and in various applications the need of scrutinizing the reasons for the rules which we follow, and of not being contented with hollow forms of words merely because they have been used very often and have been repeated from one end of the Union to the other. We must think things not words, or at least we must constantly translate our words into the facts for which they stand, if we are to keep to the real and the true. I sometimes tell students that the law schools pursue an inspirational combined with a logical method, that is, the postulates are taken for granted upon authority without inquiry into their worth, and then logic is used as the only tool to develop the results. It is a necessary method for the purpose of teaching dogma. But inasmuch as the real justification of a rule of law, if there be one, is that it helps to bring about a social end which we desire, it is no less necessary that those who make and develop the law should have those ends articulately in their mind. I do not expect or think it desirable that the judges should undertake to renovate the law. That is not their province. Indeed precisely because I believe that the world would be just as well off if it lived under laws that differed from ours in many ways, and because I believe that the claim of our especial code to respect is simply that it exists, that it is the one to which we have become accustomed, and not that it represents an eternal principle, I am slow to consent to overruling a precedent, and think that our important duty is to see that the judicial duel shall be fought out in the accustomed way. But I think it most important to remember whenever a doubtful case arises, with certain analogies on one side and other analogies on the other, that what really is before us is a conflict between two social desires, each of which seeks to extend its dominion over the case, and which cannot both have their way. The social question is which desire is stronger at the point of conflict. The judicial one may be narrower, because one or the other desire may have been expressed in previous decisions to such an extent that logic requires us to assume it to preponderate in the one before us. But if that be clearly so, the case is not a doubtful one. Where there is doubt the simple tool of logic does not suffice, and even if it is disguised and unconscious, the judges are called on to exercise the sovereign prerogative of choice. . . .

. . . If the scope of the right is already determined as absolute and irrespective of motive, *cadit quaestio,* there is nothing to argue about. So if all rights have that scope. But if different rights are of different extent, if they stand on different grounds of policy and have different histories, it does not follow that because one right is absolute, another is—and if you simply say all rights shall be so, that is only a pontifical or imperial way of forbidding discussion. The right to sell property is about as absolute as any I can think of, although, under statutes at least, even that may be affected by motive, as in the case of an intent to prefer creditors. But the privilege of a master to state his servant's character to one who is thinking of employing him is also a right within its limits. Is it equally extensive? I suppose it would extend to mistaken statements volunteered in good faith out of love for the possible employer. Would it extend to such statements volunteered simply out of hate for the man? To my mind here, again, generalities are worse than useless, and the only way to solve the problem presented is to weigh the reasons for the particular right claimed and those for the competing right to be free from slander as well as one can, and to decide which set preponderates. Any solution in general terms seems to me to mark a want of analytic power.

Gentlemen, I have tried to show by examples something of the interest of science as applied to the law, and to point out some possible improvement in our way of approaching practical questions in the same sphere. To the latter attempt, no doubt, many will hardly be ready to yield me their assent. But in that field, as in the other, I have had in mind an ultimate dependence upon science because it is finally for science to determine, so far as it can, the relative worth of our different social ends, and, as I have tried to hint, it is our estimate of the proportion between these, now often blind and unconscious, that leads us to insist upon and to enlarge the sphere of one principle and to allow another gradually to dwindle into atrophy. Very likely it may be that with all the help that statistics and every modern appliance can bring us there never will be a commonwealth in which science is everywhere supreme. But it is an ideal, and without ideals what is life worth? They furnish us our perspectives and open glimpses of the infinite. It often is a merit of an ideal to be unattainable. Its being so keeps forever before us something more to be done, and saves us from the ennui of a monotonous perfection. At the least it glorifies dull details, and uplifts and sustains weary years of toil with George Herbert's often quoted but ever-inspiring verse:

Who sweeps a room as for Thy laws,
Makes that and the action fine.

7. Anarchist Libertarianism

The native-born American anarchist Voltairine de Cleyre (1866–1912) is today completely forgotten. Not even the neo-anarchist student radicals of the last few years have read her words, though they foreshadow the contemporary mood of distrust for the centralized state in a surprisingly detailed fashion. It is for this latter reason that she and her fellow anarchists of seventy years ago merit rediscovery—not surely for their influence or their representativeness, but merely because it is highly interesting that a few Americans were saying these things when the industrial system was still so young. To the extent that an extreme demand for liberty has had a continuous tradition in the United States, persons like Voltairine de Cleyre exemplify that slender thread.[1]

She was born in a small Michigan village. Her mother was a New Englander of Puritan descent, her father a Frenchman who had recently emigrated to America. The father was a man of passionate convictions who instilled the same quality of intensity into his young daughter's mind. He named her after Voltaire because he was then an ardent socialist and freethinker, but during her girlhood he returned to the Catholic Church with a vengeance and forced the poor child, much against her will, to spend four years in a Canadian convent. Her entire youth was bitterly unhappy, partly for these reasons and partly as a result of their extreme poverty. She developed into a melancholy, nervous, headstrong adolescent, often emaciated and in poor health. So firm was her will, as she clung to her father's original atheism within

1. So of course does Randolph Bourne, never a formal anarchist, whose thinking moved in this direction under the direct impact of the First World War. Unfortunately, for reasons of balance and because of its length, I have had to omit Bourne's great essay on "The State" here, even though in literary terms it ranks with Thoreau as one of the two finest specimens of libertarian writing which have been produced in this country. Bourne's essay is readily available in Randolph Bourne, *War and the Intellectuals* (New York: Harper & Row, 1964), pp. 65–104.

the convent atmosphere, that the sisters gave up any attempt to influence her. As a young woman she became "converted" first to socialism, after hearing Clarence Darrow, and then to anarchism, by the writings of Benjamin Tucker.

Eventually she moved to Philadelphia, where she supported herself in meager fashion by teaching English to Jewish immigrants, meanwhile speaking and writing unceasingly in the anarchist cause. She travelled to the British Isles on a lecture tour, and she was also once wounded by an assassin. It was characteristic of her saintly personality that she not only refused to help identify this assassin, but worked actively for his release from jail, deliberately seeking to return good for evil. She wrote poems, short stories, and an unfinished novel, mainly on themes of social oppression. They are mournful and melodramatic, filled with vivid emotional response to the horrors of factory life in the modern city. Hippolyte Havel said of her: "A great sadness, a knowledge that there is a universal pain, filled her heart. Through her own suffering and through the suffering of others she reached the highest exaltation of mind. . . . In the service of the poor and oppressed she found her life mission."[2] Toward the question of violence and direct action, she had no fixed position. After a Tolstoyan phase during which she advocated nonresistance, she moved in her final years toward syndicalism and threw herself unreservedly into support of the Mexican Revolution. Two years after its outbreak she died in Chicago.

The tiny movement of which she was a part had already passed through many troubles by the time she came to it. In America, anarchism began as early as 1829 with the writings of Josiah Warren and continued to lead a precarious existence during the next two generations on the far margins of the New England reform tradition. (Thoreau apparently was somewhat aware of these obscure contemporaries of his.)[2a] The native American anarchists of the nineteenth century advocated a philosophy of "individualism," under which government would disappear and private property would flourish, but land would be held by local communities and distributed, presumably in town-meeting fashion, to individuals and corporations on the basis of actual requirements for use. Individualist anarchists were also, like Thoreau, much concerned

2. Alexander Berkman, ed., *Selected Works of Voltairine de Cleyre* (New York: Mother Earth Publishing Assn., 1914), p. 14.
2a. See above, p. 77.

to attack the psychological roots of deference to authority within the human mind.[3]

In the 1880's a number of immigrants began to import into America the somewhat different and more orthodox European version of anarchism, deriving from Proudhon, Bakunin, and Kropotkin, which was far more heavily influenced by the Marxist tradition and eventually became known in America as "communist" anarchism to distinguish it from the earlier "individualist" variety. These anarchists, of whom Emma Goldman was a leading figure, believed in the abolition of private property along with the state, and looked forward to a society of small, largely self-sufficient, voluntarily cooperating communes, each sharing all goods and possessions in common. All anarchists agreed in opposing marriage as an institution; sexual freedom and the liberation of women were an important element in their demands.

Factionalism thrived in these circles. At the turn of the century, "individualist" and "communist" anarchists utterly refused to recognize each other as part of the same movement. There were, moreover, still other conflicting viewpoints within the movement too complicated to relate here. "Anarchism is, in truth, a sort of Protestantism," Voltairine de Cleyre once shrewdly admitted.[4] There was an undeniable tendency for men and women whose very lives were dedicated to the overthrowing of authority not to accept easily the philosophical authority of other fellow anarchists.

The movement was further hampered by its association with deeds of violence. Spectacular individual acts to expose the vulnerability of authority, including assassination of prominent political and industrial figures, had indeed been advocated and practiced by anarchists in many countries, although not all anarchists personally believed in such deeds. These murders and attempted murders had struck a highly sensitive nerve in existing society, and as a result no group was more widely or deeply detested in the public mind. The passion with which anarchists, real and imaginary, were attacked in early twentieth-century America revealed the strong commitment of nearly all Americans, not to nonviolence (as we shall later see in exploring the San Diego scene in 1912), but to maintenance of the established social system.

Much of the energy of this small band, therefore, was directed

3. Voltairine de Cleyre, "Anarchism," *ibid.*, pp. 109–111. Not all the earlier individualist anarchists had worked out these matters as clearly in their thinking as she has in this attempt at a recapitulation of their thought.
4. Voltairine de Cleyre, "The Making of an Anarchist," *ibid.*, p. 157.

toward conflicts with other anarchists of competing persuasions (and with socialists and others on the left), or else spent in the simple necessity of fending off a hostile society on the outside. This situation has always seemingly been the fate of American radicals; the anarchists experienced it in an unusually extreme form. But one should also recall that this was not the whole of their lives, and that difficult times were often balanced by strong feelings of brotherhood. It is not commonly remembered, for instance, that an anarchist colony at Home, Washington (near Tacoma), thrived with reasonable success for nearly twenty years, between the late 1890's and the First World War, engaging in such prosaic activities as baseball games with neighboring settlements.[5] Another anarchist colony flourished for a span of several decades at Stelton, New Jersey, where the Ferrer Modern School, whose principles were anarchist, existed from 1915 until after the Second World War. As compared with socialist communitarian ventures in America, the anarchist experiments, although far less numerous, were at least equally tenacious. Despite what happened at Barcelona in 1937, when anarchists proved ineffective in running the city as a result of their own theoretical distaste for organization, it is too easy to say that anarchism leads automatically in some special fashion to its own destruction, at least on the basis of the record in America. But it is entirely fair to say that anarchists had little success in converting Americans to their doctrines. The cause declined after the First World War, although a few "communist-anarchist" journals were published thereafter in New York. Only a rather faint line of descent from the earlier movement may be traced down through Paul Goodman, Dwight Macdonald, and the decentralist community ventures of the 1950's, to the current revival of interest in anarchism among some sectors of the New Left.

But if its form was too extreme for popular taste, anarchism in some sense did keep alive the element of suspicion of authority which we saw was an important minority current in American opinion from the beginning. Anarchists sought very much to capitalize on the memory of Jefferson and Thoreau, and more generally on that of a simpler rural America. Unlike socialists, anarchists were thoroughly critical of the character of modern industrial civilization, and in that important respect they were reactionaries. Because they so strongly disliked any manifestation

5. Extensive newspaper files from this colony are in the Labadie Collection, University of Michigan, Ann Arbor.

of centralized authority, they were able to put their fingers on all those elements in modern life, including the military, which have come under attack from radicals more recently. Thus their writings are full of indictments which seem almost prophetic, even if it may strike us as amusing when Voltairine de Cleyre protests indignantly against the "menace" of a standing army of some 83,251 men! This is the paradox of the anarchist movement at the turn of the twentieth century: that it undeniably seems so backward-looking and simplistic, while at the same time it uncannily points to nearly every current criticism being made about the fundamental quality of American life. The paradox is explained, however, by the fact that the anarchists' very distance from the "realities" of industrial development gave them the ability to discern flaws and problems which are bound to figure prominently in any recurring critique of industrialism. In this light we can understand the seemingly modern ring of Voltairine de Cleyre's words when she demands that the economic system be made subservient to "free play for the spirit of change" (hardly a reactionary sentiment) and goes on to add that for the anarchist, "no system recommends itself . . . by the mere beauty and smoothness of its working; jealous of the encroachments of the machine, he looks with fierce suspicion upon an arithmetic with men for units, a society running in slots and grooves, with the precision so beautiful to one in whom the love of order is first, but which only makes him sniff—'Pfaugh! it smells of machine oil.' "[6]

Anarchism fully expressed the call for individual liberation which had begun with the Romantic movement. Despite what seems to us stilted phrasing, one may glimpse this intense vision in Voltairine de Cleyre's soaring passages on the subject of the self:

Ah, once to stand unflinchingly on the brink of that dark gulf of passions and desires, once at last to send a bold, straight-driven gaze down into the volcanic Me. . . . Once and forever to realize that one is not a bundle of well-regulated little reasons bound up in the front room of the brain . . . held in order with copy-book maxims or moved and stopped by a syllogism, but a bottomless, bottomless depth of all strange sensations. . . . To look down into that, to know the blackness, the midnight, the dead ages in oneself, to feel the jungle and the beast within . . . to see, to know, to feel to the uttermost,—and then to look at one's fellow, sitting across from one in the street-car, so decorous, so well got up, so nicely combed and brushed and oiled and to wonder

6. Voltairine de Cleyre, "Anarchism," *ibid.,* pp. 101–102.

what lies beneath that commonplace exterior,—to picture the cavern in him which somewhere far below has a narrow gallery running into your own . . . to spare all condemnation . . . because one knows the stuff of which man is made and recoils at nothing since all is in himself,—this is what Anarchism . . . means . . . to me.

And then, to turn cloudward, starward, skyward, and let the dreams rush over one . . . painting, painting endless pictures, creating unheard symphonies that sing dream sounds to you alone, extending sympathies to the dumb brutes as equal brothers, kissing the flowers as one did when a child, letting oneself go free, go free beyond the bounds of what *fear* and *custom* call the 'possible,'—this too Anarchism may mean to you, if you dare to apply it so.[7]

Extremely innocent, yes; but not the kind of innocence about human nature that afflicted her rationalist and liberal contemporaries, who shrank from the very idea of "letting go," or from recognizing the existence of bottomless caverns in the mind.

These passages have been quoted at length because the essay of hers which is printed in full below, "Anarchism and American Traditions," is a very different and more special kind of document, lacking in Voltairine de Cleyre's usual lyricism. It furnishes an anarchist perspective on the course of American history, centering in the indictment of industrialism. Her view of the past is not likely, of course, to gain much assent from historians in its literal form. The American Revolution is mistakenly idealized as a struggle against government as such, and a golden age is located somewhere during the lifespan of Thomas Jefferson. From that point forward, all is seen as declension and decline. A "modern empire" has "grown up on the ruins of our early freedom." Worse, the masses are unwilling to accept the truth of their condition, and probably cannot be reached through education or propaganda. The only hope lies in the fact that as foreign markets dry up, the capitalist economic system is bound to collapse.

The essay reveals important changes in the libertarian tradition between Thoreau's day and the early twentieth century. Practically gone is the ideal of individual aloofness. The tone is instead one of group solidarity on a voluntary basis—all the more striking because Voltairine de Cleyre was far more strongly swayed by "individualist" anarchism than was Emma Goldman. Anarchism, she says, "demands no jealous barrier of isolation; it knows that such

---

7. *Ibid.,* pp. 113–114. Alas, at one point she associates blackness with bestiality, showing that white radicals were certainly not exempt from the classic racist syndrome described by Winthrop Jordan.

isolation is undesirable and impossible." The future of mankind lies in the group, however drastically redefined. Yet the end remains the unleashing of each person's capacity for liberation.

In this phase of its development, anarchism harbored an ambiguity over the ultimate relations between group and individual which was not too dissimilar from John Dewey's. How could solidarity and consensus avoid eventually leading to a new tyranny? The elimination of all compulsory institutions was, of course, a bolder answer to this problem than Dewey and the liberals could provide. But the distinction between voluntarism and compulsion might some day become eroded, as "brainwashing" and other subtle forms of psychological manipulation began to reveal their possibilities. When the realization of freedom was linked to a willing submersion in the life-maintaining patterns of a group, not even voluntarism, small size, rural location, and the forms of participatory democracy could offer ultimate assurance against self-deception. But this is to suggest that freedom may be impossible, and it is a point which cuts as deeply against the beliefs of Americans in the mainstream as it does against those of the small band of anarchists. The anarchists, however, found no special formula which would guard them against this dilemma.

Voltairine de Cleyre,
 "Anarchism and American Traditions"

American traditions, begotten of religious rebellion, small self-sustaining communities, isolated conditions, and hard pioneer life, grew during the colonization period of one hundred and seventy years from the settling of Jamestown to the outburst of the Revolution. This was in fact the great constitution-making epoch, the period of charters guaranteeing more or less of liberty, the general tendency of which is well described by Wm. Penn in speaking of the charter for Pennsylvania: "I want to put it out of my power, or that of my successors, to do mischief."

From Alexander Berkman, ed., *Selected Works of Voltairine de Cleyre* (New York: Mother Earth Publishing Assn., 1914), pp. 118–135. Originally published in *Mother Earth* (1908–1909), vol. III, pp. 344–350, 386–393.

The revolution is the sudden and unified consciousness of these traditions, their loud assertion, the blow dealt by their indomitable will against the counter force of tyranny, which has never entirely recovered from the blow, but which from then till now has gone on remolding and regrappling the instruments of governmental power, that the Revolution sought to shape and hold as defenses of liberty.

To the average American of to-day, the Revolution means the series of battles fought by the patriot army with the armies of England. The millions of school children who attend our public schools are taught to draw maps of the siege of Boston and the siege of Yorktown, to know the general plan of the several campaigns, to quote the number of prisoners of war surrendered with Burgoyne; they are required to remember that date when Washington crossed the Delaware on the ice; they are told to "Remember Paoli," to repeat "Molly Stark's a widow," to call General Wayne "Mad Anthony Wayne," and to execrate Benedict Arnold; they know that the Declaration of Independence was signed on the Fourth of July, 1776, and the Treaty of Paris in 1783; and then they think they have learned the Revolution—blessed be George Washington! They have no idea why it should have been called a "revolution" instead of the "English war," or any similar title: it's the name of it, that's all. And name-worship, both in child and man, has acquired such mastery of them, that the name "American Revolution" is held sacred, though it means to them nothing more than successful force, while the name "Revolution" applied to a further possibility, is a spectre detested and abhorred. In neither case have they any idea of the content of the word, save that of armed force. That has already happened, and long happened, which Jefferson foresaw when he wrote:

"The spirit of the times may alter, will alter. Our rulers will become corrupt, our people careless. A single zealot may become persecutor, and better men be his victims. It can never be too often repeated that the time for fixing every essential right, on a legal basis, is while our rulers are honest, ourselves united. *From the conclusion of this war we shall be going down hill.* It will not then be necessary to resort every moment to the people for support. They will be forgotten, therefore, and their rights disregarded. They will forget themselves in the sole faculty of making money, and will never think of uniting to effect a due respect for their rights. The shackles, therefore, which shall not be knocked off at the conclusion of this war, will be heavier and heavier, till our rights shall revive or expire in a convulsion."

To the men of that time, who voiced the spirit of that time, the battles that they fought were the least of the Revolution; they were the incidents of the hour, the things they met and faced as part of the game they were playing; but the stake they had in view, before, during, and after the war, /the real Revolution, was a change in political institutions which should make of government not a thing apart, a superior power to stand over the people with a whip, but a serviceable agent, responsible, economical, and trustworthy (but never so much trusted as not to be continually watched), for the transaction of such business as was the common concern, and to set the limits of the common concern at the line where one man's liberty would encroach upon another's./

They thus took their starting point for deriving a minimum of government upon the same sociological ground that the modern Anarchist derives the no-government theory; viz., that equal liberty is the political ideal. The difference lies in the belief, on the one hand, that the closest approximation to equal liberty might be best secured by the rule of the majority in those matters involving united action of any kind (which rule of the majority they thought it possible to secure by a few simple arrangements for election), and, on the other hand, the belief that majority rule is both impossible and undesirable; that any government, no matter what its forms, will be manipulated by a very small minority, as the development of the State and United States governments has strikingly proved; that candidates will loudly profess allegiance to platforms before elections, which as officials in power they will openly disregard, to do as they please; and that even if the majority will could be imposed, it would also be subversive of equal liberty, which may be best secured by leaving to the voluntary association of those interested in the management of matters of common concern, without coercion of the uninterested or the opposed.

Among the fundamental likenesses between the Revolutionary Republicans and the Anarchists is the recognition that the little must precede the great; that the local must be the basis of the general; that there can be a free federation only when there are free communities to federate; that the spirit of the latter is carried into the councils of the former, and a local tyranny may thus become an instrument for general enslavement. Convinced of the supreme importance of ridding the municipalities of the institutions of tyranny, the most strenuous advocates of independence, instead of spending their efforts mainly in the general Congress, devoted themselves to their home localities, endeavoring to work out of the minds of their neighbors and fellow-colonists the institutions of entailed property, of a State-Church, of a class-divided people, even the institution of African slavery itself. Though largely unsuccessful, it is to the measure of success they did achieve that we are indebted for such liberties as we do retain, and not to the general government. They tried to inculcate local initiative and independent action. The author of the Declaration of Independence, who in the fall of '76 declined a re-election to Congress in order to return to Virginia and do his work in his own local assembly, in arranging there for public education which he justly considered a matter of "common concern," said his advocacy of public schools was not with any "view to take its ordinary branches out of the hands of private enterprise, which manages *so much better* the concerns to which it is equal"; and in endeavoring to make clear the restrictions of the Constitution upon the functions of the general government, he likewise said: "Let the general government be reduced to foreign concerns only, and let our affairs be disentangled from those of all other nations, except as to commerce, *which the merchants will manage the better the more they are left free to manage for themselves,* and the general government may be reduced to a very simple organization and a very inexpensive one; a few plain duties to be performed by a few servants." This then was the American tradition, that private enterprise manages better all that to which it is equal. Anarchism declares that private enterprise, whether individual or co-operative, is equal to all the undertakings of society. And it quotes the particular two instances, Education and Commerce, which the governments of the States and of the United States have undertaken to manage and regulate, as the very two which in operation have done more to destroy American freedom and equality, to warp and distort American tradition, to make of government a mighty engine of tyranny, than any other cause, save the unforeseen developments of Manufacture.

It was the intention of the Revolutionists to establish a system of common education, which should make the teaching of history one of its principal branches; not with the intent of burdening the memories of our youth with the dates of battles or the speeches of generals, nor to make of the Boston Tea Party Indians the one sacrosanct mob in all history, to be revered but never on any account to be imitated, but with the intent that every American should know to what conditions the masses of people had been brought by the operation of certain institutions, by what means they had wrung out their liberties, and how those liberties had again and again been filched from them by the use of governmental force, fraud, and privilege. Not to breed security, laudation, complacent indolence, passive acquiescence in the acts of a government protected by the label "home-made," but to beget a wakeful jealousy, a never-ending watchfulness of rulers, a determination to squelch every attempt of those entrusted with power to encroach upon the sphere of individual action—this was the prime motive of the revolutionists in endeavoring to provide for common education.

"Confidence," said the revolutionists who adopted the Kentucky Resolutions, "is everywhere the parent of despotism; free government is founded in jealousy, not in confidence; it is jealousy, not confidence, which prescribes limited constitutions to bind down those whom we are obliged to trust with power; our Constitution has accordingly fixed the limits to which, and no further, our confidence may go. . . . In questions of power, let no more be heard of confidence in man, but bind him down from mischief by the chains of the Constitution."

These resolutions were especially applied to the passage of the Alien laws by the monarchist party during John Adams' administration, and were an indignant call from the State of Kentucky to repudiate the right of the general government to assume undelegated powers, for, said they, to accept these laws would be "to be bound by laws made, not with our consent, but by others against our consent—that is, to surrender the form of government we have chosen, and to live under one deriving its powers from its own will, and not from our authority." Resolutions identical in spirit were also passed by Virginia, the following month; in those days the States still considered themselves supreme, the general government subordinate.

To inculcate this proud spirit of the supremacy of the people over their governors was to be the purpose of public education! Pick up to-day any common school history, and see how much of this spirit you will find therein. On the contrary, from cover to cover you will find nothing but the cheapest sort of patriotism, the inculcation of the most unquestioning acquiescence in the deeds of government, a lullaby of rest, security, confidence,—the doctrine that the Law can do no wrong, a Te Deum in praise of the continuous encroachments of the powers of the general government upon the reserved rights of the States, shameless falsification of all acts of rebellion, to put the government in the right and the rebels in the wrong, pyrotechnic glorifications of union, power, and force, and a complete ignoring of the essential liberties to maintain which was the purpose of the revolutionists. The anti-Anarchist law of post-McKinley passage, a much worse law than the Alien and Sedition acts which roused the wrath of Kentucky and Virginia to the point of threatened rebellion, is exalted as a wise provision of our All-Seeing Father in Washington.

Such is the spirit of government-provided schools. Ask any child what he knows about Shays's rebellion, and he will answer, "Oh, some of the farmers couldn't pay their taxes, and Shays led a rebellion against the court-house at Worcester, so they could burn up the deeds; and when Washington heard of it he sent over an army quick and taught 'em a good lesson"—"And what was the result of it?" "The result? Why—why—the result was—Oh yes, I remember—the result was they saw the need of a strong federal government to collect the taxes and pay the debts." Ask if he knows what was said on the other side of the story, ask if he knows that the men who had given their goods and their health and their strength for the freeing of the country now found themselves cast into prison for debt, sick, disabled, and poor, facing a new tyranny for the old; that their demand was that the land should become the free communal possession of those who wished to work it, not subject to tribute, and the child will answer "No." Ask him if he ever read Jefferson's letter to Madison about it, in which he says:

"Societies exist under three forms, sufficiently distinguishable. 1. Without government, as among our Indians. 2. Under government wherein the will of every one has a just influence, as is the case in England in a slight degree, and in our States in a great one. 3. Under government of force, as is the case in all other monarchies, and in most of the other republics. To have an idea of the curse of existence in these last, they must be seen. It is a government of wolves over sheep. It is a problem not clear in my mind that the first condition is not the best. But I believe it to be inconsistent with any great degree of population. The second state has a great deal of good in it. . . . It has its evils, too, the principal of which is the turbulence to which it is subject. . . . But even this evil is productive of good. It prevents the degeneracy of government, and nourishes a general attention to public affairs. I hold that a little rebellion now and then is a good thing."

Or to another correspondent: "God forbid that we should ever be twenty years without such a rebellion! . . . What country can preserve its liberties if its rulers are not warned from time to time that the people preserve the spirit of resistance? Let them take up arms. . . . The tree of liberty must be refreshed from time to time with the blood of patriots and tyrants. It is its natural manure." Ask any school child if he was ever taught that the author of the Declaration of Independence, one of the great founders of the common school, said these things, and he will look at you with open mouth and unbelieving eyes. Ask him if he ever heard that the man who sounded the bugle note in the darkest hour of the Crisis, who roused the courage of the soldiers when Washington saw only mutiny and despair ahead, ask him if he knows that this man also wrote, "Government at best is a necessary evil, at worst an intolerable one," and if he is a little better informed than the average he will answer, "Oh well, *he* was an infidel!" Catechize him about the merits of the Constitution which he has learned to repeat like a poll-parrot, and you will find his chief conception is not of the powers withheld from Congress, but of the powers granted.

Such are the fruits of government schools. We, the Anarchists, point to them and say: If the believers in liberty wish the principles of liberty taught, let them never intrust that instruction to any government; for the nature of government is to become a thing apart, an institution existing for its own sake, preying upon the people, and teaching whatever will tend to keep it secure in its seat. As the fathers said of the governments of Europe, so say we of this government also after a century and a quarter of independence: "The blood of the people has become its inheritance, and those who fatten on it will not relinquish it easily."

Public education, having to do with the intellect and spirit of a people, is probably the most subtle and far-reaching engine for molding the course of a nation; but commerce, dealing as it does with material things and producing immediate effects, was the force that bore down soonest upon the paper barriers of constitutional restriction, and shaped the government to its requirements. Here, indeed, we arrive at the point where we, looking over the hundred and twenty-five years of independence, can see that the simple government conceived by the revolutionary republicans was a foredoomed failure. It was so because of (1) the essence of government itself; (2) the essence of human nature; (3) the essence of Commerce and Manufacture.

Of the essence of government, I have already said, it is a thing apart, developing its own interests at the expense of what opposes it; all attempts to make it anything else fail. In this Anarchists agree with the traditional enemies of the Revolution, the monarchists, federalists, strong government believers, the Roosevelts of to-day, the Jays, Marshalls, and Hamiltons of then, —that Hamilton, who as Secretary of the Treasury, devised a financial system of which we are the unlucky heritors, and whose objects were twofold: To puzzle the people and make public finance obscure to those that paid for it; to serve as a machine for corrupting the legislatures; "for he avowed the opinion that man could be governed by two motives only, force or interest;" force being then out of the question, he laid hold of interest, the greed of the legislators, to set going an association of persons having an entirely separate welfare from the welfare of their electors, bound together by mutual corruption and mutual desire for plunder. The Anarchist agrees that Hamilton was logical, and understood the core of government; the difference is, that while strong governmentalists believe this is necessary and desirable, we choose the opposite conclusion, NO GOVERNMENT WHATEVER.

As to the essence of human nature, what our national experience has made plain is this, that to remain in a continually exalted moral condition is not human nature. That has happened which was prophesied: we have gone down hill from the Revolution until now; we are absorbed in "mere money-getting." The desire for material ease long ago vanquished the spirit of '76. What was that spirit? The spirit that animated the people of Virginia, of the Carolinas, of Massachusetts, of New York, when they refused to import goods from England; when they preferred (and stood by it) to wear coarse homespun cloth, to drink the brew of their own growths, to fit their appetites to the home supply, rather than submit to the taxation of the imperial ministry. Even within the lifetime of the revolutionists the spirit decayed. The love of material ease has been, in the mass of men and permanently speaking, always greater than the love of liberty. Nine hundred and ninety-nine women out of a thousand are more interested in the cut of a dress than in the independence of their sex; nine hundred and ninety-nine men out of a thousand are more interested in drinking a glass of beer than in questioning the tax that is laid on it; how many children are not willing to trade the liberty to play for the promise of a new cap or a new dress? This it is which begets the complicated mechanism of society; this it is which, by multiplying the concerns of government, multiplies the strength of government and the corresponding weakness of the people; this it is which begets indifference to public concern, thus making the corruption of government easy.

As to the essence of Commerce and Manufacture, it is this: to establish bonds between every corner of the earth's surface and every other corner, to multiply the needs of mankind, and the desire for material possession and enjoyment.

The American tradition was the isolation of the States as far as possible. Said they: We have won our liberties by hard sacrifice and struggle unto death. We wish now to be let alone and to let others alone, that our principles may have time for trial; that we may become accustomed to the exercise of our rights; that we may be kept free from the contaminating influence of European gauds, pagents, distinctions. So richly did they esteem the absence of these that they could in all fervor write: "We shall see multiplied instances of Europeans coming to America, but no man living will ever see an instance of an American removing to settle in Europe, and continuing there." Alas! In less than a hundred years the highest aim of a "Daughter of the Revolution" was, and is, to buy a castle, a title, and a rotten lord, with the money wrung from American servitude! And the commercial interests of America are seeking a world-empire!

In the earlier days of the revolt and subsequent independence, it appeared that the "manifest destiny" of America was to be an agricultural people, exchanging food stuffs and raw materials for manufactured articles. And in those days it was written: "We shall be virtuous as long as agriculture is our principal object, which will be the case as long as there remain vacant lands in any part of America. When we get piled upon one another in large cities, as in Europe, we shall become corrupt as in Europe, and go to eating one another as they do there." Which we are doing, because of the inevitable development of Commerce and Manufacture, and the concomitant development of strong government. And the parallel prophecy is likewise fulfilled: "If ever this vast country is brought under a single government, it will be one of the most extensive corruption, indifferent and incapable of a wholesome care over so wide a spread of surface." There is not upon the face of the earth to-day a government so utterly and shamelessly corrupt as that of the United States of America. There are others more cruel, more tyrannical, more devastating; there is none so utterly venal.

And yet even in the very days of the prophets, even with their own consent, the first concession to this later tyranny was made. It was made when the Constitution was made; and the Constitution was made chiefly because of the demands of Commerce. Thus it was at the outset a merchant's machine, which the other interests of the country, the land and labor interests, even then foreboded would destroy their liberties. In vain their jealousy of its central power made them enact the first twelve amendments. In vain they endeavored to set bounds over which the federal power dare not trench. In vain they enacted into general law the freedom of speech, of the press, of assemblage and petition. All of these things we see ridden rough-shod upon every day, and have so seen with more or less intermission since the beginning of the nineteenth century. At this day, every police lieutenant considers himself, and rightly so, as more powerful than the General Law of the Union; and that one who told Robert Hunter that he held in his fist something stronger than the Constitution, was perfectly correct. The right of assemblage is an American tradition which has gone out of fashion; the police club is now the mode. And it is so in virtue of the people's indifference to liberty, and the steady progress of constitutional interpretation towards the substance of imperial government.

It is an American tradition that a standing army is a standing menace to liberty; in Jefferson's presidency the army was reduced to 3,000 men. It is American tradition that we keep out of the affairs of other nations. It is American practice that we meddle with the affairs of everybody else from the West to the East Indies, from Russia to Japan; and to do it we have a standing army of 83,251 men.

It is American tradition that the financial affairs of a nation should be transacted on the same principles of simple honesty that an individual conducts his own business; viz., that debt is a bad thing, and a man's first surplus earnings should be applied to his debts; that offices and office-holders should be few. It is American practice that the general government should always have millions of debt, even if a panic or a war has to be forced to prevent its being paid off; and as to the application of its income, office-holders come first. And within the last administration it is reported that 99,000 offices have been created at an annual expense of $63,000,000. Shades of Jefferson! "How are vacancies to be obtained? Those by deaths are few; by resignation none." Roosevelt cuts the knot by making 99,000 new ones! And few will die,—and none resign. They will beget sons and daughters, and Taft will have to create 99,000 more! Verily, a simple and a serviceable thing is our general government.

It is American tradition that the Judiciary shall act as a check upon the impetuosity of Legislatures, should these attempt to pass the bounds of constitutional limitation. It is American practice that the Judiciary justifies every law which trenches on the liberties of the people and nullifies every act of the Legislature by which the people seek to regain some measure of their freedom. Again, in the words of Jefferson: "The Constitution is a mere thing of wax in the hands of the Judiciary, which they may twist and shape in any form they please." Truly, if the men who fought the good fight for the triumph of simple, honest, free life in that day, were now to look upon the scene of their labors, they would cry out together with him who said: "I regret that I am now to die in the belief that the useless sacrifice of themselves by the generation of '76 to acquire self-government and happiness to their country, is to be thrown away by the unwise and unworthy passions of their sons, and that my only consolation is to be that I shall not live to see it."

And now, what has Anarchism to say to all this, this bankruptcy of republicanism, this modern empire that has grown up on the ruins of our early freedom? We say this, that the sin our fathers sinned was that they did not trust liberty wholly. They thought it possible to compromise between liberty and government, believing the latter to be "a necessary evil," and the moment the compromise was made, the whole misbegotten monster of our present tyranny began to grow. Instruments which are set up to safeguard rights become the very whip with which the free are struck.

Anarchism says, Make no laws whatever concerning speech, and speech will be free; so soon as you make a declaration on paper that speech shall be free, you will have a hundred lawyers proving that "freedom does not mean abuse, nor liberty license"; and they will define and define freedom out of existence. Let the guarantee of free speech be in every man's determination to use it, and we shall have no need of paper declarations. On the other hand, so long as the people do not care to exercise their freedom, those who wish to tyrannize will do so; for tyrants are active and ardent and will devote themselves in the name of any number of gods, religious and otherwise, to put shackles upon sleeping men.

The problem then becomes, Is it possible to stir men from their indifference? We have said that the spirit of liberty was nurtured by colonial life; that the elements of colonial life were the desire for sectarian independence, and the jealous watchfulness incident thereto; the isolation of pioneer communities which threw each individual strongly on his own resources, and thus developed all-around men, yet at the same time made very strong such social bonds as did exist; and, lastly, the comparative simplicity of small communities.

All this has mostly disappeared. As to sectarianism, it is only by dint of an occasional idiotic persecution that a sect becomes interesting; in the absence of this, outlandish sects play the fool's role, are anything but heroic, and have little to do with either the name or the substance of liberty. The old colonial religious parties have gradually become the "pillars of society," their animosities have died out, their offensive peculiarities have been effaced, they are as like one another as beans in a pod, they build churches and—sleep in them.

As to our communities, they are hopelessly and helplessly interdependent, as we ourselves are, save that continuously diminishing proportion engaged in all around farming; and even these are slaves to mortgages. For our cities, probably there is not one that is provisioned to last a week, and certainly there is none which would not be bankrupt with despair at the proposition that it produce its own food. In response to this condition and its correlative political tyranny, Anarchism affirms the economy of self-sustenance, the disintegration of the great communities, the use of the earth.

I am not ready to say that I see clearly that this *will* take place; but I see clearly that this *must* take place if ever again men are to be free. I am so well satisfied that the mass of mankind prefer material possessions to liberty, that I have no hope that they will ever, by means of intellectual or moral stirrings merely, throw off the yoke of oppression fastened on them by the present economic system, to institute free societies. My only hope is in the blind development of the economic system and political oppression itself. The great characteristic looming factor in this gigantic power is Manufacture. The tendency of each nation is to become more and more a manufacturing one, an exporter of fabrics, not an importer. If this tendency follows its own logic, it must eventually circle round to each community producing for itself. What then will become of the surplus product when the manufacturer shall have no foreign market? Why, then mankind must face the dilemma of sitting down and dying in the midst of it, or confiscating the goods.

Indeed, we are partially facing this problem even now; and so far we are sitting down and dying. I opine, however, that men will not do it forever; and when once by an act of general expropriation they have overcome the reverence and fear of property, and their awe of government, they may waken to the consciousness that things are to be used, and therefore men are greater than things. This may rouse the spirit of liberty.

If, on the other hand, the tendency of invention to simplify, enabling the advantages of machinery to be combined with smaller aggregations of workers, shall also follow its own logic, the great manufacturing plants will break up, population will go after the fragments, and there will be seen not indeed the hard, self-sustaining, isolated pioneer communities of early America, but thousands of small communities stretching along the lines of transportation, each producing very largely for its own needs, able to rely upon itself, and therefore able to be independent. For the same rule holds good for societies as for individuals,—those may be free who are able to make their own living.

In regard to the breaking up of that vilest creation of tyranny, the standing army and navy, it is clear that so long as men desire to fight, they will have armed force in one form or another. Our fathers thought they had guarded against a standing army by providing for the voluntary militia. In our day we have lived to see this militia declared part of the regular military force of the United States, and subject to the same demands as the regulars. Within another generation we shall probably see its members in the regular pay of the general government. Since any embodiment of the fighting spirit, any military organization, inevitably follows the same line of centralization, the logic of Anarchism is that the least objectionable form of armed force is that which springs up voluntarily, like the minute-men of Massachusetts, and disbands as soon as the occasion which called it into existence is past; that the really desirable thing is that all men—not Americans only—should be at peace; and that to reach this, all peaceful persons should withdraw their support from the army, and require that all who make war shall do at their own cost and risk; that neither pay nor pensions are to be provided for those who choose to make man-killing a trade.

As to the American tradition of non-meddling, Anarchism asks that it be carried down to the individual himself. It demands no jealous barrier of isolation; it knows that such isolation is undesirable and impossible; but it teaches that by all men's strictly minding their own business, a fluid society, freely adapting itself to mutual needs, wherein all the world shall belong to all men, as much as each has need or desire, will result.

And when Modern Revolution has thus been carried to the

heart of the whole world—if it ever shall be, as I hope it will,—then may we hope to see a resurrection of that proud spirit of our fathers which put the simple dignity of Man above the gauds of wealth and class, and held that to be an American was greater than to be a king.

In that day there shall be neither kings nor Americans,—only Men; over the whole earth, MEN.

8. Conservative Mistrust of Government

Nicholas Murray Butler, president of Columbia University for four decades and Republican candidate for Vice President of the United States in 1912, wrote a rather startling essay in 1923 on the subject of lawlessness. It is startling because of its seeming affinities with the libertarian tradition. In it Butler, a kingpin in the social and political establishment, cited Thoreau's "Civil Disobedience" with approval and said, in a vein strikingly similar to Voltairine de Cleyre's, that Thomas Jefferson would turn over in his grave if he could behold the recent flowering of bureaucracy and police control in American life. Butler's conception of recent American history was again one of decline from original moral principles, and his prognosis of the future was gloomy. One suddenly wonders how widely the assumption of progress was being challenged in America during the 1920's, perhaps as a result of postwar disillusionment and very rapid social change. Or was Butler conceivably driven to such heights of despair over the trend of things because the Prohibitionists had taken away his right lawfully to enjoy a glass of wine? (It was a fact that his second wife was the daughter of a prominent wine merchant.) Read in this light, Butler's essay becomes rather amusing, but it is clear that the forces within his mind which produced it were actually more complicated.

Butler's concern over a rising tide of lawlessness in the United States since about 1890 is in itself rather understandable. Such statistics as we have indicate that this increase in crime actually occurred.[1] Butler nonetheless carries his lament to striking lengths, coming close to the position that America was a sick society, in

1. See above, p. 30.

which only a few people (presumably like himself) enjoyed full mental health. Taken alone, this assertion might run parallel to that of a radical leftist. But once Butler reveals how he conceives the nature of the sickness, we realize that his indictment of modern realities is quite different in character. For Butler equates sickness with permissiveness. And here he locks horns directly with the anarchists, despite the intriguing apparent similarities in their points of view.

A comparison between Butler and Voltairine de Cleyre on the nature of the American school system reveals the difference. To her, the schools were agents of government oppression, inculcating a blind patriotic conformity of opinion into the minds of children. To him, on the contrary, the schools, under the impact of progressivism, had begun teaching a whole younger generation that they could get away with doing as they pleased. A new spirit of permissiveness was undermining the moral fiber of the nation. Although Butler held a Ph.D. degree and was a distinguished university president, his argument was no different really from Max Rafferty's much later on.

Looking back in the opposite direction, Butler's call for discipline was a good deal more strident and frightened than anything written on the same subject several decades earlier by the likes of William Graham Sumner. Butler revealed the growing fear, among Republican New Yorkers as well as among Ku Klux Klanners, that American industrial society, with its rapidly growing cities and its throngs of alien immigrants, was in danger of veering out of control. (Butler's anti-Semitism, for instance, was discreet but very real.)

Butler differed from small-town Fundamentalists not in his analysis of the basic situation (aside from the single issue of Prohibition), but rather in the realm of remedies. Here he retained far greater confidence in the power of internal self-control, especially when bolstered by years of coercive, will-breaking education in childhood. Therefore he argued vigorously against the idea that more laws or a more intrusive law enforcement apparatus were the remedy for lawlessness.

However, the laws he singles out for attack, especially the two Constitutional amendments he couples together, will jar and puzzle the present-day reader. Can Butler claim to be a true friend of Negro suffrage when he advocates repealing the Fifteenth Amendment because it is the kind of law which "highly intelligent and morally sensitive" white Southerners can never be expected to obey? Are black political exclusion and the consumption of alcohol really comparable as areas which should be free from too much legislative interference? Or is Butler merely reflecting the random prejudices of his time and of his social class? What seems like refreshing independence of mind may turn out on closer inspection to be no more than Ivy League patricianism in the sourest phase it reached until the advent of William F. Buckley.

But Butler's mind reveals more than either of these things. In it one glimpses the emerging right-wing disposition in the United States, here expressing itself in its most measured and respectable form. Before the Russian Revolution of 1917, there had long been a political left in America, but no sharply discernible right. Stand-patters—however much they might seek to destroy anarchism, labor unions, and certain forms of progressivism—were still usually attacking concrete targets in a spirit of political realism. Bolshevik victory in Russia, the emotional crisis of the First World War, the great labor strikes of 1919, all created an atmosphere in which American conservatism rapidly grew more panicky and careless. Thereby the outlines of future polarization of sentiment in this country became completely visible.

Beneath his gentlemanly façade, Butler seems to have been accommodating himself to certain aspects of the new postwar mood. In terms of his own immediate past, it was an about-face. The academic administrator who fired professors from Columbia if they showed lukewarmness toward the First World War was now suspicious of governmental constraint, veering toward a hasty embrace of Jefferson and Thoreau. Clear-cut intellectual distinctions, such as those between liberty and authoritarianism, seemed to dissolve in a muddle. But even the new muddle possessed some telltale outlines. Right-wing sentiment would frequently call, as Butler did, both for more discipline and more freedom; it would simultaneously fear moral breakdown and big government. Butler at least managed to avoid the cruder excesses of this new frame of mind.

Butler did tacitly retain a positive vision for the future of American society, which might be set against Voltairine de Cleyre's left-wing alternative. In Butler's ideal civilization, few people would rebel or turn criminal because few would conceive of the possibility of such things. Children would be docile, well laundered, eager to obey both the spirit and the letter of what they were told. Business would continue to flourish. Voters, from whom the unintelligent would be politely barred, would thoughtfully elect leaders from the nation's elite. This elite would command automatic grateful deference; therefore, few laws would be necessary. Variegated expressions of personal taste would remain, because no one would be barred from taking that graceful sip of wine. This was meaningful freedom. And the police could remain tactfully out of sight, patrolling the slums.

Nicholas Murray Butler, "Law and Lawlessness"

. . . That disregard of law, disobedience to law, and contempt for law have greatly increased and are still increasing in this country, is not to be doubted. Similar happenings are taking place in other parts of the world, but one may wonder whether the unenviable supremacy of the people of the United States in this field is not fixed for the time being. In all parts of the country judges and lawyers are discussing the prevalent spirit of lawlessness, and usually end by asserting emphatically that the law must be and shall be enforced exactly as it is written without fear or favor. This has a fine sound and is universally applauded, but it contributes absolutely nothing to an understanding or solution of the grave problem which wide-spread lawlessness has raised. An examination of the proceedings of the recent annual meetings of Bar Associations throughout the country establishes the fact that almost all of them have been hearing discussions of this topic. Its importance, therefore, and its nation-wide character may be taken for granted.

It is rather a sorry outcome of our century and a half of existence as an independent nation, proclaiming to the world the discovery of the best possible method of providing for liberty under law, that we should now be pointed to as the law-breaking nation *par excellence*. At the meeting of the American Bar Association held in San Francisco in August last, I listened to the report of a special committee on law enforcement. That committee called at-

An address before the Ohio State Bar Association, Columbus, January 26, 1923. From Nicholas Murray Butler, *The Faith of a Liberal* (New York: Charles Scribner's Sons, 1924), pp. 105–120, 122–125. Reprinted by permission of the publisher.

tention first to the fact that we in this country are without adequate and accurate statistical information as to crime, and will remain so until the Department of Justice is in position to establish a Bureau of Records and Statistics where all relevant information may be assembled and preserved, and to which recourse may be had by courts and public officers throughout the nation. That committee offered a most disheartening and indeed shameful comparison between the law-abiding character of the people of the Dominion of Canada and that of the people of the United States. They seemed to feel that the situation was somewhat relieved by the fact that when Canadians cross the border they become proportionately less law-abiding than when at home. Some of us might think that, contrary to the adage of the poet Horace, these immigrants had changed both the sky above them and the spirit within them, and that the inference was not complimentary to the United States. However that may be, the Dominion of Canada, with a population of some nine millions, stands in most enviable contrast to Cook County, Illinois, with a population of some three millions, when burglaries, larcenies, and homicides are taken as standards of comparison.

It was of particular interest to hear in that report the statement that particularly since 1890 there has been and continues to be a constantly widening and deepening tide of lawlessness in the United States. I hold that date, 1890, to have marked the turning point for the worse in more than one field of thought and action, and to be a truly significant date for any one who would understand the prevalent lawlessness among our people. It seems clear that the remedies usually suggested for this lawlessness are very superficial, and can have none but superficial and temporary results. It is well enough to increase the number of judges, to make criminal trials more speedy and sentences after conviction more severe, and in various other conventional ways to strengthen the administration of justice. We may, however, do all these excellent things, and lawlessness will still continue to exist and to grow unless its underlying causes be reached and dealt with. Human experience has long since exploded the doctrine that a severe punishment will deter from the commission of crime. The fear of detection will so deter, but the fear of punishment will not.

In order to get at the fundamental facts in respect to lawlessness, we must dig down somewhat deeper than ordinary. There is, first, the body of new information just being brought to general public attention, which appears to indicate that during the past hundred years and more the material progress of man and his power to control and apply the forces of nature have far outrun both his intellectual and his moral capacity and competence. One of the most distinguished of American scientists recently said in my hearing that he had about come to the conclusion that all his discoveries and advances were harmful rather than helpful to mankind, because of the base and destructive uses to which they were likely to be put. He insisted that, in the present state of public intelligence, if there was a lofty use and a lower use of his discoveries and inventions, evidence multiplied that the lower use would be the first chosen. He pointed, among other things, to the fact that the Great War, with all its destructiveness and appalling loss of life and treasure, could never have been fought except by the use of two of the most beneficent and striking of modern inventions, namely, the telephone and typhoid prophylaxis. What, he added, is the use of inventing and improving the telephone or of discovering and applying typhoid prophylaxis, if the killing of millions of men is the best use that can be made of them?

Frankly, we must face the possibility that we are living in a material world to which but a portion of the people are intellectually and morally adjusted. These, and these alone, be they few or many, are in a state of mental health. The others are pathologic cases from the intellectual and the moral point of view. They are not mentally defective as that term has been understood, nor are they in any technical sense insane; but they are sufficiently maladjusted to their environment to be lacking in complete mental and moral health. If conditions like these be superadded to the general temperament and known characteristics of the people of the United States, it is not difficult to see how a widespread spirit of restlessness, of dissatisfaction with law, and eventually of disregard for law might be brought about. The more advanced of our students and investigators of mental life and mental health are quite alive to these conditions, but as yet they are voices crying in a wilderness.

The report of the American Bar Association's committee on

law enforcement mentioned the year 1890 as significant in the history of the development of lawlessness in this country. That happens to be about the time when the standards and methods of general education which had existed in the United States for more than a half-century began to give way before those that have since become increasingly influential not only in our schools and colleges but in our homes. For various reasons which need not be gone into here, there then began to be an increasingly sympathetic response to the doctrine, which had for some time been preached, that no youth should be asked to follow any course of study that he did not like and that was not of his own choosing. His tastes and early capacities, or perhaps his whims, were to take the place of human experience and the general interest in determining how he should spend his time while in the process of formal education. A quick effect, and indeed an almost unconscious effect, of the practice of such a doctrine is to displace discipline and to arouse in the mind of youth contempt and disregard for those things which he has not chosen to know, regardless of what may be the opinion of others concerning their value and importance. In this way the individual learns to separate his own tastes, his own interests, his own occupations from those of the community of which he is a part, and only to prefer and to follow his own. That subtle and many-sided influences would in this way be set in motion to make for lawlessness seems obvious.

Until about 1890 the ruling notion in American education was that there existed such a thing as general discipline, general knowledge, and general capacity, all of which should be developed and made the most of by co-operation between the home and the school. As a result of a few hopelessly superficial and irrelevant experiments, it was one day announced from various psychological laboratories that there was no such thing as general discipline and general capacity, but that all disciplines were particular and that all capacities were specific. The arrant nonsense of this and the flat contradiction given to it by human observation and human experience went for nothing, and this new notion rapidly spread abroad among the homes and schools of the United States, both to the undoing of the effectiveness of our American education and to the spread of a spirit which makes for lawlessness. It would surprise a great many excellent persons to be told that the schools upon whose maintenance they are pouring out almost unlimited sums raised by public tax were, quite unconsciously, doing all that they reasonably could to implant a spirit of lawlessness in those who come under their influence. And yet that is the sober truth. If a youth be taught at home or in school that there are no fundamental underlying principles, but that the world is his oyster, to be consumed at such time and in such fashion as he may see fit, or that it is to be made over to his heart's desire, one need not wonder when a spirit of lawlessness and restlessness under order and constraint find expression in his life. The platitude-makers tell us sometimes that education is preparation for life, and sometimes that education is life; take either horn of the dilemma, and the sort of education to which we are now subjecting our youth is too often a training in the spirit of lawlessness. No person can be called educated who will not do effectively something that he does not wish to do at the time when it ought to be done.

If these considerations be correctly stated, a secure foundation for lawlessness has been laid in our national life, and an invitation to lawlessness has been extended by the recent material progress of man and by the changes that have come over our national system of education. The sum total of the effects of these causes is to predispose to lawlessness. In such case there is no effective barrier raised against human passion, human greed, human revenge, or human cupidity. First comes individual interest and individual satisfaction; then group or class privilege or advantage; and last of all, the interest of the general public, which in a healthy and law-abiding society will always be supreme.

Upon the foundation so laid there has been rising for some time past a structure making for lawlessness, which has had the co-operation of many builders, most of whom have been quite unconscious of the part they were playing. Our legislatures, both State and national, and our various administrative boards and bureaus, are largely made up of those whom Thomas Jefferson wittily described as demi-lawyers. Their ruling passion is a statute or an administrative order. Their constant appeal is to force, to what has come to be known as the police power of the state, and they exercise it with a ruthlessness and a ferocity from which kings and emperors have been accustomed to draw back. Shortly before retiring from public life former Senator Thomas of Colorado, himself a learned lawyer of high type, made a speech in the Senate in which he pointed out that within a relatively short period of time we Americans had some seventy thousand statutes, State and national, passed for our guidance and government. To state this fact is to name a powerful force making for the spread of lawlessness. When the temporary is confused with the permanent, and when the unimportant and trivial is mistaken for that which has broad reference and wide implication, intelligent citizens must not be expected to look seriously upon statutes and statute-making or to treat all statutes with equal respect. The strain is quite too much for common sense and for a sense of humor to bear. I well know that it is the opinion of lawyers that whatever enactments are duly made by a legislature and upheld by a competent court, are part of the law. But that is an illusion. They are only part of the law if general public opinion supports and upholds them. There is a silent referendum in the hearts and minds of men on every important enactment by a legislature and on every important decision by a court which involves a fundamental principle of civil liberty. Without a favorable issue in that referendum, the statute and the decision alike are written in water. It must not be forgotten that law is but one form or type of social control.

It is not so many years ago that Americans used to laugh at the Prussian bureaucracy and to point with scorn at the signs Verboten that were to be seen on every hand in Prussia. Our bureaucracy is quite as bad as that of Prussia ever was, without being so efficient, and now we have a dozen Verboten signs in the United States to every one that Prussia can show. Not a few of the printed forms addressed to citizens by various bureaus of the national and State governments are rude and peremptory to the point of insolence, and are justly resented by self-respecting citizens. The multiplication of petty crimes has gone on until the list includes scores of perfectly innocent departures from the conventional and scores of perfectly harmless infractions of good manners and good conduct. No longer do the demi-lawyers stop with defining these acts as misdemeanors. Not infrequently they are elevated to the rank of felonies. Is it any wonder that an intelligent and self-respecting public revolts at that sort of official treatment? It may just as well be frankly stated that a very distinct contribution to the spread of lawlessness is made by the ease and inconsequence with which we make and modify the law. Did time serve, it would be possible to give illustration after illustration drawn from the statute books and administrative codes of States in all parts of the Union. Thomas Jefferson would rise in his grave if he could know what is now going on in the United States, not infrequently at the behest and under the influence of the political party which still professes allegiance to his name and principles.

In this respect things have come to such a pass that the really public-spirited legislator who should vote No on every roll-call in respect to the final passage of a bill would be rendering public service nine times out of ten. The common law will take care of our developing needs in far better fashion than will statutes in all but a very small class of cases. The influence of a sound education and a true religion, if really believed in instead of being merely talked about, would in time build up a spirit of obedience to law which no possible system of law enforcement can ever bring about. Through centuries a habit of obedience to the Ten Commandments may be built up among men, but the Ten Commandments cannot be enforced by all the governments and armies in Christendom.

This is but one more phase of the never-ending struggle between reason and force in human life. Civilized states, and particularly those which rest upon a basis of popular government, are always steadily aiming to widen the area in which reason rules and to narrow that in which force controls, both as to their internal policies and as to their international relationships. We in this country, however, have of late been pursuing the reactionary policy of widening the area where force controls, and this is justly resented by a very large number of Americans. Their resentment leads naturally, in the case of not a few, to lawlessness in one of its many forms. It is no answer to say that these statutes and these administrative orders are made in pursuance of law, and that at bottom they rest, through the medium of our representative institutions, on the will of the majority. The will of the majority is under precisely the same limitations as was the will of the monarch. In the process of gaining freedom, it has never been the intention of modern men to substitute a tyrant with many heads for a tyrant with one head. They have endeavored and have struggled to mark out and to define an area of civil and political liberty into which no tyrant may enter, whether he have one head or many. The invasion of that area by the many-headed tyrant under the ostensible forms of law is just as repugnant to the lover of liberty as is its invasion by the monarch claiming to enter by divine right. When the law commits a trespass, it can hardly expect that sort of hospitable welcome which is cheerfully offered to an invited guest.

These were once fundamental principles of American public polity. They were universally accepted by the fathers, and were laid down as the chart by which our ship of state was to be guided as it set out on its memorable voyage across the seas of political experience. It needs no argument to prove that we are tending to lose sight of these fundamental principles and to try all over again, although in new forms, the world-old experiment of tyranny and despotism, and interference with personal life and private conduct. It has been settled and generally accepted law in the United States for nearly two generations that when an undertaking privately organized becomes charged with a public interest, then public supervision and control may rightly be established over it. Similarly, it is only when the private life and personal conduct of an individual become so charged with a public interest that public authority has any proper concern with them at all. It would not be unbecoming for us all to reread at intervals the Declaration of Independence and to reflect seriously upon its words. If the American of to-day were to read Thoreau's essay on Civil Disobedience he might be startled, but he certainly would be enlightened.

It would be lacking in frankness and sincerity not to point out two important and law-made influences which are now making, and seem likely long to make, for lawlessness in American life. The American people as a whole cannot escape full share of the responsibility for these two influences, although they are in part due, no doubt, to what Walt Whitman described as "the never-ending audacity of elected persons." The first is the Fifteenth Amendment, proclaimed in 1870, and the second is the Eighteenth Amendment, proclaimed in 1919. In form and in fact, and judged by all the usual tests and standards, these two amendments to the

Constitution of the United States are part of the organic law, with all the rights and authority which attach thereto. Nevertheless, they are not obeyed by large numbers of highly intelligent and morally sensitive people, and there is no likelihood that they can ever be enforced, no matter at what expenditure of money or of effort, or at what cost of infringement or neglect of other equally valid provisions of the same Constitution. The purpose of those who advocated and secured the adoption of these two amendments was excellent, but they did not stop to deal with the realities of politics and of public morals.

When the Thirteenth Amendment abolished slavery, and when the Fourteenth Amendment provided for the reduction of the representation in Congress from any State which abridged the right of any citizen to vote, except for participation in rebellion or other crime, the matter might well have rested there. All that was needed was the courage and the public opinion to enforce the Fourteenth Amendment, and speedily the several States would have made provision for their own protection by which the intelligent colored man would have been permitted to vote. General Robert E. Lee himself testified in this spirit before the Reconstruction Committee of the Congress. The Civil War had but just ended, however, and passion ran high. Therefore, the Fifteenth Amendment was proposed and ratified, and the right of suffrage was given a national basis and protected by a national guaranty. What has been the result? After a half-century the colored man votes in those States where he voted when the Fifteenth Amendment was passed, but he rarely votes, and certainly does not freely participate in public life, in those States where he did not vote then. Every attempt to enforce the Fourteenth or Fifteenth Amendment has been denounced as a force bill. Oddly enough, it has been so denounced by those very Senators and Representatives who will go to any length to enforce the provisions of the Eighteenth Amendment. The practical question is not whether or not the colored man should vote in the Southern States, but whether the American people will frankly face the problem presented by the nullification throughout a large part of the land of a most important provision of the Constitution of the United States. Every one knows what political results follow from the failure to enforce the provisions of the Fourteenth Amendment and from

the skilful measures which have been enacted to escape its provisions without actually violating it. All this is a matter of history.
No one in his senses wishes to overturn white government in the
Southern States; but every one with the American spirit in his
heart wishes fair play and a fair chance for the colored man and
the removal of any continuing cause of lawlessness which has its
foundation in the organic law itself. It is elementary that an
individual or a community may not defy law in one respect without developing a habit of disregard for all law. If the American
people stand idly by and see the Fifteenth Amendment unenforced
and unenforceable because it runs counter to the intelligence and
moral sense of large elements of the population, must they not
either remove the offending cause from the law or leave off be-
wailing the lawlessness to which its presence naturally leads? This
generation has become so accustomed to the cavalier treatment
of the Fourteenth and Fifteenth Amendments that it rarely weighs
and little understands, the influences flowing from them for lawlessness. It is a fair question whether, if the Fifteenth Amendment
were repealed and the Fourteenth Amendment were enforced, the
political and social condition of the colored man in the Southern
States would not be vastly improved. Certainly, a powerful and
continuing cause of lawlessness would have been eliminated, and
the political condition of the colored man would be no less ad-
vantageous than now.

The situation with regard to the Eighteenth Amendment is even
worse, because the revolt against it is not confined to men and
women of intelligence and moral sensitiveness in one section alone,
but is nation-wide. It will not do to attempt to silence these persons by abuse or by catch phrases and formulas of the hustings.
These men and women dissent entirely from the grounds upon
which the case for the Eighteenth Amendment was rested, and
they regard its provisions and those of the statutes based upon it
as a forcible, an immoral, and a tyrannical invasion of their private
life and personal conduct. They have no possible interest in the
liquor traffic, and they are without exception opposed to the
saloon. But they are equally opposed to making the Constitution
of the United States the vehicle of a police regulation affecting the
entire country, and dealing not alone with matters of public interest and public reference, but with the most intimate details of

personal and private life, including food, drink, and medical treatment. The moral sense, as well as the common sense, of very many people is affronted by a policy which will expend millions of dollars and use the methods of Tsarist Russia and of the Spanish Inquisition to enforce one provision of law, while others of far greater significance and public importance are accorded conventional treatment or less. . . .

. . . The answer which is made is instant and resounding. We are told that the Eighteenth Amendment was adopted in accordance with the provisions of the Constitution itself, and that its validity as an amendment has been affirmed by the United States Supreme Court. We are told then that all that those who disagree with its principles and purposes have to do is to accept defeat, to recognize themselves as in the minority, and to obey the law. Parhaps this ought to be the case, but it is not, and I greatly doubt if it ever will be, at least within the lifetime of any man now living. The majority is not always right, nor is its verdict final. The Old Testament records a leading case in which four hundred and fifty prophets of Baal were worsted single-handed by the prophet Elijah, who had God and right on his side. Four hundred and fifty to one is a very unusual majority, but it was not enough.

As Abraham Lincoln pointed out in his argument against the finality of the decision of the United States Supreme Court in the Dred Scott case, he was not violating the law or urging its violation. He did not propose to set Dred Scott free by force, in opposition to the court's decision. What he did propose, however, was to agitate and to lead an agitation for such political action as would make impossible the conditions which had led the Supreme Court to make its decision in that particular case. It is lawless openly to affront the law. It is not lawless to agitate for its modification or repeal.

No one who is familiar with the practical workings of our political system would expect either the Fifteenth or the Eighteenth Amendment to be repealed at an early day. So far as one can see, therefore, we are shut up to the alternative of their attempted enforcement by soldiers and police and special agents and detectives and spies, or to their abrogation over a great part of the land by local initiative and common consent. Either alternative is humiliating and degrading. If our people have taken untenable and harmful positions in respect of securing suffrage for the colored man, and in respect of promoting the cause of temperance and total abstinence and in removing the abuse and the nuisance of the public bar, they should be willing to retrace those steps and start toward their wise and splendid goals by other and more practicable paths. I know of no one who dares to hope for any such fortunate outcome of the unhappy conditions that now confront us.

Speaking for myself, I may say that my first political activity in my native State of New Jersey was in co-operation with colored men and on their behalf, and in support of movements to restrict and to abolish the saloon, or public bar. In my own Congressional district there were large numbers of colored voters who were eager, intelligent, and public-spirited. To see colored men of that type participate freely in the public life of other districts and other States would be a great satisfaction. But it is now plain to me that the road which was taken to that end was a wrong road. It has delayed, not hastened, the political participation of the colored man in the public life of the United States. Similarly, it was my fortune, as a member of the Committee on Resolutions of the New Jersey State Republican Convention of 1886, to give the casting vote in favor of the platform declaration which declared war on the saloon. That platform declaration is supposed to have cost the Republican Party that election, but it was a sound and true declaration none the less. Later, in the State of New York, it was my lot to work vigorously with those who attempted to drive out the saloon by use of the power of taxation. Therefore, I am personally committed through many years of practical political action to the cause of universal suffrage and to the abolition of the saloon. Perhaps, for that very reason, I feel so strongly as I do the disastrous mistakes that have been made, and the evil consequences that have followed and are certain long to follow in the life of the people of the United States. Surely there can be no more distressing and no more disintegrating form of lawlessness than that which arises from the resistance of intelligent and high-minded people, on grounds of morals and fundamental principle, to some particular provision of law.

The American people must learn to think of these things and to give up that unwillingness, which seems so characteristic, to discuss or to deal with the disputed and the disagreeable. We have almost gotten to a point where public men, and those who should be leaders of opinion, hesitate to speak until they know what others are likely to say, and how what they say will probably be received by the press and the public. There are not so many as there should be who are willing to take the risk of being unpopular for the sake of being right.

Beyond All Forms of Liberalism

Questions of liberty and authority continued to be debated in varying contexts during the last several decades of American history. But for much of this time they were not posed very freshly or interestingly. The outcry of businessmen against Franklin D. Roosevelt produced the American Liberty League in 1934, but its arguments did no more than echo a traditional desire of entrepreneurs to be left free from onerous forms of governmental interference, and there was a speciousness about invocations of laissez faire uttered by spokesmen for giant, semimonopolistic industrial combines.

During the Cold War period, the issue of freedom in the political sense again came to the fore, but also in a dreary fashion, entirely within the context of anti-Communist emotions. In several shorter essays and in his book *The Vital Center* (1949), Arthur M. Schlesinger, Jr., went through some torturous fence-straddling on this question from a liberal point of view. However, at bottom Schlesinger's reasoning added little to the majoritarian assumptions of George Bancroft a hundred years earlier, aside from Schlesinger's evident awareness that a problem in the area of individual dissent did at least theoretically exist.[1] During the McCarthy era, few Americans felt impelled to probe the matter of political obligation to its depths.

All this changed enormously, as we know, in the 1960's. The

1. Any single quotation from Schlesinger is bound to be somewhat unfair. But the following reveals quite a bit of his state of mind: "The cold war and the Soviet threat have necessarily narrowed alternatives; and the indulgence of freedom must inevitably take second place in the real world to the harsh requirements of survival. And the intellectuals themselves, in many cases, have forfeited sympathy or respect because of the arrogance and egotism they displayed when they were riding high—an arrogance too often accompanied by political imbecility, if not by political guilt. Yet the demagogues of the right, trying to pluck power out of anxiety, have narrowed the alternatives far beyond the point of necessity." Arthur M. Schlesinger, Jr., "The Highbrow in American Politics" (first published in 1953), in *The Politics of Hope* (Boston: Houghton Mifflin, 1963), p. 227.

majoritarian consensus, seemingly stable ever since the early days of industrialization, now faced a quickening confrontation from without. Two issues, the emerging self-awareness of black people and the need for many individuals to define their position toward a war which deeply offended them, brought forth a double-pronged challenge to the basic liberal attitude of working gradually for change within the machinery of the existing system. "Liberalism" became a swear word among an angry, highly intelligent minority of blacks, student radicals, and dropouts from the middle class. In these circles, law was unambiguously identified with an unjust political establishment. Sometimes it was sweepingly rejected on these grounds. As John Gerassi, a former professor at San Francisco State College, expressed this mood in 1968:

That is the liberal position: respect for Law. The law doesn't have to be moral because it defends that which already exists. The liberal's myth is that through the rule of law justice ultimately triumphs. And although he can be shown that it is under the rule of law that we butcher people in Santo Domingo, that it is under the rule of law that we go into Vietnam to wipe out a population with napalm,[2] nevertheless the liberal will insist that it must be under the rule of law that we must put an end to all these crimes. . . . A system of law has always been essential to the American Way of Life. This system justifies repressions, rationalizes oppressions, codifies frustrations.

Hemmed in by law, Gerassi went on to argue, American would-be radicals frequently reacted "by focusing on our inner selves," that is, were diverted into the politically innocuous "hippie" route toward liberation.[3]

Both among militant radicals and their hostile critics, it was apparent that a conflict had developed over fundamentals of loyalty and dissent. Driven by concern over certain particular issues, a small minority of Americans had begun subconsciously thinking of themselves not foremost as Americans, but instead, however vainly, as human beings (or as black people) who happened to be born in America. The shifting frame of reference was crucial,

2. Both these last assertions of Gerassi's are factually highly questionable. If he had asserted that America adopted these policies with the tacit consent of a majority (even if at times somewhat after the fact), he would have been on much firmer ground.

3. John Gerassi, "Imperialism and Revolution in America," in David Cooper, ed., *To Free a Generation: The Dialectics of Liberation* (New York: Collier Books, 1968), pp. 88–89.

even though it by no means equalled a direct embrace of revolution. Government, for these persons as for Thoreau, had lost its sacredness. Their opponents, sensing this, demanded that submission to authority be reasserted above all else. The phrase "law and order," which had already been casually used in the nineteenth century and which was perhaps influentially repopularized in the text of the nightly sign-on to the "Lone Ranger" radio dramas of the 1940's, now sprang onto many politicians' lips. These words were invoked not merely to suppress actual violent uprisings, but more broadly to force a universal acknowledgment in men's minds that the needs of the state must reign supreme.

9. Rejection of a Closed Society

Liberalism—in its more moderate senses—and nationalism were the two cornerstones of majority belief in America. In the 1960's white radicals tended more often to reject nationalism, while black militants—caught up in their own nationalist yearnings—more decisively cast aside liberalism instead.

White radicals did indeed often speak contemptuously of liberalism, and a few of them—in particular the Weatherman faction of Students for a Democratic Society—deliberately courted a martyr's death in the streets. Yet most of them found it hard to exorcise the habit of taking ordinary political tactics seriously. Liberal upbringings were always showing through radical intentions. Most white youth, unless temporarily prodded by the draft, did not conceive of themselves as outlaws. Whether their protest against the Vietnam War was violent or nonviolent, their usual assumption was that they would have to face the legal consequences of their action. They would fight willingly in the courts for a maximum recognition of their rights under the American legal system.[1] When defeated, they would accept the consequence

1. Thus at the trial of the Chicago Seven in 1969–70, there was much more effort to argue within the terms of the legal system (e.g., over the right to appoint one's own counsel) than at the Black Panther trial early in 1970, where the disruption attempted to dramatize hostility toward the entire system. At their trial in 1918, I. W. W. leaders had refused to accept courtroom protocol. For an interesting discussion of this issue see

—punishment in jail. Further, if their specific grievances were ever met, a strong likelihood existed that all but a small hard core would prove surprisingly receptive to resuming the game of mainstream politics.

Black radicals, on balance, tended to reject the American system at a deeper level of the self. Having been forced into the consistent role of outsider, rather than voluntarily adopting that role, their alienation was probably more deep-seated and perhaps more profound. At the same time, they were less intellectual than many of the radical whites. They had enlisted at birth in a group struggle, and as they came to full political consciousness they tended to become angrier, and sometimes more scornful, but not often abstractly philosophical. Their war was not 6,000 miles away, and it would not likely be over as soon. Their emotional stake in America, while not entirely lacking, was apt to be less. Majoritarianism was never an issue about which they needed to feel ambivalent. In these respects, it was easier for them to take a clear-cut position at odds with past traditions.

The essay on violence by the black author and playwright LeRoi Jones thus requires little direct comment. Unlike, for instance, Voltairine de Cleyre, Jones has no need to wrestle with American history; its meaning for him, from Jamestown to the present, is perfectly obvious, and Thomas Jefferson is no hero. On the question of violence itself, Jones is perhaps a bit ambiguous, because he defines its target in impersonal terms ("society," or "the American socio-political stance"), thereby softening the impact of the phrase "literal murdering," which at one point he employs. But if one reads the whole essay, there is little softness to be found. There is also little concern for the individual as such, and therefore no connection with Thoreau. Individualism is apt to be a lively concern for men whose sense of group identity is already automatically assured within their minds. In that respect, individuality (of all kinds, not merely economic) is after all a value closely connected with the liberal tradition. Breaking decisively with this, Jones ushers in an era of group conflict in America, in which allegiances and loyalties count for more (on both sides) than questions of personal fulfillment.

Yet there is a further major irony about the struggle for black

---

R. Thomas Breckenridge, "Defiance of Law," *Mother Earth,* IX (1914), 49–53, pointing out how seldom radicals up till that time had been non-cooperative in court.

liberation which Jones announces. At its root, the ideal of black identity is but one more instance of the concept of nationalism, which first emerged in early nineteenth-century Europe. Only a position of actual powerlessness separates black nationalists from the leaders of existing governments. Ironically, therefore, the white man's way of thinking still dominates the mental processes of black nationalist spokesmen, for it was the white man who first promoted the idea of ethnicity and, as in the case of Woodrow Wilson, argued that territorial lines should wholesomely reflect cultural entities. White Americans have been fascinated by black separatism because it turns their own logic against them. But for this same reason, however urgent its appeal and however final its break with liberalism, black nationalism reveals itself as the dated product of the specifically European imagination. Only in something like tribalism could the black militant truly manage to escape the impact of Western forms on his own consciousness.

Yet black radicals would probably reply that the present racial situation in the United States is not one to permit the luxury of such historical-mindedness. Jones speaks directly from an awareness of injustice. This awareness tends to wither the white man's logical (and liberal) scruples, perhaps even those on the subject of nationalism itself.

LeRoi Jones, "What Does Nonviolence Mean?"

1

There is a war going on now in the United States. Anyone who does not understand how this could be possible is more naïve, fortunately, than one would think this century would permit.

Recently in that war, four Negro children were blown to bits while they were learning to pray. The leader of the Jackson, Mississippi, NAACP (himself a reluctant convert to "the doctrines of nonviolence") was assassinated in front of his home. Police dogs, fire hoses, blackjacks, have been used on Negroes, trying to reinforce a simple and brutal social repression. And all these

From LeRoi Jones, *Home: Social Essays* (New York: William Morrow, 1966), pp. 133–148, 150–154. Copyright © 1963 by LeRoi Jones. Reprinted by permission of the publisher.

terroristic tactics are used, finally, toward the same end: to make young bucks and tutering school marms confess to the same lie the racks and iron maidens of the Inquisition demanded—that there is something other than reality. While a Negro is under a hose or thrown against a building by some dumb brute, he is supporting that lie as well as the lie of his own inferiority. The inferiority of the suppliant. The readiness of the weak to repeat themselves. To be no more than weak, or no smarter than their torturers. Yet in spite of this, and in the face of such brutality, certain elements in America ask the Negro to be Nonviolent. But who are these elements, and what are they really asking?

On all levels the white man insists that there is no Negro in America like the one that claims now to be here. Or at least there has been a constant and unfailing effort on the part of almost every white man in America (and the West) to have his own qualified version of a black man exist, and not just any black man who might like to appear under his own volition. To the Southern white (and many Northerners) the sit-ins are liars, the pickets and boycotters, all are fiendish liars. There is no such Negro who would want anything but what we've always given them, the white Southerner says. The Negro who wants the foot off his neck must be inspired by Communists. It is a simple lie to say otherwise, they say. We know what Negroes are, what they want. Governor Wallace, on television, admonishes his black housekeeper warmly, "Y'all take care of everything, heah?" The old woman smiles, and goes off to take care of his baby. That is the Negro that really exists for him. No other. The smiling convicts raking up leaves in his yard. He waves as he crosses to his car. More real Negroes. He is on his way to the University to make the fake Negroes disappear.

The liberal white man insists also that there is no such thing as a Negro, except the thing he has invented. They are simply underprivileged, the have-nots, the emerging. They are the same as we, given an education, a livelihood, etc. And this is the rhetoric. But where did all these underprivileged people, these have-nots, come from? What, for instance, are all these black people doing in this country in the first place? It is questions like these that the rhetoric is supposed to erase from the liberal white man's mind. The fact that the Negro was brought here as an

African slave, and that he labored some two hundred years in slavery, is by now supposedly forgotten. (During slavery a liberal, or a moderate, was a man who didn't want the slaves beaten. But he was not asking that they be freed.) Certainly the Negro middle class has forgotten, or at least it is their job to pretend they have forgotten, and for this reason even the low moan of blues from some un-American tenement is almost as much of a social affront as a sign on a water fountain. This is the missionaries' legacy, the last pure remnant of the slave mentality—cultural shame.

What the liberal white man does is to open a door into the glittering mainstream of white American life as a possibility for the middle-class black man. All the Negro need do is renounce his history as pure social error and strive with the rest of the strivers, so that he too can help in erecting a monolithic syndrome of predictable social values, based on the economic power and hegemony of the American (Western) white man.

In order for the Negro to achieve what I will call an "equality of means," that is, at birth to be able to benefit by everything of value in the society, of course the society would have to change almost completely. What the liberal white man wants is to change the Negro so he can be included in the existing system. Richard Nixon is an example of what the liberal wants the Negro to become. A drab lower middle-class buffoon who has no more political power or cultural significance than his social interment petty ambition allows. Very few American white men want the system itself changed, and that change complete, or occurring with the rudeness of sudden reality. Abracadabra, a family of twelve Negroes is living in the next lot. What shall we do? the cry goes up from the kindest hearts.

It is the same kind of spurious and pragmatic realism that motivates most American "reformers," *e.g.,* most of the socio-economic policies of Roosevelt's New Deal were not meant to change the society, but to strengthen the one that existed. Roosevelt, in this sense, like a man who when fire breaks out in his apartment immediately builds a stove around it, gave a flexibility to the American ruling class that it could not have survived without.

So far the most serious battles in the war I spoke of are being waged between two classes of white men, although the middle-class Negroes are the semi-conscious pawns in these struggles. (The rest of the black population are pawns by default.) The battles are being waged now, have been waged for the last three hundred years, between those white men who think the Negro is good for one thing and those who think he is good for another. This same fight went on during the early days of slavery between the missionaries, those who would give the slave Christianity, thereby excusing the instance of slavery as a moral crusade (with concomitant economic advantages) and those who felt that as animals the black men had no need for God, since as animals they had no souls. The fight continues today, with the same emphasis. Except in earlier times the liberal forces, the God-carriers, had only the house slave, or occasional freedman, to show off as end products of a benevolent Christian ethic, but now the Kennedys and the Rockefellers have a full-fledged black bourgeosie to gesture toward as an indication of what the social utopia of the West should look like.

So the war goes on, from battle to battle, but with essentially the same things at stake, and for the same reasons. The forces of naked repression, on the one hand, have always been out in the open. What they want, have wanted, is common knowledge to Negroes once Negroes have gotten old enough to find out that the world as they will come to know it is basically unfriendly if you are black. Each "class" (of white people) has its own method of making that world unfriendly, which makes the quarrel. But nothing is really to be changed. Complete socio-economic subjugation is the goal of both white forces. What the liberal sees as evil about this program is the way it is being carried out. Liberals want to be leaders rather than rulers.

The black middle class, and its spiritual forebears, the freedmen and house slaves, have always "fought" to maintain some hegemony and privilege, and as a privileged class within the American system as defined by the Liberal/Missionary class of American white men. And because of this they have always had to be pawns and tokens in the white class war that constantly goes on over the question of what to do with Negroes. The NAACP, SCLC, CORE, and any other group who advocate moral suasion as their weapon of change (reform) have been members of the Negro middle class, or at least bound by that class's social sentiments. These organizations, and others like them, are controlled by the Negro middle class and sponsored by white liberal monies. All these people treat history as if it were autonomous and had nothing to do with people or ideas. Old slavery, for instance, and its legacy, contemporary social and economic slavery, are looked at as hideous accidents for which no one should be blamed. (The liberal mind is such that it is already trying to persuade us that no one was to blame for Hitler, or for that matter, Joe McCarthy, but "the times.") But the fact is that Negroes in America are still either field slaves or house slaves, the mode of oppression depending on the accident of social breeding, one group having easy chairs in its cells.

The puppet uses to which the historic Liberal/Missionary syndrome has put the black middle class have grown more bizarre through the years simply because of the increasing dead weight of the black poor which this artificial middle class is supposed to exercise. But this weight, if anything, has gotten heavier, and is felt by all the elements of this society. The Welfare State was the reformer's answer. It was, and is, like a rotten blimp attached to the sleek new airliner. Thirty-five dollars a month and carfare to the Welfare office is available to each poor Negro who rides in this quasi-lighter-than-air ship called Ghetto. Each scream of agony that comes from the airship causes the black middle class, who ride in a special airtight compartment of the airliner, to ask for more Zweibacks in their gleaming bowls. So that now there must be a Negro Asst. Press Secretary, a proposed Negro chief of Urban Affairs, a Negro for housing, etc., all of which creates a tiny transistor-like industry, for the placing of Negro tokens.

Booker Washington prepared the way for such utilization of Negroes. Martin Luther King, as a faceless social factor, is the same man. Both men are simply public servants. Washington solidified the separate but equal lie, when that lie was of value to the majority of intelligent white men. King's lie is that there is a moral requirement to be met before entrance into the secular kingdom of plenty. This is the reason Washington said Negroes had to labor in the wings in the first place: to *get ready* for this entrance. Rev. King, who is formed very clearly and expertly from the same missionary fabric, comes bearing the same message of goodwill—that once this moral requirement is met by all Negroes (*i.e.*, the poor and brutalized will immediately rise once they understand this) then they might pass easily and joyously into that burning building which he insists on calling Heaven, even though gasoline is being spread on the blaze on all sides by every suffering man in the world. The reward for piety and high moral concern then is to be a membership in Gomorrah. . . .

For every token offered in the general interest of keeping goodwill between the black middle class and the Liberal/Missionary power structure, the gap between this invented bourgeoisie and the majority of black men in this country is widened. The tokens are more and more bizarre, have more and more supposed power and influence, but at each instance the poor black man gets even statistically poorer and less accessible to utopian propaganda. But the public servant function of the black middle class, especially as indicated by the performance of its chiefs like King, Roy Wilkins, Whitney Young, etc., is one of communication and control. That is, they present the "demands" of the black middle class to the white ruling class, and in exchange, as payment for the meeting of some of these demands—usually such social treachery as token integration which involves the creation of a lucrative civil rights *industry*—they relay that ruling class's wishes to the great mass of Negroes, while making sure that none of this mass becomes autonomous enough to make demands of its own. . . .

. . . Absence of violence was the commitment these leaders asked, have always asked, and again it was given, by poor and lower middle-class Negroes and those strivers who had to be on the scene. And if word got back to the leaders that the silent weight, the poor blacks, were uneasy at being left to rot in the same ghettoes (without the slightest hope or chance of their misery being eased, except by making that symbolic leap into Bourgeois commitment, which is the local utopia) and dwelt by such uneasiness upon the impossibility of such advice, then King would walk among them praying, seeking to involve the most oppressed people in this country in a sham ethic that only has value for the middle-class power structure, and that even in those uses remains artificial, except as it maintains local and national social evils with an admirable stability. When this uneasiness would manifest itself as actuality or actual possibility, then these bearers of the missionary legacy would quickly seek to turn whatever energy that existed into confusion, and always shame. "Let it be our blood," King says to the poor, making an opportunistic identification he trusts even "backward" white people will understand as *leadership*. And when that cry of "passive resistance" is translated into common social activity, it means very simply, "Do as you have been doing, and some white miracle will prove your suffering was accidental, and finally worthwhile."

2

Violence or nonviolence as actualities have never been real categories. Rather, their use is symbolic in discussing possible goals of any Negro "progress" in this country (and the white West). Negroes, except for isolated, *i.e.,* limitedly organized and unconnected, incidents, have never been anything else but nonviolent. There have been race riots, when the "liberalizing" elements of the white power structure have been briefly stalemated, and the brainwashed lower class and lower middle-class whites have clashed with those economically similar groups of Negroes. (In purely idealistic terms the real tragedy is that these two groups could not find goals that were mutually attainable in some kind of egalitarian "revolution" that would simply kill off their mutual oppressors and resurrect a "system" that would be workable for men who could utilize all their energies within it. Such a revolution was possible at the end of the Civil War . . .)

But for the most part there has been no violence from the black man. American Indians tried violently to defend their lands from white expansionism, but the material superiority of Western culture, and of the peculiar aggressiveness of humanist industrialism, was, of course, much too powerful. It is a humanist industrialism that has always longed for the twentieth century, *i.e.,* a century when man really is the measure, and literally has his fate clutched quite tightly in his spastic hands. A century where the only gods are immediately useful, and grow angry only as their worshipers do. The moral priggishness of the Western white man, which grows to insane proportions in America, is displayed religiously in every part of the world he has exploited. The ritual murders in the name of reason and progress go on every hour, in every part of the globe. How many nonwhite peoples have been killed in Asia, in Africa, in Latin America, just since 1945, in the name of some almost mystical need for a consistently accommodating order? The "Free World" is merely that part of the world in which the white man is free to do as he wants with the rest of the people there. And he has ruled this way since the Elizabethans.

When the white man says *violence,* he means first of all violence to his system, the possibility of outright war to change the political and economic categories of rule. But this has to do with thought, primarily, rather than the actual utilization of arms by Negroes to attain some arbitrary political and economic goals. The middle-class Negro's first word on the subject of violence, as it is sheepishly (and unintentionally) given reference as a possibility in the real world, is that, "We couldn't win anyway." But the real idea expressed here is that the bourgeois black man does not believe he could benefit by a total withdrawal from white society, which could be manifest by simple political rebellion. And in this sense any attempt at such rebellion represents "violence." (In the same sense, the political overtones of the Muslim movement represent this kind of violence against the liberal middle-class missionary power structure, as withdrawal and actual political rebellion. This is why the intelligent white man and the middle-class Negro are so frightened of this group. Because, certainly, the only real terror in Elijah Muhammad's program is the fact that even though it utilizes a fancied ethnic hegemony as its catalyst, its "goals" and its version of U.S. social history are quite practical, as even a thinker like Thomas Jefferson has attested. "The slave . . . when freed . . . is to be removed beyond the reach of mixture. . . .")

But a political rebellion within the existing social structure is impossible. Any energy seen to exist within the superstructure of American society is almost immediately harnessed within acceptable motifs, and shaped for use by the mainstream, whether the results of this process are called Swing music or CORE. The intent is the same: *white music.* There is no way the black man can be heard, or seen clearly, in the existing system. Muslims would be rounded up and dropped in the Grand Canyon before any kind of territorial gift would be made. Absolutely no "violence," no real social or political rebellion, will be tolerated by the static center, and for this reason this center assumes a flexibility which allows it to sweep from right to left without actually moving at all. It merely gets stronger and essentially more intransigent. "We will risk our cities to defend Berlin," is one answer.

Since Negroes have never tried to mount any organized physical violence, and any political violence to the system is, by the nature of the black man's oppression almost impossible (even though there are attempts from time to time, such as the new all black Freedom Now party, which by the very exclusivity of its form proposes a very practical dissent, hence violence, to the existing party system) one might wonder just why it is so necessary for white liberals and the Negro middle class to exhort Negroes constantly to follow a path that, willingly or not, they have always followed? It would seem, if one examines the history of black men in the West, and especially in the United States, that they have most often been objects of violence rather than perpetrators. It would seem too that if there were any need to caution some group against violence, and influence them toward a path of righteous passivity and moral indignation, it would be the white man, at this point, who needed such persuasion. As exiled ex-NAACP leader Robert Williams has said, "How much money has been expended to convert the racist brutes of the social jungle of the South to the ism of nonviolence and love? How many nonviolent workshops are being conducted in Ku Klux Klan dominated communities and racist strongholds of hate and violence against Afro-Americans?"

Nonviolence, as a theory of social and political demeanor concerning American Negroes, means simply a continuation of the *status quo*. As this "theory" is applied to define specific terms of personal conduct Negroes are supposed to utilize, it assumes, again, the nature of that mysterious moral commitment Negro leaders say the black man must make to participate as a privileged class among the oppressed. Nonviolence on this personal (moral) level is the most sinister application of the Western method of confusing and subjugating peoples by convincing these peoples that the white West knows what is best for them. Since the Negro exists at a particular place in American society, which has been constantly redefined by the warring elements in white society.

Nonviolence and Passive Resistance are only the echoes of a contemporary redefinition of the Negro's place, as seen by the most powerful of those elements, the industrial-liberal née missionary element, which since the Civil War has held the upper hand in the overall power structure of the society. But even couched in purely secular terms, the emphasis on passive resistance and moral suasion is an undiluted leftover from the missionary era, and its intentions are exactly the same. Only God has been replaced, as he has all over the West, with respectability and air conditioning. The Negro must have both before he is "ready" for equality is the way another answer goes. To enter into the mainstream of American society the Negro *must* lose all identity as a Negro, as a carrier of possible dissent. He must even assume a common cultural liability, and when the time comes for this white society to die, he will be asked to die with it, and for the same reasons it will die. But there is no indication that the poor have any such communal suicide in mind, not that they have any theories or bodies of social reasoning to the contrary; it is merely that in most parts of America the social system still hews to the intransigence of its beginnings and no real advance into that mainstream is really being offered. The white liberal's plan is still too academic to really work. But then what *will* happen? What will Negroes do? Are there any alternatives?

3

All black political thrusts, that is, any that could issue from the actual needs of the masses of Negroes are blocked, either by the sham "leadership" of the middle-class Negro, whose whole tradition is based on selling out his poorer brothers, or by the intransigence of those whites who are "behind the times," as any liberal spokesman will tell them. An America made up strictly of such backward types of white men would survive only a few more years before internal disorder and/or external pressures resulted in out-and-out racial wars. (Asia, Africa, Latin America, and Black America versus the white West.) But the feigned flexibility of the center permits a certain toughness for the American way that will take some pushing to topple completely. Nonviolence is such a feigned flexibility. It allows some gesture of social and political "protest," but offers no real alternative to the existing order. But, again, what is the black man's alternative? Very simply, either he must find some way to do political and social violence to the existing system, even though he is hampered at every step by the black middle class and the white power structure, or an actual physical violence will result.

When those four children were killed in the Birmingham bombing, the US Steel plant in that city should have been shut down by Negroes. Black workers should have walked out of every job they hold in the city. A general strike should have been called. An attempt should have been made to shut down completely the city's industrial resources. That city should have died, should have been killed by Negroes. At this writing the bombers have still not been found, and no attempts have been made toward finding an "equitable" position for Negroes in that city, if that's what was supposed to have happened. All of this happened two or three weeks after the great March On Washington. And nothing else could have shown the moral sham involved in that lugubrious display as horribly as that bombing. Martin Luther King arrived in Birmingham hours after the bombing to quiet the crowds and give a quiet light of hope to the middle class. But no real hope or stance is offered by black leaders in the face of such treachery. Talks in poolrooms with "the 4th St. toughs," about the dignity of man, to men whose dignity consists in their constant resistance to the yoke of cultural compromise white men call their place. One young slick-haired cat chalking his cue and looking straight into the television camera, after that same bombing, said, "There's a whole lotta' people ain't gonna stand for much more 'a this." Meaning: "I am not the president's Assistant Press Secretary nor the first Negro to appear in a Chemical Corn Bank television commercial, but nobody's gonna run over me because of it."

The point is, I think, that the poor black realizes, at least instinctively, that no matter what deal goes down, *i.e.,* no matter which side "wins out," the "Crackers" or the Government, no help at all is being offered to him. The desegregation of schools has been largely a lie, the increase of employment among chronically unemployed Negroes has also not happened. The battle of housing is to determine whether a Negro who is able to buy a $12,000 house can live in it. There is no doubt that soon he might be able to, but that means little to most Negroes. . . .

In the United Nations a few days ago only the United States, Great Britain, France, and the white "Free World" abstained from voting on a resolution to make illegal any organization that promotes race prejudice. In Latin America governments change hands monthly, and no matter how repressive, illegal, and non-representative a government might be, as long as it plays ball with the United States, is "anti-Communist," we say nothing. It is only in Cuba that something is going on of which we disapprove. But why? In South Vietnam and South Korea the United States supports the most brutal governments in the world. Part of the sugar quota is transferred to South Africa. We sign a new contract with Franco. And this is the society Rev. King wants to get the poor Negro ready to enter. Better Hell itself. But "partnership" in Gomorrah is the best thing offered by the white man to the Negro in America today. This is in essence what the promoters of Nonviolence represent to the Negro masses. The March On Washington, for instance, began as an idea of protest against the system, but was quickly turned into a night-club act, and a "moral victory" for the middle classes, with marines and plainclothesmen on the scene just to make sure the audience liked the show they were going to put on.

Nonviolence then is not a protest at all, in the context it has been promoted into in America. It has to do with India too, just as Rev. King thinks it does. And just *what* did nonviolence accomplish there? The Germans were our enemies and they are better off than the great majority of Indians. Plague and hunger still ravage India: and for all the lies and rhetoric that issue from the West about that country's independence and the political individuality of Mr. Nehru, India for all practical purposes is still a crown colony. It is still very much exploited by Great Britain and the rest of the Western world. . . .

What other goals can the Negro realize in America? The "out of date" white man, who is perhaps in one manner of speaking more honest, is offering the Negro nothing at all, except what has always been offered the black man in white society. He is saying if the Negro wants *anything* further than what the white man has always given he is going to have to take it. And this kind of white man will take steps immediately to see that such taking remains, as it has always remained, in the context of an "orderly" American society, unheard of. The liberal white man does not even offer the possibility of such "taking." His only goal for the Negro is that the Negro remain nonviolent. In exchange for this non-violence this liberal power structure will send an army into Mississippi to see that its symbols are accepted by white and black alike, but in essence this is all this power structure offers and what it hopes Negroes will continue to accept. It offers Negroes nothing further in their or its life time. Nonviolence, then, is not being offered as a means to an end, but as the end in itself.

The Negro's real problem remains in finding some actual goal to work toward. A complete equality of means is impossible in the present state of American society. And even if it were pos-sible, the society is horrible enough without Negroes swelling its ranks. The only genuine way, it seems to me, for the Negro to achieve a personal autonomy, this equality of means, would be as a truly active moralizing force within or *against* American so-ciety as it now stands. In this sense I advocate a violence, a literal murdering of the American socio-political stance, not only as it directly concerns American Negroes, but in terms of its stranglehold on most of the modern world.

The Negro must take an extreme stance, must attack the white man's system, using his own chains to help beat that system into submission and actual change. The black man is the only revo-lutionary force in American society today, if only by default. The supposed Christian ideal of Nonviolence is aimed at quieting even this most natural of insurrectionary elements. As an actual moral category all rational men are essentially nonviolent, except in defense of their lives. To ask that the black man not even defend himself (as Robert Williams tried to defend himself and the rest of the black community of Monroe, North Carolina, a few years ago, before he was framed in a bogus kidnapping charge by local whites with the aid of the Federal Government) is to ask that that black man stay quiet in his chains while the most "liberal" elements in this country saw away at those chains with make-believe saws. The Negro, again, in this instance, is asked to be what the white man makes of him. Not only does the white man oppress the Negro, but he is even going to tell him how to react under the oppression. Surely, however, the most patiently Christian man must realize that self-defense in any situation is honest and natural. It is also obligatory, otherwise there is no use in asking for any right since the asker will probably not be around to benefit by its granting.

But if the most violent political and social protests are muffled (and the exile of Robert Williams seems to me one notable example of such muffling; the attempted jailing of newsman William Worthy for trying to find out about China and Cuba another) and the moral bankruptcy of the black middle class continues to be used by the white ruling class as its cynical symbol of Negro "progress," then it seems to me that quite soon an actual physical violence *will* break out. For every lie that the liberal power structure tells itself, the black bourgeoisie, and the rest of the world about the majority of Negroes in this country, alienates that majority even more critically. By not allowing a real "grassroots" protest to issue from the core of the oppressed black masses, the American white man is forcing another kind of protest to take shape. One that will shake this whole society at its foundations, and succeed in changing it, if only into something worse.

Soon, for every sham gesture like the March On Washington or the still impending "deal" King and the other black "leaders" made with white Birmingham, there may be twice that many acts of unorganized responsive violence. How much longer does anyone in this country, black or white, think that the "4th St. toughs," *i.e.,* the oppressed black man, who has made no deals with the white power structure, nor received any favors, is going to run from policeman and dogs, or stand by and watch while "unknown assailants" blow up their pitiful homes? Is it possible that the American white man knows so little about Negroes, from whatever level he does his observing, that he thinks these Negroes believe or have ever believed in the justice and morality of the white man? Left to their own devices, the masses of Negroes will finally strike back, perhaps even kill, in a vertiginous gesture of fear and despair. Their anger will not even matter, since it has been a hopelessly familiar element in their emotional lives.

Nonviolence can be your "goal" if you are already sitting in a comfortable house being brought the news of your oppression over television. It *can* be the normal conduct of rational men if they can believe in the literalness and effectiveness of what they are trying to accomplish by such conduct. But walk, on any night, from one end of 125th Street (in New York's Harlem) to the other, and count the hundred policemen and figure out the climate of rational conduct that is being cultivated by such an environment.

A legitimate Negro protest movement unstalemated by the sham of tokenism and filthy bourgeois intention might succeed in remaking this society, and establishing an honest connection between it and the rest of the nonwhite world. But most of the leaders of what passes as such protest, the middle-class Negroes and white liberals, who have access to courtrooms and picket lines, have already sold their souls. Finally, it would seem that for the mass of Negroes such leadership as they need will be spawned within their own ranks, bolstered by those young Negroes from the middle class who recognize themselves the hopelessness of their social connections. But this leadership is most likely to take solid form only in the most repressive and irrational of circumstances. The most horrible vision I have is that the white man, in growing terror of those suddenly ubiquitous acts of unorganized violence to which the most oppressed black men might resort, will become even more repressive, and even the veneer of the liberal establishment will be stripped away (in much the same way that such veneer has been worn away in international affairs or in dealing with the possibility of actual domestic political dissent. The Communist party is already outlawed. Mail is being opened. Phones are being tapped. The penalty for traveling to Cuba is five years in prison and five thousand dollars fine, they say. Where will such insanity lead?) And in such instances these unconnected acts of responsive violence would increase, and perhaps even gradually find their connection. The result of such chaos is anybody's guess. Guerilla warfare, concentration camps? But one of our congressmen has said recently that our only real ally in Africa is South Africa. And the only "foolproof" way to completely stop legitimate Negro protest, especially as it grows more agitated by the lies and malice of most of America, and agitated, I am saying, into actual bloodletting, would be to follow the South African example (or Hitler's). I hope this is ugly fantasy too. But there are very few white men in this country who are doing anything to prevent this. The present emphasis on Nonviolence rather than honest attempts at socio-economic reconstruction will only speed the coming of such horror.

Part Two

Patterns of Confrontation
Outside the Law

Most Americans, especially since the time of the First World War, have become suspicious of rhetoric. Action, they believe, furnishes the only valid test of a man's convictions. There is an enormous difference, from this point of view, between talking about revolution in Herbert Marcuse's parlor and actually throwing up barricades. It is this very distinction, between words and action, which formed the basis for the Supreme Court's "clear and present danger" ruling on the issue of free speech in 1920.

And yet of course the meaning of this dividing line may easily be exaggerated. Actual revolutions, except for palace coups, always require verbal slogans and images. Existing legal systems similarly depend for their survival upon patriotic concepts as well as upon a monopoly of physical force; a pledge of allegiance is a more economical guarantee of civil order than a soldier standing on every corner. Words can play a crucial role both in exciting people and in lulling them. A more significant boundary than that running between words and action may well be that between private thought and public verbal commitment.

In turning, therefore, from rhetoric about law and order to accounts of Americans who have concretely flouted the law for a significant purpose, we are not moving from one distinct universe to another. The connections between intellectual attitudes and practical consequences are constantly worth seeking out. These connections especially reveal themselves in the motives of the actors on all sides of each historical drama. One should not forget the need for carefully assessing these motives while exploring the controversial and sometimes almost melodramatic episodes which this part of the volume contains.

Here one may find evidence which bears directly on the question of what limits existed in the treatment of unpopular minorities by the democratic majority in America. In pondering those limits, one should recall that, while radicals like Ben Reitman usually (though not always) escaped with a coat of tar and feathers, dozens of black Americans each year were tortured, mutilated, and killed under similar circumstances.[1]

1. "In the ten years from January 1, 1918, through 1927, American mobs lynched 454 persons. Of these, 38 were white, and 416 were coloured. Eleven of the Negro victims were women, three of them at the time of lynching with child. Forty-two of the victims were burned alive. . . . Eight of the victims were beaten to death or cut to pieces. Sixty-six of 454 lynchings, therefore, were executed with . . . bestiality. . . . Of the sixty-six cases—instances of drowning or of tying the body to an automobile and dragging it through the streets are not included—four were of white victims, three burnings and one beating to death. The remaining sixty-two victims were Negroes." Walter White, *Rope and Faggot* (New York: Knopf, 1929), pp. 20–21. The rate of lynching was far higher in the late nineteenth century and the Progressive Era; from 1889 to 1899 it averaged 187.5 persons per year. In the earlier period the proportion of whites lynched was much larger, and so was the proportion of lynchings that took place outside the South. Arthur Raper, *The Tragedy of Lynching* (Chapel Hill, N.C.: University of North Carolina Press, 1933), p. 25, quoted in Hadley Cantril, *The Psychology of Social Movements* (New York: Wiley, 1941), p. 81, which contains a good brief summary article on the subject of lynching. Lynching largely disappeared after the Second World War.

Extralegal Majorities

Vigilantism as a mainstream tendency in nineteenth-century America was described at some length in an opening essay to this volume. Also discussed were the effects of romantic attitudes toward emotional release, both on a popular level in shaping responses to the violence of the Wild West, and on a very different level among a small minority of radical intellectuals.[1]

These themes may now be traced in a series of concrete settings which extend from frontier vigilantism down into the modern urban environment.[2]

10. The Frontier Outlaw and the Community

"The Hanging of 'Captain' Slade" is a beautiful vignette. It captures, perhaps more fully than any other single document, the personality of the Western outlaw and the character of community responses to him in the period of the frontier. Not, of course, that all outlaws were alike, but one gains a strong feeling that the town and the episode here recounted were nearly archetypical. Perhaps one is swayed toward such a judgment by Dimsdale's almost Thucydidean prose, simultaneously embodying restrained detachment, painstaking factual care (in a locale dependent largely upon oral history), and an obviously deep concern for all the characters in the drama.

In this episode, then, one may find much suggestive evidence

1. See above, pp. 18–29.
2. First-hand accounts of a far larger number of occurrences of this kind are contained in John W. Caughey, *Their Majesties the Mob, op. cit.* Unlike Caughey, I have sought to include only a few unusually vivid and representative episodes and to present each of them in some depth.

for a discussion of pre-industrial American attitudes toward violence, law, and social control. The problem of interpretation immediately divides itself into three aspects: Slade's own make-up,
the temperament of his loyal supporters, and the attitude of the
rest of the community. (His followers of course often blended
into the community structure.)

As for Slade himself, a modern reader is apt to conclude that
he was mentally ill. Not merely do his uncontrollable spasms of
violence imply this, but also the rapid switches he made between
two quite separate personalities. Further, there is the fact that
on at least one occasion he mutilated his murder victim—a rare
occurrence which went against the grain of the usual code of outlawry. There is, it is true, a certain amount of contrary evidence.
He was warmly attached to his friends and seems to have sacrificed himself for them on occasion; he was happily married to a
devoted wife; and he appears to have been both rational and
somewhat apologetic during the intervals between his destructive
bouts. But these complications, interesting as they are, do not
seem to tip the balance.

What partially disguises Slade's madness, however, is that its
form embodied the romantic version of "individualism" which
was so widely implanted in the popular American mind. When
most Americans thought of self-assertion, they did not envision
retreating to Walden; their mental image was much closer to one
of galloping down Main Street wildly firing their revolvers. Thus
Slade could be admired by many men who knew him, up to a long
point, not just for one but for both of his twin personalities—the
warm, comradely one and the other one which we now tend to
label sick.

All this emphasizes the vast gulf between popular and intellectual forms of Romanticism in America. Radicals like Voltairine
de Cleyre (and in our own day Herbert Marcuse or Norman O.
Brown) could speak passionately of a need for human 'liberation," yet by it they meant a heightening of consciousness usually
as an aftermath to prolonged study or contemplation. More than
these intellectuals liked to admit, they looked forward to a utopian
universalization of their own rigorous and highly premeditated
style of thinking and living. These mental projections might sometimes include an element of revolutionary violence. Yet the deliberate, calculated throwing of a bomb by an anarchist has
almost nothing in common with the nonreflective, shoot-'em-up
form of release with which "Captain" Slade and his followers

casually identified themselves. Or, to put this another way: latter-day anarchists attend art films, not formula Westerns.

In the realm of the popular imagination, by contrast, "liberation" has meant little more than going berserk. Such a state may be admired or it may be feared, but in either case that is its total extent as a conception. For a great many people, release still takes the form of a spree. It is a phase in a cycle of limited duration, after which one puritanically identifies oneself as a "backslider." In this alternation, the countertug of Sunday morning defines the pull of Saturday night. The activities of "Captain" Slade revealed this rhythm in an extreme fashion. Every once in a while he felt an absolutely uncontrollable urge to ride through the town, smashing things destructively and asserting his supremacy.

Was this entire spasmodic pattern, involving not only himself but his followers, an intrinsically sick form of release from authority? Intellectuals are prone to label any form of liberation other than their own as "false consciousness," as a profound symptom of social malaise rather than merely as an alternative mode of expression indulged in by a group with a different life style. My own conviction is that "Captain" Slade was sick as an individual, but that a historian should exercise caution in applying blanket psychological judgments to his many Montana admirers. Psychological indictments, especially of groups, are weapons to be used only sparingly. It would be more to the point, by way of establishing a proper distance between these frontier Montanans and ourselves, simply to affirm that Slade's lure over his community now seems distasteful, and leave it at that. Further, to understand Slade's power over men's minds, one should not forget that the frontier, due mainly to its low population density, attracted an unusual number of "Slade" types, enabling them to fulfill themselves with far more immunity than would have been permitted in thickly settled regions.

The ambivalence with which much of the town regarded Slade is central to the meaning of the story. Despite its torn feelings, the community eventually closed in on Slade with a sure instinct. Vigilantism was here the device which almost ritualistically brought a spree to its close after it had run its course. The puritanical, or "spasmodic," form of liberation may often have required such policing; indeed, it may have been bound into its very logic. The sober miners and townsmen seem to have known when it was appropriate for them to play their parts. All this remains true even though one may also wonder whether, if only Slade had not gone quite so far, the community might not willingly have deferred to him for a much longer period of time

Thomas J. Dimsdale, "The Hanging of 'Captain' Slade"

J. A. Slade, or, as he was often called, Captain Slade, was raised in Clinton County, Ill., and was a member of a highly respectable family. He bore a good character for several years in that place. The acts which have given so wide a celebrity to his name were performed especially on the Overland Line, of which he was for years an official. Reference to these matters will be made in a subsequent part of this chapter.

Captain J. A. Slade came to Virginia City in the spring of 1863. He was a man gifted with the power of making money, and when free from the influence of alcoholic stimulants, which seemed to reverse his nature, and to change a kind-hearted and intelligent gentleman into a reckless demon, no man in the Territory had a greater faculty of attracting the favorable notice of even strangers, and in spite of the wild lawlessness which characterized his frequent spells of intoxication, he had many, very many friends whom no commission of crime itself could detach from his personal companionship. Another and less desirable class of friends were attracted by his very recklessness. There are probably a thousand individuals in the West possessing a correct knowledge of the leading incidents of a career that terminated at the gallows, who still speak of Slade as a perfect gentleman, and who not only lament his death, but talk in the highest terms of his character, and pronounce his execution a murder. One way of accounting for the diversity of opinion regarding Slade is sufficiently obvious. Those who saw him in his natural state only would pronounce him to be a kind husband, a most hospitable

---

Originally published in Thomas J. Dimsdale, *Vigilantes of Montana, or Popular Justice in the Rocky Mountains* (Virginia City, Mont.: D. W. Tilton & Co., 1866); reprinted in Joseph Kinsey Howard, ed., *Montana Margins: A State Anthology* (New Haven, Conn.: Yale University Press, 1946), pp. 113–122. It is printed here in its entirety.

host and courteous gentleman. On the contrary, those who met him when maddened with liquor and surrounded by a gang of armed roughs, would pronounce him a fiend incarnate.

During the summer of 1863 he went to Milk River as a freighter. For this business he was eminently qualified, and he made a great deal of money. Unfortunately his habit of profuse expenditure was uncontrollable, and at the time of his execution he was deeply in debt almost everywhere.

After the execution of the five men on the 14th of January the Vigilantes considered that their work was nearly ended. They had freed the country from highwaymen and murderers to a great extent, and they determined that in the absence of the regular civil authority they would establish a People's Court, where all offenders should be tried by a judge and jury. This was the nearest approach to social order that the circumstances permitted, and though strict legal authority was wanting, yet the people were firmly determined to maintain its efficiency and to enforce its decrees. It may here be mentioned that the overt act which was the last round on the fatal ladder leading to the scaffold on which Slade perished, was the tearing in pieces and stamping upon a writ of this court, followed by the arrest of the judge, Alex Davis, by authority of a presented derringer and with his own hands.

J. A. Slade was himself, we have been informed, a Vigilanter; he openly boasted of it, and said he knew all that they knew. He was never accused or even suspected of either murder or robbery committed in this Territory (the latter crimes were never laid to his charge in any place); but that he had killed several men in other localities was notorious, and his bad reputation in this respect was a most powerful argument in determining his fate, when he was finally arrested for the offense above mentioned. On returning from Milk River he became more and more addicted to drinking; until at last it was a common feat for him and his friends to "take the town." He and a couple of his dependents might often be seen on one horse, galloping through the streets, shouting and yelling, firing revolvers, etc. On many occasions he would ride his horse into stores; break up bars, toss the scales out of doors, and use most insulting language to parties present. Just previous to the day of his arrest he had given a fearful beating to one of his followers; but such was his influence over them that the man wept bitterly at the gallows, and begged for his life with all his power. It had become quite common when Slade was on a spree for the shopkeepers and citizens to close the stores and put out all the lights; being fearful of some outrage at his hands. One store in Nevada he never ventured to enter—that of the Lott brothers—as they had taken care to let him know that any attempt of the kind would be followed by his sudden death, and though he often rode down there, threatening to break in and raise ——, yet, he never attempted to carry his threat into execution. For his wanton destruction of goods and furniture he was always ready to pay when sober if he had the money; but there were not a few who regarded payment as small satisfaction for the outrage, and these men were his personal enemies.

From time to time, Slade received warnings from men that he well knew would not deceive him, of the certain end of his conduct. There was not a moment, for two weeks previous to his arrest, in which the public did not expect to hear of some bloody outrage. The dread of his very name, and the presence of the armed band of hangers-on who followed him, alone prevented a resistance which must certainly have ended in the instant murder or mutilation of the opposing party.

Slade was frequently arrested by order of the court whose organization we have described, and had treated it with respect by paying one or two fines, and promising to pay the rest when he had money; but in the transaction that occurred at this crisis, he forgot even this caution, and goaded by passion and the hatred of restraint, he sprang into the embrace of death.

Slade had been drunk and "cutting up" all night. He and his companions had made the town a perfect hell. In the morning, J. M. Fox, the sheriff, met him, arrested him, took him into court, and commenced reading a warrant that he had for his arrest, by way of arraignment. He became uncontrollably furious, and seizing the writ, he tore it up, threw it on the ground, and stamped on it. The clicking of the locks of his companions' revolvers was instantly heard and a crisis was expected. The sheriff did not attempt his capture; but being at least as prudent as he was valiant, he succumbed, leaving Slade the master of the situation, and the conqueror and ruler of the courts, law and lawmakers. This was a declaration of war, and was so accepted. The Vigilance Committee now felt that the question of social order and the preponderance of the law-abiding citizens had then and there to be decided. They knew the character of Slade, and they were well aware that they must submit to his rule without murmur, or else that he must be dealt with in such fashion as would prevent his being able to wreak his vengeance on the Committee, who could never have hoped to live in the Territory secure from outrage and death, and who could never leave it without encountering his friends, whom his victory would have emboldened and stimulated to a pitch that would have rendered them reckless of consequences. The day previous, he had ridden into Dorris's store, and on being requested to leave, he drew his revolver and threatened to kill the gentlemen who spoke to him. Another saloon he had led his horse into, and buying a bottle of wine, he tried to make the animal drink it. This was not considered an uncommon performance, as he had often entered saloons, and commenced firing at the lamps, causing a wild stampede.

A leading member of the Committee met Slade, and informed him in the quiet, earnest manner of one who feels the importance of what he is saying, "Slade, get your horse at once, and go home, or there will be ———— to pay." Slade started and took a long look with his dark and piercing eyes, at the gentleman—"What do you mean?" said he. "You have no right to ask me what I mean," was the quiet reply, "get your horse at once, and remember what I tell you." After a short pause he promised to do so, and actually got into the saddle; but, being still intoxicated, he began calling aloud to one after another of his friends, and at last seemed to have forgotten the warning he had received and became again uproarious, shouting the name of a well-known prostitute in company with those of two men whom he considered heads of the Committee, as a sort of challenge, perhaps, however, as a single act of bravado. It seems probable that the intimation of personal danger he had received had not been forgotten entirely; though, fatally for him, he took a foolish way of showing his remembrance of it. He sought out Alexander Davis, the Judge of the Court, and drawing a cocked derringer, he presented it at his head, and told him that he should hold him as a hostage for his own safety. As the Judge stood perfectly quiet, and offered no resistance to his captor, no further outrage followed on this score. Previous to this, on account of the critical state of affairs, the Committee had met, and at last resolved to arrest him. His execution had not been agreed upon, and, at that time, would have been negatived, most assuredly. A messenger rode down to Nevada to inform the leading men of what was on hand, as it was desirable to show that there was a feeling of unanimity on the subject, all along the Gulch.

The miners turned out almost en masse, leaving their work and forming in solid column, about six hundred strong, armed to the teeth, they marched up to Virginia. The leader of the body well knew the temper of his men on the subject. He spurred on ahead of them, and hastily calling a meeting of the Executive, he told them plainly that the miners meant "business," and that, if they came up, they would not stand in the street to be shot down by Slade's friends; but that they would take him and hang him. The meeting was small, as the Virginia men were loath to act at all. This momentous announcement of the feeling of the Lower Town was made to a cluster of men, who were deliberating behind a wagon, at the rear of a store on Main street, where the Ohling-house stone building now stands.

The Committee was most unwilling to proceed to extremities. All the duty they had ever performed seemed as nothing to the task before them; but they had to decide, and that quickly. It was finally agreed that if the whole body of the miners were of the opinion that he should be hanged, the Committee left it in their hands to deal with him. Off, at hot speed, rode the leader of the Nevada men to join his command.

Slade had found out what was intended, and the news sobered him instantly. He went into P. S. Pfouts' store, where Davis was, and apologized for his conduct, saying that he would take it all back.

The head of the column now wheeled into Wallace street and marched up at quick time. Halting in front of the store, the executive officer of the Committee stepped forward and arrested Slade, who was at once informed of his doom, and inquiry was made as to whether he had any business to settle. Several parties spoke to him on the subject; but to all such inquiries he turned a deaf ear, being entirely absorbed in the terrifying reflections on his own awful position. He never ceased his entreaties for life, and to see his dear wife. The unfortunate lady referred to, between whom and Slade there existed a warm affection, was at this time living at their ranch on the Madison. She was possessed of considerable personal attractions; tall, well-formed, of graceful carriage, pleasing manners, and was, withal, an accomplished horsewoman.

A messenger from Slade rode at full speed to inform her of her husband's arrest. In an instant she was in the saddle, and with all the energy that love and despair could lend to an ardent temperament and a strong physique, she urged her fleet charger over the twelve miles of rough and rocky ground that intervened between her and the object of her passionate devotion.

Meanwhile a party of volunteers had made the necessary preparations for the execution, in the valley traversed by the branch. Beneath the site of Pfouts' and Russell's stone building there was a corral, the gate-posts of which were strong and high. Across the top was laid a beam, to which the rope was fastened, and a dry-goods box served for the platform. To this place Slade was marched, surrounded by a guard, composing the best-armed and most numerous force that has ever appeared in Montana Territory.

The doomed man had so exhausted himself by tears, prayers, and lamentations, that he had scarcely strength left to stand under the fatal beam. He repeatedly exclaimed, "My God! my God! Must I die? Oh, my dear wife!"

On the return of the fatigue party, they encountered some friends of Slade, staunch and reliable citizens and members of the Committee, but who were personally attached to the condemned. On hearing of his sentence, one of them, a stout-hearted man, pulled out his handkerchief and walked away, weeping like a child. Slade still begged to see his wife most piteously, and it seemed hard to deny his request; but the bloody consequences that were sure to follow the inevitable attempt at a rescue, that her presence and entreaties would have certainly incited, forbade the granting of his request. Several gentlemen were sent for to see him in his last moments, one of whom (Judge Davis) made a short address to the people; but in such low tones as to be inaudible, save to a few in his immediate vicinity. One of his friends, after exhausting his powers of entreaty, threw off his coat and declared that the prisoner could not be hanged until he himself was killed. A hundred guns were instantly leveled at him; whereupon he turned and fled; but, being brought back, he was compelled to resume his coat, and to give a promise of future peaceable demeanor.

Scarcely a leading man in Virginia could be found, though numbers of the citizens joined the ranks of the guard when the arrest was made. All lamented the stern necessity which dictated the execution.

Everything being ready, the command was given, "Men, do your duty," and the box being instantly slipped from beneath his feet, he died almost instantaneously.

The body was cut down and carried to the Virginia Hotel, where, in a darkened room, it was scarcely laid out, when the unfortunate and bereaved companion of the deceased arrived, at headlong speed, to find that all was over, and that she was a widow. Her grief and heart-piercing cries were terrible evidences of the depth of her attachment for her lost husband, and a considerable period elapsed before she could regain the command of her excited feelings.

J. A. Slade was, during his connection with the Overland Stage Company, frequently involved in quarrels which terminated fatally for his antagonists. The first and most memorable of these was his encounter with Jules, a station-keeper at Julesburg, on the Platte River. Between the inhabitants, the emigrants and the stage people, there was a constant feud, arising from quarrels about missing stock, alleged to have been stolen by the settlers, which constantly resulted in personal difficulties, such as beating, shooting, stabbing, etc., and it was from this cause that Slade became involved in a transaction which had become inseparably associated with his name, and which has given a coloring and tone to all descriptions of him, from the date of the occurrence to the present day.

There have been so many versions of the affair, all of them differing more or less in important particulars, that it has seemed impossible to get at the exact truth; but the following account may be relied on as substantially correct:

From overlanders and dwellers on the road we learn that Jules was himself a lawless and tyrannical man, taking such liberties with the coach stock and carrying matters with so high a hand that the company determined on giving the agency of the division to J. A. Slade. In a business point of view, they were correct in their selection. The coach went through at all hazards. It is not to be supposed that Jules would submit to the authority of a newcomer, or, indeed, to any man that he could intimidate; and a very limited intercourse was sufficient to increase the mutual dislike of the parties, so far as to occasion an open rupture and bloodshed. Slade, it is said, had employed a man discharged by Jules, which irritated the latter considerably; but the overt act that brought matters to a crisis was the recovery by Slade of a team "sequestrated" by Jules. Some state that there had been a previous altercation between the two; but, whether this be true or not, it appears certain that on the arrival of the coach, with Slade as a passenger, Jules determined to arrest the team, then and there; and that, finding Slade was equally determined on putting them through, a few expletives were exchanged, and Jules fired his gun, loaded with buckshot, at Slade, who was unarmed at the time, wounding him severely. At his death, Slade carried several of these shots in his body. Slade went down the road, till he recovered of his wound. Jules left the place, and in his travels never failed to let everybody know that he would kill Slade, who, on his part, was not backward in reciprocating such promises. At last, Slade got well; and, shortly after, was informed that his enemy had been "corralled by the boys," whereupon he went to the place designated, and tying him fast, shot him to death by degrees. He also cut off his ears, and carried them in his vest pocket for a long time.

One man declares that Slade went up to the ranch where he had heard that Jules was and, "getting the drop on him," that is to say, covering him with his pistol before he was ready to defend himself, he said, "Jules, I am going to kill you"; to which the other replied, "Well, I suppose I am gone up; you've got me now"; and that Slade immediately opened fire and killed him with his revolver.

The first story is the one almost universally believed in the West, and the act is considered entirely justifiable by the wild Indian fighters of the frontier. Had he simply killed Jules, he would have been justified by the accepted Western law of retaliation. The prolonged agony and mutilation of his enemy however, admit of no excuse.

While on the road, Slade ruled supreme. He would ride down to a station, get into a quarrel, turn the house out of windows, and maltreat the occupants most cruelly. The unfortunates had no means of redress, and were compelled to recuperate as best they could. On one of these occasions, it is said, he killed the father of the fine little half-breed boy, Jemmy, whom he adopted, and who lived with his widow after his execution. He was a gentle, well-behaved child, remarkable for his beautiful, soft, black eyes, and for his polite address.

Sometimes Slade acted as a lyncher. On one occasion, some emigrants had their stock either lost or stolen and told Slade, who happened to visit their camp. He rode, with a single companion, to a ranch, the owner of which he suspected, and opening the door, commenced firing at them, killing three and wounding the fourth.

As for minor quarrels and shootings, it is absolutely certain that a minute history of Slade's life would be one long record of such practices. He was feared a great deal more, generally, than the Almighty, from Kearney, west. There was, it seems, something in his bold recklessness, lavish generosity, and firm attachment to his friends, whose quarrel he would back, everywhere and at any time, that endeared him to the wild denizens of the prairie, and this personal attachment it is that has cast a veil over his faults, so dark that his friends could never see his real character, or believe their idol to be a blood-stained desperado.

Stories of his hanging men, and of innumerable assaults, shootings, stabbings and beatings, in which he was a principal actor, form part of the legends of the stage line; nevertheless, such is the veneration still cherished for him by many of the old stagers, that any insult offered to his memory would be fearfully and quickly avenged. Whatever he did to others, he was their friend, they say; and so they will say and feel till the tomb closes over the last of his old friends and comrades of the Overland.

It should be stated that Slade was, at the time of his coming West, a fugitive from justice in Illinois, where he killed a man with whom he had been quarreling. Finding his antagonist to be more than his match, he ran away from him, and, in his flight, picking up a stone, he threw it with such deadly aim and violence that it penetrated the skull of his pursuer, over the eye, and killed him. Johnson, the sheriff, who pursued him for nearly four hundred miles, was in Virginia City not long since, as we have been informed by persons who knew him well.

Such was Captain J. A. Slade, the idol of his followers, the terror of his enemies and of all that were not within the charmed circle of his dependents. In him, generosity and destructiveness, brutal lawlessness and courteous kindness, firm friendship and volcanic outbreaks of fury, were so mingled that he seems like one born out of date. He should have lived in feudal times, and have been the comrade of the Front de Boeufs, De Lacys, and Bois Guilberts, of days almost forgotten. In modern times, he stands nearly alone.

The execution of Slade had a most wonderful effect upon society. Henceforth, all knew that no one man could domineer or rule over the community. Reason and civilization then drove brute force from Montana.

One of his principal friends wisely absconded, and so escaped sharing his fate, which would have been a thing almost certain had he remained.

It has often been asked, why Slade's friends were permitted to go scot free, seeing that they accompanied him in all his "raids," and both shared and defended his wild and lawless exploits. The answer is very simple. The Vigilantes deplored the sad but imperative necessity for the making of one example. That, they knew, would be sufficient. They were right in their judgment, and immovable in their purpose. Could it but be made known how many lives were at their mercy, society would wonder at the moderation that ruled in their counsels. Necessity was the arbiter of these men's fate. When the stern Goddess spoke not, the doom was unpronounced, and the criminal remained at large. They acted for the public good, and when examples were made, it was because the safety of the community demanded a warning to the lawless and the desperate, that might neither be despised nor soon forgotten.

The execution of the road agents of Plummer's gang was the result of the popular verdict and judgment against robbers and murderers. The death of Slade was the protest of society on behalf of social order and the rights of man.

11. Local Anti-Radical Vigilantism

San Diego, California, in the year 1912 might superficially have
seemed a quasi-frontier environment. But this was not in fact
the case. San Diego at that time was an established city of more
than 40,000 people, stratified into a discernible middle class and
working class. Politically it was progressive Republican. (In the
primary election that year, whose result was announced on the
same day that the anarchist Ben Reitman was tarred and feathered
by local vigilantes, the city-wide totals were as follows: La Fol-
lette, 2083; Roosevelt, 2064; Taft, 1126; Wilson, 611; Clark,
298). The several newspapers of San Diego represented the entire
political spectrum, but the two leaders in the race for circulation,
the *Union* and the *Sun,* clearly reflected the basic social division
which existed. The *Union,* owned by the locally powerful Spreckles
interests, supported a conservative version of middle-class ideals
and aspirations. The *Sun,* which boasted the largest circulation
and whose reporting was the most detailed and impartial, claimed
to speak for the working man within an overall context of progressivism. Of the other smaller papers, the *Tribune* was extremely
conservative; the weekly *News* was reticent but conservative; and
the *Herald,* furthest to the left, had its typefaces destroyed by
vigilantes on at least one occasion.

During the period between February and June 1912, San Diego
was nakedly polarized into rival camps. Law temporarily broke
down. Mob scenes occurred. At least two radicals were killed.
Major episodes of violence, threatening to break out in full daylight in the center of the city, were only narrowly averted. For
several weeks, until Governor Hiram Johnson threatened to bring
in the state militia to restore order, local police and public officials openly colluded with vigilante groups who were themselves
composed, from all indications, of respectable businessmen. The
vigilantes and the police both threatened and administered bodily
harm to radicals who would not immediately leave the city.

The issue which gave rise to this open warfare on the streets was
not San Diego's alone, although its effects there were extreme.
At stake was the attempt of radicals, mainly members of the
syndicalist labor union, the Industrial Workers of the World, to

mount soapboxes on busy intersections and speak freely against the capitalist system. These free speech fights, as they were known, occurred in at least twenty cities, particularly on the West Coast, during the period between 1909 and 1913. They usually followed a quite similar pattern. They would begin when local authorities, out of fear and revulsion over the organizing efforts of the I.W.W., passed ordinances outlawing public speaking in neighborhoods where audiences might be attracted. I.W.W. members would then deliberately pour into town, speak in violation of the ordinance but otherwise behave nonviolently, and thereby court arrest. Their aim was to clog the jails beyond capacity and thus to dramatize their position, placing an unwelcome burden on the local tax rate while making the authorities appear ridiculous.[1]

In San Diego the free speech fight began in January 1912, when the local grand jury, after first investigating I.W.W. activities and in turn being attacked by radical orators, requested the City Council to pass an ordinance prohibiting street speaking within the downtown area. As radicals arrived in increasing numbers to test the ordinance, vigilantes and police responded by forcibly taking many of them out of town, beating them, and turning them loose with a warning never to return. On one such occasion it is reported that "fifteen to sixteen autos were found" at the edge of the city limits, "with lights burning low. There were between sixty and seventy-five men there, some with lanterns, while others openly displayed revolvers, knives, nightsticks, blackjacks and blacksnakes. None wore disguises. The insignia of the order, or band, was a white handkerchief, tied at the elbow of the right arm, probably worn for the purpose of distinguishing the so-called vigilantes from the I.W.W." A flagpole had been erected, and radicals were often made to kiss the American flag. Some groups of radicals were placed in cattle pens without food or drink for eighteen hours, during which time they were beaten. One man was severely kicked by policemen in the San Diego jail, then denied medical attention, after which he died. The coroner's jury declared that "death was caused by tuberculosis of the lungs and valvular disease of the heart." A second man was killed by police during a raid on his house. Some victims of police brutality were not I.W.W. members but mere bystanders or cases of mis-

1. See Paul F. Brissenden, *The I.W.W.: A Study of American Syndicalism* (New York: Columbia University Press, 1920), pp. 262–266; Melvyn Dubofsky, *We Shall Be All: A History of the I.W.W.* (Chicago: Quadrangle Books, 1969), pp. 173–197.

taken identity. These events had been occurring for some weeks by the time that the anarchist Emma Goldman decided to come to San Diego and try to speak there, with the results that are described in the following documents.[2]

The role of the judicial system, incidentally, was not such as to give any comfort to the radicals. The federal grand jury in Los Angeles announced soon after May 14 that it would take no action in the resultant tarring of Ben Reitman (who was Emma Goldman's lover-companion), claiming that it lacked jurisdiction. The local grand jury, the original promoter of the anti–free speech ordinance, continued to investigate the I.W.W. but failed to subject the vigilantes to similar scrutiny. Governor Johnson at first tried to put pressure on this grand jury to adjourn, so that a special grand jury, presumably of a more impartial complexion, could replace it, but the original grand jury refused to disband itself, and the governor's agent admitted defeat on the issue on June 5. The governor's threat to call in state troops did bring about a noticeable change in the attitude of the local police, who around June 3 began offering street speakers more genuine protection and asked the vigilantes, in effect, to "cool it." But, so far as is known, the community never pressed any charges against the vigilantes for what they had already done.

What would make so many leading San Diegans react to radicalism in this violent and extreme fashion, especially when the legal system seemed so clearly to be operating in their favor? There was the practical problem that I.W.W. tactics had exhausted the capacities of the local jails. But the wellsprings of the community's response must have run a good deal deeper. In this instance an economic explanation of motives is actually quite convincing. If one reads the less sensational columns of the San Diego newspapers in this period, or the similar publications elsewhere in Southern California as a whole, one is constantly impressed by the promotional atmosphere in which these people lived. To make land values rise was the steady underlying aim of a great number of daily words and actions. The influx of tourists was never-ceasing. The "right" kind of tourist, the substantial, stable kind, was being encouraged by realtors and bankers (occupations figur-

2. The most trustworthy narrative of all these episodes is in Harris Weinstock, *Report to the Governor of California on the Disturbances in the City and County of San Diego* (Sacramento, Calif.: State Printing Office, 1912). Weinstock was sent to San Diego on a fact-finding mission by Governor Johnson immediately after Emma Goldman's visit.

ing prominently among the vigilantes) to return to the area to stay. A "boom atmosphere," in which one's own existing stake would pleasantly increase, depended upon retaining for the city the sort of reputation that would continue to attract the "right" people to it. This meant an image of wholesome calm, undisturbed by such repulsive downtown sights as saloon drunkenness or shabby orators on soapboxes brazenly haranguing crowds. An urban environment was for these reasons no less anxious to avoid a "wide-open" reputation than were rural ranchers or farmers, who feared I.W.W. organizing efforts for even more direct economic causes. The conspicuous presence of the I.W.W., even for a few hours or days at a time, on principal downtown streets where tourists were constantly passing by, visibly threatened the conception of community which its solid citizens were so anxiously trying to maintain. These town leaders felt so threatened, indeed, that they could not wait for the slow machinery of the judicial system to operate.

This is why early twentieth-century urban vigilantism had so little in common with the same phenomenon on the Montana frontier. The memory of the earlier history remained alive, so that the term and the tactics could be conveniently borrowed. But the substance was entirely different. In Montana, vigilantes had come into being in the near absence of usual agencies of law enforcement and had operated (though in an arbitrary and potentially dangerous fashion) against a deranged individual. In San Diego, vigilantes functioned, one must say, as the instruments of class warfare (however harsh this term may appear when applied to conditions in America). They were the agents of the middle-class American dream of success, determined to obliterate any traces of a contending dream. They were passionate men, but they were also the products of a relatively stable and structured society, even though it was then in its early and less secure phases of rapid urban growth. Thus their actions sprang from the specific conditions of modern American life more than they did from "human nature" (as the San Diego Congregational minister tries to argue below) or from purely psychological desires. Only a growing sense of security about property and about civic image could reduce the pressures that would otherwise lead to such "excesses." But this sense of relaxation was always fragile, and perhaps always would remain so in America. In succeeding decades, vigilante groups might not so often be headed by civic leaders as apparently was the case in San Diego; their appeal might shift instead toward the lower middle class or the white working class. But the impulse to destroy offensively radical troublemakers remained at bottom the same. And because the police themselves remained lower-middle-class in origin, their own role in these situations would continue to be ambiguous.

Emma Goldman and Ben Reitman in San Diego, Selections from the San Diego Sun, Mother Earth, the San Diego Tribune, the San Diego Union, and the San Diego News, March to June, 1912

EMMA GOLDMAN IN; HOOTED BY CROWD; CAN'T GET A HALL
(San Diego Sun, May 14, 1912)

Emma Goldman, the famous anarchist, is today in San Diego.

While some cheered and others hooted, Miss Goldman stepped from a Santa Fe train at the foot of D street at 1:10 this afternoon and was driven at once to the U.S. Grant hotel, followed by an excited crowd.

Many did not wait for the streetcars, but ran pell mell after the 'bus from the station to the hotel. The police made no attempt to arrest the woman.

As Miss Goldman climbed to the top of the 'bus at the station, a fashionably dressed woman rose to a standing position in an automobile and yelled: "Soak her, soak her, soak her!" at the top of her voice. She kept this up for some time, but although there were muttered threats in the crowd against the woman, no attempt was made to molest her. Miss Goldman was the least excited person in the crowd. She sat erect in her seat on top of the 'bus and made no attempt to answer those who called at her. She didn't seem to be aware that there was any crowd there.

A crowd of nearly a thousand people, including leading Socialists, vigilantes, police and deputy sheriffs and common people, were at the station.

Shortly after the train arrived Detective Shepherd, who was in charge of the police, announced that Miss Goldman would not be arrested at the train. The police were there, he said, to preserve order. . . .

Miss Goldman left the train without attracting attention, and edged her way through the crowd, through the waiting room of the depot, and climbed to the top of the big auto bus of the Grant hotel before she was recognized.

Those who had gathered to greet her thought that she had been taken off the train north of here by detectives, but when they got sight of her on the 'bus, they ran in that direction. The crowd then saw them running and surged towards the 'bus. It was a crush, and the police were afraid that somebody would be hurt. They kept the crowd back as best they could.

"There she is. What will happen to her before she leaves San Diego will be a-plenty," cried one man. Another man shook his fist in the air and declared that Miss Goldman had gone too far. A sympathizer of the woman tried to cheer, and came near being roughly handled. Several cheers, however, rose up from sympathizers. Miss Goldman remained unmoved. . . .

Passengers who came down on the train did not know what all the excitement was about. They asked many questions which no one had time to answer. As the 'bus swung out into the street five detectives climbed on the steps and rode to the hotel. They had instructions, it is said, to protect Miss Goldman against a mob. At the hotel Miss Goldman was given a room, despite a report that she would not be admitted. . . .

Miss Goldman was plainly attired. She wore a brown sweater vest and looked slightly stouter than when here last. . . .

About 200 people, mostly men, followed Miss Goldman into the hotel. A number of them called her an "anarchist," and advised her to get out of town. She paid little attention to them, and went at once to the room that was assigned to her.

When the crowd was going in the door, the negro porter shoved a boy off the sidewalk who had an I.W.W. button on. This almost started a riot. The boy declared he didn't want any protection from the American flag, and some people in the crowd declared they would send him out of town.

Chief [of Police] Wilson said this afternoon that he had not made up his mind what he would do if Miss Goldman attempted to speak. He said that he did not think she should have come here at this time.

Feeling was high against Miss Goldman in the crowd at the station. She was called names that would not look well in print, and there were many threats made. . . .

TARRY COAT FOR DR. REITMAN AS

EMMA GOLDMAN LEAVES CITY

(San Diego *Sun,* May 15, 1912)

Wearing blue overalls and a checkered jumper, and showing unmistakeable signs of mistreatment at the hands of the vigilantes, Dr. Ben Reitman, manager for Emma Goldman, limped into Escondido this afternoon from Bernardo.

Reitman had failed in an attempt to hide the traces of the mob's work. On his face and in his whiskers were splotches of tar. The clothes he wore were evidently borrowed from some farm house. . . .

With Emma Goldman, the famous woman anarchist, safe in the Antlers hotel in Los Angeles, and with her manager, Ben Reitman, going in the same direction as fast as he could, San Diego was as quiet this morning as if the famous "red" and her companion had never visited the city.

Last night all was excitement and turmoil around the U.S. Grant hotel where Miss Goldman and Reitman were, but the morning—a beautiful sunny morning, so typical of San Diego—dawned to find their rooms at the hotel empty and the people of the city again calm. She escaped violence only by the narrowest margin, leaving the city a little more than 12 hours after she had entered it.

Reitman, who announced that he would come to San Diego despite Police Chief Wilson's warning to stay away, was not so fortunate. Treatment that the vigilantes would not give the woman was accorded to the man. Reitman was mysteriously spirited away from the hotel some time near midnight, taken in an automobile to a point near the Penasquitas ranch, and, it is reported, tarred and feathered and branded on the back with the letters "I.W.W." He is furthermore said to have been forced to kneel and kiss the

American flag. The branding was done with a lighted cigar, which was traced through the tar. . . .

The manner in which he was taken out of the hotel, probably between 11 and 12, was today a much discussed question. The police declare that they did not see him go, and it is certain that none of those in the hotel lobby or the street without knew that the manager was being taken. . . . Before the man was taken away, he is declared to have been in a highly nervous condition, saying that he would not have come to San Diego had he realized the intense feeling of the people. . . . The tar and feathers which were used upon Reitman are known to have been prepared in advance, and are said to have been hidden in an automobile not far from the hotel. . . .

Chief of Police Wilson was this morning inclined to discredit the tar and feathers story. He said he believed that Reitman was taken out of the hotel by sympathizers. . . .

Chief Wilson disavowed a story that Miss Goldman had broken down and begged for police protection.

"She was nervous but stubborn," said the chief today, "and tried to put on a bold front. She declared that she didn't need the protection of the police, but seemed willing to get out of town. I told her that I would not attempt to take her out in that crowd, but that if she would wait until morning I would have my men escort her to the train and protect her from harm. I do not know who took her to the Owl train. I had gone home at that time. . . ."

EMMA GOLDMAN, "THE OUTRAGE OF SAN DIEGO"
(*Mother Earth*, VII [June 1912], 115–122)

On my previous trips to California I never failed to speak in San Diego, and I have never been disturbed. This time I had a double reason for visiting that city. First, to lecture; and, secondly, to learn for myself of the outrages which had been committed against the I.W.W. men during the last three months. Dr. Reitman and I could have slipped in quietly, but we had nothing to hide. Besides, we wanted to give the authorities a chance to make good their claim that they were not in league with the savagery and cruelties committed by the so-called patriotic citizens of San Diego.

We wrote the Mayor, notifying him of the time and the place of the lectures, and asking him to keep his subordinates from suppressing the right of free speech. In reply we heard from Chief of Police Wilson, ordering us to stay away from San Diego. As we could not possibly recognize the high-handed authority of this uniformed cossack, we determined to carry out our schedule as originally planned.

On arriving in the city we saw a large crowd, but paid no further attention to it, quietly passing to the auto-bus of the U. S. Grant Hotel. Then the mob outbreak began, the moment our presence became known. I shall not attempt to describe the language, the madness, the atrocities that raged around us. It seemed as if the entire city had turned into an insane asylum.

But for the pluck of the chauffeur, we would have been mobbed there and then. He raced at wild speed, with several cars full of vigilantes in mad pursuit, screaming, yelling, and cursing the chauffeur. Finally we reached the U. S. Grant Hotel, in our company being Mr. and Mrs. E. E. Kirk. Mr. Kirk, though under indictment himself, showed wonderful bravery in meeting us at the depot—an act which was certainly as heroic as that of Wendell Phillips, who rushed out to the rescue of Lloyd Garrison.

No objection was made at the hotel. We were assigned to our rooms and, after some rest, we went down to the grill-room for our luncheon. Everything seemed quiet, when about 4 P.M. the head clerk announced that he would have to transfer us to other rooms, as the vigilantes had gotten hold of the registry and were determined to get us out of the hotel. Later the manager himself, Mr. Holmes, arrived, assuring us that we were perfectly safe under his roof, but that he could not permit us to go down to the lobby or restaurant, or anywhere in the hotel, which meant nothing less than incarceration. Again we waited for some time to map out a plan of action, but at 7.30 P.M. the horror of our reception was repeated, only in a more hideous manner.

Five thousand people, preceded by a hundred autos, with fashionably-dressed women and men as their occupants, with American flags, their riot-whistles creating a deafening noise, surrounded the hotel. Five hundred of these maniacs, led by a good Christian and American patriot, Francis Bierman, reporter on the San Diego *Union,* entered the hotel lobby, unfurled the American flag, compelled everybody to sing the "Star Spangled Banner" as an inspiration for their heroic work, then walked up to Manager Holmes and demanded: "Turn over the two damned Anarchists to us, or we will take you." Mr. Holmes replied that he couldn't do that. That it was the custom of the hotel to protect its guests; but that if they would quiet down, he would see Miss Goldman and induce her to leave the city. Thereupon the committee said they would wait, but would return, reinforced, raid the hotel, drag every guest out of the rooms until they would locate us. If they should fail in that, Mr. Holmes would have to pay for it with his life.

About 10 o'clock Mr. Holmes came to us and told us that he could no longer guarantee our safety, but that if we would leave he would give us protection. That we refused to do. Equally so, to act upon his suggestion to ask the Chief of Police for protection. We said that when we decided to go, we would leave as we had arrived—openly and without the support of the authorities. While we were discussing the matter, we were interrupted by violent knocks on the door, and a man (whom we took for a detective, but who afterwards proved to be a vigilante) stepped in and informed Mr. Holmes that the Chief of Police, with other men from the department, were at Mr. Holmes' office and demanded to see us.

Strange to say, Reitman showed greater intuition than myself, immediately suspecting foul play. He said that the Chief should come to us, but to avoid argument I suggested that we go down to the office of Mr. Holmes. There we found six men; one, a certain J. M. Porter, I recognized as the leading vigilante of the afternoon mob, and also the one who threatened E. E. Kirk's life in my presence in the hotel lobby. We were then informed that the Chief was in the next room and would see me first. Even then I did not suspect the conspiracy to which the police and even Mr. Holmes himself had lent a willing hand. How could I? We were not in Russia. We were in San Diego, in an American city, in the leading hotel of the town, at 10 o'clock in the evening. How could I for a moment suspect that human beings would be so bestial and degenerate as to commit a thing which would put to shame even Russia?

My conversation with the Chief of Police, his assistant, the head of detectives, and some other officers lasted but a few minutes. They offered their protection, which I refused, telling the Chief that all he had to do was to invoke the ordinance which has made it a felony to gather in the business districts of the city and for which three hundred I.W.W. men had been beaten, clubbed, arrested, and subjected to every cruelty and indignation imaginable. But the Chief replied that he couldn't do that, because the mob had outgrown his power. I then suggested that he resign, as he declared himself unfit to be a protector of so-called law and order. I asked him to let me speak to the mob from the window, as the office was on the first floor. I have faced mobs before in my life and have invariably succeeded in soothing them. But even that he wouldn't do, and so the conversation came to an end, the Chief giving me the cheerful assurance that he would turn me over to the mob the following morning. I replied that if I had to die, I was just as willing to die at the hands of the mob as at the hands of the police.

I immediately went to tne room where I had left the Doctor. I found it locked, and then I suddenly realized the whole contemptible conspiracy. I demanded that the door be opened, and of course there was no Ben Reitman. I turned to the Chief of Police and told him that if any serious injury should come to Reitman, or if he should lose his life, I would hold the Chief responsible for it; and, furthermore, that I would come to San Diego and take his miserable life; nor would I run away, as I am always ready to stand the consequences for anything I say or do. The brave Chief grew pale and said, "Why, we had nothing to do with it. You know yourself, we were in the next room." Which only added to his cowardice, as the whole wretched business was carried out with the consent and connivance of the police department.

For four hours I paced the floor of my room in agony, not knowing what had become of Ben Reitman, and knowing still less what to do, because I could not communicate with our friends in San Diego, as that would have meant turning them over to the police. At 2 A.M., May 15th, the house detective and another man came to the room. Nature does create some freaks. The man with the house detective had a most wonderful face, kind, tender, and human, but he introduced himself as a detective. He reminded me of a beautiful woman with a rotten soul. He said that he would

not lie in telling me that he came from Ben Reitman, but that
he was given absolute assurance on the part of some authoritative
people that no harm had come to him, although he had been
taken out of town and was now on his way to Los Angeles. I
then called up Mrs. Estelle Kirk, giving the name of the detective,
whom she evidently knew, as she told me that he was the only
decent man in the entire department; that therefore it might be
possible that he was telling the truth. But I did not feel inclined
to believe, as I never yet have found a detective who can tell the
truth. But the manager of the hotel begged and pleaded with me
to leave. He said that he had sheltered us as long as he could;
that he didn't ask us to come in the first place; that we were taking undue advantage of him; and that we were ruining the hotel
and jeopardizing his life—all of which was true. I felt I had no
right to drive the man into a still more desperate position, and
therefore I decided to leave on the 2.45 train for Los Angeles. I
ordered a taxi. On the way to the depot I could see nothing of a
suspicious character. The streets were deserted, and San Diego
had returned to its normal sleepy state.

I was just about to enter the car when six automobiles with
the same maniacs—patriotic citizens—whisked up to the station,
and then I felt myself bodily lifted up by the trainmen, pushed
into the car, and the door locked. The train did not pull out for
another eight minutes, the most terrible, the most hideous eight
minutes of my life. There were the good Christian, law-abiding,
respectable citizens, and the howl they raised, the language they
used, the efforts they made to break into the train, are beyond
description, beyond anything that the most depraved human beings
could be capable of. After a seemingly endless trip, in the desperate hope that Reitman would join me at some of the stations,
I finally landed in Los Angeles, only to find that he had not
arrived. Later I learned of the horrible things that happened to
him, the details of which our readers will find in his own article.

I have, of course, been interfered with on previous occasions
in a number of American cities. Free speech in this country de-
pends entirely on the whims and arbitrary will of ignorant police
officials. But it was left to San Diego, a town which Nature herself
has intended man to be happy and peaceful in, to suppress the
right of free speech and assemblage and to outrage every vestige

of personal liberty in a manner which would have put to shame the Spanish Inquisition. It was left to citizens who swear by law and order to break not only their own written laws, but every principle of decency and humanity.

Ostensibly the organization now known as the I.W.W. is responsible for the excitement and the blood-thirsty attitude of the people of San Diego. But after all, that is the indictment made against every organization and idea which the popular mind has not yet accepted. But whether the I.W.W. be right or wrong, they cannot possibly be so wrong as the people of San Diego who are brutally suppressing the right of free expression and who are committing acts of violence and outrage which would put every one of them, including the entire police department, into the penitentiary for life, if the judiciary of that city were not as cowardly and craven as its citizens.

Men and women who are not ready to listen to contrary opinion on any given subject, thereby condemn themselves to the grossest ignorance and the most outrageous tyranny. If what the I.W.W., or any other undesirable, have to say is wrong, it will die of itself a much quicker death than if these people are beaten, clubbed, tarred, and driven out like wild beasts. Nor can anything I stand for be killed by mob-butchery or by police violence. The issue of Free Speech is one of the most vital and fundamental in America, and the very moment any given section of the country undertakes to suppress freedom of expression, it at the same time undermines every principle of liberty and condemns itself to death.

Fortunately for Reitman, he had money and his return ticket to Los Angeles. He could at least help himself somewhat after the terrible experience. But what about the hundreds of men, without friends or money, who were subjected to the same terrible outrage, except that their bodies were not burned or tarred? I understand that the Savior of the Christian people said, "Whatsoever ye do unto the least of these my children, ye do unto me." And yet the people who call themselves Christians and worship the memory of Christ, continue in a brutal, savage manner to outrage life, to beat and club men, to drive them out of town, to leave them penniless and without food on the deserts of California.

Verily, man's power of endurance is a very elastic thing, or the vigilantes would have long ere this been given a dose of their own medicine.

However, it has been said that if there is one innocent man in a city, that city will be saved. And there is such a man in San Diego—Mr. George Edwards, who is at the head of the Music Institute. At the critical moment, when even the bravest people lost their courage, this man, who had never before seen or heard me, offered me his hall for a lecture. I felt, however, that to accept Mr. Edwards' kindness and hospitality would have meant to endanger his life, which I certainly could not do. But it was his spirit of kindliness and the great friendship shown by the Kirks that gave the only spark of life and warmth in that benighted, maddened town, San Diego.

Life under our present system is not so great a thing that he who has an ideal and loves liberty should not be willing to part with it. But life in San Diego is worse than death. I cannot believe that the number of intelligent people in the United States is so small that they could not bring moral pressure upon that city to stop its atrocities. It was the intelligent minority which forced the Southern planter to stop his murderous treatment of the black man. Surely the same can be done to-day. It is with that in view that this article is written, and not in complaint of anything we have endured. It is also because I feel that the crimes, the savagery, and the unspeakable cruelties perpetrated by the San Diego thugs, with the connivance of the police and the support of the San Diego *Union* and *Tribune,* must be brought to an end. Crime begets crime, and violence inevitably gives birth to violence. If San Diego is justified in violence, why not its victims? To avoid both, I appeal to all fair-minded and liberty-loving people throughout the country to join in a determined campaign against San Diego and its horrors.

LEADERS OF THE MURDEROUS VIGILANTES PILLORIED
(*Mother Earth,* VII [June 1912], 108)

Some of the Participants in the Outrages Against Life and Liberty Perpetrated in San Diego.

J. M. Porter, of Porter & Forbes, real estate.

Walter P. Moore, Assistant Superintendant of Streets.

Francis Bierman, reporter on the San Diego *Union*.

Colonel Jack Dodge, theatrical man, slated for the management of the new Spreckles Theatre. His brother ———— Dodge is a real estate man.

Clark Braly, rancher. Owner of a large ranch close by San Diego. Suggested that the I.W.W.'s should be met at the county-line by men on horseback, armed with whips.

George Sears.

Amy Johnson. A male, despite the name.

George W. Fishburn, president of the Marine National Bank of San Diego.

Carl I. Ferris, of Ferris & Ferris, drug store.

———— Julian, a one-armed man, who drove an auto at the service of the vigilantes.

R. J. Walsh, of the firm of R. J. Walsh Real Estate Company.

———— Brodnax, of Brodnax & Neale, real estate firm.

W. Litzenberg, of the Homeland Real Estate Company.

———— Parker, a contractor.

Supervisor Fisher.

Col. Fred Jewell, retired banker.

J. F. Forward, Jr., F. J. Lea, W. F. Ludington, S. C. Payson. Dr. Chamberlain, John Burkham, George Burnham, Percy Goodwin.[1]

BEN L. REITMAN, "THE RESPECTABLE MOB"
(*Mother Earth*, VII [June 1912], 109–114)

After four years of active Anarchist propaganda, I am beginning to understand that which is difficult for every American to appreciate; namely, that there is only as much freedom in America as the authority and property interests are willing to grant. And it is very plain to me now that whenever the police permit "too much" free speech, the capitalist class will step in and take matters

---

1. The source of this list cannot be found. Newspaper accounts give no specific information about the composition of the vigilantes, though the respectful way in which they manage to avoid the subject strengthens one's impression that they were indeed community leaders.

into its own hands. Our San Diego experience not only burned industrial unionism into my flesh, but also engraved on my heart and soul that this is a country of the master class, and that the latter controls free speech.

The San Diego mob that tried to tear us to pieces and kidnapped me was a typical respectable mob, made up of retired bankers, retired army officers, real estate men, lawyers, doctors, business men, and saloon keepers. Most of the active vigilantes own an automobile and property. To the credit of the working class it can be stated that the few workingmen who were in the mob were there at the bidding of their masters and not on their own initiative. In relating my experience I want our readers to know that that which was done to me was done in a measure to 300 other men, mostly members of the I.W.W. When the manager of the U. S. Grant Hotel, in San Diego, came to our room and said, "the Chief of Police wants to see both of you," I at once became suspicious. When Miss Goldman and the hotel manager left the office to go into another room, I was left alone with six respectable citizens. As soon as the door was closed, they drew out six cold steel revolvers, that some workingmen had made, and pointed them at me. They said, "If you utter a sound, or make a move, we'll kill you." Then they gathered around me. One man took my right arm, the other the left; a third man grabbed the front of my coat, another the back, and I was taken out into the corridor, down the elevator to the main floor of the hotel, and out into the street past a uniformed policeman, and then thrown into an automobile. When the mob saw me in the automobile, they set up a howl of delight. The auto went slowly down the main street and was joined by another one containing seven law-abiding, respectable business men. This was about 10.30 P.M.

I wish I could describe the terror of that twenty-mile ride in the beautiful California moonlight. I was in an automobile with six men and a chauffeur, and as soon as we were out of the business district, these Christian gentlemen started cursing, kicking, and beating me. Each one seemed to vie with the other to get a blow at me. My long hair was a favorite spot for attack. They took turns at pulling it. These Christian patriots put their fingers into my eyes and nose; kicked, pounded, bit me and subjected me to every cruel, diabolical, malicious torture that a God-fearing respectable business man is capable of conceiving. Space will not permit me to make a detailed report of that ride, but there was not a second but what some new torture was inflicted upon me. In fact, so many different blows poured in on me, and impressions came so fast, that I was unable to register all of them in my mind. I must ask our readers to listen to a part of the conversation:

"Why did you come here, you damned Anarchist outlaw?"

"We telegraphed you and that woman to stay away from here."

"Don't break his nose. I promised the doctor in the other automobile that he could have this pleasure."

"Oh, we like this; it's a treat for us to get a dog like you; you are one of them editors, one of them leaders that have been sending these men here. We have been beating up those I.W.W. hobos, and now we've got you. We like to beat you."

"We could kill you and tear out your guts and no one would know who did it, but we promised the Chief of Police that we wouldn't kill you or beat up your face too much."

"Why did you come here, you dago, you ignorant foreigner? We don't want you here. This is our town. We own property here. We've got money in the bank. We are not workingmen; we are business men, doctors and lawyers, and we've got the law and the police on our side; and even if we didn't, the business men in San Diego are able to keep out all the I.W.W. Anarchist outlaws."

"You thought we wouldn't hurt you, huh? You came here and you thought you'd get locked up and get free advertisement. But we are done locking men up. We arrested 300 of those I.W.W. outlaws and we had every jail in the county full of them, and they wouldn't work while they were in jail. They sang songs and they broke up the jail; so we ain't going to arrest anybody else; we're just going to club hell out of all who come here to take part in this free speech fight and we'll brand them."

"You won't kiss the American flag, eh? By God, we'll make you: we'll ram it down your throat. Now you —— —— —— Anarchist, sing the Star Spangled Banner! No, that ain't the way. Sing it with feeling. Now, you Anarchist editor; you go back east and you tell all the I.W.W. Anarchists and Socialists and agitators how we treated you. Tell them what to expect when they come here. We own this town and we'll run it to suit ourselves, and there ain't none of your outlaws who can come here and interfere with our business. Understand?"

In the last twenty years I have traveled more than half a million miles; but that ride with the business men of San Diego on the night of May 14th, 1912, was the most excruciating in my not uneventful career. When we reached the county line, some twenty miles out of town, the two automobiles drove to a deserted spot, off the main road, and then they all got out of their machines, and put the two automobiles together, so the lights from the auto lamps made a sickly stage light. Then these fourteen brave defenders of their country formed a ring around me and commanded me to undress. They tore my clothes from me, and in a minute I stood before them naked, and the naked stars looked painfully on "how men their brothers maim."

When I read of the horrors of the Spanish Inquisition I could hardly believe it was true, and when I was told about the barbaric treatment the Russian revolutionists were subjected to, I felt that these gruesome tales must be exaggerated. And so when I relate to the readers of *Mother Earth* the cruel and inhuman treatment I received at the hands of fourteen American citizens, who are not only business men but also loving husbands and kind fathers, many will question my statements.

At first I refused to kiss the American flag. I was knocked down and compelled to kiss the flag which I had been taught to love in my boyhood days. Once I joyfully sang, "My Country 'Tis of Thee, Sweet Land of Liberty." Twenty-five years ago I was thrilled when I took part in a chorus which sang, "Oh, the Star Spangled Banner, long may it wave." Now when I hear those songs I want to weep; to me they are hollow mockery,—covering all the sins and crimes of a cowardly nation. I was taught to loathe my native flag, not by Anarchists, or by ignorant foreigners, but by law-abiding, respectable business men.

When I lay naked on the ground, my tormentors kicked and beat me until I was almost insensible. With a lighted cigar they burned I.W.W. on my buttocks; then they poured a can of tar over my head and body, and, in the absence of feathers, they rubbed handfuls of sage brush on my body. One very gentle business man, who is active in church work, deliberately attempted to push my cane into my rectum. One unassuming banker twisted my testicles. These and many other things they did to me, until I forgot "whether I had done a great or little thing." When these business men were tired of their fun, they gave me my underwear for fear I should meet some women. These respectable citizens are very considerate of their women. They also gave me back my vest, in order that I might carry my money, railroad ticket, and watch. The rest of my clothes they stole from me in highwayman fashion. I was ordered to make a speech, and then they commanded me to run the gauntlet. The fourteen vigilantes were lined up, and as I ran past them, each one, in a businesslike manner, gave me a parting blow or kick.

My suffering was terrible, but my greatest pain was anxiety about E. G. I took it for granted that she would leave San Diego on the 2.45 A.M. train, and I attempted to walk towards the next station, hoping to board the train which I supposed she would be on. I walked blindly, like one mad, over the hills and through the canyons, and finally when the sun came up at 5 A.M., I saw by a sign post that I was fifteen miles from the nearest railroad. At 7 A.M. I came to the village of Renando and, timidly going into a store, I bought a pair of overalls and a jumper, a large bottle of turpentine and some tar soap. Under a bridge, knee deep in a soft running stream, I began the process of removing the evidence of the business men of San Diego. Turpentine and tar soap and two hours of hard work made me half-way presentable. I called up E. G., who had reached Los Angeles by this time, and notified her that I was alive. Then I walked to Esconditte very cautiously. I was afraid of the business men of California. I caught the 2.30 P.M. train and arrived at Los Angeles at 5.30 P.M.

All this happened in the year of Our Lord 1912, in the most beautiful and best organized State in America.

Many lessons can be drawn from our San Diego experience, but none more important than this: the business men and the property owners will *fight* for their "rights." The historian who analyzes the cause of the San Diego trouble will have to record that it was property, and the fear that it may be taken from them, that roused the savagery of the San Diego vigilantes.

Another lesson is that the business mob can always depend upon the police and the press to back them up. The most active men among the vigilantes is Harvey, a detective-sergeant, and Bierman, a newspaper man on the San Diego *Union.*

Comrade Joseph Mikolasek was wantonly killed by a policeman's bullet. Michael Hoey, an I.W. man, was knocked down by a stream of water, and died soon after. An innocent child was washed out of the buggy by a hose held by the police, and killed. Nearly four hundred men have been jailed on charges varying from vagrancy to murder. Practically all those men were innocent. Three hundred men have been beaten, kidnapped, and forced to undergo Spanish Inquisition tortures. The vigilantes and police have had a great deal of fun. None of them has been as much as slapped on the wrist. They proved to us that we were a lot of cowards, unable to protect ourselves. All that has been done in the way of retaliation has been to appeal to the government and the public for sympathy. We didn't even get that. The revolutionary movement of America has not justified its existence, at least so far as San Diego is concerned. For myself, I weep. I am ashamed that that great, big, strong giant, Labor, can be so readily bullied and beaten, and will not strike back.

A friend, whom I saw last week in San Quentin prison, asked me: "Why don't somebody do something?" I answered: "We are all cowards, I guess."[1]

Editorial in San Diego *Tribune,* March 4, 1912

Hanging is none too good for them [I.W.W. members] and they would be much better dead; for they are absolutely useless in the human economy; they are the waste material of creation and should be drained off into the sewer of oblivion, there to rot in cold oblivion like any other excrement.

Editorial in San Diego *Tribune,* March 5, 1912

Why are the taxpayers of San Diego compelled to endure this imposition? Simply because the law which these lawbreakers [in

---

1. In evaluating this testimony by Reitman, one should be aware of the fact that Reitman, unlike Emma Goldman (who was deeply in love with him), had the almost universal reputation within the anarchist movement of being untrustworthy and cheaply theatrical. But would these character traits necessarily affect the credibility of the above account?

the free speech fight] flout prevents the citizens of San Diego
from taking the impudent outlaws away from the police and hanging them or shooting them. This method of dealing with the evil
that has fastened itself on San Diego would end the trouble in
half an hour. Possibly when the . . . [I.W.W. members] resort to
crimes of violence, as is obviously their intention when enough of
them have "arrived," as their orators have threatened, the citizens
will be permitted to take the law into their own hands, which will
be bad for the Industrial Workers of the World and permanently
good for San Diego.

Editorial in San Diego *Union*, April 7, 1912

In the absence of legal machinery for dealing with so anomalous
a situation [as the free speech fight], citizens of San Diego fell
back upon their "inalienable rights" under the State constitution to
protect themselves. They have deported many an Anarchist from
the city and turned back many who sought to come here. There is
every reason to believe that this plan of averting a deadly menace
will be continued as long as may be deemed necessary for the
safety of the community. If this action be lawlessness, make the
most of it.

Editorial in San Diego *News*, May 16, 1912

Violence at any time is to be condemned, but there are mitigat-
ing circumstances. A lion's cage is safe for the keeper when the
beast is quiet and at rest. But when it has been starved and tormented until its fury is almost ready to break he who enters is
unwise and foolhardy and cannot claim "visciousness" [*sic*] if the
lion tears his frame.

Editorial in San Diego *Sun*, May 17, 1912

The *Sun* does not stand for violence or lawbreaking, or direct
action foolishness, or any such policy as that evidently adopted by
Bill Haywood [I.W.W. leader] and his kind. It does not stand for
dynamiting, gun-men, or anything of the kind. It does not stand
for any "I-won't-work" policy. Nor does it stand for anything
that encourages that kind of thing—no matter from what source
that encouragement comes.

The *Sun* can see, by the way, as many good citizens here see, as members of the vigilance committee can see and do see, that there may be a serious trouble here if great care is not taken—that some building may be dynamited by a crazed fanatic, or some one in authority shot by some equally misled anarchist. Some such deed might have been encouraged by the coming of Emma Goldman or her press-agent companion, Dr. Reitman, and it was bad that they came here, although *The Sun* is inclined to believe that what she and Reitman came for was not to stir up trouble, but to get some advertising, for Emma and the doctor are out for the hard, iron dollar the same as any other show, tented or otherwise. Anyway, now is a time for cool counsel to prevail, for every effort to be made to stop bitter talk and violence, for the constituted authorities to stand firm for law and order.

For there are powerful interests at work here which do not want law and order here. Some are anarchists of the common kind. Others are in—Wall street—Big Business. Let's make this plain. . . . What better could big business pull off than to start a bitter fight here and compel Gov. Johnson to send troops here, possibly to start shooting of workers—not industrial Workers, but workers with the small "w."

UP TO SEHON TO STOP VIOLENCE, SAYS THORP
(San Diego *Sun,* May 20, 1912)

The Rev. Willard R. Thorp, pastor of the First Congregational church, in his sermon last night put it up to Capt. Sehon, head of the police department, to stop "aggressions and intimidations" by vigilantes, and to get back to law and order. These are extracts from Mr. Thorp's sermon:

"After all these centuries of human progress there is only a slight barrier that protects civilization from barbarism. How easily broken through it is, even in a highly civilized community like this, we have sad occasion to see within the past few days.

"That protective barrier we call law. By it we agree to restrain our passionate feelings, our vengeful hatreds, and under the shelter of it we live our ordered lives. . . . The experience of humanity has been that when under stress of passionate feeling we brush aside the laws and act regardless of them, we set in motion wild and ungovernable forces that sweep away the frail but precious guarantees which society has established and bring us in an incredibly brief time into a condition of anarchy. And that is the great peril in which this community is at the present moment.

"What is the lesson the people of this city most need to learn just now? Is it the danger from anarchistic revolutionists? No. Of that danger we are all fully convinced, and to it we are intensely alive. The lesson we need most sorely to learn is the danger involved in abandoning orderly and legal measures and resorting to lawlessness. We cannot afford to indulge in the anarchy of the vigilantes in order to overthrow the anarchy of the I.W.W.'s.

"It has been necessary to resort to extraordinary measures to protect our community against those who were coming here for the express purpose of breaking down our laws. It was under this plea that volunteer vigilance committees came forward. That good men were on these committees and were actuated by conscientious motives, cannot be questioned. But this is a method which is exceedingly dangerous. Human nature cannot be trusted to act in matters like this without the restraint of law and of responsible direction. When soldiers are called out, we know who is commanding them and we know the soldiers themselves by their uniforms, and they are held strictly accountable for what they do. But when self-constituted vigilance committees undertake the work, we know not who they are, and a feeling of distrust and intimidation runs through the community. We have been playing with fire. We hoped we should not be burned. But alas, we have been disappointed. Human nature among us has turned out to be no better than elsewhere.

"It was right that Emma Goldman and her companion should be made to leave this city. It was the duty of authorities to see that they were safely out of it. This they did in the case of the woman. The man the vigilantes were permitted to take out of the city and subject to abuses and indignities of the most insulting character.

"It is not what happened to him that troubles me, but what happened to us as a city when we permitted it to be done.

"But how has it served us? Let us not deceive ourselves. It was an act of lynch law, and it sends the name of our city out over the country as a city where lynch law is countenanced.

"It will be said: 'It will show the world what San Diego thinks of anarchists.' As a matter of fact it has the world thinking not about the problem of anarchists, but about the problem of San Diego vigilantes.

"Other intimidations have been practiced, most serious of all the intimidation of the counsel for the men who are on trial. The right of counsel is an inalienable right for any man, no matter what is the crime committed. . . .

"Let Capt. Sehon give the word to the vigilantes that he no longer needs their assistance, and that aggressions and intimidations must cease. If he ever needs them again, let them be commissioned as special police and let them act solely under his direction and within the law. Let us have peace and order under those forms of law which alone are the guarantee of our civilization."

GOVERNOR SAYS HE'S FOR EXACT JUSTICE TO ALL
(San Diego *Sun*, May 21, 1912)

SACRAMENTO, May 21.—Gov. Johnson this morning issued a statement that he has directed Attorney General Webb to proceed to San Diego, "that justice may be done, that the law may be enforced, that a solution of the problem confronting San Diego may be found. . . .

"I wished to learn the facts concerning the I.W.W. and its propaganda, as well as to investigate the alleged acts of cruelty and lawlessness in San Diego, so that we might properly and effectively deal with the problem hereafter, and so that if mistakes had been made in one community in dealing with the problem, they should not be repeated subsequently in other communities of the state. Beyond this, however anarchistic the I.W.W.'s might be, no organized government can tolerate the administration of the law by vigilantes or by any extrajudicial body. . . ."

REITMAN NOT TORTURED, SAYS THE REV. DR. THORP
(San Diego *Sun*, May 22, 1912)

Answering the charges made by Ben Reitman, Emma Goldman's manager, that he was not only tarred and badly scared by a party of vigilantes here, May 14, but was also beaten, cruelly mistreated and subjected to unmentionable indignities, a statement was issued here today by the Rev. W. B. Thorp, pastor of the First Congregational church. Mr. Thorp has been consistently opposed to the I.W.W. anarchistic program and to the violent work by vigilantes or by any other extralegal body. His statement follows:

". . . With two other gentlemen, I have had an extended interview with one of the men who took Reitman out. He related to us in detail everything that was done, offered to support his statements with an affidavit, and to take us to the scene and corroborate his story by such evidence as could be obtained. This we did not feel was necessary, for we were entirely satisfied of the truthfulness of his narrative.

"A coat of tar, even if applied cold, as it was in this case, is a bad enough indignity to deserve the words I used. But for the credit of our city, let it be known that it was not accompanied with branding or anything to cause physical pain or bodily injury, except that once the end of a lighted cigar was touched to his flesh.

"WILLARD B. THORP"

TRIES STREET-SPEAKING, AND SMALL RIOT STARTS
(San Diego *Sun,* May 27, 1912)

A. B. Carson of Los Angeles, who didn't say whether he was an I.W.W., started trouble at Seventh and E streets at 1:05 this afternoon when he attempted to speak from a soap box. Carson was knocked off his box by a motorcycle policeman, who knocked and kicked him for nearly half a block. A body of citizens, who had apparently heard in advance of the proposed speaking, were present and serious trouble seemed likely. Had it not been for the presence of mind of Walter P. Moore, there is no telling what would have happened to Carson. . . .

"I shall take my text from the Bible," said Carson in opening. " 'Ye shall know the truth, and the truth shall make you free.' " He then started to make some remarks about the free speech situation here in San Diego.

At that time Motorcycle Policeman Hathaway came up and

leaning his motorcycle against the curb, walked around to the west side of Carson and knocked him off his box. Hathaway followed the first blow with several others, and Carson struggled and turned until he faced the policeman and cried: "Am I under arrest?"

"No, you are not under arrest," answered Hathaway, "but you go on and get out of here!" Saying this, Hathaway continued to beat Carson in the face and to kick him. Carson attempted to struggle and fight back, and he fell over the curb. Before he could get up, he received several kicks.

Then the crowd started, and surging after the man, some members of it struck at him and attempted to kick him.

Cries of "get him," "hit him," "take him out of town," and "get an auto and take him out," were heard. Many tried to reach the man in order to "handle" him.

Carson ran around from E street and started north on Seventh, with men on every side trying to get hold of him. They were held back by Walter P. Moore, who got in their way and shouted: "Don't do that boys! That is not what we want."

Turning to Carson, he said:

"Go on, get out of here while you have a chance. Get out quick. Get out of town."

This was repeated every time when the crowd got close to Carson until he backed against the wall of a building.

He was evidently scared and wanted police protection, for he kept crying:

"I don't mind being arrested. I will go with the officers. If I am under arrest, I will not resist. I will go with the officers."

As he stood against the building, two men made a rush for him and before Moore could interfere one landed a kick on Carson.

Then the officers broke through the mob and took Carson in charge. He was hustled up Seventh street to D and about half way up the block the police attempted the turn the mob back. Most of the people stopped, but the members of a committee, with their American flags, stayed close to the police. . . .

Midway between Sixth and Seventh, on D street, Moore turned to the other men who were following and called out:

"Come on boys; let us turn back. We have gone far enough. We are not needed here."

To a man the men with the American flags dropped out and turned back around the corner from whence they came. . . .

Carson stated this morning that his home is in Los Angeles and that he had come here to take part in the free speech fight.

He was informed [by local socialists] . . . that he had a legal right to speak at Sixth and E streets, but they did not think it would be wise for him to go there at this time. . . .

Capt. of Detectives Joseph Meyers this afternoon instructed his men to take charge of the street-speaking situation themselves and especially commanded them not to let the citizens get their hands on any street speaker in case of trouble.

The detectives are now all dressed in uniform so that they can be plainly recognized. . . .

12. Federal Vigilantism

Vigilantism at the federal level was apt to appear in twentieth-century America whenever the forces and pressures tending toward it at the local level became prominently represented in the national government through the operation of the democratic process. Personal political ambitions were noticeable, both in the case of Wilson's Attorney-General, A. Mitchell Palmer, in 1920, and in that of Joseph McCarthy in the early 1950's. But politicians of this kind are least likely to make an appeal which is believed to be lacking in wide popular sympathy. Federal vigilantism is therefore a much simpler phenomenon to explain than local vigilantism.

A national context, nonetheless, offered the chance for a more grandiose attack against subversive conspiracy. The existence of the Bolshevik regime in Russia after November 1917 provided objective evidence of a threat to traditional American institutions on a worldwide scale. In 1919 and early 1920, it became especially easy to confuse the intent of the optimistic Russian revolutionaries with the very different matter of their practical capabilities. In the highly emotional aftermath to World War I, American society showed deceptive signs of breaking at the seams. Race riots occurred. One-seventh of the labor force went out on strikes (which usually ended up being unsuccessful); worker "soviets" were briefly established in a handful of American cities. Two rival Communist parties were founded, their miniscule memberships tending to harbor in their own minds exaggerated hopes for rapid success in precisely the same way that Palmer (and his lieutenant, J. Edgar Hoover) harbored exaggerated fears over what they could accomplish. Making a dramatic try for the presidency, Palmer initiated a nationwide dragnet operation for alien radicals, starting on November 7, 1919. As so often happens in such situations, the arrests (and the consequent police indignities) fell upon many relatively casual bystanders as well as upon dedicated revolutionary activists. On December 21, 249 aliens and citizens, many of them leading anarchists, were arbitrarily deported to Russia aboard the *Buford*. Emma Goldman was among their number. On January 2, 1920, new raids collected more than 4,000 suspected radicals in thirty-three major cities across the nation. Families were separated; prisoners were held incommunicado, and the right to legal counsel was ignored.[1] This was the immediate background to Palmer's half-boastful, half-admonitory article written for a wide audience in February, 1920. But as the spring wore on, public passion on the issue suddenly cooled, and by mid-year Palmer found himself in the uncomfortable position of the distrusted wolf-crier. Only the more genuine military might of the Soviet Union thirty years later enabled Joseph McCarthy, by contrast, to remain a major popular hero for over four years at a single stretch.

Palmer's anti-radical appeal contains the same ambiguity about law which one could find among San Diego spokesmen in 1912, though in a more flagrant form. On the one hand, he appeals to law and order; on the other, he chides Congress for refusing to pass enough relevant legislation, thus "forcing" him to act in advance of it. He is partly the law's avenger, partly the outsider presuming to judge its inadequacies. He is the would-be spokesman for the American majority. Thus on balance it is probably fairer to see him as a George Bancroft gone sour than as a Rufus Choate brought up to date.

Worthy of regard is Palmer's clever use of psychology in the creation of a thoroughly unsavory view of his targets. In Palmer's writing, the imagery frequently relates to cleanliness and social hygiene; in this the parallel to Adolf Hitler's attacks upon the

---

1. See Robert K. Murray, *Red Scare* (Minneapolis, Minn.: University of Minnesota Press, 1955), esp. pp. 191–222.

Jews is striking. Twice, moreover, Palmer labels radicals as "hysterical." One is tempted to suggest that he is unconsciously projecting onto his opponents the very term which historians now most often apply to him. But in Palmer's own context, the device is actually an effective means for banishing any possibility of rational debate or argument. His reference to "the moral perverts and the hysterical neurasthenic women who abound in communism" furnishes an especially good illustration. However dimly and crudely, these phrases presage the increasing use of Freud as a weapon against political extremists. Amateur psychologists of this intent did actually begin to appear in the year 1919, and an early peak in this form of intellectual endeavor was reached in 1923, when a New York psychologist named Joel Rinaldo published a book called *Psychoanalysis of the Reformer,* in which he confidently claimed to connect a great number of specific personality traits, most of them highly unpleasant, with a disposition toward left-wing activity. To desire drastic change in the social system under which one lived was to be labelled scientifically as abnormal.

Palmer's attitudes and his tone of voice became the standard ones for at least a half century of government-sponsored extralegalism in America, usually backed by a majority of public opinion. They reveal the longstanding indifference toward legal niceties in which a very large share of Americans have concurred whenever they have felt their society and their main interests to be endangered. Behind these emotions lies the nationalism which Bancroft, like most Americans, had so enthusiastically celebrated a hundred years earlier; behind them also lies the perception of direct threat to a climate of growth which the leading citizens of San Diego had experienced so vividly in 1912. By persistently countenancing anti-Communist crusades, a great many Americans showed that sternness toward dissenters, not respect for law as such, lay uppermost in their minds.

As the *Buford* sailed, the New York *Times* applauded deporting those aliens "guilty of not merely overt act, but advocacy of the destructive and murderous doctrine, the propagandist in the press, the helper with the purse as well as the maker of the bomb. . . . The Federal authorities . . . are now acting with a vigor which the American people heartily appreciate and sustain."[2] No public opinion polls existed in 1920; however, in mid-

2. Editorial in New York *Times,* December 23, 1919.

1954 some 54 percent of all Americans reportedly supported Joseph McCarthy.

A. Mitchell Palmer, "The Case Against the 'Reds' "

In this brief review of the work which the Department of Justice has undertaken, to tear out the radical seeds that have entangled American ideas in their poisonous theories, I desire not merely to explain what the real menace of communism is, but also to tell how we have been compelled to clean up the country almost unaided by any virile legislation. Though I have not been embarrassed by political opposition, I have been materially delayed because the present sweeping processes of arrests and deportation of seditious aliens should have been vigorously pushed by Congress last spring. The failure of this is a matter of record in the Congressional files.

The anxiety of that period in our responsibility when Congress, ignoring the seriousness of these vast organizations that were plotting to overthrow the Government, failed to act, has passed. The time came when it was obviously hopeless to expect the hearty co-operation of Congress, in the only way to stamp out these seditious societies in their open defiance of law by various forms of propaganda.

Like a prairie-fire, the blaze of revolution was sweeping over every American institution of law and order a year ago. It was eating its way into the homes of the American workman, its sharp tongues of revolutionary heat were licking the altars of the churches, leaping into the belfry of the school bell, crawling into the sacred corners of American homes, seeking to replace marriage vows with libertine laws, burning up the foundations of society.

Robbery, not war, is the ideal of communism. This has been demonstrated in Russia, Germany, and in America. As a foe, the anarchist is fearless of his own life, for his creed is a fanaticism that admits no respect of any other creed. Obviously it is the creed of any criminal mind, which reasons always from motives impos-

From the *Forum*, LXIII (1920), 173–185.

sible to clean thought. Crime is the degenerate factor in society.

Upon these two basic certainties, first that the "Reds" were criminal aliens, and secondly that the American Government must prevent crime, it was decided that there could be no nice distinctions drawn between the theoretical ideals of the radicals and their actual violations of our national laws. An assassin may have brilliant intellectuality, he may be able to excuse his murder or robbery with fine oratory, but any theory which excuses crime is not wanted in America. This is no place for the criminal to flourish, nor will he do so, so long as the rights of common citizenship can be exerted to prevent him.

Our Government in Jeopardy

It has always been plain to me that when American citizens unite upon any national issue, they are generally right, but it is sometimes difficult to make the issue clear to them. If the Department of Justice could succeed in attracting the attention of our optimistic citizens to the issue of internal revolution in this country, we felt sure there would be no revolution. The Government was in jeopardy. My private information of what was being done by the organization known as the Communist Party of America, with headquarters in Chicago, of what was being done by the Communist Internationale under their manifesto planned at Moscow last March by Trotzky, Lenine and others, addressed "To the Proletariats of All Countries," of what strides the Communist Labor Party was making, removed all doubt. In this conclusion we did not ignore the definite standards of personal liberty, of free speech, which is the very temperament and heart of the people. The evidence was examined with the utmost care, with a personal leaning toward freedom of thought and word on all questions.

The whole mass of evidence, accumulated from all parts of the country, was scrupulously scanned, not merely for the written or spoken differences of viewpoint as to the Government of the United States, but, in spite of these things, to see if the hostile declarations might not be sincere in their announced motive to improve our social order. There was no hope of such a thing.

By stealing, murder and lies, Bolshevism has looted Russia not only of its material strength, but of its moral force. A small clique of outcasts from the East Side of New York has attempted this, with what success we all know. Because a disreputable alien— Leon Bronstein, the man who now calls himself Trotzky—can inaugurate a reign of terror from his throne room in the Kremlin; because this lowest of all types known to New York can sleep in the Czar's bed, while hundreds of thousands in Russia are without food or shelter, should Americans be swayed by such doctrines?

Such a question, it would seem, should receive but one answer from America.

My information showed that communism in this country was an organization of thousands of aliens, who were direct allies of Trotzky. Aliens of the same misshapen caste of mind and indecencies of character, and it showed that they were making the same glittering promises of lawlessness, of criminal autocracy to Americans, that they had made to the Russian peasants. How the Department of Justice discovered upwards of 60,000 of these organized agitators of the Trotzky doctrine in the United States, is the confidential information upon which the Government is now sweeping the nation clean of such alien filth. . . .

Sedition Reached by Espionage Act

It was shown in my report to the Senate that the Espionage Act, approved June 15, 1917, and amended May 16, 1918, was invoked to be used against seditious utterances and acts, although I felt that it was limited to acts and utterances only which tended to weaken the waging of actual hostilities. . . . Nevertheless, I caused to be brought several test prosecutions in order to obtain a court ruling on the Espionage Law and its application to seditions committed since the cessation of the armed activity of our forces.

I did this because our general statutes as to treason and rebellion do not apply to the present radical activities, with the exception of Section 6 of the Federal Penal Code of 1910, which says:

If two or more persons in any State or Territory or in any place subject to the jurisdiction of the United States conspire to overthrow, put down or to destroy by force, the Government of the United States, or to levy war against them, or to oppose by force the authority thereof, or by force to prevent, hinder or delay, the execution of any law of the United States, or by force to seize, take or possess any property of the United States, contrary to the authority thereof, they shall each be fined, not more than $5,000 or imprisonment not more than six years, or both.

Although this Act by no means covered individual activities, under this law I prosecuted the El Arieto Society, an anarchistic organization in operation in Buffalo, N.Y., indicting three of its members for circulating a manifesto which was an appeal to the proletariat to arise and destroy the Government of the United States by force, and substitute Bolshevism or anarchy in place thereof. It was printed in Spanish. Phrases such as, "the proletariat of all countries to invite to participate the revolution," "for all others who suffer the evils of servitude must join in the conflict," "to attack the State directly and assail it without hesitation or compunction," were uncompromisingly seditious advice. In threatening the officers of the Government, the manifesto went on to say, presumably addressing the officers themselves:

Cannibals, your hour of reckoning has arrived. You have fattened before having your throats cut like hogs. You haven't lived and consequently cannot die decently like men. You are at your wits ends and at the prospects of millions of human beings everywhere rising and not only asking, but demanding and executing vengeance for the promotion of your usurpt interests. Yes, they will overwhelm you. We are convinced that rebellion is the noble vindication of slaves, that from generation to generation the shameful reproach of slavery has now come. Make way for Bolshevism, for the Department of Labor, Mines, Railroads, fields, factories, and shops. Let the Soviet be organized promptly. The ideal is not converted into facts until it has come to consciousness after having been acquired by the sacrifice of innumerable voluntary victims.

On motion to dismiss the indictment this case came before Judge Hazel of the Western District Court of New York, July 24, 1919, who, after hearing counsel, dismissed the case and discharged the defendants. In his opinion the Court, after citing Section 6, said:

I do not believe that the acts and deeds set forth in the indictment and the evidence given in support of it establish an offense such as this Section which I have just read contemplates.

However, the language of this Spanish document was so violent and desperate in its declarations of defiance to the existing Government of the United States, that I, at once, placed the entire record of this case before the Commissioner of Immigration, with a recommendation that the defendants involved be deported as undesirable aliens.

All deportation activities conducted since by the Department of Justice against the "Reds" have been with the co-operation of the Department of Labor, which issued the warrants of arrest and deportation recommended by evidence that meets the conditions of the Federal Penal Code of 1910. I pointed out to the Senate certain classes of radical activities that might come under certain sections of this Penal Code:

1. Those who have 'attempted to bring about the forcible overthrow of the Government of the United States have committed no crime unless their acts amount to treason, rebellion or seditious conspiracy.' This is defined in Section 1, 4 and 6 of the Criminal Code above quoted.

No Laws Against Some "Red" Crimes

There were other activities of the Reds, however, for which there was no legislation. These were:

2. The preaching of anarchy and sedition is not a crime under the general criminal statutes of the United States.
3. Advising the defiance of law is not a crime under the general criminal laws whether the same be done by printing and circulating literature or by the spoken word.
4. Nor is the advising and openly advocating the unlawful obstruction of industry and the unlawful and violent destruction of property a crime under the United States general statutes.

These conclusions were reached after wide consultation with the best criminal lawyers in the country. In my testimony before the sub-committee of the Judiciary Committee of the Senate on July 14, 1919, at its request, I had fully outlined the conditions threatening internal revolution in the nation that confronted us. Legislation which I then recommended to meet this great menace has not been enacted. This is not my fault, for I knew that Congress was fully aware of the "Reds'" activities in this country.

Many States passed certain acts which embodied the basis of my request to Congress for national legislation bearing upon radicalism. California, Indiana, Michigan, New York, Ohio, Pennsylvania, Washington and West Virginia have passed State laws governing the rebellious acts of the "Reds" in their separate territories. These States have infinitely greater legal force at their command against the revolutionary element than the United States Government, for detecting and punishing seditious acts. In their equipment of men to carry out their laws, they far surpass the facilities of the Department of Justice. New York City alone has 12,000 policemen charged with the duty of investigation, and the District Attorney of New York County has a force of over fifty prosecuting attorneys.

Under the appropriations granted by Congress to the Department of Justice, the maximum number of men engaged in the preparation of the violation of all United States laws is limited to about 500 for the entire country. Startling as this fact may seem to the reader who discovers it for the first time, it is the highest testimony to the services of these men, that the Department of Justice of the United States, is today, a human net that no outlaw can escape. It has been netted together in spite of Congressional indifference, intensified by the individual patriotism of its personnel aroused to the menace of revolution, inspired to superlative action above and beyond private interests.

One of the chief incentives for the present activity of the Department of Justice against the "Reds" has been the hope that American citizens will, themselves, become voluntary agents for us, in a vast organization for mutual defense against the sinister agitation of men and women aliens, who appear to be either in the pay or under the criminal spell of Trotzky and Lenine.

Deportations Under Immigration Laws

Temporary failure to seize the alien criminals in this country who are directly responsible for spreading the unclean doctrines of Bolshevism here, only increased the determination to get rid of them. Obviously, their offenses were related to our immigration laws, and it was finally decided to act upon that principle. Those sections of the Immigration Law applicable to the deportation of aliens committing acts enumerated in the Senate Resolution of

October 14, 1919, above quoted, were found in the Act of Congress, approved October 16, 1918, amending the immigration laws of the United States.

By the administration of this law deportations have been made, the law being as follows:

Be it enacted by the Senate and House of Representatives of the United States of America in Congress assembled:

Sec. 1. That aliens who are anarchists; aliens who believe in or advocate the overthrow by force or violence of the Government of the United States or of all forms of law; aliens who disbelieve in or who are opposed to all organized government; aliens who advocate or teach the assassination of public officials; aliens who advocate or teach the unlawful destruction of property; aliens who are members of or affiliated with any organization that entertains a belief in, teaches, or advocates the overthrow by force or by violence of the Government of the United States or of all forms of law, or that entertains or teaches disbelief in or opposition to all organized Government, or that advocates the duty, necessity or propriety of the unlawful assaulting or killing of any officer or officers, either of specific individuals or of officers generally, of the Government of the United States, or of any other organized Government, because of his or their official character, or that advocates or teaches the unlawful destruction of property, shall be excluded from admission into the United States.

Sec. 2. That any alien who, at any time, after entering the United States, is found to have been at the time of entry, or to become thereafter, a member of any one of the classes of aliens enumerated in Sec. 1 of this Act, shall upon the warrant of the Secretary of Labor, be taken into custody and deported in the manner provided in the Immigration Act of Feb. 5, 1917. The provisions of this Section shall be applicable to the classes of aliens mentioned in this Act irrespective of the time of their entry into the United States.

Although this law is entirely under the jurisdiction of the Department of Labor, it seemed to be the only means at my disposal of attacking the radical movement. To further this plan, as Congress had seen fit to refuse appropriations to the Department of Labor which might have enabled it to act vigorously against the "Reds," I offered to co-operate with the immigration officials to the fullest extent. My appropriation became available July 19, 1919. I then organized what is known as the Radical Division.

Briefly this is a circumstantial statement of the present activities of the Department of Justice, co-operating with the Department of Labor, against the "Reds."[1] They require no defense, nor can I accept as true the counter claims of the "Reds" themselves, who, apparently indifferent to their disgrace, violent in their threats against the United States Government, until they are out of sight and sound of it, betray the characterless ideas and purposes that Trotzky has impressed upon the criminal classes which constitute communism.

Will Deportations Check Bolshevism?

Behind, and underneath, my own determination to drive from our midst the agents of Bolshevism with increasing vigor and with greater speed, until there are no more of them left among us, so long as I have the responsible duty of that task, I have discovered the hysterical methods of these revolutionary humans with increasing amazement and suspicion. In the confused information that sometimes reaches the people, they are compelled to ask questions which involve the reasons for my acts against the "Reds." I have been asked, for instance, to what extent deportation will check radicalism in this country. Why not ask what will become of the United States Government if these alien radicals are permitted to carry out the principles of the Communist Party as embodied in its so-called laws, aims and regulations?

There wouldn't be any such thing left. In place of the United States Government we should have the horror and terrorism of bolsheviki tyranny such as is destroying Russia now. Every scrap of radical literature demands the overthrow of our existing government. All of it demands obedience to the instincts of criminal minds, that is, to the lower appetites, material and moral. The whole purpose of communism appears to be a mass formation of the criminals of the world to overthrow the decencies of private life, to usurp property that they have not earned, to disrupt the present order of life regardless of health, sex or religious rights. By a literature that promises the wildest dreams of such low aspirations, that can occur to only the criminal minds, communism distorts our social law.

1. In this summary, Palmer omits mentioning that he had been greatly encouraged to begin his deportation raids by a unanimous Senate resolution on October 17, 1919, which in effect asked him to deport those aliens more rapidly. The Congress was thus by no means as restrained as Palmer (probably for his own political purposes) wishes to picture it.

The chief appeal communism makes is to "The Worker." If they can lure the wage-earner to join their own gang of thieves, if they can show him that he will be rich if he steals, so far they have succeeded in betraying him to their own criminal course. . . .

These are the revolutionary tenets of Trotzky and the Communist Internationale. Their manifesto further embraces the various organizations in this country of men and women obsessed with discontent, having disorganized relations to American society. These include the I.W.W.'s, the most radical socialists, the misguided anarchists, the agitators who oppose the limitations of unionism, the moral perverts and the hysterical neurasthenic women who abound in communism. . . .

It has been inferred by the "Reds" that the United States Government, by arresting and deporting them, is returning to the autocracy of Czardom, adopting the system that created the severity of Siberian banishment. My reply to such charges is, that in our determination to maintain our government we are treating our alien enemies with extreme consideration. To deny them the privilege of remaining in a country which they have openly deplored as an unenlightened community, unfit for those who prefer the privileges of Bolshevism, should be no hardship. It strikes me as an odd form of reasoning that these Russian Bolsheviks who extol the Bolshevik rule, should be so unwilling to return to Russia. The nationality of most of the alien 'Reds" is Russian and German. There is almost no other nationality represented among them.

It has been impossible in so short a space to review the entire menace of the internal revolution in this country as I know it, but this may serve to arouse the American citizen to its reality, its danger, and the great need of united effort to stamp it out, under our feet, if needs be. It is being done. The Department of Justice will pursue the attack of these "Reds" upon the Government of the United States with vigilance, and no alien, advocating the overthrow of existing law and order in this country, shall escape arrest and prompt deportation.

It is my belief that while they have stirred discontent in our midst, while they have caused irritating strikes, and while they have infected our social ideas with the disease of their own minds and their unclean morals, we can get rid of them! and not until we have done so shall we have removed the menace of Bolshevism for good.

For whatever reasons, a certain number of twentieth-century Americans have displayed a persistently negative attitude toward coercive authority. Such persons have sometimes faced daily hazards of a kind which make Thoreau's brief jail experience seem like the play acting of a gentleman novice. The full weight of the machinery of the modern state has been turned against these stubborn and obscure noncompliants, especially in time of national emergency.

The details of what these men have willingly gone through combine to create a powerful impression of the consequences of defying the state while continuing to live in it. However, the coercion which they faced does not have a simple or uniform character. It is compounded of several elements: bureaucratic regulations; the uncertain role of the courts; the special requirements of the state in wartime; the varying personalities of the often lowly people who enforce the regulations; the personalities and the practical means of bystanders and sympathizers; the constantly shifting interplay between all these people and the mind of the resister.

What is it that sets the role of the determined resister apart from other social roles? The resister lives a life which is continually unsettled because it is extremely vulnerable. Even in prison, where the scale of activity must appear tiny, it is an unusually active form of life. Only for brief periods can there be relaxation into the comfort of a stable routine. The individual will, having laid itself on the line, is always being tested by large and small events. Thus, to achieve a principled consistency of self-direction, another kind of consistency, which habit automatically furnishes and which is strongly attractive to most men, is sacrificed. Paradoxically, the resister, as the very consequence of his extreme degree of self-direction, finds himself placed at the mercy of a shifting external environment to an unusual extent. Of course he will reply that this loss of control has to do solely with externals, and that in the essential things his is indeed a stable life. But the purely physical aspects of survival figure prominently in the narratives of such individuals; they are apt also to dominate our own minds as we read them. And in this highly important regard these men are victims. Having shed the normal layers of self-protection which guard most of us from being similarly buffeted, they have thrown themselves on the slender and uncertain supply of community good will. Those whom they encounter are constantly forcing them to go through the motions of a highly special dance, by which they reaffirm their integrity.

No one can say whether their sacrifices have been worth the price. Attitudes toward martyrdom generally vary with the political context. Millions of Americans would admire Philip Grosser if his act of resistance had been performed in Nazi Germany. But these same people are likely to find his deeds puzzling and gratuitous when performed in their own country. Again, other Americans, thinking of the Vietnam War, will discover a heroic quality in the strikingly parallel refusals of compliance on earlier occasions. There is, however, no guarantee that in the future we will never collectively return to the mood of 1942.

These documents, therefore, cannot pretend to offer an ultimate clue as to how the spirit of extreme self-determination should be regarded. They can only illustrate the typical consequences, both physical and psychological, of throwing oneself squarely against the modern state. This they do in a way that is both resonantly universal and appallingly specific.

13. Resistance in Wartime

The mood of national conformity which swept over America during and shortly after the First World War is well known. Woodrow Wilson did much to foster it; A. Mitchell Palmer represented it at its most extreme. Now we shall observe it from its other side, in terms of its effects upon a man who directly collided with it.

Since nationwide military conscription was a novelty in 1917 (its only predecessor, the Civil War draft, had been very loose in application), contemporaries were surprised at how little resistance developed to it. Members of historically pacifist religious groups were allowed to become conscientious objectors, but Wilson rejected pleas to grant a wholly secular basis for receiving this status. Only about 4,000 men refused to serve in the army, out of more than 24 million who registered for the draft during the

First World War. Of these, uncompromising secular pacifists of a radical or humanitarian persuasion totalled only a few hundred; these were given the severe kind of treatment which Philip Grosser, one of their number, describes below.

In the Second World War, the treatment of conscientious objectors was somewhat less harsh, although nonreligious grounds for avoiding military service were again rejected. Typical prison terms ran five years, as compared with the thirty years to which Grosser was originally sentenced. Only about 18,000 men rejected any form of affiliation with the army, and only 6,000 (of whom 4,000 were Jehovah's Witnesses) refused to serve in civilian work camps and entered jails.

Except on an abstract plane for a time in the mid-1930's, conscientious objection did not become a major public issue until the Vietnam War. Whether the new debate over it represented a fundamental loosening of American attitudes in this area remained extremely doubtful. Treatment of objectors has become far more routine and bureaucratic in the period since Grosser underwent his ordeal; there is less savage fierceness directed against the individual. But the essential elements in the situation have not greatly changed.[1]

Philip Grosser, "Uncle Sam's Devil's Island"

I was never a soldier, yet I spent three years of my life in military prisons. After I registered for the draft as an objector

1. Grosser's account of his ordeal in the First World War might profitably be compared with narratives of more recent draft resistance which cannot all be mentioned here for lack of space. Lowell Naeve, *A Field of Broken Stones* (Denver, Col.: Alan Swallow, 1959), is a highly readable book-length account of the same kind of experiences during the Second World War; the files of the magazine *Pacifica Views,* published by objectors in California during that war, should also be examined. For the Vietnam period, see Willard Gaylin, *In the Service of Their Country: War Resisters in Prison* (New York: Viking Press, 1970), and, Murray Kempton *et al., Trials of the Resistance* (New York: Vintage Books, 1970), containing a number of essays which originally appeared in *The New York Review of Books.*

Subtitled, "Experiences of a Conscientious Objector in America During the World War." An undated, privately published pamphlet, apparently written after 1929, printed below in its entirety. It is in the Labadie Collection at the University of Michigan Library, Ann Arbor.

to war on political grounds, I refused to submit to a physical examination for military purposes and refused to sign an enlistment and assignment card. Instead of being tried for violation of the war-time conscription act, which was a Federal civil offence, I was turned over to the military and was subjected to all forms of punishment as an erring soldier, not as a civilian who refused to participate in a war waged "to make the world safe for democracy."

My name was called among the first five per cent of the draft quota in August, 1917. The military machine was not quite ready at that time, and the local Draft Board did not know what to do with me when I reported to them and told them that I was opposed to war and that I would not participate in military life; that to be examined physically for military purposes was to me the same as a military order and that I refused to submit to it. Chairman Burroughs of Local No. 5 Draft Board, Boston, told me that my case would be turned over to the Federal District Attorney. A few days later I reported to the Federal District Attorney and submitted to arrest for violation of the conscription act. I was released on a five hundred dollar bond to await the action of the Federal Grand Jury. Provost Marshall General Crowder, however, defined the draft act so that a man could be automatically inducted into the "selective" army, and in December, 1917, I was notified to report for military service, that I was a soldier under the automatic ruling of General Crowder, that failure to report according to notification received constituted desertion, and desertion in time of war was punishable by death. I still refused to obey the military call and surrendered to the Federal District Attorney. He in turn notified the military, and a soldier from the Irvington Street Armory, Boston, with fixed bayonet on a rifle, was sent to the Federal Building to bring me in as a deserter.

The desertion charge was not pressed, and I was transferred to Ft. Banks, Boston Harbor. Arriving at the harbor fort the guard took me to the guard house, yelled out, "Corporal of the Guard, one prisoner." A Corporal came out and answered "Turn him in." Next morning I refused to obey military orders and was put in solitary confinement on bread and water diet and tried by a special court-martial. Before being sentenced, however, I was transferred, not as a prisoner, to Ft. Andrews, Boston Harbor, where my objections to the military were to be overcome with kindness. Lt. Stanley G. Barker, the officer of tact, was to take charge of me. After being in the guard house at Andrews, not as a prisoner, the officer of tact decided that the situation was impossible. I refused to don the uniform of a soldier, refused to stand in military formation and behaved in general as a civilian in a military post in time of war. I was not a very good example to other drafted men. An agent provocateur, posing as a Conscientious Objector, was placed with me in the guard house. He talked about blowing up the place, running away from the Island and other silly stuff. I was not taken in on that and the so-called C. O. (Conscientious Objector) suddenly disappeared. Immediately thereafter Lt. Barker and Post Adjutant Lt. Chase came to the guard house, searched me, took away all my letters, newspaper clippings, the book "Under Fire" by Henri Barbusse, and placed me under arrest by order of the Northeastern Department without preferring specific charges against me. All the prisoners in the guard house were ordered not to talk with me, and the order on the guard report was that I shouldn't be allowed to leave my cell unless a noncommissioned officer accompanied me. So to be taken from my solitary cell to the wash room in the same building a Corporal or Sergeant had to be my valet. For about ten weeks I underwent all forms of torture. I was dragged with a rope around my neck to the Quartermaster's Office to be given a pair of government shoes. I was beaten with a rifle butt. A couple of soldiers used to carry me out to stand in military formations, and when the soldiers were not holding on to me, I used to sit down on the parade ground and spoil the whole show. I was chained by my hands to the bars of my cell. My arms were stretched upward till I had to stand on tiptoe. The blood was pushed back into my muscles and shoulders. Besides the twisters were tightened so that I could not move. For nineteen hours I was not even allowed to go to the toilet. At intervals the Officer of the Day, Lt. Carpenter, came to ask me whether I'd submit to military authority, and upon my refusal he would order the Sergeant to leave me in my misery. After the first nineteen hours in chains, the Commandant, Lt-Col. Ayers, ordered that the chaining to the bars should be three hours off and three hours on, day and night. All my belongings were removed from the cell, the straw sack taken out and the three hours I was off the chains I had to rest on the iron bunk with nothing to lie on and no blankets to cover up with. Between the cold and the chaining up, I did not sleep for nights.

On April 25, 1918, I was taken before a court-martial, charged and found guilty of the following military crimes:

"Refusing to obey a lawful command of Lt. Stanley G. Barker to go to work.

"Saying in the presence of officers and enlisted men that I would not obey any military orders.

"Refusing to stand at attention when ordered to do so by Lt. Carpenter.

"Attempting to create mutiny in the United States Army, by writing letters to other objectors, and urging them to stand fast, and not to submit to military authority."

My punishment, according to Court-Martial Order No. 152, Northeastern Department, Boston, was:

"To be dishonorably discharged from the service, to forfeit all pay and allowances due and to become due, and to be confined at hard labor for *Thirty Years* at such place as the reviewing authorities may direct."

The place of confinement was designated at Ft. Jay, Governor's Island, New York. On June 11, 1918, chained to another prisoner, who was found guilty of desertion and of throwing a live cat into a hot furnace and whose punishment was, four years imprisonment, I was brought to "Castle Bill," as the military prison at Ft. Jay is known in the army. My stay here was not of long duration. The place getting overcrowded, one hundred fifty of us were put "in irons" and, after a three day-and-night travel being chained, we arrived at Ft. Leavenworth military prison.

The mistreatment of the C. O.'s and the abuse of all other military prisoners at Leavenworth, with the resulting "prisoners' general strike" of February, 1919, is a story by itself. The Commandant blamed the revolt of the general prisoners on the Objectors, and soon after the strike all Objectors were removed to a stockade which was connected with the prison. We were practically left to do as we damned pleased, so on May 1, 1919, some of us even celebrated the International Workers' Holiday. The lining of our prison caps was red, so we turned our caps inside out, and carrying a few magazine photographs of Lenin and Trotzky and singing revolutionary songs, we went round and round the stockade enclosure. The guards notified the Commandant and he came running with a dozen officers, and told us not to be parading. We promised, and that was that.

Some of the boys imprisoned had newspaper experience. Many of them had office work assigned to them by the prison authorities and had access to typewriters, and spontaneously a crude sheet appeared for general distribution among the prisoners. It was called *"Wire City Weekly,"* one of the numerous underground Bolshevik weeklies in America, circulation subterranean, printed in the United States Disciplinary Barracks, Ft. Leavenworth, Kansas. Somehow the Department of Justice got hold of a copy and immediately an agent came to fort, with full power to unearth the printing press. Of course they couldn't find a press because there wasn't any. The *"Wire City Weekly"* was made almost in the Commandant's office, on government paper and on typewriters owned by the United States Army Quartermaster Corps. Col. Rice, Commandant of Leavenworth military prison, got good and sore and decided that he had about enough of the slackers. Officers were heard to say with great sincerity that they cursed the day that Conscientious Objectors were ever sent to them. Col. Rice obtained permission from the War Department to get rid of all the undesirable prisoners. In June, 1919, thirty one prisoners and myself were transferred from the disciplinary barracks to the post guard house, and at two o'clock the following morning we were called out and some of us were chained in pairs by the wrists and others were in addition shackled in twos by the ankles. We were taken to a side track where a couple cars were ready for us. The commissioned and non-commissioned officers accompanying us wouldn't tell us our destination. "Sealed orders," they claimed. To outside inquiries, however, they gave the information that we were a gang of German prisoners being transferred to a concentration camp. We were in "irons" all the time, confined in the cars from the morning we were placed at Leavenworth until we reached Oakland, California, where we were taken to Ft. Mason docks, and placed aboard a government boat to sail to "Uncle Sam's Own Devil's Island." At all stations, windows and doors of our cars were locked, and guards were posted to watch us. At railway junctions, where transfer to other lines had to be made, our cars were shifted to make the proper connections. Four train seats were allotted to each pair of convicts, and by having two vacant seats facing us we managed to fix up a "comfortable" sleeping place. If my partner, who happened to be an Oxford University graduate, forgot in his sleep that he was Uncle Sam's passenger and wanted to turn in his sleep he had to drag me along. The first day of our journey I suffered from diarrhea, and my partner had to go along with me quite often, for the bracelets were not taken off for any purpose whatsoever. The trip from Leavenworth to Alcatraz took us three days and three nights.

Alcatraz Island is a 12 acre rock at the mouth of the Golden Gate, capped with a white "house of silence." The fascination of the horrible clings about the misty Gibraltar whose history reaches back to the time when it was a military post in the day of Spanish domain. The Island is reached by government boats only, and the visitor must obtain a pass from the Commandant. The place is known as "The Rock," and sometimes as "Uncle Sam's Own Devil's Island."

On my arrival at Alcatraz I refused to work or to stand military formations. I was taken before Executive Officer, Lt. J. J. Meskill. He gave me the formal military order to go to work at once, and when I refused he sentenced me to 14 days solitary confinement in the "hole" and a bread and water diet. He said, "If Jesus Christ were to come to this Island and refuse to work, I would put him in the dungeon and keep him there."

Sergeant Cole, overseer in charge, switched on the electric light and took me down a flight of stairs to the basement, hollowed out of the rock under the prison. He ordered me to take up a bucket, and when I wasn't quick enough he lifted his club and yelled, "I'll knock your God damn brains out!" He showed me into a cell, locked the iron barred door behind me, and I heard his footsteps going up the stairs as I was left alone in the dungeon. Then he switched off the lights and I found myself in complete darkness. I tried to investigate the place which was to be my abode for the next fourteen days. Attempting to walk through the cell I bumped my head against the ceiling. Feeling my way, I found that the cell roof was arched and lower at the sides than a man's height, so that it wasn't safe to walk around in the dark. I sat on the door-sill waiting for something to happen. After awhile the lights were turned on and a guard came down with a few slices of bread and a pitcher of water. Trying to have a good look at my cell while the lights were still on I found that there was no furniture or toilet facilities, the only things that were to be seen were the pitcher of water, the few slices of bread, and the "old wooden bucket" which the guard told me would be emptied only once every twenty-four hours. The dungeon cells were under the prison, situated so that not a ray of daylight ever penetrated them. The air in the cell was stagnant, the walls were wet and slimy, the bars of the cell door were rusty with the dampness, and the darkness was so complete that I could not make out my hand a few inches before my face. It seemed eternity until the officer of the day and a guard came about nine o'clock in the evening. The cell door opened and the guard threw in a pair of lousy army blankets, wholly insufficient, as was evidenced by the fact that four blankets were provided for the warmer and drier cells upstairs. The prison officer had to put a searchlight on me to note that I was "present and accounted for." The light was switched off, and as no other prisoners were at that particular time confined in the dungeon I was left alone with the rats for company. The water and sewer system of the pails were located in the center of the underground dungeon in front of the cells and in case of accident, as the bursting of a pipe, a prisoner could have been drowned like a rat before anyone in the jail proper could have noticed it. I took off my shoes and coat and used them as a pillow, wrapped myself in the two blankets, and with the concrete floor as a mattress made myself a nice comfortable bed.

Next morning, a guard took me up to the wash room to empty my bucket. Behind the guard's back I managed to beg some of the prisoners around to give me some tobacco. A few minutes later I was back in the "hole," searched by the guard and locked in safely again. I planted a part of the bootleg tobacco under a loose brick in the wall and "rolled my own." As soon as I lit my cigarette, however, the guard returned, searched me and confiscated the tobacco. The part that I had hidden in my cell he did not get, and I managed to have smokes for the next twenty-four hours in spite of the unexpected raid.

The things hardest to endure in the dungeon were the complete darkness, the sitting and sleeping on the damp concrete floor, and the lack of sight or sound of any human being. The eighteen ounces of bread was quite sufficient for the first few days, and towards the last I had some of the bread left over. The rats were quite peaceful and friendly. The fact that the dungeon was made a store house for the "ball and chain," straightjacket, wrist chains and other implements of medieval torture was not very pleasant.

After serving fourteen days in the rat-infested dungeon I was taken out in a weakened condition to the prison hospital. The prison doctor thought that eating too much bread was the cause of my sickness. I knew better. To place any human being in the "hole" for fourteen days, even if one were given a chicken diet, was enough to weaken him. It felt good to be given a soft hospital bed after the concrete floor as a sleeping place. The food, which was quite good in the hospital, was also a treat compared with the eighteen ounces of bread. Then the daylight and the association with human beings again made me feel as if I were on a holiday.

After a two-day stay in the hospital the Doctor transferred me back to the cell-house and I was assigned to "make little ones out of big ones" on the rock pile. I did not refuse to file out with the workers, but I refused to accept tools or to perform any labor when I got there. Under military regulations no prisoner can be kept in solitary for more than 14 consecutive days, and must have at least 14 days in the regular cell or normal diet before he can be returned to solitary. Being unable, therefore, to send me back to the "hole" at once, the authorities placed a special sentry over me and I was forced to parade around the windiest side of the Island for eight hours a day, while the other prisoners worked. At the end of 14 days of grace I again disobeyed a formal order to work and was returned to the dungeon. During my interval out of solitary, a charge of disobeying a military command, under the 96th article of war (not of peace) was preferred against me. The specific offence was that I did not obey Lt. J. J. Meskill's order to go to work. I was also placed in "yellow numbers" (3rd class prisoner), which meant being segregated with the degenerates in the cell block and being seated in the mess-hall at the same table with them. For one offence I was subjected to three-fold punishment: 14 days in the "hole", court-martial under the 96th article of war and "yellow numbers." On being called for trial I refused to plead or to say anything to the military judge. He (his honor, the judge) was quite perplexed. Then he said, "The prisoner stands mute." I was found guilty and three more months of hard labor were added to my original thirty-year sentence.

Visitors were allowed to see prisoners on Sunday provided they procured a pass from the Commandant. Men in the "hole" were not entitled to have visitors. The first visitors to the Island were Anna Coggins and Margaret Stanislowsky of Oakland, Cal. They came to see Clark Getts, underground postman of Leavenworth fame, who had informed the outside world of the torture and chaining to cell bars of Objectors in that prison, and was punished with solitary for fourteen days when found out. Capt. Chambers, psychiatrist at Leavenworth, confined him in a cell with the violently insane after his fourteen days solitary was served. It was only the news smuggled out that procured his release from the "nut" factory. At Alcatraz, Getts again started the underground ball rolling and the Commandant, Col. Jos. Garrard, started to receive protests against the use of the dungeon from all over the country. My brother and other friends in Boston, and the Civil Liberties Union of New York protested to President Wilson and Secretary of War, Baker. Friends in California tried to obtain a pass to visit me, but the Commandant, abiding by the rule that no prisoner in solitary confinement was entitled to a visitor, refused passes. Alice Park, of Palo Alto, wired to Senators, to Newton D. Baker, and to the President of the United States until Col. Garrard allowed her and two other friends, Robert Whitaker and Marion Alderton, to visit me although I was in solitary. On the second term of my fourteen days solitary I was treated to the most unusual thing, a visit of three friends. I was taken up to the library by an old soldier who was to listen in, and my visitors talked with me for about three hours, or rather, I talked and they listened. After one is denied the privilege of talking, as at Alcatraz, where the silence system prevailed, when one is given the opportunity, one talks a mile a minute. The old soldier became rather tired and snoozed a little. That gave my visitors a chance to take notes.

In a letter to my brother David, Lt. J. J. Meskill, Executive Officer of Alcatraz prison, states: "Your brother Philip has assumed the role (sic) of a Conscientious Objector and when given an order by me to go to work he persistently refused. He also refused to recognize military authority. For his persistent refusal, he was placed in solitary confinement for 14 days on a bread and water diet. When not in solitary your brother has the freedom of the air and sunshine, notwithstanding the fact that he persistently refuses to work and bores his fellow inmates, who labor arduously while he stands looking on."

On account of the protests of the Civil Liberties Union and others the War Department ordered an investigation and assigned Col. Phillips to investigate the doings of Col. Garrard. The Alcatraz authorities got wind that an investigation was contemplated and prepared for it. Other Objectors and I, who were serving time in the dungeon, were transferred to solitary dark cells on the ground floor of the prison. These are ordinary cells with no bed to sleep on and the barred cell door boarded up to shut out the light. Through the cracks of the boarded door I could see prisoners carrying cement bags and beds with iron springs to the dungeon. I did not know the reason. It seemed, however, that the authorities of the jail knew the reason. At the same time the Colonel allowed four blankets for men in solitary. A few days later the investigator arrived. Everything was nicely prepared, the dungeons were floored with concrete smoothly polished, all rat-holes were blocked up, the iron springs and beds arranged. A plate of freshly grated cheese was placed in one of the cells over night to prove that there were no rats. Col. Phillips had an army stenographer with him and all those in solitary that were previously confined in the dungeon were called before the investigator. I told Col. Phillips that there was no bed in the dungeon cell where I served my 14 day stretch in, also that the concrete floor polishing was done in anticipation of his arrival, and though all my testimony, was taken down by the stenographer not a word of it was reported to the Secretary of War who ordered the investigation. Col. Phillips, the military man, could hardly be expected to be dissatisfied with Col. Garrard's methods of handling men who refused to recognize military authority and who according to army regulation were justly punished. The dungeon was not officially condemned, but on the investigator's departure the dungeon, so far as Objectors were concerned, was done away with.

On completing the third term of solitary, which was served in the dark cells, I was chased out again on the rock piles. The number of non-working C. O.'s increased to nine and all of us at that time were out of solitary. We were assigned to work on the rock pile, but refused to accept tools or to perform labor. The sentry paraded our army of the unemployed right near the quarry laborers, until one day we simply struck on the guard, refused to obey his orders to parade, sat down and did as we damned please. After numerous threats of bodily violence, the guard turned us to the Executive Officer. He, not being able to place us again in solitary until our fourteen days of grace was over, locked us in the cells and did not order us out to the quarry any more.

A group of young men and women in Oakland and San Francisco organized regular visiting parties to the Island. Many of the civilian visitors were penalized for their sympathy with the slackers. Thus Prof. W. W. Lyman and Prof. Anderson of the University of California were not reappointed as teachers. Prof. Witter Bynner was denied the privilege of being annual poet laureate at the Bohemian Club of San Francisco. Some of the visitors were questioned by Department of Justice agents. When the district attorney of Oakland decided to try Anita Whitney, liberal and social reformer for the violation of the criminal syndicalism law, he made a trip to the Island to get evidence against her from us whom she had visited. Of course we were not taken in and his trip was useless. Most of the visitors got by, by giving fictitious names. Others who were recognized by the guards as undesirables even disguised themselves in order to get to the Island.

Liberal, radical, even "bolshevik" literature was received by us underground regularly. A few tricks of the trade. We had some one in New York insert a two-sheet I. W. W. paper in a N. Y. Sunday Times, and the censor was fooled. Some of our papers were mailed to a Sergeant on the Island, and a trusted prisoner who was not suspected of radicalism and who worked for this noncom got hold of the papers ahead of the Sergeant and brought them in to us. A copy of the Communist Manifesto was bound in the covers of the Holy Bible, etc. Why, when the right and left wing controversy in the Socialist Party culminated in the forming of the Communist Party, some of us even signed the roll and joined the Communist Party in jail.

A change of administration at Alcatraz. Brigadier General James B. McDonald was appointed Commandant in place of Col. Garrard. Major Johnson became Executive Officer to replace Lt. Meskill. Old Colonel Garrard was about 80 years and in his second childhood. He had been retired long before the war began. On declaration of war, however, he was called back to service and appointed Commandant of the Pacific Branch United States Disciplinary Barracks, and the destinies of hundreds of young Americans were placed in the hands of an old, deaf Southern Gentleman, who was physically unable to handle the situation. The result was that Alcatraz Prison was mismanaged by Col. Garrard's subordinates. The notoriety and publicity Alcatraz received after the arrival of the war Objectors may have been the cause of Col. Garrard's going back into retirement.

Executive Officer, Maj. Johnson, and the newly appointed Commandant thought that the army regulations for the punishment of military prisoners were too mild when applied to Objectors. The chaining up of prisoners to cell doors had been abolished by Sec. Baker in 1918, as a result of the undue attention attracted by the publicity given that practice by the C. O. prisoners at Leavenworth. The War Department News Bureau release No. 9, Dec. 6, 1918, read:

The Secretary of War authorizes the following statement: Disciplinary regulations in force in military prisons have been modified by the War Department order. Fastening of prisoners to the bars of cells will no more be used as a mode of punishment. This and milder devices have been effective in the past in breaking the wilful or stubborn opposition of prisoners of the usual military type, who would not submit to work requirement of disciplinary barracks. Instead of being allowed to lie in the bunks while others worked, they were compelled to choose between working or standing in discomfort during working hours. Practically, under usual conditions, this has been more of a threat than an actuality, and as such it has been effective, but during recent months with the influx of political prisoners to the disciplinary barracks, particularly Fort Leavenworth, Kansas, extremity of attitude on the part of this new type of prisoner has at times led to extremity of discipline, as provided by military regulations. These clearly were not formulated with the political type of prisoner in mind, and their effectiveness as deterrents has been questionable. Men have returned for repeated experiences of the severest form of discipline. The most extreme of these is discarded and the order is comprehensive. It applies to not merely political prisoners, but to every other type.

Not being able to chain us up, therefore, McDonald and Johnson conceived the idea of building "Iron Cages," which they afterwards named "vestibule doors," in which to confine men who still refused to work after repeatedly enduring dungeon and solitary punishment. These "coffin cages" were 23 inches wide and 12 inches deep. Each cage was made of iron bars bolted to the doors of the cells. The prisoner stands upright, with an adjustable board at his back to reduce the depth to about nine inches so as to make a tight fit,—a veritable iron straight jacket. A religious Objector named Simmons and I were placed in the "Iron Maiden" for eight hours a day, alternated by sixteen hours of solitary confinement in dark cells on a bread and water diet.

By that time our underground news traveled fast, and the American Civil Liberties Union managed to have the news of the cages on the Associated Press wires the first day they were used at the Island. The cage form of punishment for Objectors to war was introduced about a year and a half after the war for democracy was fought and won, and many of our liberals thought that it was safe to protest against this form of cruel and unusual punishment. Newspaper reporters came to the Island and the authorities had to find a way to explain the torture chambers to the War Department and to the press. Commandant McDonald's explanation was as follows: "In other prisons they chain prisoners to the cell doors when they refuse to work. We place them in those standing cages, "vestibule doors," and compel them to remain in an upright position during working hours only." All along the war, Objectors had puzzled the authorities. Col. Garrard had complained to a reporter, "I have had more trouble with the C.O.'s, I. W. W.'s, than with any other prisoners. I came here from West Point in '77 and had many prisoner soldiers under my charge, but the C.O.'s I cannot understand. They refuse to work, some of them even refuse to eat. Now what are you going to do when you are faced with a situation like that? . . . These so called C.O.'s are yellow men not white men, and as yellow men, sir, we are so treating them when they seek to break the rules of this institution."

The undue attention or publicity was, however, successful to the limited extent that the cage punishment was not thereafter given in combination with solitary, and we who were "caged" and put in an ordinary cell, were allowed regular rations, and were placed in the torture chambers only for eight hours every day. I endured it for about two months, until I saw my reason going, and realized that brain and body could stand no more. I had made my protest—I gave in and agreed to work and was taken out of the torture cage.

Adjutant General Harris sanctioned the use of the Iron Cages. In a letter to Beatrice Kinkhead, of Palo Alto, Cal., dated April 27, 1920, he says that the cage punishment was "not cruel or unusual." The Iron Maidens are still at Alcatraz, though they have not been used of late. Adjutant General Lutz Wahl, at Washington, replied to an inquirer about the cages under date of Nov. 1928:

"The arrangement of the 'double cell door' as a punishment for the military prisoners at Alcatraz, was discontinued shortly after 1920, not because punishment was believed to be severe, but rather because of the undue attention attracted to it by misrepresentation as to its severity."

Though it may be true that no one has been confined in the cages recently, I have reliable information, as late as 1929, that the "Iron Maidens" four steel cages erected in Alcatraz military prison in January, 1920, are still in their proper places as before, ready for use.

Time and again my friends were advised that if I'd ask for clemency my release might have been granted. I never asked for mercy. On November 23, 1920, Wilson and Baker were magnanimous enough to release all Objectors. My release also was signed and forwarded to Alcatraz.

On Dec. 2, 1920, the authorities of Alcatraz Island, San Francisco, California, were ordered by the War Department to set me free. They put me in solitary confinement for refusing to sign soldier's release papers which stated that I was a recruit unassigned not eligible for re-enlistment, had no previous enlistment, no horsemanship, no markmanship, etc. My answer was that I never consented to obey the draft act, that I did not recognize the government's right to make me a soldier automatically, that I did not sign any papers to get into military jails and that I would not sign any papers to get out. A wire was sent to the War Department to have my release cancelled and to have me courtmartialed again for disobedience to military orders. Evidently the War Department did not care to keep me any longer, for an order was given to let me go free without my signature. So I was inducted into the service of the United States Army automatically and was

released from the service also automatically, after being transferred from one military prison to another, without serving a
single day in a military barracks.

The government gave me a new prison-made suit of clothes, a
Dishonorable Discharge and a "donation" of $10. I was free to
face the world and the American Legion.

14. Economic Noncompliance

Persistent refusal to lend the state economic support by failing to
pay one's taxes has been rarer than conscientious objection in
wartime. During the Vietnam War, a number of radicals deducted
the portion of their income tax which they believed supported the
war, put it aside in special trust funds, and waited for the government to seize the amounts. But this was a mild version of tax
refusal; it forced no change in one's standard of living. Consider
by way of contrast the case of the well-known pacifist A. J. Muste,
who refused to pay any income tax from 1948 until his death in
1967. Though the courts cleared Muste of charges of fraud and
dismissed the extra penalties for lateness which the government
wanted to collect, they continued to insist that Muste pay the
actual amount of back taxes which he owed. The only way in
which Muste could avoid such an involuntary contribution to the
Cold War was to live year after year with virtually no personal
assets that could be seized. The state thus allowed even people
such as Muste to remain out of jail, though only at the cost of
forgoing any property or possessions.[1]

Still more extreme is the instance of Ammon Hennacy, perhaps
the most persistent of all articulate radicals in recent years, who
paid practically no taxes of any kind between 1943 and his death,
which occurred in January 1970 at the age of seventy-seven.
Hennacy also had to forgo any possessions, even making special
arrangements for the printing of his books so that they could not
be seized by the government. He hitchhiked long distances to avoid
paying the former federal transportation tax. He was obliged to
shun any form of employment which might withhold taxes from

1. George Thayer, *The Farther Shores of Politics: The American Political Fringe Today* (New York: Simon and Schuster, 1967), p. 463.

his wages, thus being practically confined to odd jobs and occasional farm labor. At the end of his life he owed $1,500 in back income taxes, boasting that "I always turned in a true report and did not lie or evade." From time to time he would be mildly harassed by the F. B. I.

Hennacy's manner of living and thinking superbly illustrates the possibilities of pronounced nonconformity. He was raised on a farm in eastern Ohio, of mixed Irish and Quaker background; it is surely no accident that the name of John Brown was worshipped in his parents' household. Converted in his youth to socialism, Hennacy attended the University of Wisconsin for a year during its golden period, getting acquainted with many of the radicals then living in Madison. Forced to drop out of college to help support his family, he lapsed into the study of yoga, spiritualism, and astrology. The next spring was that of 1917, and Hennacy, by now an ardent pacifist, began devoting his full energy to propaganda against the war. Like Grosser he refused to register for the draft and spent nearly two years in Atlanta penitentiary, over eight months of it in solitary confinement. He emerged an anarchist. Only after all these experiences, incidentally, in 1921, did he first read Thoreau and Walt Whitman. For a time much later on, under the influence of Dorothy Day and the Catholic Worker movement, Hennacy was converted to Roman Catholicism, but he renounced it in 1967. He readily admitted that, despite his extreme concern for consistency, his life contained anomalous compromises; for instance, although an anarchist, he worked for the county government in Milwaukee as a social worker during the 1930's. His marriages, however, were common law, as he refused to seek the state's sanction for such a purpose.

The following excerpts from Ammon Hennacy's autobiography, which he published several times under varying titles, reveal the fiber of such a man. Though they may seem somewhat disjointed (both as a result of his own style and the requirements of editing), his mind comes through clearly, often revealing itself in small asides and incidental details. Throughout his account, there is a matter-of-factness and a reportorial honesty which is engaging. His itinerant life, which moves from Wisconsin to a kind of Walden in New Mexico and Arizona, then abruptly to New York (and most recently, to Salt Lake City, where he long ran a storefront hospitality house for tramps), may reveal what one gains and what one loses by truly setting one's own course. Here, one suspects, was a man who thoroughly enjoyed himself (except for his initial imprisonment) through many adventures. Perhaps he proves that a man of boundless confidence and simple tastes can indeed still do very much as he wants, unless he is of draft age. And this is no doubt to the credit of the American majority.

Ammon Hennacy, "Tax Refusal and Life on the Land"

Before World War II income taxes were not paid by those in the lower brackets so it was not a problem to think about. I was still too nervous from jail to work steadily, so to get the jail out of my system my wife and I started from New York City on June 21, 1921 (the anniversary of my entrance into solitary in Atlanta in 1918) with packs on our backs and $100 in our pockets. We never asked for rides but took them if offered and went 22,000 miles in every state in the union distributing pacifist propaganda, with stickers "Stop the Next War Now." We stopped to work most of the time, but on my birthday, July 24, 1925, we bought 10 acres with $100 down near Waukesha, Wisconsin, built one room in the woods, and another next year. I helped Carmen get born there June 17, 1927, and Sharon on Oct. 23, 1929. (The very day the depression started.) I had led in a strike in a dairy where I worked and lost my job. Friends suggested that I become a social worker in Milwaukee. I thought this work was too bourgeois, but for me it was either take relief or hand it out. I told my examiners for the job that I was an anarchist and would break rules when I thought it best to do so. They needed male social workers badly it seemed and I got a job with the county of Milwaukee. I organized a union and was active in pacifist circles.

In 1936 a client locked me up in a room and came after me with a butcher knife because I would not give him something that he didn't have coming. After a time I dared him to knife me (I didn't double dare him) and I shook hands with him. He put

From a pamphlet, *Two Agitators* (New York: The Catholic Worker, 1959), pp. 22–27, 29, 31, 32, 34–35; and Ammon Hennacy, *Autobiography of a Catholic Anarchist* (New York: Catholic Worker Books, 1954), pp. 89, 253–254.

the knife away and we became friends. My boss was a Catholic and head of the American Legion in Wisconsin. He wanted me to take this man to court. I refused for he had been in jail twice for knifing social workers and had done time for it, and had not learned anything. My boss thought I should get acquainted "with those crazy Catholics in New York." I asked Father Kennedy in the same block, editor of the *Herald-Citizen* about the *Catholic Worker* and he gave me a copy. Then I became acquainted with Nina Polcyn and Dave Host and worked with the CW House formed there the next year, where my daughters sang Christmas carols, and I took Muriel Lester, the English pacifist to bless our CW house. I met Dorothy Day and Peter Maurin that same year as they spoke in Milwaukee. I liked their pacifism and radicalism but not their church. In fact I sold *CW's* every Sunday in front of churches but would not go inside except to get warm.

When World War II came the American Legion wanted to have me fired from my job because I sold *CW's* on the street. I had a private hearing for an hour with a court stenographer taking notes before the Corporation Counsel. I told him that I would not quit my job nor would I cease selling *CW's* on the street, and that I would insist upon a public hearing. They dropped the charges that week. However, when the time came for me to register for the draft on April 27, 1942 I openly refused to do so and resigned my job. I thought I would get 5 years but the government had secretly made a rule that those over 45 would not be prosecuted. I was 48, and was only in jail a few hours. My wife and daughters were in the west at that time so I went to Denver and got a job at a dairy. Selling *CW's* on the street I was imprisoned incommunicado for 4 days for not carrying a draft card, and I was re-arrested a week later for selling *CW's* at the same place.

On Jan. 1, 1943 the withholding tax went into effect. About the only place where a person could work without paying taxes for war was on a farm. For here the tax was to be paid at the end of the year. The brackets had been lowered so that even a dishwasher in a restaurant had to pay about a dollar a day for war. *The New York Times* in a recent editorial declared that 83% of the income tax went for past, present or future wars.

I found work on a farm near Albuquerque with a farmer whose wife was a Quaker and at the end of the year when I refused to pay my tax I was fired but got a job with another farmer. I also sold *CW's* on the streets in Albuquerque for 4½ years and the police never bothered me.

I moved to Phoenix in July of 1948. Here the tax man was a Quaker and I was at once arrested for picketing the tax office in 1949. Again in 1950 on August 6th I picketed the tax office and fasted for 5 days because it was 5 years since we had dropped the bomb at Hiroshima. I turned in a report to the tax office, not as my duty or their right, but as a courtesy to my enemy, the State, saying: "This is my name, this is where I live, this is what I made. Try and get it." I had sent all of my money to my daughters who were taking music at Northwestern University.

Finally in 1953 I came to New York City and the *Catholic Worker* as my daughters had graduated, and since then I have not earned enough by speaking to owe any tax. The tax men have been here several times to investigate my income and have called me into the tax office when I have been picketing them. I can get 5 years for each of the 12 times that I have refused to pay my income tax. Young toughs have threatened me at times as I have picketed in New York City. Now on August 6, 1959 I will fast 14 days until the 20th as it is 14 years since Hiroshima. I do this as a penance for the sin of our country in continuing atomic testing and warfare. The following is a chapter from my life as a laborer near Phoenix, Arizona.

Life on the Land

My entrance into Phoenix, Arizona, with one cent in my pocket in July of 1947 is typical of the method by which one who "bootlegs" work must act. I walked around that morning asking for work at each farm. Around noon a Japanese farmer gave me as much watermelon as I could eat. Later on I ate some peaches at another farm, and ended up by eating cantaloupes that I picked up crossing a field. Just about dark I met a young Molokon who had read my Tolstoy booklet, "Thou Shalt Not Kill," while in a conscientious objector camp. These Molokons are a dissident sect from Russia, somewhat like the Doukhobors, who came to this country at the turn of the century, bought land and lived communally. They were pacifists and went to prison for refusing to register. Now most of them were prosperous and owned land individually, but they were still pacifists.

I put my sleeping bag under the trees in his yard and the next day worked for his uncle in the harvesting of beet seed. It was very hot and I drank plenty of water and had only melon for breakfast. After three days I worked on a farm in the middle of the desert cleaning ditches for ten hours a day at 60c an hour for 18 days straight. Then I walked for miles seeking another job which I finally got in a dairy. The farmer had wanted to go on a vacation so he taught me the work and when he came back from his vacation fired me. Then I went to the cabin of an old time anarchist in Phoenix and slept on his floor and got up early before daylight in order to get down to the slave market at Second and Jefferson, jumping on the first truck which was there to pick up workers. I did not know if I was going east, west, north or south. I was packed in this closed truck with about thirty others of all nationalities. I worked in a field for a big produce company, trimming beet plants which were to be planted. At quitting time I asked the foreman if I could sleep in one of the company shacks and he said they were only for "Nationals" by which is meant imported Mexican laborers. Native workers had to find their own place to live. He said that maybe some Molokon had a shack vacant. I walked down the road and asked the first person I met if he knew a Molokon who had a vacant shack. He laughed and said he was a Molokon and had a shack I could live in up the road in the middle of a cabbage field. My presence there might keep people from coming in and taking the cabbage wholesale. No one minded the "gleaning" of a few cabbage heads or any other field product for much went to waste anyway.

I was soon sleeping on an old spring mattress. I got an old stove from a neighbor and fixed the place up. I worked day by day for the produce company at 60c an hour at different kinds of stoop labor in the fields. One Saturday an old man across the road asked me to cut wood for 75c an hour. This was Lin Orme, the Old Pioneer, who was my friend until he died in 1953. I moved into a shack on his property not long after. . . .

"It's good to have you around; you give one confidence in life, you live off the land like an Indian," said the Old Pioneer when he saw me come home from work for a neighbor and gather my cap full of peas from our garden, and a bowl of mulberries for breakfast from the huge tree by the Lateral. I replied that I had never bought any canned goods, although at times my fare might seem monotonous to the glutton who thought only of variety and out of season vegetables. After peas came fine red tomatoes. Then there is corn, regular sweet corn, Hopi Indian corn, and popcorn, okra, a little of which goes a long way, and always onions and carrots. The chard wilts in this hot weather after being on hand since last November. We surrounded some of the tomato plants with stakes and a small mesh wire, and these plants did better than before. Bell and chili peppers are now on hand until frost, and egg plant will be my staple in about a month. These are difficult to start but grow like weeds when they have passed a certain stage. We have five rows of watermelons. Banana and hubbard squash established ownership at one end of the garden. The oven in my stove is no good, so often when I come home from work the Old Pioneer has baked a squash for me. He has electric stove but claims that food tastes better with a fragrant wood fire of desert mesquite.

Today, May 15, I received a notice that I owe $2.15 interest and penalty on my $192 tax bill for 1951 and unless paid within ten days my property and wages will be attached. This is an old runaround and I am not worrying. Today I ate the first Irish potatoes from our garden, which is more important in the life of man than paying taxes. The persimmon tree which the Old Pioneer's daughter-in-law gave me last winter now bears premature fruit. Watermelon, eggplant, tomatoes, squash, peppers and onions are doing fine.

While cutting lettuce in the fields one morning the boss told us to get in the closed truck and we would all go to the sheds. I had never been there. I found there was broccoli to pack. We finished all there was in a few hours. Meanwhile, I had heard the conversation of the workers and had picked up a bulletin of the union and found that there was a strike of the shed workers. The fields are not organized but the sheds are. I then looked outside and saw the pickets. The foreman told us he would take us home early for dinner and pick us up and pack lettuce until late that day. I told him that I was not working in the shed that afternoon because I did not want to be a strikebreaker. He replied, "you are already a strikebreaker." My answer was that because I was dumb I didn't have to stay dumb. Here the pay was $1.25 an hour but in the fields it was 60c and at times 85c. Afterwards they never asked me to work in the sheds and did not discriminate against me because of my refusal to scab, although the foreman would at times jokingly refer to me as a strikebreaker. Two I.W.W.'s, one of them also a Mormon, also refused the next day to scab. The strike was finally lost and the head of the union resigned and started a tavern.

During this winter I did not have steady work. Ordinarily Mexican men will not chop wood and it is up to the woman to do it. The Mexican neighbor women were scabbing at the sheds so had plenty of money and did not feel that they had to chop wood, so they asked me, an "Anglo," to do it. I chopped for several days while the Mexican men sat by laughing at an Anglo working for them. I like to chop wood. Some of my friends accuse me of pride but if they could see me chopping this wood they would not see much pride. Although I am really glad and proud in the right way, to do useful labor.

"Doing it the hard way, eh?" spoke the Mexican goodnaturedly as he was driving the huge caterpillar disc in the field next to the 75 by 75 feet garden which I was spading.

"Yes, but I eat from this garden every day of the year and don't plow under my crop like you folks do," I replied.

True, the disc was ten thousand times more efficient than my primitive method, but for what? Their lettuce and melons are not raised to be eaten but only for the profit to be made. If the price drops the crop is plowed under or the sheep are turned in on the field. Three years ago my Molokon neighbor received $5,000 for the cabbage on his 20 acres. Next year he put in 40 acres and did not sell a head.

Having nearly fathomed the mysteries of the harness which equipped the blind and deaf mules borrowed from a neighbor (I milked his cow while he caught the wild animals), I hitched them to a disc and prepared the garden, irrigated two weeks before. A clump of Johnson grass here and there definitely showed remnants of green after the rest of the garden was a pleasant brown.

A harrow leveled off the ground nicely. One row of egg plant and peppers remained from the summer garden. The hot August weather had nearly burned them up, but now near the end of September they were blooming again and would produce until heavy frost. The Old Pioneer brought twine and we measured out straight rows. We hitched the blind mule to the plow and the Old Pioneer led as I made—not the straightest row in Missouri or Arizona—but one good enough for the purpose. We came back over the furrow to make the ground even on both sides of it. By 1 p.m. I had turned the mules and had started to plant. The rows are 81 feet long. I have never worked elsewhere in such fine mellow ground: not a hard lump to be found. It had rained recently thus any clods that remained from the plowing were now dissolved. The furrows were about a foot and a half in depth. I leveled off the ground between them with a rake, then took a hoe and chopped half way down the edge of the furrow to make sure the ground was fine and crumbly as a bed for the seeds. Then I made an inch furrow along this edge where I judged the line of irrigation water would about reach. First I planted a row of radishes. Then taking a chance that we would have a late frost I planted 46 hills of Irish potatoes in the next row. Last year I had planted them in August, and it was so hot that they dried up in the hill instead of growing. The trick with potatoes is to have the ground loose and high enough above the furrow so that the top is always dry; the water on either side subbing up and making sufficient moisture. Next I planted two rows of chard, the green leaves of which would mix well with the carrots, to be pulled each day for a salad, from the next two rows. A row of onion seed and onion sets provided a different shade of green in the garden, followed by three rows of beets. We had made four rows for the planting of peas in November, two beds for the tomatoes in the spring, and two beds for watermelons in the spring. Very few times in my life have I had such a feeling of satisfaction as when after dark I looked over the even rows that I had just planted. All had been planted except two rows of beets. Supper tasted especially fine that night.

Long before I had known that Gandhi ate from one bowl—the aluminum one which he brought from prison—I had told women folks that they cluttered themselves up with too many dishes. Sometimes my sister-in-law at whose home I lived for a year in

Milwaukee, called me "one-bowl-Hennacy," and cut down the quantity of utensiles [sic] around my place at the table. To my mind the simple life means that one should eat that which is at hand and buy from the store only what is absolutely necessary. As long as I have Irish potatoes in the garden they form the bulk of my main meal. When they are gone I do not buy potatoes but eat egg plant, peppers and onions, which are delicious fried. When I worked in a dairy I made my own cottage cheese, but now that is one thing that I buy at the store. Except for the months of August, September and October I have chard and spinach and carrots which make a fine salad, so then I really have two bowls instead of one. When I worked at a chicken ranch in Albuquerque I ate cracked eggs by the dozen. Since then I seldom buy eggs. When I worked in a large apple orchard I had apples every day of the year—and apple dumplings—and apple cider part of the time, except in April, May and June. Here also I had asparagus seven months of the year. It grew wild in the orchard and all that was needed was to cut the shoots every few days and not allow them to go to seed. Apples do not grow around Phoenix and I never buy them. Orange and grapefruit trees are nearby and I have worked picking them, and pomegranates and figs in season. The Old Pioneer will plant some grapevines this month. We had watermelon each day from June first to August twelfth. And of course we had free access to the hundreds of acres of cantaloups and other vegetables around us. We have used no commercial fertilizer as I have a small compost pit and chicken manure. . . .

During the month of May 1945 and around that period I lived on $10 a month, sending the rest of my income to my daughters in Santa Fe. Of this $1 was for electric lights; $2.40 for *Catholic Worker's* and the *Conscientious Objector* paper that I distributed, and $2.05 for postage stamps and haircut. The balance of $4.55 was as follows:

Whole wheat flour, 25 pounds (could grow own wheat)	$1.25
Vegetable shortening, 3 pounds	.68
Cornmeal, 5 pounds (could grow own corn)	.46
Oleomargarine, 2 pounds	.38
Rice, 4 pounds (price is too high)	.58
Raisins, 2 pounds	.23
Syrup, 5 pounds	.47
Yeast, sugar, salt, etc.	.50

"There's only one way the poor class of folks can beat this system," said the poor tubercular Oakie as we shivered together on the cotton truck on a dull February morning.

"What is that?" I asked.

"I could take my wife and six kids; rent me a few acres in Arkansas away from the main highway; get me a mule, a cow and an old sow, and no one could boss me and starve me like they do now. I did it once, and I'll do it again one of these days if I ever get away from this damned desert."

"I agree with you. Many professors have written books about just that way of life but few have gone back to the land," I answered.

"Folks hereabouts was talking the other day of breaking in the stores to get something to eat. But I told them they are beat before they start at that game. Got to get back to the land. That's what I told them, but they didn't want to get too far away from the dime stores, shows and taverns," he continued as we came to the cotton field.

"You can't farm in this commercial valley though. Takes too much for machinery and if you lose a crop through lack of water, bugs, or poor prices, then the big company grabs your land for what they want to give. Have to get to the sticks," he added with a smile, "away from the places where you think you have to spend money. And the more noise, the more traffic and the more big whirring machinery, the more we seem to forget that the man next to us is our brother. I know folks back home in the country who never saw a city, who feud like all blazes though, so it isn't only where you are or what you do that counts; it must be what you have inside," my friend said as we ended another row.

A huge fat man said as we were waiting for the cotton truck that there was an ad in the paper the day before asking for 300 women to sew parachutes in nearby Goodyear. When hundreds of applicants arrived they sorted them out and hired 25 which was all they wanted in the first place. Any who were over 30 or under 20 or weighed more than 120 pounds were not wanted. He added: "A fat woman I know who is about my size has had 20 years experience in sewing could not get a look in there. Getting's so people's got to be all one size and one age, and I suppose pretty soon they'll want them all to look just alike."

We met some Oakies on the way home clustered around a woodpile in their yard enjoying the sun. One boy was wielding an ax and the father rested, snuggled a few inches away against a log, much as cartoons depict certain long-whiskered hillbillies. The subject of continued rain here and snow further north came up. One young man remarked that it wasn't fair to drop food to the Indians while the white ranchers got nothing. How much he knew of white ranchers was another thing. The inference seemed to be that no airplanes dropped anything near this particular woodpile. All the poor kid knew was depression and war so for him to think of an all time Santa Claus was understandable. . . .

I slept in a cot-house in Eloy, Arizona one night so as to be up early for the cotton trucks. In the morning as I had hot cakes and coffee in the crowded restaurant a saintly looking middle aged man sat next to me greeting me with a southern drawl. His kind voice was in keeping with his countenance. Old, decrepit and un-shaven men; stocky kids; white women, colored women and a few Indians around the L shaped counter. I am not especially hard-boiled and there have been a few times since I left Atlanta prison that I have shed tears. I have seen much of suffering and misery and I know that the poor do not have many of the common virtues which the rich applaud. Yet this morning I could hardly eat as the tears came because of the spectacle of those faces around me. . . .

At times I have steadily cut lettuce without straightening up for the quarter of a mile row. Generally there are enough immature heads to give you a rest in between. This work pays from 75c to a dollar an hour depending upon how many hours you are able to work in a day, for at times there is frost until noon. When there is no frost you can commence at daylight, but when it is hot in the afternoon it is best not to handle the lettuce. If touched when frosty it leaves a black mark on the lettuce. No portal to portal pay in this agricultural work as when you enter a mine and pay starts at the time of entrance. You stand around shivering and waiting on the frost to melt and if it is then not too hot you can work until dark. . . .

The next day I was told to work in the cauliflower dry package stand at the other end of the field. Coming to work that morning I was picked up by my Basque friend in his truck and the radio told of Gandhi's assassination. "Our Gandhi is dead," he exclaimed. I had worn a white cap similar to that which Gandhi and Nehru wore, with the words in small red script "Free India Now" upon it, for years until India was free, and my Basque friend recognized my interest in Gandhi. Amplify the Fellowship of Reconcilation, a pacifist group to which I belong, had members wear this cap as a protest to British rule in India. Arriving at the field where cart loads of cauliflower were dumped and sorters quickly discarded the small, broken and discolored heads I found that my job was to fork the culls away so that new cart loads could be emptied. Farmers came and got the culls for their cattle. The good heads were thrown on a table where four packers put them in crates and slid them over rollers to the cutter who with an enormous knife cut off the tops even with the crate. The man at the end of the slide put on the tops, and several fellows loaded the boxes on the truck.

The mystery which I never did get explained, by boss or workman, was why the packers, who had the easiest job of all with no stooping or even skill of sorting out culls, were paid from $18 to $40 a day and the rest of us got 85c an hour. It was a custom for the packer to get more was all the answer I could get. I worked here for three weeks and as the Indian lives off the country wherever he may be, this vegetarian had the one dish of cauliflower every night for supper. A one-track mind and a one-track stomach. I found a combination of cheese and jelly made good sandwiches for lunch. . . .

I had been called to the tax office and told that I should pay something down on my bill. I replied that I did not intend to pay anything, as per my notice to them. The tax man was a Catholic veteran who thought I was a Communist. He said that I would have to go to jail if I did not pay. I told him that I had been there before and was willing to go again.

"Do you think you are right and every one else is wrong?" he asked. "Just about!" was my quick reply. "How could that be?" he queried. "I already have figured it out; it is up to you to figure it out," I replied. "What kind of a country would we have if everyone thought like you?" he asked. "We would have a fine country; no government; no war; no tax man; no police; everyone living according to Christ and the Sermon on the Mount!" was my answer. At this he became angry and said "If you don't like this country why don't you go back to Russia?" "I like this country; it is my country; I want to stay here and fight you fellows who are trying to spoil it," I replied quickly.

"I don't wear a label! I'm for all good causes," replied a young conscientious objector, who, passing through Phoenix, had called the local paper to find my address, and found me one evening when I was caretaker of Jersey cows at the sale of purebreds at the State Fair grounds. Many people write to me, or come to visit me, who are drawn by different phases of my philosophy. So as to save time, I try to find out if their emphasis is I.W.W., *Catholic Worker,* pacifist, anarchist, vegetarian, life on the land, or tax refusal. This slogan of not wearing a label is fine for kids, I told my new friend, but at his age of 31 he ought to begin to have ideas that lead to some definite belief or action. . . .

In the Market Place

In the spring of 1953 the Old Pioneer died, being baptized a Catholic by Father George Dunne a few days previously. Coming to New York City I began to sell *CW's* on the street and to write about my adventures. My fellow editor Tom Sullivan suggested that I entitle my column, "In The Market Place."

One day when I was soapboxing at Broad and Wall Streets a man asked me what came first with me: Catholicism or anarchism? I replied that Catholicism came *First* and daily Mass and Communion. *Second,* to live poor as we did at the *CW. Third,* to love your enemy, for as Dorothy [Day] quotes some saint: "You love God as much as you love the person you love the least." *Fourth,* to bring this out in some association with others. *Fifth,* Don't be a parasite, which of course cuts out all Wall Street. *Sixth,* to be an anarchist for if one lived a dedicated life and put first things first, to vote for one millionaire or another whose business was to return evil for evil in courts, prisons and war, was a poor way of being a Christian. *Seventh,* in order to be effective in the spiritual and radical life I do not smoke, drink, eat meat, or take medicine.

Selling *CW's* at 43rd and Lexington a cop arrested me for selling papers without a license. I told him that according to the

Supreme Court decision in the forties the Jehovah Witnesses had won the right to sell papers without a license. He said to tell it to the judge. The magistrate let me out on my own name for trial in three weeks. I went back next Friday and another cop said I had to have a license but I talked him out of it. The next Friday Eileen Fantino and Bertha Tisius stood on one corner and I was on my regular corner when the first cop arrested me when the girls were not looking. Dorothy came up to help and finally discovered that I was in jail. They sold *CW's* all afternoon and Jackson MacLow, an anarchist friend came along and helped also. They were not arrested. I got 5 days in jail or a $10 fine and as I never would pay money to the state I did the time on Rikers Island. The American Civil Liberties Union wanted to use me as an example to provide freedom for those who always moved on when told to do so. After six months, although losing the first appeal, the highest court in the state affirmed my right to sell the *CW* and my book as I was not doing it for profit.

Across the street from St. Patrick's Cathedral a policeman told me that I should not sell "that Communist paper." I told him it was not a Communist paper, and if it was I had the right to sell it there, and I showed him a press clipping of the court decision.

"I don't care anything about the law. If I don't want you here I'll have you pinched and you'll be in jail, you won't be here. If the judge lets you out as you say, I'll arrest you again, and if he frees you, I'll arrest you again. I'll wear you out."

"What if I wear you out?" I replied.

He shrugged his shoulders and walked away. You have to be ready to die or you are not ready to live. I was never bothered again on that corner.

In 1955 there came the first air raid drill in New York City. The state law says that if you do not take part you can get a year in jail and $500 fine. I called up Ralph DeGia of the War Resister's League and other pacifists and we told the authorities that we would openly refuse to take part in their war game and would sit in the City Hall Park. Television and radio gave our message as we handed out our leaflets. 29 of us were arrested. Dorothy, being a better basic radical than I, persuaded me to plead guilty instead of not guilty. We Catholic Workers and some atheistic anarchists pled guilty and the others carried the case on appeal and it is still in the courts. We all got suspended sentences. The next year we had our demonstration in Washington Square and 19 of us got 5 days in jail. Those of us who pled guilty served them. In 1957 there were only 12 of us in the demonstration in the park across from our house on Chrystie Street and we got 30 days in jail from a Catholic judge who told us to read the Bible. Dorothy spoke about the terrible conditions in the woman's prison on NightBeat on television, and I spoke twice on the same program later. So in 1958 when 9 of us were arrested while picketing the Atomic Energy Commission near Columbus Circle during the air raid drill our sentence was suspended. In 1959 five of us who had been demonstrating annually were accompanied by 14 others at City Hall Park during the drill and we got 10 days in jail, after waiting 5 days in jail for our trial. The newcomers got a suspended sentence. This time when the judge asked me about "rendering unto Caesar" I answered that Caesar was getting too much and God was getting very little so I would render unto God by disobeying Caesar as St. Peter did.

For several years, Bob Steed, my fellow editor, and I and others have picketed the Kohler Company uptown and also the Atomic Energy Commission. More recently we picketed the hospitals in the strike of Local 1199. I have met thousands of people on the street corners as I have been out every day selling *CW's*. And I have spoken at Fordham University seven times and in hundreds of schools and colleges and churches in Canada and nearly every state in the union.

In June 1957 I went to Las Vegas, Nevada and fasted for 12 days and picketed the AEC with its atomic tests there. (The Bishop of Nevada publicly stated that my position was not in line with the Catholic Church but I did not see this paper until I came back to New York.) The terrific heat weakened me but the AEC folks were kind and I rested a lot. On the last day when the biggest bomb of all was to explode it did not go off. The army captain in charge told me, "You stopped this one, Hennacy; you better get back home and let us get to work." And the headline in the paper said: "Pacifist wins 'moral' Victory; bomb didn't go off."

In 1958 I along with others picketed the missile base at Cape Canaveral, Florida. We gave out leaflets at the different churches and the ushers at the local Catholic Church had me arrested twice and said they would tar and feather or drown me. I didn't run and nothing happened.

During this past year I fasted 40 days in Washington, D.C. and picketed the AEC there, and also 46 days during Lent, going about my regular daily work. This is not a fast against the authorities, but is a penance for our sin of exploitation and atomic war. This is my way of doing what the Quakers call Speaking Truth to Power.

15. The Spirit of Revolution

Undiscouraged by the fate of earlier radical resisters, a small but highly visible group of genuine revolutionaries appeared on the American scene during the 1960's. Something about the times made them careless of personal consequences. Many of them feared that hydrogen warfare would soon destroy civilization in any event. They also believed that mainstream American society was rotten to the core. Beyond these assumptions, their styles differed. Some continued to agitate in the classical pattern of the European Marxist tradition—purposefully, in a calculated manner, constantly with an eye to making converts from the most likely elements in the population, hoping to expand outward from such a power base. Other revolutionaries, exemplified by the Yippie movement, adopted instead the surrealist strategy of immediate shock and surprise, usually in a context of sexual exhibitionism. For them, the four-letter word and the nude human body were weapons against the sacredness of polite authority, extensions of Thoreau's attack upon America's "civic religion." Their knife thrust was directed at the very fundamentals of existing social morality. Yippies liked to hold this morality (and themselves prominently in the process) up to a mirror. They thought they could destroy the old order by exposure and ridicule. By most standards, they were "further out" than the rather square revolutionaries in such groups as Students for a Democratic Society or the Progressive Labor Party.

The cleverness of the Yippies' tactical suggestions for revolution lay in their skillful dramatization of defiance at what was really quite a low level of escalation. Anyone can play with dynamite, as certain other revolutionaries were doing early in 1970, with thoroughly predictable results (New York anarchists had similarly blown themselves up by mistake in 1914). Abbie Hoffman, on the other hand, proposed a series of small but telling public actions, unmistakable in intent yet not defined in conventional terms as major crimes, which would brazenly challenge the older way of life. He counted upon the spreading psychological impact of these episodes to create a revolutionary momentum without need for much bloodshed. Even though this strategy appeared greatly to overestimate the rebellious potential of large masses of American youth, there was an imaginative quality to it which made this movement quite special in the history of such radical groups.

Above all, Yippies took pride in displaying a firm sense of the psychic distance between themselves and others. This enabled them to perform the outrageous at just those times and places which mattered most to the normal functioning of the American system —at the Pentagon during a critical period in the Vietnam War, at Chicago during a professionally managed Democratic Party convention. On such occasions they could hope to win maximum attention, especially from liberals who might envy their daring. (The cafeteria line at Cornell, described below by Abbie Hoffman, offered a similar opportunity in miniature.) It thus seems no accident that Yippies wasted none of their energy parading in such locations as Grand Island, Nebraska. The vitals of the American political system captivated their attention. Like all political revolutionaries, they found themselves locked into an unceasing struggle with the most conspicuous agents of authority. In this sense, their lives were hardly free.

Yet they had a definite enough conception of "liberation." Manifestly it was supposed to mean the freedom of the individual continuously to gratify his impulses without hindrance—to do whatever might come into his head, without suffering social consequences. Life was to consist of a constant and unrestrained flow of self-expressive deeds. In actual practice, however, the Yippie style revealed the continued presence of a number of inhibitions. Freedom was equated with certain kinds of bold acts (nudity, stealing) and not with others (murder, torture).[1] On a deep level, the Yippie imagination was therefore reassuringly fas-

1. I do not mean to deny that Hoffman toyed with the idea of revolutionary violence, though he appears to have broken quite decisively with this notion in *Woodstock Nation* (New York: Vintage Books, 1969). In-

tidious. Certain marks of a conventional upbringing revealed themselves despite the most thoroughgoing of radical platforms.

And thereby the social scientists who had long proclaimed the universal importance for mankind of socialization into a patterned group identity seemed to get in the last word. If Yippies appeared automatically to identify "liberation" with only some forms of release while shunning others, then they were promoting a new social ethic which would continue to have tacit limits of its own on what was done and not done—and not an ethic under which literally "anything goes." The debate over Yippie goals would thus properly center on the specifics of their alternative way of life, not on the idea of eliminating the superego from human consciousness. All this is to say that Yippies could not altogether escape from the more prosaic heritage of the revolutionary tradition as it had developed since the Enlightenment. At the very least, their conception of human nature remained as optimistic as that of earlier anarchists and socialists.

What was somewhat new about them, and what made them appear so shocking to unliberated Americans, was the brazen defiance which characterized their tone. This, joined with an apparent need for a periodic public form of release, reminds one oddly of the spasmodic outbursts of "Captain" Slade. Could it be that Yippies combined some elements of the popular version of "liberation" along with that of anarchist intellectuals? If so, the influence was largely subterranean and indirect, for Yippies did not celebrate American mass culture in the spirit of pop art or the early Andy Warhol; their acts of outrage were seemingly of a different kind. But the spirit of exhibitionism, which implies periodicity, was indeed an element common to the frontier wildman and to the Yippie demonstrator. Perhaps actively to engage in revolution (in itself a sudden, highly climactic event) is to identify with a form of struggle which remains at bottom Faustian

---

stead I refer to the character of his implicit eventual utopia, which is recognizably leftwing libertarian, rather than one that glorifies killing or torture in a fascistic manner. (Spiro Agnew, in the passage below, would be confined and ridiculed, but not physically harmed.) Jason Epstein, in a sophisticated discussion of Hoffman's motives (*The New York Review of Books*, February 12, 1970, pp. 25–28), questions whether Hoffman really has desired to see his 'moral fantasies' acted out in a literal, public manner. But his very enthusiasm for the Woodstock festival seems clearly to answer this, so far as a *cultural* revolution leading toward his utopia is concerned.

and developmental. There was nothing truly contemplative about the Yippie, despite all the talk of sexual ecstasy.

No chance existed in practical terms, of course, for a successful revolution in America. This was true not just because of the sheer power of the Establishment (though this was unprecedented in world history) but also because the great majority of Americans—however wisely or foolishly—remained firmly attached to their present way of life. Militants, whether black or white, comprised only a tiny fraction of the population, and there was almost no likelihood that these statistics would ever change decisively. Revolutionaries like the Yippies were thus knocking their heads against a solid wall, even if the bricks could be conveniently labelled "false consciousness."

In America, therefore, the urge toward revolution becomes no more than one final category of pronounced individual nonconformity. It is the most active form of resistance, but like all other such forms it is a symptom at most of desperate tenacity rather than of prophetic insight. The existence of revolutionaries on the American scene in recent years testifies to the incapacity of the present civilization to satisfy certain deep aspirations, including a demand for simple equality of treatment to minorities who are in our midst. But revolutionary activity is futile except as an honest statement of the intensity of one's moral convictions.

Here is the final irony about the Yippies: that ultimately their significance is as moralists. Just as atheists constantly demonstrate how seriously they in fact take religion, Yippies reveal in every shocking action their earnest involvement with the moral pattern of the American majority. They would not abandon morality, only one particular ingrained version of it. This makes them no less subversive from the majority's point of view. But it means that in discussing the revolutionary challenge, one should be discussing the substantive nature of such issues as property rights, human rights, sexual freedom, sexual restraint—and not the nebulous, impossible dream of "total" liberation. Yippies (and such other groups as the Living Theater) have helped to encourage such basic discussions to take place. However, if this is their real contribution, and if the real contribution of conscientious objectors is similarly to force the rest of us to rethink the fundamentals of a war policy, then the resister is merely an extreme variety of social critic. By exposing himself, by making himself vulnerable to retaliation from the state, he is showing how deeply he cares about the future and how anxious he is that it conform to his own conception of moral rectitude. In effect, if not in his own mind, he is therefore one kind of reformer.

In countries where revolutions can really happen (and they may be becoming fewer), the role of the revolutionary is a serious and very special one. In America, the call for revolution may in part be a clever advertising device to force the layman's fleeting attention upon a socially just alternative. It is a hard-sell campaign for basic social change. The Yippie is an ingenious promoter with a hundred gimmicks. In this respect the Yippie's version of anarchism is truly native-born.

"Free" [Abbie Hoffman],
"Revolution for the Hell of It"

The Rising of the Pentagon

We are throwing everything we've got at the Pentagon—evil hulk that sits like a cancerous death-trap on the beautiful Potomac. An Exorcism to cast out the evil spirit on October 21st. The Pentagon shall not survive, neither for that matter will the fag-ridden peace movement. "Ring-around-the-Pentagon-a-pocket-full-of-pot." Wrote a beautiful poem that I lost last week when Marty Carey and I got arrested there. Met a Digger in San Francisco who went to the Chicago New Politics mess. He sat on the stage with a flute in one hand and a tire iron in the other, drawing an imaginary circle around himself. "I declare this area a liberated zone. Anyone enters and I'll kill him." A total political stance. I am ready for the struggle. As far as the revolution goes, it started when I was born. Broke with the Mobilization coalition for Washington (which means I don't go to their meetings anymore). At one meeting I declared, "The truth lies through insanity." They are scared shitless of the mystery. They suppressed an article by Keith Lampe because of the word "SUCK." My Lord, what fucking prudes. Our suck magic is much too strong medicine for the middle-class peace movement.

Many wild happenings are planned in preparation: circling of Washington Monument, Empire State Building (vertically), Make Love Day orgy leading up to October 21st. On Columbus Day a mighty caravan of wagons will roll East out of San Francisco to rediscover America complete with real live Indian scouts, compliments of Chief Rolling Thunder of the Shoshone. Junk cars, stolen buses, motorcycles, rock bands, flower banners, dope, incense, and enough food for the long journey. Wagon train East. Yahoo! We will dye the Potomac red, burn the cherry trees, panhandle embassies, attack with water pistols, marbles, bubble gum wrappers, bazookas, girls will run naked and piss on the Pentagon walls, sorcerers, swamis, witches, voodoo, warlocks, medicine men, and speed freaks will hurl their magic at the faded brown walls. Rock bands will bomb out with "Joshua fit the Battle of Jericho." We will dance and sing and chant the mighty OM. We will fuck on the grass and beat ourselves against the doors. Everyone will scream "VOTE FOR ME." We shall raise the flag of nothingness over the Pentagon and a mighty cheer of liberation will echo through the land. "We are Free, Great God Almighty, Free at last." Schoolchildren will rip out their desks and throw ink at stunned instructors, office secretaries will disrobe and run into the streets, newsboys will rip up their newspapers and sit on the curbstones masturbating, storekeepers will throw open their doors making everything free, accountants will all collapse in one mighty heart attack, soldiers will throw down their guns. "The War is over. Let's get some ass." No permits, no N.Y. *Times* ads, no mailing lists, no meetings. It will happen because the time is ripe. Come to the Day of Judgment. Forget about degrees, they are useless scraps of paper. Turn them into Litter Art. Don't hold back. Let the baby-Beatles shut your mouth and open your mind. On October 6th the Diggers in S.F. will present the Death of the Hippie and the Birth of the Free Man. S.F. will become the first Free City extending the boundaries of the Haight-Ashbury ghetto. Extend all boundaries, blow your mind. . . . Skulldiggery shoots up the media. Chaos. Riots, earthquakes, black men grabbed in Philadelphia with enough poison for 4,000 people or cops, Digger hurls pie at colonel at University of California. "Splash." Last night at the Straight Theater in Haight-Ashbury sheer beauty of mind-body dancers acting out fears of paranoid America, huddled in a corner and casual as can be they take their clothes off and continue the dance. "We are free, we are Men, we are Women, we love, we hate, we are real"—plastic-coated America. America let's see your balls, America can I only see them on a tiny screen in a superjet acted out by John Wayne and Robert Mitchum in a land called El Dorado. El Dorado is now at the Straight Theater and it's all free.

The Night the Red Sox
Attacked the U.S. Embassy

. . . America will lose more than its face in Vietnam rice paddies hunting jackknife warriors with napalm machines. Where will be our Alamos? Where even our brave men planting flag on Iwo Jima hilltop? America is a mythic land. Dreamed up by European beatniks, religious fanatics, draft dodgers, assorted hippie kooks, and runaways from servitude off to the New World of milk and honey. Europe said, "If you don't like it here, why don't you leave." Echoed three hundred years later by a middle-aged veteran with sagging ass and sagging belly hunched over sign reading IF YOUR HEART IS NOT IN AMERICA GET YOUR ASS OUT. Sagging crudeness of Joe McCarthy national policy. And even as we slaughtered the Indians, as children we could accept the encircled group of covered wagons fighting to defend themselves and wanting simply to make it to a little pastureland in the green hills and valleys of California.

The myths of America are strong and good but the institutional machine is a trap of death. Can you believe I was eighteen before I even knew this country had a Depression but at thirteen I could list with correct dates all Revolutionary War battles and discuss in detail the battle at Lexington and Concord which took place just thirty miles from my hometown? . . . America lost its balls in the frontier and since then there have been no mighty myths and now we hunt for them in lonely balconies, watching *Bonnie and Clyde*. Tragic figures, born out of rejection of a machine-mad American sterility, like James Dean and Marilyn Monroe crushed by plastic Hollywood. . . .

Plans for the Destruction
of the Universities

Last fall I spoke at Cornell and announced, "The food here is free!" and twenty of us walked into the cafeteria, loaded our trays with hamburgers, Cokes, and pies and walked out without paying. We sat in the dining hall laughing and slapping each other on the back stuffing our faces with Digger shit. I told them of epoxy glue and what a great invention it was. And at another school we asked them why they were there and they said just to get a diploma and so we passed out mimeographed sheets that said "This is a diploma," and asked the question again.

We appeared at Brooklyn College and announced, "The classroom environment is free," unscrewed desk tops and transformed them into guns, passed out incense and art, wrote Black Board on the door, switched off the lights and continued in darkness, announcing that the security guard was one of us, freeing him through the destruction of his identity, and in general doing whatever spontaneously came to his mind. Our message is always: Do what you want. Take chances. Extend your boundaries. Break the rules. Protest is anything you can get away with. Don't get paranoid. Don't be uptight. We are a gang of theatrical cheerleaders, yelling Go! Go! Go! We serve as symbols of liberation. That does not mean that at times we do not get caught. Everyone's been arrested or stomped on or censored or shot at or fired from a job or kicked out of school or all that and more. "We've all been snuffed," as Ed Sanders says. It is not the snuffing but the notion that we can get away with taking chances that keeps us going. The reason I believe world revolution is inevitable is because the National Liberation Front is doing so well, not because they are getting slaughtered. Ché Guevara went to Bolivia because they got away with it in Cuba. The Movement grows through successes, not through frustration. The ability to withstand frustration is what keeps us alive.

Our brothers and sisters are in the prisons of the universities. It is our duty to rescue them. Free men draw a line in Harvard Yard and dare President Pusey to "cross over the line." Students burst into the dean's office and when he asks them what they want they all hold a finger in the air. At San Francisco State, Black Panthers and even White Panthers wait on the rooftop ready to shoot if the administration calls the police onto campus. Make war on bells in school. Bring alarm clocks to class and have them ring on the half hour instead of the hour. You can buy a small Japanese tape recorder and a few speakers from a junkyard for about twenty-five dollars. Some careful camouflaging and you can suddenly turn the school into a huge discothèque.

. . . What would happen if large numbers of people in the country started getting together, forming communities, hustling free fish on Fulton Street, and passing out brass washers to use in the laundromats and phones? What if people living in slums started moving into abandoned buildings and refusing to move even to the point of defending them with guns? What if this movement grew and busy salesmen sweating under the collar on a hot summer day decided to say fuck the system and headed for welfare? What if secretaries got tired of typing memos to the boss's girl-friend in triplicate and took to panhandling in the streets? What if when they called a war, no one went? What if people who wanted to get educated just went to a college classroom and sat-in without paying and without caring about a degree? Well, you know what? We'd have ourselves one hell of a revolution, that's what. "Who would do the work?" Fuck it. There's always some schmuck like Spiro Agnew lying around. Let him pick up the garbage if he's worried about the smell. We'll build a special zoo for people like that and every weekend we'll take the kiddies over to Queens to watch them work. . . .

Part Three

The Police as Contemporary Symbol
of Authority

Because resisters and revolutionaries have had no chance for
general success in America, their importance has actually lain in
dramatically testifying to the existence of alternative policies or
philosophies. Their challenge, in other words, has mainly been
a symbolic rather than a literal one. However, the defenders of
authority cannot be viewed in the same light. For these men have
actually held effective power, and the way in which they have
exercised it has greatly shaped the quality of American life on a
large scale. Any firmly established regime, such as the Soviet
Union or the United States, will most fairly be interpreted not
on the abstract plane of ideology but in terms of how it treats the
entire population which is subject to its physical control.

Thus the recent debate over the legitimate limits of authority
in America—as distinct from debate over substantive issues such
as foreign policy—properly centers on the upholders of law and
order, not upon the small groups of radical militants. The question again becomes one of how extremely unpopular people are
treated in practice. The stakes in such a judgment are high. If
one concludes that the general picture is one of great harshness
and disrespect for individual rights, then one may reluctantly be
led in the direction of defining America as a garrison state, in
local as well as worldwide terms. If, on the other hand, coercion
is minimal and sparing, America will tend to be confirmed as a
society in which, perhaps, not everything "goes," but in which
there is a steady subtle encouragement of diversity, experiment,
and self-pride among widely disparate individuals and groups.

All aspects of the political system—Congress, the courts, the legal profession—are relevant to such an evaluation. But the local police department has become an increasingly prominent test case in assessments of this kind. The police are unusually visible among agents of authority because they are most in evidence during the routine course of our existence and also because they take on a major role in dramatic moments of confrontation with dissidents. Thus they come first to mind when the question of submission to authority is discussed by persons of all persuasions. In purely practical terms, too, their role has for some time been regarded as a national problem, extremely difficult to solve or to affect.

What is the history of this "police problem"? Why has the behavior of American policemen lately come to seem such an important issue? Are the police the spokesmen for the majority or do they in some important respects constitute still another minority, despite the unusual power they wield? These are questions that soon spring to mind in any down-to-earth debate about liberty and authority in the United States at the present day. Americans are therefore beginning to study their police machinery with a new degree of interest.

16. The Police Tradition in America

An appropriate starting point for the study of the police is Ernest J. Hopkins's assessment of them, written in 1931. Hopkins was a journalist who toured the major cities of the nation interviewing law enforcement officials and closely observing the practices of police departments at that time. His resultant book, *Our Lawless Police,* was not a scholarly work in the narrow sense, but its accuracy is highly regarded by legal historians who know the period well. In it, Hopkins tried not only to describe the concrete situation he found—for instance, low standards, prevalence of street brutality and the third degree, and denial of basic rights to the accused—but also to explore the previous history of police attitudes, and of public responses to them, in the United States. Though somewhat speculative, his account of these matters is shrewd, balanced, and believable.

Hopkins's description of the police mentality and his insights into its earlier origins take on unusual interest when they are read forty years later. The continuities between the nineteenth century and the 1930's are what Hopkins himself emphasizes, and the further continuities between his day and ours also become striking. The police emerge as a curiously static enclave, protected by the dependence upon them of elected public officials, somewhat like the army in a small nation. Isolated from many sectors of the public, poorly paid, and offering a dangerous and unpleasant life, city police forces could only hope to attract men of little education or ambition. The main rewards of the job were security of tenure, the status of the uniform, and (doubtless for some) the satisfaction of literally throwing one's weight around. These incentives might be sufficiently powerful to men of a certain background and temperament, but they created an atmosphere from which the more independent-minded were bound to recoil. And thus police departments became highly self-selecting.

A casual acceptance of violence was deeply ingrained in the American police tradition. The policeman's convenient theory of human nature, which divided mankind into two categories, citizens and "crooks," enabled a no-holds-barred strategy to develop in dealing with those who were defined, often arbitrarily, in the latter category. Police, at least in 1931, did not hesitate to push "crooks" around. But the violence was usually controlled, routinized, supervised, in the manner (though not to the degree) of the German SS, rather than resembling the spree of the frontier outlaw.[1] From time to time, to be sure, individual policemen would go beyond these limits; Hopkins's book abounds in well-substantiated gory incidents, including beatings, emasculations, and various forms of torture practiced upon prisoners. But, while such episodes seem to have been distressingly common, at least in those years, they are still exceptional when placed against the backdrop of daily police routine. The style of police violence is probably best summarized as that of a stable bureaucracy which by its particular nature condones intimidation and within which from time to time a minority of the personnel can gain a full temporary release of their private feelings.

Who was a citizen and who was a "crook"? Hopkins's assertion that "crooks" were usually immigrants from southern and eastern Europe is extremely suggestive, especially because it runs parallel to the role of the black man in the police imagination, both then and more recently. Hopkins's argument that many immigrants

---

1. It is well known that sadists were systematically eliminated from the SS, so that bureaucratic control could be maintained at all times.

accepted crime as a way of life because of the casual violence and discrimination vented upon them in their childhoods by slum-hardened policemen seems highly plausible, though it can never be directly substantiated. If one does accept this theory, then the police have indeed been partially to blame for the long-term atmosphere of violence—among both whites and blacks—in our major cities. But one must not forget that the cultural traditions of the different ethnic groups undoubtedly played some part in producing this overall picture as well.

Harsh methods against those identified as "crooks" were constantly justified, as Hopkins points out, by the metaphor of a "war" against crime. If so, then police should have directed their energy, especially at that time, toward the really big criminals, the heads of major syndicates. That is what J. Edgar Hoover wanted the nation to believe was actually occurring. But, elsewhere in his book, Hopkins shows that this was not the case. Not simply because of graft, but often out of fear or helplessness, police departments accorded the really big gangsters the kind of treatment reserved for persons of high status. When apprehended, large-scale criminal operators were not subjected to the third degree or any other form of brutality. And for the most part, these men were left entirely alone. Brutality was instead characteristically practiced against youngsters just beginning a life of crime, boys and young men without connections, immigrants and Negroes. This must somewhat qualify our picture of an impersonal or "objective" police bureaucracy.

Though conditions have changed in many details, the 1931 account by Hopkins reveals the seedbed of today's police problem.

Ernest Jerome Hopkins, "Police Tradition and Mentality"

Behind the psychology of the police as a group or class there may be distinguished three formative influences: the tradition of the profession, the character of the personnel, and the stimuli peculiar to police work. In the last twenty years these underlying

From Ernest Jerome Hopkins, *Our Lawless Police: A Study of the Unlawful Enforcement of the Law* (New York: The Viking Press, 1931), pp. 324–347, 361. Copyright 1931 by The Viking Press, Inc., renewed 1969 by Ernest Jerome Hopkins. Reprinted by permission of the publisher.

psychological factors have been subjected to an entirely new set of circumstances which have, on the one hand, only augmented the professional sense of authority and, on the other, have tended to deprive this sense of general social support. The result has been an acute emotional opposition between the police, the public, and the law.

I. The Police Tradition

American police originally were town watchmen and, as the law provided, constables. By necessity, our larger cities—roughly a century ago, in many cases less—established police departments. The reason for the new form of organization was disorder—street violence of a degree hardly known today. Atlantic seaports were riotously rough; western towns were rough in the way of all frontiers. So, at the outset, actual fighting was the main job of American law enforcement. There had to be rudimentary order before there could be law. And we were a disorderly people. Promptly, then, the municipal policeman lost the constabulary attitude, became something more than the arrest-making agent of the courts, and formed the habit of inflicting direct and violent punishment himself. It was a drastic departure; its importance is clearly seen today.

Vigilantism might have ended, constables might once more have become constables, but that immigration began before native disorder was quelled. For a half-century police work, increasingly punitive, centered in the "tough districts" and foreign slums. Shillalah-battles with the old-fashioned street gangs that fought the police with stones and fence-posts, mêlées in waterfront saloons, brawls in brothels—these formed American police work. The disorder of a nation in motion required such police. The memoirs of veterans yet living are filled with accounts of these battles of the roaring days. By natural attraction, the work called unto itself happy warriors who loved the fray and who, further, knew nothing and cared less about Anglo-Saxon law. Police work meant, not law enforcement primarily, but fighting.

Almost as early, municipal police departments became adjuncts to corrupt boss-politics. This, too, was an obvious consequence; the cities were full of singularly flagrant vice; vice needed protection, and that meant the police. Control of the police department was the primary objective of politics; it was as lucrative in gathering tribute as any other source of revenue in the days before the franchise scandals, and much more valuable in gathering votes. So the policeman found himself a personage of no mean political importance; he was essential to carrying elections, and since these were spoils-system days, he had to carry them or be ousted by the rival machine. The intimate alliance between bossism, vice, and the police department was fully developed at the time of the Tweed Exposure in 1871. It exists, of course, today, but it may be regarded as vestigial. Only the more completely boss-ridden cities approach what is past.

In the era of the great bosses, the police lost entirely their purely constabulary relationship to government. An addiction to force, plus an authority over politics, are the two classic elements in official tyranny; very early, our police acquired both.

What prevented the public of the times from recognizing the trend was the extreme good-nature of the policeman of the day. Although his position now had tyrannic elements, he was no tyrant except in a narrow sphere. The general public knew and loved him as the crossing-cop with an Irish quip for ladies and children, and the catcher of runaway horses. The crime world and vice world and political world in which he lived existed as a thing far apart from average life. Respectables hardly admitted that it was there. So, while they turned their backs, the tradition became fixed. It brought with it some features still retained:

Two causes determined that the policeman should be a large, heavy man: the hand-to-hand "roughhouse" fighting, without guns, that prevailed; and the parade of power wanted by the machine for the purpose of impressing the public and keeping the voters in line. The first was necessary before disorder took to firearms. And the idea of "The Finest" originated as Tammany propaganda. So did the idea of charity work and doing good turns to widows and the poor; Tammany, prototype of all machines, was always a charitable institution in its public-relations aspect. Police work everywhere has maintained this side; policemen are open to every sort of charitable and sentimental appeal. The strange inconsistency of this fact with the frequent over-riding of simple human rights in the cases of arrested unfortunates finds its explanation in the political tradition.

So, too, does the large tolerance toward vice and the underworld, which has made the anti-vice laws so hopeless of enforcement. Toleration once meant votes; the purpose today may be clouded, the traits remain. And the police detestation of "reform" and "reformers" may be easily traced to the days when political movements, hostile to the dominating machine, always took the name of "reform," as the Ruef-Schmitz regime did to begin with in San Francisco and the Penrose machine in Pennsylvania. The very word "reform," in those spoils-system days, threatened the policeman's job. And, of course, the obtaining of promotion through political rather than law-enforcing activity was intrinsic in the situation. It, too, survives.

A vitally important factor on the moral side of the tradition must be noted. In that era of a gulf-like separation between the good and the bad, the pure and the outcast, the black and the white, there was thoroughly established in police work a moral code recognizing the existence of two categories of people, sharply and forever defined. A more sophisticated age has recognized, under compulsion of fact, that humanity in general is more or less gray; but if you think the black-and-white concept is dead in the land, you should become better acquainted with policemen, even of the fairly modern school.

You would find, repeatedly and unconsciously expressed, the nineteenth-century moral concept that once a man has committed crime he is a criminal; once a woman has sinned she is a "fallen woman"; and its obvious corollary is that justice does not apply to outcasts, hence that the classes most subject to law enforcement have no rights. I have referred to the order against false arrest, issued in the Chicago department in 1931, as a milestone in progress toward lawful enforcement, and it was such, but in that order was the following language: "This regulation shall not be construed to mean that professional criminals, gunmen and hoodlums who have police records" [note: the wording is not "penitentiary" records] "shall not be arrested and held for investigation . . . This regulation shall not be construed to mean that persons with criminal records, hoodlums, and suspicious characters, shall be accorded this consideration" [the legal right of communicating with the outer world].

There are, in short, by police tradition, two sets of law; one for good people, one for bad; and the restraints upon official conduct accordingly apply only to those persons whom the police consider eligible to constitutional protection. This dualistic concept of humanity is, literally, a major tenet in the policeman's creed today; it is rooted in the past, finds unconscious expression in the speech and actions of law-enforcing officials, and, even more vigorously than the somewhat relinquished tradition of violence, it is the inspiration of lawless law-enforcement and of the extremes to which it goes.

This school of thought is very much at the heart of this entire problem. Its symbol is the word: "crooks." No word is more perpetually on the policeman's lips, no concept more constantly in his mind—and his emotions. There are citizens, and there are "crooks." There are good people and "crooks." This hard-and-fast moral code is, of course, not unique with the police; but it lives in police tradition in its simplest and most extreme form. Prevailing, the policeman is something of a moralist. He reflects much upon right and wrong, sorting people into the two great classes as definitely as he books them for robbery or murder. Such was the picture of American society as it really was in the black-and-white days. And it is a straight, simple concept, with plenty of adherents throughout the ages.

In police work, this belief in "crooks" and in the morality of making life miserable for "crooks" thoroughly predominates. It is a free-will concept. It outweighs, of course, all considerations urged by the environmental school of criminology. "Crooks" are not to be excused in any degree on the score of environment; favorable influences are wasted on the "crook." And it outweighs, as we have seen, the considerations of constitutional justice, individual rights, at times (as this concept has done historically) humanity. The crook "knows only one language and laughs at the detective who tries any other. . . . Protect the good people and treat the crooks rough. . . . Make a good friend of every business man and a bitter enemy of every crook." The phrases are from Captain Willemse's book, so often quoted in these pages. They will be repeated to you, in essence, by nine out of ten policemen with whom you discuss the age-old problem of crime.

And the tradition, finally, developed the strong idea that our courts of law are wrong and, in no slight degree, immoral. The courts "gave crooks a chance," "set crooks free." Defense lawyers, too, of course, are under the same imputation. I hold no brief for the legal profession; it has given us lawless defense quite as often as police have given us lawless enforcement. But the policeman's attitude toward courts and the law is founded in his moral code. No consideration more greatly illuminates the lawless enforcement of law than this: that the incredibly simple pigeon-holing of people as exclusively righteous or unrighteous pervades this profession as it does no other.

Long ago, too, this idea acquired heat. This was the direct result of our system that makes a trial a form of combat. The more acute that combat in the courtroom has been, the more have police become determined to cut through the forms, step outside the restrictions, and win the victory somehow. Crooks should be punished; the courts might not punish them; so the police would. Crooks would perhaps not be convicted in court; so the police would make them confess, and force the court to convict. Again, it is a moral issue. The Constitution itself, in that it regards crooks as equal before the law, is in no small measure viewed as immoral. Lawless law-enforcement thus expresses an emotional complex, and every endeavor of the public to curb it encounters a resistance cemented in morality.

II. Survival of the Tradition

Into the influence of this tradition there have come, through the years, replacements of man-power of a type excellently calculated to keep it alive in all its features. This is a volunteer service; men of large stature and bulk selected this calling by natural affinity. Fighters selected it because it gave promise of the chance to fight. Individuals of the exhibitionistic proclivity were naturally attracted by the uniform, star, parading, publicity, and the gratifying petty authority. Politically-minded youth flocked to it, or were helped into it, as a matter of course.

One does not see an intellectual enthusiasm for the principles of justice exerting any marked attraction, or the general idea of restraint which is the general idea of law. Quite definitely, the attraction of police work has always been its less lawful aspect. It has been the alluring promise of personal unrestraint—whether along lines of violence, display, authority and prestige, politics, membership in an influential group with secret-society characteristics, or downright profit. All are summed up in the concept of privilege: privilege easily attainable by physical and political talents alone.

I asked a Western detective what drew young men into police work. He answered without hesitation: "Adventure"; then, after a pause, added, "and graft." In an Eastern city, a veteran patrolman returned in a mood of indignation from escorting a new recruit around his first beat. He had shown the entrant what alleys to inspect, what signboards to look behind, what doors to test; toward the end of the circuit the lad had turned to him and demanded: "What I want to know is, what speakeasies come through?"

One element of attractiveness in police work, which has developed in the years since Lincoln Steffens and Ray Stannard Baker exposed " the shame of the cities," presents a challenge. Civil service, "taking municipal employees out of politics," became the lever of the municipal-reform movement that began about 1905. Quite generally, although latterly, it was extended to cover police departments. Now, civil service has two aspects: it selects men by competitive examination, and it makes it extremely difficult to get rid of them, once selected. The two must go together, for success.

In police work, the latter aspect of civil service certainly has predominated. It seems beyond question that the man-power given to police departments by the examining boards has been inanely and insanely selected in many localities; while at the same time the old and strong tradition has been cemented through the lifetime protection against discharge. And insofar as inertia is implied by the civil service status itself, it may have worked for inertia in police work.

A tragic loss of opportunity for thoroughly renovated and modernized police departments occurred, in city after city, when the police departments, already out-dated, were first put under civil service. By allowing major credits for "experience," commissions simply gave the old ways life-tenure. Examinations, since then, usually have had little to do with law, little with enforcement. There have been physical tests: running a hundred yards in twelve seconds, and the like. But the mental requirements have been the classic despair of enthusiasts for the civil service. Bruce Smith, an expert on police administration, cites such questions as the

following: "Where is the Tropic of Capricorn?" "Who was the
Duke of Wellington?" "What is a felony?" "How much wall-paper
will be required for a room ten feet high—" etc. Some of these
are, no doubt, general-intelligence questions; but there is no search
for specialized aptitudes. In Boston, the examinations (held by
the State) are severe; only one applicant passes in three. In Milwaukee, a Socialist administration in control for a quarter-century
has had a rigid civil service. (Can it be altogether by coincidence
that these are probably the two most law-abiding and effective
police departments in the country?) But the civil service system,
normally, has selected this one all-important municipal department for the emphasizing of its weaker side. It has not weeded out
incompetent applicants; it has let them in. Once they were in, it
has operated to keep them in. Civil service commissions have acted
as obstacles to departmental renovation in more than one city,
and for political reasons. By the device of selecting new men
from the topmost three on the list, and moving others up, politics
has entered in the selection. Men fully meriting discharge must be
discharged twice—once by the police trial-board, once by the
civil service commission—so that unless the two work together,
discipline itself is blocked.

Records show that policemen are recruited mainly from the
unskilled callings. They have been motormen, conductors, chauf-
feurs, truck-drivers, ice-men, factory-hands, garage and service-
station employees, warehouse workers, clerks. It is an entrenched
political custom for politicians to keep an eye open for husky lads
with friends and get them "on the Force." The favor will be
returned later, perhaps, in a pinch. San Francisco's department
recruited a good many preliminary fighters and amateur pugilists.
Seattle's ran to longshoremen and ex-sailors from the navy. New
York's has gone increasingly to clerks. Boston's strike, occurring
just when overseas divisions were demobilizing, filled the department with ex-soldiers, who made excellent policemen. In cities
where the reputation of the local department is low, the volunteers
tend to reflect that reputation; similarly where it is high, or markedly political, or markedly violent. In Chicago, the civil service
commission arbitrarily added 10 per cent to each man's grade
in the examination, simply in order to "qualify" enough men to fill
the vacancies.

Police executives generally express concern. Several have stated

that they felt that the level of ability entering police work was declining. One told me that a "flippant" type of youth was entering
the service—this in one of the best departments. Another stated
that unemployment, since 1929, was giving him some excellent unemployed mechanics; but that during the high-wage period a
mechanic content to earn a policeman's wage usually had other
disqualifications not connected with trade-skill. A third, who had
just put eighty-three new men on the force, was sitting at his desk
wondering what they were doing on the streets—he and an officer
had gone over the list, found six first-class, ten moderately good,
and the rest, as he expressed it, "out."

Some striking facts given in the fourteenth report of the Wicker-
sham Commission, that on "Police," are properly interpreted as a
critique upon the civil service rather than upon departments mentioned. This section, consisting of August Vollmer, David G.
Monroe, and Earle W. Garrett of the University of Chicago, found
that "more than 60 per cent of the present police personnel have
never entered high school, and the status of the officers is little
or no better." Alpha tests, taken by the departments of Los
Angeles, Minneapolis, Kansas City, and Cleveland, were contrasted
with the same test taken by the freshmen at the University of
California. An intelligence-rating of 120 in a possible score of
212 was taken as the minimum standard for a competent policeman. Here is the table, in which, said the report, "the lack of
passable material is tragically exemplified":

Group	Number of men	A 135-212 Per cent	B 105-134 Per cent	C+ 75-104 Per cent	C 45-74 Per cent	C- 25-44 Per cent	D 15-24 Per cent	D- 0-14 Per cent
Freshmen, University of California	1,760	60	31	7	2	0	0	0
Los Angeles police department	1,712	9	18	29	28	12	2	2
Minneapolis police department	473	7	19	29	27	11	3	4
Kansas City police department	623	5	13	24	33	15	6	4
Cleveland police department		4	13	28	33	15	6	1

There is always the chance that policemen, already secure in
their jobs, do not take such tests seriously at the time they are

given. But the results of the intelligence tests nevertheless amount to a terrific indictment of the civil service as applied to the selection and after-elimination of policemen. The lawless enforcement of law, involving the overriding of public liberties, has been entrenched behind civil service status. And the man-power selected has been psychologically designed to respond with great readiness to the forceful, dominating, emotional, and direct-action traits in the police tradition, and to interpose a mental barrier against change.

Of late years there has been a movement for police training. Several departments have established schools. Some are limited to a three-months' course in firearms for the neophyte policeman. A few have established some degree of training for the regular men, and some even include the officers. Probably the most hopeful sign in the picture of police work, it remains true that this movement is yet young and is hardly conscious, as yet, of the larger function of the policeman. Shooting, wrestling, courtesy, are taught, with some smattering of how to get evidence and prepare it for presentation in court. But the preservation of American institutions intact, while so doing, is seldom in the curriculum so far, and the cursory teaching of the "rights of an accused," as seen in the average police manual or textbook, is given no significance. It can hardly be, in view of the fact that the teachers in these schools are police officers, themselves in the tradition. I know one police school where the work in "law" is given by the same desk lieutenant who writes out the confessions which suspects are made to sign. . . .

Cross-fertilization with the ideas of the outside world is at once the thing most greatly needed and the least sought for by this inbred profession. The concepts of law, as we have seen, have not penetrated. The concepts of criminology are sometimes met with a sneer: "Do they expect us to feed ice cream to baby-killers?" The policeman's real education is derived from the men he works with, under, and, one should add, against. Still, the schools offer hope.

III. Modern Pressures and Conflicts

In the era when the police tradition was fixed, it worked out in practice with little serious friction. The violence was exerted against roisterers, outcasts, and immigrants. Policemen dealt out punishment to these groups with social sanction, if not with the sanction of the law. Municipal politics and graft went by default, as far as the "disorganized respectables" were concerned. The concept of "crooks" as a different race of human beings, to be visited with brutality in prisons or out, prevailed in the sociology of most Americans.

Moreover, it was then quite easy to define or identify "crooks." They were those who broke the penal laws and not in connection with municipal politics. So the policeman could be sure as to his sanctions. He lost no friends, jeopardized no public support, by punishing and maltreating crooks. His own violations of the law were socially encysted.

It is the general breaking-up of this condition, the bringing of police work into contact with the whole population, that has thrown the lawless enforcement of the law into sharp collision with general standards, whether of modern criminology, old-established law, or what is viewed as actual justice today. Neither public nor police has reacted well to that encounter. The public has become cynical about its own legal agents and its law; departments have become aloof, egotistical, and arbitrary. It is possible to trace this unfortunate development by the series of collisions that have occurred between the law-enforcers and the people; each resulting on the one hand in a swelling of the policeman's authority-complex, on the other in a new birth of antagonism in some large group. The demonstration has shown the old tradition recoiling upon the police themselves, exacting penalties in failure and in isolation to the exact extent that the tradition was outside the law.

The first collision has been mentioned. Many years ago the American policeman undertook to make enemies of the vast numbers of foreign-born people whom we were inviting to our shores. There is no blacker page in American history than that which tells of our reception of the immigrant; and that page must be shared equally between those who exploited the newcomers economically, and the police. This was not true of the first waves of immigration which brought us the Irish and the Germans; it was the great influx of people from the Slavic and Latin countries that saw the policeman regarding the immigrant as his natural prey. Granted that the problem of policing the slum was extremely difficult, it must also be granted that the brutal methods unanimously adopted helped to raise the whirlwind of crime in the second immigrant generation today. The sons of men who were clubbed, bullied, browbeaten and harassed by our representatives of law under the serious delusion that here was a class without rights, grew up with an antagonism learned in childhood and ready to flower into crime. Perhaps nothing is more directly responsible for the violent character of much present-day crime than the lawless police work that was visited upon the immigrant in the past.

Shortly after the World War, I was in a position to see this process in operation. The California State Commission of Immigration and Housing, with which I was connected, had the general function of trying to adjust the foreign-born people to American life. Immigrant education (they called it "Americanization" then) was one route to that end; another was through a State Bureau of Immigrant Complaints, devoted to hearing individual grievances and engineering the adjustments. The files of the complaint bureau grew clogged with cases in which the abusers of the immigrants were the police. "The Law" was refuting, in daily practice, exactly those principles of American justice which immigrants were learning in the "Americanization" classes. What was true in California was true everywhere. Blackjack, club, false arrest, incommunicado, the third degree, wreaked upon the foreign-born, must assume heavy responsibility for the failure of assimilation. Lawless law-enforcement bred both crime and anarchism in the second immigrant generation. The task of bringing races of differing legal mores within our code was difficult at best; against such official contradiction of the code, it was impossible.

A second large-scale alienation followed the next great extension of police authority. This occurred when the masters of our economic destinies undertook to define economic dissent as crime. With the growth of industrialism, strikes occurred; the disorders of the eighteen-nineties saw the participation of police in strike activity, upon the employers' side. This function came by a natural sequence: the cities had political bosses, the bosses had police departments at their disposal, disorder in strikes lent a pretext for constabulary involvement. The individual policeman may or may not have felt personal sympathy with the working class from which he sprang; but political orders and his own love of the fray decided his course, and the long succession of anti-labor activity began.

How profound has been the social effect of a situation that saw each step in labor's progress taken in the face of police intervention, it is difficult to determine; but today this trend is kept vigorously alive. As I write, striking garment-workers in New York, including women and girls, are being manhandled by police under color of an anti-picketing ordinance, and there are strike battles involving police in the coal-fields. In this connection, of course, our police have collided squarely, not only with an important section of our population engaged in an upward struggle, and their white-collar sympathizers, but also with the First Amendment to the Constitution, guaranteeing free speech and free assemblage. It was not law, but political control, that doomed the police to take ever the reactionary side. Police tradition determined the methods to be used in this tragic extension of the lawless enforcement of the law.

With the immigrant, and militant labor, added to the victims of arbitrary authority, only a collision with the average citizen was needed. It came, by the automobile—the eternal bugbear of traffic. Here, at last, the well-to-do middle class was brought into contact with the police. The capacity of the old direct-action methods to breed human antagonism now became generally demonstrated.

Memory is yet vivid in the older auto-driving public, as to details of that first contact with authority. It was nobody's fault. Here were fighting-men suddenly thrown upon a new and strenuous problem, with neither training nor precedent to guide them. Of course, at first, they applied the same forms of speech and authority which tradition had given them as the forms to be employed. Now, in this connection, police history was made: for at last, in traffic regulation, the tradition of force was found wanting and was definitely reversed. Its failure when applied to the so-called middle class was too emphatic to be overlooked. Traffic, and nothing else, bred the new school of courtesy in police work; stimulated the police-school movement, yet young, of which much may be expected; shocked police departments for the first time into some appreciation of the inadequacy of mere domineering as a substitute for law. But it gave the police, too, a new appreciation of the willingness of the American public to smash its own laws, to "cut corners," and to pay for the privilege. Out of this first general contact, both police and public came with a mutual disillusion. We knew, now, that police were lawless. They knew we were, too.

There was the new factor in the situation: we were all candidates for membership, now, in the policeman's category of "crooks." And since the tradition exempting crooks from the protection of law persisted untouched in its field, complexities were increasing. At least, before traffic arrived, the policeman was fairly safe in applying uniform direct action to all within his purview. Now his task was spreading greatly; so were the workings of influence; police work became highly personal. It all fostered the authority-complex, though with a new need of making exceptions. Another trend began:

City councils, and State legislatures, beginning with the wave of progressive reform about 1905, began to create new laws in the *mala prohibita* category: housing laws, health laws, inspection laws, truant laws, welfare laws, sumptuary laws, freak laws. In an average city today, there are 1500 laws under which policemen may make arrests; almost any one of us is subject to arrest at some time for infraction of some of those laws. Many of them were and are necessary; many are of highly debatable necessity; some are outrageous and foolish. But the common quality of all has been, that groups have wanted them passed, that the large public has been indifferent, and that their proponents have reposed under the innocent illusion that the police were neutral-minded automata with some universally applicable and mysterious technic —that they would, and could, obligingly put life into any laws that might be adopted. This is our modern legislative trend, during the past quarter-century, and such was the fallacy upon which it was based.

Passing a law with no adequate study of its problems of enforcement is the height of practical folly. It has so been proved, surely, to the national satisfaction. It cannot be said that our law-enforcers resisted this trend. New authority was aggrandizing the American policeman, giving him power and position, far beyond any other policemen on earth: why should he resist? Housing laws made him a slum inspector. Sanitation laws put him in charge of garbage-cans, milk-bottles, and food piled on fire-escapes. Moral laws made him the supreme critic of plays, motion-pictures, and literature new and old, the arbiter of sex morality and the judge of seaside dress. Anti-vice laws gave him a fruitful field of exploitation; on the one hand he was literally forced to hire stool-pigeons as *agents provocateurs,* on the other he had protection to sell. Some day the story of our sumptuary legislation, and its working out, will be fully told, and it will be seen that the conditions legislated against in no case have disappeared; what has disappeared is the integrity of public, policeman, and government within the field of operation of such laws. By this entire process, men of the tradition and type described above have received an extension of authority that has, first, inflated the dominant attitude; second, engendered friction with the public at point after point of normal life; third, set a public against its own police in a continual hunting for the holes in law enforcement; and, finally, because the size and scope of the police task have grown impossible, created an all-around exhibit of failure and a general popular disgust at the pass to which "the Law" has come.

On top of it all, the evil genius of our destinies put attempted prohibition—the supreme example of blind faith in automatic law enforcement and ignorance of the contra-suggestible nature of a people educated to self-rule. Which brings us to the final item in pressure upon the police: the pressure of an amazing new intensity of crime.

The bases for modern crime had already been laid. There was the definite antagonism in groups of foreign origin against our law, created in no small part by the police. There were the older sumptuary laws and the graft which they bred. There was the very serious diversion of police energies away from the control of crime, with lack of progress in the skill of solving crime. Prohibition emphasized all these factors. The child of the slum became a paid gangster. The violation of the sumptuary laws became big business. The public greatly connived at the breaking down of its own over-reaching laws. Crime became what we know it to be.

What is the connection between all this familiar picture and the street brutality, false arrest, and third degree? To me, it seems altogether direct and obvious. Let me summarize.

There was a lawless tradition, centering on the concepts that the crook had no rights in law, also that the police had the right to punish independently of the courts, and that force was the patent medicine for crime.

There was a man-power precisely designed to keep this tradition alive, entrenched in a position to keep it alive in fact, and usually resistant to change; especially to any change meaning a reduction in direct-action authority.

There was an old inability to get results through the courts; made more acute by shysterism, and by police lawlessness itself.

There was a series of events which, by antagonizing first one great section of the public and then another, made it difficult to the verge of impossibility for the policeman to call upon the general public for the normal degree of assistance necessary in curbing crime.

Simultaneously there was a great extension of the paper authority of the policeman; it inflated his sense of power, even while the reality of power, namely the co-operation of the public, was being withheld.

There was a tremendous diversion of police energy away from its central task; plus a new viciousness, difficulty, and danger in crime itself: so that our police have shown a bravery not surpassed by any other set of men on earth.

Lawful police work relies, simply, upon the ability of the policeman to gather evidence against each criminal and to produce it in court. But a diffusion of his interests made this impossible, or at least extremely difficult. An antagonized populace would not bear witness against its neighbor. An exalted police would not, in common parlance, "get out and rustle" except on prominent crimes. The easier course was to perform "busy-work," make countless arrests on the non-essential laws, depend no longer on the laborious gathering of evidence—and rely on direct action.

Insofar as the third degree and its allied malpractices are not simply the modern form of the old brutal tradition, they are the direct-actionist outburst of an authority at once too large and badly swamped, cut loose from its normal sources of support and, against terrific obstacles, "going it alone." Solutions lie along the path of altering the tradition—relieving the pressures—restoring the broken contact with the public and with its fundamental law. There is risk to our institutions if solutions are not found. . . .

We have a strange country, with a heterogeneous population. It is extremely vital to our national future, perhaps to national survival, that a loyal attitude be inculcated in our semi-alien groups toward our fundamental and peculiar national institutions. Anarchy for the coming years is being bred today by the lawless practices that have entered the enforcement of law. Our national need is a police who can and will put statute law into effect without at the same time tearing down our fundamental individual rights that underlie the law of the land.

17. A Police View of Society and Morals

Police spokesmen minimize the continuities between the state of police activity four decades ago, as described by Hopkins, and that of the very recent period. They point to the increasing professionalization of police work, the development of new techniques which rely upon sophisticated technology, and a concomitant growth in pride and morale. They claim that police work has been effectively divorced from politics in most American cities, and that it has become increasingly efficient and impersonal (hence impartial). There is no doubt, in actual fact, that far more attention is now being paid to the training of policemen than was the case in the 1930's. As in so many other occupational areas, an image is being created of computerization, planning, and nonpartisan expertise.

But in the instance of police work, there are severe doubts about the credibility of this image. The educational level of policemen, although it has risen, continues to be relatively low. Pay scales are still not adequate enough to attract many highly talented or ambitious men to the force. As in the case of teachers, the least well-qualified personnel tend to be placed in the undesirable assignments located in ghetto neighborhoods. Persistent reports occur, many of them well documented, of rampant right-wing political extremism and racial prejudice within a number of large police departments.

The four documents which follow seek to illuminate this confusing situation. The first reveals the social philosophy of a renowned police chief, William H. Parker of Los Angeles, who, until his death in 1966, was widely admired in police circles. Parker's perspective was one which seemed not only forward-looking but pace-setting, representing the very best ideals within the profession. The Los Angeles force was looked to as a model of what training, efficiency, and scientific expertise could do in transforming the policeman's role.

Parker's admirers nonetheless pointed with pleasure to the fact that his grandfather had been a law enforcement officer on the great plains frontier and that Parker himself grew up in Deadwood, South Dakota. It was assumed that the Wild West tradition, at least as a pleasant memory, meshed well with the new spirit of technological control and professionalism. Parker's public relations awareness also drew favorable attention. It was noted that as police chief he spent a great share of his time addressing groups of businessmen and other citizens, and that he was unusually active in the American Legion and the Boy Scout movement, as well as in the Community Chest and in State Department activities involving contact with overseas visitors. Wounded on the beach in Normandy, Parker was all-American.

Parker's mind, as revealed in speeches he made in 1950 and 1952, interestingly mingles the old-fashioned with the up-to-date, and in a way which manages to be surprisingly consistent and self-contained. To begin with, he announces his acceptance of the starkly dualistic view of human nature which Hopkins had identified with the police mentality of 1931. Society is fundamentally healthy, but there are "evil forces" lurking within it like germs. "Wicked men" sometimes even find their way into police departments and thereby give those departments a bad public name. For this reason, Parker frankly admits, "police history is not a pretty thing." But the remedy lies in an even sterner and more efficient rooting out of these foul people, both within the police and in the larger society.

Yet Parker also dallies with moral relativism. He admits that law is often arbitrary, and that reasonable men may disagree about its validity in particular instances. Law enforcement is simply to prevent anarchy, not to impose an ethic which is intrinsically just in philosophical terms. Criminals have their own belief system, at odds with that of the majority of citizens.

What, then, gives Parker the right to refer so casually to "evil forces" and "wicked men"? Because, he would reply, no matter how arbitrary the law and how relative the moral standards on which it is based, no man has the right willfully to break it, for it (the law itself, the product of the majority at any given time) is the one absolute. Everything is morally relative, in other words, except democratic legalism. The advocate of change must work within the law, trying to convince his fellow citizens that such change is desirable. To step outside this framework is to join "the criminal element." This element must be fought ruthlessly and with great cleverness. A long-range solution is to educate, or brainwash, criminals into an acceptance of the beliefs of the majority.

From within the confines of this perspective, Parker can even go on to praise the idea of individuality. His answer to the problem of individualism is the one which powerfully appeals to all American moderates: namely, that there is already sufficient scope for all legitimate forms of individual self-expression within the context of obedience to existing laws as determined by the majority. Believers in more radical forms of individual behavior (drinking alcohol in the 1920's, smoking marijuana today) can scarcely justify doing something so serious as repeatedly breaking the law merely to gratify such private inclinations. For the law permits a great many diverse forms of personal pleasure, and there is a gratuitousness about consistently selecting a form of pleasure which lies outside it. Disobedience of the law in any form tears at the fabric of society. This line of reasoning is enormously persuasive to American liberals as well as to conservatives. Parker emerges as no right-wing extremist in social philosophy, but instead as yet another heir of George Bancroft and, to a large extent, Oliver Wendell Holmes.

Where Parker is less liberal is in his rejection of a socioeconomic interpretation of crime. "Hunger, poverty, maladjustment, and other physical problems do not incite crime," he says; they merely "incite beliefs that may produce crime." There is good reason for him to insist on the importance of this distinction and for him to emphasize the role of intellectual history, rather than of social structure, throughout his analysis. For if physical shortcomings directly produced crime, then he would be forced to admit that a massive program of social improvement offers the best hope of attacking all these diseased germ cells in our midst. But such a conclusion would be deeply alien, for on this practical level Parker was scarcely a liberal. Therefore he had to locate the genesis of crime in the human mind, where it could be linked with free will (hence hated). Parker stressed the reassuring idea that individual morality is the basis of social morality, to be altered only by a long and paternalistic process of education. If evils are at bottom moral rather than physical or social, it is much easier to adopt the posture of the righteous crusader, a role which, despite mechanization, is still highly appropriate to the social life of the police chief. Because educational campaigns are difficult, ineffective, and above all respectable, they have long tended to be favorite remedies among essentially moderate men in positions of power. For one thing, their results are so hard later to pinpoint that they spare the public official embarrassingly concrete disclosures of failure. Unfortunately for Parker, however, the Watts riot of 1965 did eventually furnish just such a rare negative verification of the efficacy of his approach.

Parker has been called, by a hostile academic critic, a man "whose professional views were extremely conservative even for an extremely conservative profession," and a man whose behavior in the aftermath of the Watts crisis "bordered . . . on the paranoid."[1] Toward the end of his sixteen-year administration in Los Angeles, Parker's right-wing sympathies became far more apparent. He tolerated a large and open John Birch Society membership within the department; he was explicitly hostile toward the civil rights movement; he identified himself with anti-Communist crusades and refused to meet with liberal community spokesmen. Though he did all these things, the present documents show that these later actions do not adequately reveal his social philosophy at an earlier and happier point in his career. (And these essays were, after all, written during the heyday of McCarthyism.) These earlier writings were reasonably sophisticated, and it is only fair to judge Parker (as the model for the "new" kind of policeman) on their basis.

But even so the continuities with Hopkins's much earlier description of the police mentality remain impressive. At least it can be said that Parker was initially aware of the shameful aspect of the police tradition and that, within his limits, he tried for a while to come to terms with it, before ultimately giving way to the much easier posture of an A. Mitchell Palmer.

1. Robert M. Fogelson, "White on Black: A Critique of the McCone Commission Report on the Los Angeles Riots," *Political Science Quarterly*, LXXXII (1967), 350. For an extended critical discussion of Chief Parker, see William W. Turner, *The Police Establishment* (New York: Putnam, 1968), pp. 70–106.

William H. Parker, "Crime and Belief"

People have organized themselves into our present society in order that each person may contribute to the welfare of the others and thus provide a full and protected life. But social contacts create friction. There are wicked men with evil hearts who sustain themselves by preying upon society. There are men who lack control over their strong passions, and thus we have vicious assaults, many times amounting to the destruction of the life of a fellow man.

To control and repress these evil forces, police forces have existed, in some form or another, throughout recorded history. On the surface it would appear that complete harmony should reign between the good citizens of the community and their police. But there are frictions even in this relationship.

As society increases in number, it becomes more complex and additional regulations become necessary to preserve it from disintegration. But it must be remembered that this great nation of ours was founded by men and women who fought their way across the Atlantic to escape the harsh and oppressive restrictions under which they lived in Europe. From these hardy pioneers we have developed a nation of people who are deeply conscious and rightfully jealous of their individual liberties and the dignity of man. The resultant conflict between increased regulation and individual liberty gives rise to a problem of serious proportions.

The police, in an attempt to obey legislative mandate and enforce regulations, are often brought to grips with the individuals to whom these measures are applied. The American people possess a greater degree of sympathy for the "under-dog" than any of the

---

Portions of two addresses, the first a radio speech following his appointment as Chief of Police in Los Angeles, August 9, 1950, and the second, with the above title, delivered at the Fifty-Ninth Annual Conference of the International Association of Chiefs of Police, September 1952, in O. W. Wilson, ed., *Parker on Police* (Springfield, Ill.: Charles C. Thomas, 1957), pp. 5–7, 12–17. Reprinted by permission of the publisher.

other peoples on earth. Thus, when police measures are applied against an individual, we are inclined to extend sympathy to that individual and are therefore prone to overlook the deeds of the individual that made police action necessary.

The police enforcement burden is therefore in two parts: they must enforce regulations on one hand and maintain public support on the other. It has been aptly stated by an eminent judge that the success of any police department rests largely upon the confidence of the people whom it serves.

There is another factor that enters into the delicate relationship of the police and the public. It is axiomatic that a police force is judged by the acts of its individual members. Sometimes wicked men elude the detection devices of the selective processes and find their way into police service. Their evil acts, when discovered, cast disrepute upon the entire force and sometimes result in a sharp break between the community and the police. The infrequent contact between the individual citizen and the police is usually with only one or two members of the force. The nature of that contact builds within the mind of the individual a concept of the entire organization. When the experience is satisfactory, the citizen praises the force and is pleased with his police establishment. When the experience is unpleasant, all members are grouped together as the object of his castigation.

In an endeavor to build a superior police department in the City of Los Angeles, we have applied recruiting standards and a measure of selectivity probably more stringent than has been used in any other part of the country. For example, in a recent examination for the position of policeman, in which over 2300 applicants participated, only seventeen achieved a passing grade in the written test. Credits in the oral examination and the application of veteran credits qualified less than 150 men out of the original group. Subsequent thereto, many of these failed to pass our rigid medical examination and others failed to perform in accordance with our high standards during their probationary period.

Those receiving appointments have been sent through a comprehensive training period at the police academy and, in addition to the other phases of the policeman's craft, these officers have been inculcated with a deep appreciation of the relationship between the police and the public. It is the considered opinion of authorities in the police field that about five years of service are required before an officer, through training and experience, develops the sense of judgment that enables him to handle almost any situation with a minimum of conflict and friction.

Ours is a young department. Over 3000 young men have entered the department since the cessation of hostilities in World War II. With rare exception, all are veterans of the War. It is a radical change to relieve a man from a fighting armed force, where he is imbued with a deep sense of preservation of self and destruction of the enemy, and to place him in the peacetime role of a police officer where he must refrain from the use of physical force unless it becomes absolutely necessary for the protection of society.

In the administration of the affairs of your police department, it will be my earnest endeavor to provide you with an honest and efficient police force, dedicated to the service of the community. The law will be enforced in a reasonable fashion, with full consideration given to the individual rights of every citizen. We will continue in our attempts to eradicate from the community those parasites who prey upon us and whose nefarious activities drain huge sums of money from local channels of trade. . . .

. . . The public does not rest great responsibility upon those in whom it does not rest great faith. Police history is not a pretty thing; it does not inspire confidence. However bright the present and promising the future, the past hangs as a millstone about the neck of . . . professional-minded police leaders. . . .

. . . The prevention of crime is not one of the traditional police tasks. Law enforcement officers are neither equipped nor authorized to deal with broad social problems. We do not control economic cycles; we are not equipped to deal with racial, religious, or political prejudice; we are not arbiters of right and wrong. In short, we are not healers of social ills. Our job is to apply emergency treatment to society's surface wounds; we deal with effects, not causes. . . .

. . . I will disappoint anyone who expects to find here an easy formula for preventing crime. As a problem in ethics (the third branch of philosophy) crime has received attention from the best minds of all the centuries. Not only has man failed to find a solution, he has been unable to agree on a common definition. To one man it is a crime to steal a penny but good business to steal a fortune. To another it is a crime to gamble at cards but recreation to gamble at horse races. And to another it is a crime to betray a political party but idealism to betray a nation. What is a crime? We do not know; we have only our personal concepts.

As policemen we are guided by an artificial definition of right and wrong—the law. We do not pretend that it is all-wise, all-inclusive, or all-just. The student of ethics will find in it many flaws. The student of theosophy [sic] will find in it many deviations from fundamental religious principles. The student of logic will find in it many contradictions. It is probable that no man exists who agrees with all the statutes. This creates a remarkable paradox. Law exists, not because we do agree on what is right and wrong, but because we do not agree. A universally accepted standard of ethics does not exist. To prevent anarchy, it is necessary to impose this artificial standard based on majority agreement.

When a majority of persons do not accept these imposed concepts, the law is changed, either by democratic process or by force, and new standards are adopted. The minority who do not accept them, however, are said to be the criminal element.

Crime has its birth in this clash between individual and group ethics. I submit that the volume of crime is proportional to the quantity and breadth of this variance. I believe that this hypothesis is susceptible of proof. As practicing policemen we are familiar with the fact that the average criminal does not believe that he is doing wrong. As he views the situation, he is doing right. However faulty his premises, however weak his logic, however selfish his reasons, and however transitory his beliefs, he acts in accord with his own concepts.

Therefore, if we are to approach crime at its most vulnerable angle, we must recognize that man is a creature of belief. If anyone doubts the power of belief, let him turn to his history book and watch man rise and fall, love and kill, exalt and fear—all on this basis. In the arena of war, conflicts that have arisen from empty stomachs have been mere skirmishes compared to those holocausts incited by confused minds. Kings rule, martyrs suffer, and merchants prosper according to their own convictions. Like other men, the criminal acts in response to his own beliefs. The fact that his beliefs differ from those of the majority and that they may be completely illogical does not alter the primary fact that they are the mainspring of his life. Hunger, poverty, maladjustment, and other physical problems do not incite crime—they incite beliefs that may produce crime.

This subtle difference may be regarded by some as hair-splitting. In reality, the distinction is of enormous importance. If criminal acts are symptoms of a conflict between individual morals and accepted morals, then the problem can only be solved by resolving the conflict. Either the law, our artificial standard of morals, must be altered, or the individual's standard must be brought into closer conformity with popular requirements. The two in conflict invariably produce crime.

It is apparent that our way of life cannot survive if we so relax and broaden our laws that almost any individual's standard will conform with them. Such a course would be little more than anarchy. Therefore, the only alternative is to alter individual standards.

A question immediately arises: Can individual ethical standards be altered? The answer is unreservedly "Yes!" Men's ideas are constantly being revised. Our great religions are founded on this fact. Science, philosophy, and art depend upon it for their creative sustenance. Discarded ideas, like burned-out torches, litter mankind's path, and its future way is lit by those freshy kindled. Ideals, morals, ethics, or by whatever name you call man's convictions—they are the indispensable tools of life.

Another question: How may beliefs be altered? It is no secret to practical men that beliefs are altered by stronger beliefs. Grecian philosophy altered the convictions of the Mediterranean; Roman practicality dominated Europe and Africa; and, in turn, the minds of both were captured by a small band of Hebrews who preached the ideals of Christianity. America was conceived in the rupture of old beliefs and nurtured by new ones.

Small beliefs are also changed. Bathtubs, chewing gum, chrome bumpers, and vitamin tablets all represent new convictions. Police administrators improve their departments by implanting new convictions.

Ideas great and small are susceptible to change. To a nation that daily uses the press, radio, and television with such frightful potency, this should come as no surprise.

This is not a call to fit men into identical patterns. There is a divine dignity in individuality. If the price of eliminating crime is to cast all men from a common mold, the price is too great. It is better to bolt the door in fear of the criminal than to bolt the mind in fear of an all-powerful state. Fortunately it is unnecessary to suffer from either extreme. In a democratic society, ample latitude exists within the law to exercise creative diversities.

During the 1930's the German dictatorship successfully imposed upon an entire generation of youth, and with only slightly less success upon older generations, completely new concepts of moral values. More recently the Soviet Union, undoubtedly encouraged by Germany's success, has improved and expanded the program internationally. That these are false concepts, we know. But the activities of our enemy demonstrate something we once knew but have forgotten. Men want desperately for something to believe in. This desire is so great that they will flock to new concepts, even though they be evil and illogical, so long as they are strong concepts.

America has concepts that are vital and that are compatible with the natural desires of men and in accord with the Law of God. We have developed these concepts within a broad framework of democratic law that leaves room for the dignity which only liberty can bestow. Moreover, we constantly improve these laws, altering them when they are found to be in the least oppressive. It is the hope of our enemies that we will fail to demonstrate to ourselves the advantages of life within these concepts.

Americans who know how to sell people on the largely mythical values of luxury commodities can also sell them on the obvious values of majority ethical convictions. Would the burglar be reduced to tears and deterred from his crime by a thirty-second radio announcement on the advantages of virtue? We well know he would not, no matter how clever the writer and forceful the announcer. But neither did the citizen rush to the market to buy chlorophyl the moment the new deodorant was first advertised. It took ten years of conditioning to do the job. Americans, who a few years ago were convinced that they were the sweetest smelling persons in the world, today regard honest perspiration with deep suspicion and, as a result, consume advertised chemicals on a grand scale. Is it impossible that the odor of crime could be brought to the same public's attention?

The eager critic will point out, of course, that various criminal acts are in response to natural urges and are therefore beyond the reach of gentle persuasion. Rape, theft, murder, and the like, he will say, result from inadequate housing, lack of recreation, hunger, ignorance, bad companions, or some combination of them. He will speak of secret urges in the dark recesses of the mind. But he will not explain how most of us here, and indeed a significant portion of our countrymen, have endured one or many of these hardships without yielding to those secret desires. It is the truth, as our critic will some day discover, that a man's convictions will carry him over adversity as surely as his faith carries him over doubt.

I do not oppose social improvement. If an equitable way can be found, give every man three bedrooms and a green lawn, fill his belly, and while away his leisure hours with entertainment—but if you fail to find for him something to believe in, if he and his neighbors do not share convictions within which to live, that physical Utopia will lack the vital necessity of ordered life.

Whether or not the time, material, and funds for a comprehensive crime prevention program will ever be available, is debatable. Surely it would be an enormous undertaking. However, there is an immediate way that can yield much in the future. Youth is the key. Their beliefs are not yet fortified behind the concrete shell of certainty that adults call maturity. Growing minds are capable of immense faith. They are eager to believe, so eager that when we fail to supply convictions for them, they go out and seek them on street corners and in back alleys. So great is this desire that our juvenile officers, sometimes using only a day in the mountains, a baseball and a sandlot, or a few sticks of wood and a pot of glue to excite curiosity, have left indelible convictions of right and wrong on these young minds, which have fortified them for the remainder of their lives. Since law enforcement's pitifully few juvenile officers have done so much, is there any doubt what the great resources of this nation could accomplish?

If I have pointed the way to a solution, it is no easy one. I wish that crime were a simple plague to be solved by isolating a troublesome microbe, but it is not. I wish it could be eliminated materialistically, by continually supplying Americans with chrome fixtures, softer beds, and shorter work hours, but I know that it cannot be thus eradicated. Certainly I do wish that the police had it within their power to solve the problem alone, but I know they cannot. Crime in America is not a surface disorder—a minor irritation. It is indicative of deep conflicts which enervate the vital strength of the republic. In a nation regulated by brute force, a crime problem is not fatal. But in a nation founded upon faith and held together solely by belief, it is a potent threat.

It is the clear duty of the American police to work to prevent crime by all means at their disposal. We have accepted that obligation, and we will continue to perform the task to the best of our ability. But this does not discharge our obligation completely. It is imperative that every American recognize crime, not as a police problem, but as a departure from the deep convictions that bind 150 million persons into a secure, prosperous, and happy nation. The police must help them understand.

18. The Perception of the Police in Black Neighborhoods

But the police looked very different from the outside, and especially from the standpoint of their most persistent and indiscriminate victims, the black people of America. The evidence which James Baldwin presents concerning certain events in Harlem in the spring of 1964 is again perfectly consistent with the picture of the American police tradition presented in 1931 by Ernest Hopkins. The new element is an aroused black consciousness which specifically pinpoints the police as the hired agents of racial oppression. White Americans, reacting to the extreme terms of Baldwin's indictment, would do well to imagine their state of mind if they had grown up from early childhood in the daily atmosphere which Baldwin depicts.

James Baldwin, "A Report from Occupied Territory"

On April 17, 1964, in Harlem, New York City, a young sales-man, father of two, left a customer's apartment and went into the streets. There was a great commotion in the streets, which, espe-cially since it was a spring day, involved many people, including running, frightened, little boys. They were running from the police. Other people, in windows, left their windows, in terror of the police because the police had their guns out, and were aiming the guns at the roofs. Then the salesman noticed that two of the police-men were beating up a kid: "So I spoke up and asked them, 'why are you beating him like that?' Police jump up and start swinging on me. He put the gun on me and said, 'get over there,' I said, 'what for?' "

An unwise question. Three of the policemen beat up the sales-man in the streets. Then they took the young salesman, whose hands had been handcuffed behind his back, along with four others, much younger than the salesman, who were handcuffed in the same way, to the police station. There: "About thirty-five I'd say came into the room, and started beating, punching us in the jaw, in the stomach, in the chest, beating us with a padded club—spit on us, call us niggers, dogs, animals—they call us dogs and animals when I don't see why we are the dogs and animals the way they are beating us. Like they beat me they beat the other kids and the elderly fellow. They throw him almost through one of the radiators. I thought he was dead over there."

"The elderly fellow" was Fecundo Acion, a 47-year-old Puerto Rican seaman, who had also made the mistake of wanting to know why the police were beating up children. An adult eyewitness reports, "Now here come an old man walking out a stoop and asked one cop, 'say, listen, sir, what's going on out here?' The cop turn around and smash him a couple of times in the head." And one of the youngsters said, "He get that just for a question. No reason at all, just for a question."

From *The Nation*, CCIII (July 11, 1966), 39–43. Reprinted by per-mission of the author.

No one had, as yet, been charged with any crime. But the nightmare had not yet really begun. The salesman had been so badly beaten around one eye that it was found necessary to hospitalize him. Perhaps some sense of what it means to live in occupied territory can be suggested by the fact that the police took him to Harlem Hospital themselves—nearly nineteen hours after the beating. For fourteen days, the doctors at Harlem Hospital told him that they could do nothing for his eye, and he was removed to Bellevue Hospital, where for fourteen days, the doctors tried to save the eye. At the end of fourteen days it was clear that the bad eye could not be saved and was endangering the good eye. All that could be done, then, was to take the bad eye out.

As of my last information, the salesman is on the streets again, with his attaché case, trying to feed his family. He is more visible now because he wears an eye patch: and because he questioned the right of two policemen to beat up one child, he is known as a "cop hater." Therefore, "I have quite a few police look at me now pretty hard. My lawyer he axe (asked) me to keep somebody with me at all times 'cause the police may try to mess with me again."

You will note that there is not a suggestion of any kind of appeal to justice, and no suggestion of any recompense for the grave and gratuitous damage which this man has endured. His tone is simply the tone of one who has miraculously survived—he might have died; as it is, he is merely half blind. You will also note that the patch over his eye has had the effect of making him, more than ever, the target of the police. It is a dishonorable wound, not earned in a foreign jungle but in the domestic one—not that this would make any difference at all to the nevertheless insuperably patriotic policeman—and it proves that he is a "bad nigger." ("Bad niggers," in America, as elsewhere, have always been watched and have usually been killed.) The police, who have certainly done their best to kill him, have also provided themselves with a pretext *derisoire* by filing three criminal charges against him. He is charged with beating up a schoolteacher, upsetting a fruit stand, and assaulting the (armed) police. Furthermore, he did all of these things in the space of a single city block, and simultaneously.

The salesman's name is Frank Stafford. At the time all this

happened, he was 31 years old. And all of this happened, all of this and a great deal more, just before the "long, hot summer" of 1964 which, to the astonishment of nearly all New Yorkers and nearly all Americans, to the extremely verbal anguish of *The New York Times,* and to the bewilderment of the rest of the world, eventually erupted into a race riot. It was the killing of a 15-year-old Negro boy by a white policeman which overflowed the unimaginably bitter cup.

As a result of the events of April 17, and of the police performance that day, and because Harlem is policed like occupied territory, six young Negro men, the oldest of whom is 20, are now in prison, facing life sentences for murder. Their names are Wallace Baker, Daniel Hamm, Walter Thomas, Willie Craig, Ronald Felder and Robert Rice. Perhaps their names don't matter. They might be my brothers: they might also be yours. My report is based, in part, on Truman Nelson's *The Torture of Mothers.* . . . My report is also based on what I myself know, for I was born in Harlem and raised there. Neither I, nor my family, can be said ever really to have left; we are—*perhaps*—no longer as totally at the mercy of the cops and the landlords as once we were: in any case, our roots, our friends, our deepest associations are there, and "there" is only about fifteen blocks away.

This means that I also know, in my own flesh, and know, which is worse, in the scars borne by many of those dearest to me, the thunder and fire of the billy club, the paralyzing shock of spittle in the face; and I know what it is to find oneself blinded, on one's hands and knees, at the bottom of the flight of steps down which one has just been hurled. I know something else: these young men have been in jail for two years now. Even if the attempts being put forth to free them should succeed, what has happened to them in these two years? People are destroyed very easily. Where is the civilization and where, indeed, is the morality which can afford to destroy so many?

There was a game played for some time between certain highly placed people in Washington and myself before the administration changed and the Great Society reached the planning stage. The game went something like this: around April or May, that is as the weather began to be warmer, my phone would ring. I would pick it up and find that Washington was on the line.

WASHINGTON: What are you doing for lunch—oh, say, to-morrow, Jim?

JIM: Oh—why—I guess I'm free.

WASHINGTON: Why don't you take the shuttle down? We'll send a car to the airport. One o'clock all right?

JIM: Sure. I'll be there.

WASHINGTON: Good. Be glad to see you.

So there I would be the next day, like a good little soldier, seated (along with other good little soldiers) around a luncheon table in Washington. The first move was not mine to make, but I knew very well why I had been asked to be there.

Finally, someone would say—we would probably have arrived at the salad—"say, Jim. What's going to happen this summer?"

This question, translated, meant: Do you think that any of those unemployed, unemployable Negroes who are going to be on the streets all summer will cause us any trouble? What do you think we should do about it? But, later on, I concluded that I had got the second part of the question wrong; they really meant, what was *I* going to do about it?

Then I would find myself trying patiently to explain that the Negro in America can scarcely yet be considered—for example—as a part of the labor unions—and he is certainly not so considered by the majority of these unions—and that, therefore, he lacks that protection and that incentive. The jobs that Negroes have always held, the lowest jobs, the most menial jobs, are now being destroyed by automation. No remote provision has yet been made to absorb this labor surplus. Furthermore, the Negro's education, North and South, remains, almost totally, a segregated education, which is but another way of saying that he is taught the habits of inferiority every hour of every day that he lives. He will find it very difficult to overcome these habits. Furthermore, every attempt he makes to overcome them will be painfully complicated by the fact that the ways of being, the ways of life of the despised and rejected, nevertheless contain an incontestable vitality and author-ity. This is far more than can be said of the middle class which, in any case, and whether it be black or white, does not dare to cease despising him. He may prefer to remain where he is, given such unattractive choices, which means that he either remains in limbo, or finds a way to use the system in order to beat the system. Thus, even when opportunities—my use of this word is here limited to the industrialized, competitive, contemporary North American sense—hitherto closed to Negroes begin, very grudgingly to open up, few can be found to qualify for them for the reasons sketched above, and also because it demands a very rare person, of any color, to risk madness and heartbreak in an attempt to achieve the impossible. (I know Negroes who have gone literally mad because they wished to become commercial air-line pilots.) Nor is this the worst.

The children, having seen the spectacular defeat of their fathers —having seen what happens to any bad nigger and, still more, what happens to the good ones—cannot listen to their fathers and certainly will not listen to the society which is responsible for their orphaned condition. What to do in the face of this deep and dangerous estrangement? It seemed to me—I would say, sipping coffee and trying to be calm—that the principle of what had to be done was extremely simple; but before anything could be done, the principle had to be grasped. The principle on which one had to operate was that the government which can force me to pay my taxes and force me to fight in its defense anywhere in the world *does not have the authority* to say that it cannot protect my right to vote or my right to earn a living or my right to live anywhere I choose. Furthermore, no nation, wishing to call itself free, can possibly survive so massive a defection. What to do? Well, there is a real estate lobby in Albany, for example, and this lobby, which was able to rebuild all of New York, downtown, and for money, in less than twenty years, is also responsible for Harlem and the condition of the people there, and the condition of the schools there, and the future of the children there. What to do? Why is it not possible to attack the power of this lobby? Are their profits more important than the health of our children? What to do? Are textbooks printed in order to teach children, or are the contents of these textbooks to be controlled by the Southern oligarchy and the commercial health of publishing houses? What to do? Why are Negroes and Puerto Ricans virtually the only people pushing trucks in the garment center, and what union has the right to trap and victimize Negroes and Puerto Ricans in this way? None of these things (I would say) could possibly be done without the consent, in fact, of the government, and we in Harlem know this even if some of you profess not to know how such a hideous state of affairs came about. If some of these things are not begun—I would say—then, of course, we will be sitting on a powder keg all summer. Of course, the powder keg may blow up; it will be a miracle if it doesn't.

They thanked me. They didn't believe me, as I conclude, since nothing was ever done. The summer was always violent. And in the spring, the phone began to ring again.

Now, what I have said about Harlem is true of Chicago, Detroit, Washington, Boston, Philadelphia, Los Angeles and San Francisco—is true of every Northern city with a large Negro population. And the police are simply the hired enemies of this population. They are present to keep the Negro in his place and to protect white business interests, and they have no other function. They are, moreover—even in a country which makes the very grave error of equating ignorance with simplicity—quite stunningly ignorant; and, since they know that they are hated, they are always afraid. One cannot possibly arrive at a more sure-fire formula for cruelty.

This is why those pious calls to "respect the law," always to be heard from prominent citizens each time the ghetto explodes, are so obscene. The law is meant to be my servant and not my master, still less my torturer and my murderer. To respect the law, in the context in which the American Negro finds himself, is simply to surrender his self-respect.

On April 17, some school children overturned a fruit stand in Harlem. This would have been a mere childish prank if the children had been white—had been, that is, the children of that portion of the citizenry for whom the police work and who have the power to control the police. But these children were black, and the police chased them and beat them and took out their guns; and Frank Stafford lost his eye in exactly the same way The Harlem Six lost their liberty—by trying to protect the younger children. Daniel Hamm, for example, tells us that ". . . we heard children scream. We turned around and walked back to see what happened. I saw this policeman with his gun out and with his billy in his hand. I like put myself in the way to keep him from shooting the kids. Because first of all he was shaking like a leaf and jumping all over the place. And I thought he might shoot one of them."

He was arrested, along with Wallace Baker, carried to the police station, beaten—"six and twelve at a time would beat us. They got so tired beating us they just came in and started spitting on us—they even bring phlegm up and spit on me." This went on all day. In the evening, Wallace Baker and Daniel Hamm were taken to Harlem Hospital for X rays and then carried back to the police station, where the beating continued all night. They were eventually released, with the fruit-stand charges pending, in spite of the testimony of the fruit-stand owner. This fruit-stand owner had already told the police that neither Wallace Baker nor Daniel Hamm had ever been at his store and that they certainly had had nothing to do with the fruit-stand incident. But this had no effect on the conduct of the police. The boys had already attracted the attention of the police, long before the fruit-stand riot, and in a perfectly innocent way. They are pigeon fanciers and they keep—kept—pigeons on the roof. But the police are afraid of everything in Harlem and they are especially afraid of the roofs, which they consider to be guerrilla outposts. This means that the citizens of Harlem who, as we have seen, can come to grief at any hour in the streets, and who are not safe at their windows, are forbidden the very air. They are safe only in their houses—or were, until the city passed the No Knock, Stop and Frisk laws, which permit a policeman to enter one's home without knocking and to stop anyone on the streets, at will, at any hour, and search him. Harlem believes, and I certainly agree, that these laws are directed against Negroes. They are certainly not directed against anybody else. One day, "two carloads of detectives came and went up on the roof. They pulled their guns on the kids and searched them and made them all come down and they were going to take them down to the precinct." But the boys put up a verbal fight and refused to go and attracted quite a crowd. "To get these boys to the precinct we would have to shoot them," a policeman said, and "the police seemed like they was embarrassed. Because I don't think they expected the kids to have as much sense as they had in speaking up for themselves." They refused to go to the precinct, "and they didn't," and their exhibition of the spirit of '76 marked them as dangerous. Occupied territory is occupied territory, even though it be found in that New World which the Europeans conquered; and it is axiomatic, in occupied territory, that any act of resistance, even though it be executed by a child, be answered at once, and with the full weight of the occupying forces. Furthermore, since the police, not at all surprisingly, are abysmally incompetent—for neither, in fact, do they have any respect for the law, which is not surprising, either—Harlem and all of New York City is full of unsolved crimes. A crime, as we know, is solved when someone is arrested and convicted. It is not indispensable, but it is useful, to have a confession. If one is carried back and forth from the precinct to the hospital long enough, one is likely to confess to anything.

Therefore, ten days later, following the slaying of Mrs. Margit Sugar in Mr. and Mrs. Sugar's used-clothing store in Harlem, the police returned and took Daniel Hamm away again. This is how his mother tells it: "I think it was three (detectives) come up and they asked are you Danny Hamm? And he says, yes and right away—gun right to the head and slapping him up, one gun here and one here—just all the way down the hall—beating him and knocking him around with the gun to his head." The other boys were arrested in the same way, and, again of course, they were beaten; but this arrest was a far greater torture than the first one had been because some of the mothers did not know where the boys were, and the police, who were holding them, refused for many hours to say that they were holding them. The mothers did not know of what it was their children were accused until they learned, via television, that the charge was murder. At that time in the state of New York, this charge meant death in the electric chair.

Let us assume that all six boys are guilty as (eventually) charged. Can anyone pretend that the manner of their arrest, or their treatment, bears any resemblance to equal justice under the law? The Police Department has loftily refused to "dignify the charges." But can anyone pretend that they would dare to take this tone if the case involved, say, the sons of Wall Street brokers? I have witnessed and endured the brutality of the police many more times than once—but, of course, I cannot prove it. I cannot prove it because the Police Department investigates itself, quite as though it were answerable only to itself. But it cannot be allowed to be answerable only to itself; it must be made to answer to the community which pays it, and which it is legally sworn to protect; and if American Negroes are not a part of the American community, then all of the American professions are a fraud.

This arrogant autonomy, which is guaranteed the police, not only in New York, *by the most powerful forces in American life* —otherwise, they would not dare to claim it, would, indeed, be unable to claim it—creates a situation which is as close to anarchy as it already, visibly, is close to martial law.

Here is Wallace Baker's mother speaking, describing the night that a police officer came to her house to collect the evidence which he hoped would prove that her son was guilty of murder. The late Mrs. Sugar had run a used-clothing store and the policeman was looking for old coats. "Nasty as he was that night in my house. He didn't ring the bell. So I said, have you got a search warrant? He say, no, I don't have no search warrant and I'm going to search anyway. Well, he did. So I said, will you please step out of this room till I get dressed? He wouldn't leave." This collector of evidence against the boys was later arrested on charges of possessing and passing counterfeit money (he pleaded guilty to a misdemeanor, "conspiring" to pass counterfeit money). The officer's home in Hartsdale, N.Y., is valued at $35,000, he owns two cars, one a Cadillac, and when he was arrested, had $1,300 in his pockets. But the families of The Harlem Six do not have enough money for counsel. The court appointed counsel, and refused to allow the boys counsel of their own choice, even though the boys made it clear that they had no confidence in their court-appointed counsel, and even though four leading civil rights lawyers had asked to be allowed to handle the case. The boys were convicted of first-degree murder, and are now ending their childhood and may end their lives in jail.

These things happen, in all our Harlems, every single day. If we ignore this fact, and our common responsibility to change this fact, we are sealing our doom. Here is the boy, Daniel Hamm, speaking—speaking of his country, which has sworn to bring peace and freedom to so many millions: "They don't want us here. They don't want us—period! All they want us to do is work on these penny-ante jobs for them—and that's *it*. And beat our heads in whenever they feel like it. They don't want us on the street 'cause the World's Fair is coming. And they figure that all black people are hoodlums anyway, or bums, with no character of our own. So they put us off the streets, so their friends from Europe, Paris or Vietnam—wherever they come from—can come and see this supposed to be great city."

There is a very bitter prescience in what this boy—this "bad nigger"—is saying, and he was not born knowing it. We taught it to him in seventeen years. He is draft age now, and if he were not in jail, would very probably be on his way to Southeast Asia. Many of his contemporaries are there, and the American Government and the American press are extremely proud of them. They are dying there like flies; they are dying in the streets of all our Harlems far more hideously than flies. A member of my family said to me when we learned of the bombing of the four little girls in the Birmingham Sunday school, "Well, they don't need us for work no more. Where are they building the gas ovens?" Many Negroes feel this; there is no way not to feel it. Alas, we know our countrymen, municipalities, judges, politicians, policemen and draft boards very well. There is more than one way to skin a cat, and more than one way to get bad niggers off the streets. No one in Harlem will ever believe that The Harlem Six are guilty—God knows their guilt has certainly not been proved. Harlem knows, though, that they have been abused and possibly destroyed, and Harlem knows why—we have lived with it since our eyes opened on the world. One is in the impossible position of being unable to believe a word one's countrymen say. "I can't believe what you say," the song goes, "because I see what you do"—and one is also under the necessity of escaping the jungle of one's situation into any other jungle whatever. It is the bitterest possible comment on our situation now that the suspicion is alive in so many breasts that America has at last found a way of dealing with the Negro problem. *They don't want us—period!*" The meek shall inherit the earth, it is said. This presents a very bleak image to those who live in occupied territory. The meek Southeast Asians, those who remain, shall have their free elections, and the meek American Negroes—those who survive—shall enter the Great Society.

19. Police Response to Criticism

Confronted by the attacks of people like Baldwin, the police in the mid-1960's grew noticeably edgier and more inclined toward sweeping self-defense. In this their mood paralleled that of a large segment of the American public as it rallied around the phrase "law and order." A polarity developed between those who accepted the view that police were often oppressors of the innocent and those who just as instinctively honored and supported the police as a safeguard against violence and radical excess.

At stake in this conflict of interpretations was the basic issue of skepticism toward established authority. Although very few Americans were real revolutionaries, we have seen that the sacredness of symbols of authority came into dispute on an unprecedented scale during the mid-1960's. Should an individual, in most situations, believe what his government officers tell him? In the national arena, Lyndon B. Johnson's credibility over the Vietnam War was being questioned. Some Americans were afraid that too much of this skepticism would further undermine the social order at a time when it already seemed to be under direct attack from vocal groups of radicals. Others openly mistrusted the veracity of spokesmen in high places, for instance on the subject of police brutality, because they retained an ingrained suspicion of official leadership as such.

A pronounced challenge to one's basic trust in something, social psychologists tell us, does not tend to open most men's minds. When one's faith is suddenly undermined or disconfirmed, particularly if that faith had been of an intense character, one is likely to go on reiterating it in a heightened fashion rather than announcing that one has changed one's mind in the light of new evidence.[1]

1. For striking evidence of this, see Leon Festinger, Henry W. Riecken, and Stanley Schachter, *When Prophecy Fails: A Social and Psychological Study of a Modern Group that Predicted the Destruction of the World*

Especially is this to be expected when, as in the present case, many crucial facts were simply missing. The individual newspaper and magazine reader had to choose whether to believe a man like Quinn Tamm (in the next selection) or a man like James Baldwin. In factual terms, either police brutality was rare or it was extensive. Unfortunately, since all initial sources of information are heavily biased (consisting either of the claims made by victims, sometimes long afterward, or else of official police reports), irrefutable confirmation or disconfirmation of brutality is rarely available. In this situation, most people found it easy to go on believing what they already wanted to believe, reacting to the atmosphere of factual dispute by clinging all the more rigidly to their previous beliefs. Only a few academics and similar persons, trained deliberately to subject themselves to the constant possibility of the disconfirmation of their ideas, might postpone taking a firm position, and radicals and conservatives alike would dismiss such persons as weak-minded. From a psychological perspective, this is the manner in which widespread polarization of viewpoints over the issue of police power came into being in America.

Meanwhile, much has been done in the way of a painful if tardy accumulation of facts.[2] But these additional facts will probably change few persons' minds. For one reason, the increasing forwardness of radical groups and the heightening mood of black retaliation made police behavior seem like a less important issue to moderates and conservatives. A certain amount of police brutality and disrespect for the rights of suspects will be tacitly forgiven or even condoned by those who defend the necessity of an alert and unfettered police force.

We are left, then, with two sharply differing public attitudes

---

(Minneapolis, Minn.: University of Minnesota Press, 1956); see also Milton Rokeach, *The Open and Closed Mind: Investigations into the Nature of Belief Systems and Personality Systems* (New York: Basic Books, 1960).

2. See, for instance, *Rights in Conflict: The Violent Confrontation of Demonstrators and Police in the Parks and Streets of Chicago During the Week of the Democratic National Convention of 1968: A Report Submitted by Daniel Walker . . . to the National Commission on the Causes and Prevention of Violence* (New York: Bantam Books, 1968); and, on black violence, Terry Ann Knopf, "Sniping—A New Pattern of Violence?" *Trans-Action,* VI (July–August 1969), 22—29. Unfortunately, studies like the latter can only testify indirectly as to the "appropriateness" of various forms of police response in ghettos, rather than directly establishing the frequency of police brutality.

toward the police, and with little apparent chance that either of them is vulnerable to rapid change. Quinn Tamm, for some years the executive director of the International Association of Chiefs of Police, provides an excellent summary statement of the "hard-line" position on authority as it has recently developed in this country. One must indeed choose whether one accepts his view of reality or that of James Baldwin, for the two are utterly incompatible.

Quinn Tamm, "Police Professionalism and Civil Rights"

I know of no period in recent history when the police have been the subject of so many unjustified charges of brutality, harassment and ineptness. It almost seems that the better we do our jobs of enforcing the law the more we are attacked. The more professional we become, the more effective we become and the more effective we are, the more we impinge upon the misbehavior of society.

But for this we should offer no apology. A police force is established, among other things, for the purpose of enforcing existing laws. In this respect, we are duty-bound.

Those who damn our actions in this regard must be made to understand that the police do not make the laws, that laws are the direct product of public desires and if the public does not like those laws or believe them to be fair, then the public should change the laws rather than criticize the police.

It is in this context that I offer the fervent hope that we will not be known as the "Silent Generation."

The time has passed when we can sit silently by or protest feebly to those who unfairly criticize us when what we do is legally and morally right. We can no longer afford to answer unjust criticism with thinly veiled innuendos and pusillanimous generalities. If we are right, let's say so.

This was the philosophy behind one of our recent editorials in

Originally published in *The Police Chief* (September 1964); reprinted in David Stahl, Frederick B. Sussman, and Neil J. Bloomfield, eds., *The Community and Racial Crises* (New York: Practicing Law Institute, 1966), pp. 120–126. Reprinted by permission of the author

The Police Chief, entitled "Police Brutality—Or Smokescreen?" In it we referred to baseless charges of police brutality which have been made to cover excesses and illegal conduct on the part of some demonstrators involved in the current racial tension.

The editorial is, I believe, forthright and simple enough in expression. It is merely an assertion of facts, and it needed to be said. Of course, it would have been politic to say nothing, and some of our leading law enforcement executives have chosen this tactic. At the same time, other practicing police executives have had the courage, if indeed that is what it takes, to speak unemotionally and factually of our responsibility of upholding the law. To do so is not to align oneself with one side or the other of a sociological argument. It is merely to state the police position with regard to breaking the law, whether the violation be robbery or illegal conduct while engaging in a public demonstration.

Columnist David Lawrence wrote an understanding analysis recently when he commented, "Perhaps the most difficult phase of the whole problem is the situation which confronts the local police. If they do not arrest the demonstrator, lots of innocent persons are injured, but, on the other hand, if the police try to use force to deal with those who are threatening violence, these same law officers are accused of 'brutality.' "

Never before in the history of the police service have we been singled out so mercilessly and so wrongfully as the whipping boys by demonstrators for so-called sociological evolution and by out-and-out hoodlums who have abandoned the banner of civil rights to engage in senseless insurrection.

The police of the nation have no quarrel with peaceful demonstrations by responsible groups. An excellent example of planning and purposefulness was the "March on Washington, D.C." last August, at which time demonstration leaders and the authorities charged with maintaining law and order insured peace through co-operation and planning. That human dignity prevailed is a tribute both to law enforcement and to the leaders of the March.

A moment ago I used the term insurrection. I can think of no other word which would describe the recent outrages against life, property and authority which we have seen perpetrated by hoodlums in Harlem and other sections of New York City and in Rochester, New York. It has been clearly established, I believe, that these mob actions involving destruction of property, looting and assaults on peaceful citizens and the police have transcended the hopes and purposes of responsible civil rights leaders. Cloaking themselves falsely in the mantle of civil rights, the rabble of society in these two communities have used so-called resentment against police to engage in savagery seldom witnessed in this country's history.

One lachrymose female reporter for a Washington, D.C., newspaper, who became an "expert" on the cause of Harlem's riots in something like a 48-hour visit to that area, has opined that, "In the beginning, both the good and the bad in Harlem had a common bond and it was not so much their color as it was their seething rage at the New York City police force." She also quoted a Harlem youth worker who declared that the riots were a rebellion against the New York City police and that they were the result of "act upon act of police brutality." She added that "True or false, Harlem believes that it is a fact of life that cops are on the take and cops will 'brutalize' you—bash your heads in for no provocation."

She, like so many other journalistic observers, cites the slaying of a 15-year-old Negro youth by a white police officer as the spark which ignited the dry tinder of so-called frustration in Harlem.

And, like so many other erudite, journalistic observers, she dips deeply into her store of sensational adjectives and adverbs to describe the police action. The state of our so-called objective press is sad to behold as one peruses the mostly biased and tongue-clucking accounts written by journalists whose writing prowess appears to be titillated only by violence and sensationalism. Subtly, too many so-called objective news writers attempt to excuse the actions of minorities even when their unlawful rioting causes death, injury and carnage which no other society would condone for a moment. For instance, the female reporter wrote, "And they (Harlem's inhabitants) again renewed demands for a civilian review board to guard against any cover-up. Instead, the city answered their requests by sending wave after wave of white-helmeted, white-faced police officers into Harlem."

She continued, "And a Negro youth said: 'When I see a helmet I think of war and so I act like it is war.' Thus, bottles, bricks, stones, garbage, even lethal Molotov cocktails were thrown on police from the rooftops and the cellars." Abruptly, this reporter changes her mood and goes on, "Police retaliated by scorching the air with round after round of ammunition, fired over the heads of the rioters." She then deplores this police tactic apparently to back up her earlier contention that "billy clubs and bullets are not the way to halt New York City's hemmed-in youth."

At the same time, however, she offers no alternative which might have had the immediate effect of containing and restraining the rioters.

This pompous tone of reporting and the avid search by movie and still photographers for pictures of police battling "frustrated" rioters are an appalling and dishonest journalistic treatment of the police and the mission which they are duty-bound to carry out.

Try as I might, I cannot accept the so-called news media's contention that the police are responsible for society's failures to provide better opportunities for minority groups, and it is hypocritical and morally wrong for the police to be singled out by virtually all factions as the symbol of all society's failures.

Louis Lomax, a Negro journalist and author who writes for the North American Newspaper Alliance, Inc., has injected some reason into the Harlem picture. He said in a recent article, "The killing of a 15-year-old Negro boy by an off-duty white policeman was not the cause of the riots; rather, this incident was only an excuse for the rioting to occur. For Harlem, USA, is little more than a bloody race riot looking for somewhere—and a reason—to take place."

He goes on to say, however: "Then there are, to be sure, the police. Most of them are white, many of them are rookies, and so many of them seem to have what New Yorker Barbara Benison called 'an irrational fear of black men.' Harlemites disrespect the police with vigor and hate them with passion. They disrespect the police because they know—after all, they see it with their own eyes every day and night—the police are in league with the vice and crime that flaw their community; they hate the police because most of them have either experienced or witnessed some act of flagrant police brutality."

Such a sweeping indictment of police is a smear of the first magnitude. Such general comments beg specifics to be brought to light and presented to the proper authorities.

It is not surprising that these charges come from a group which Mr. Lomax describes as follows: "The Harlem masses, more than any people I have encountered anywhere, simply don't believe in anything or anybody. They applaud but do not follow Malcolm X and the Black Nationalists; Harlemites rejoice when there is a victory by their brothers in the Deep South, but they refuse to support the organizations involved in the civil rights struggle; Harlem's newspaper has a smaller circulation than either of the white dailies in the community; the area brims with churches and bars, but the ministers have no more community-wide influence than the bartenders. . . . The ultimate irony is that Harlem rioted at the very time when its citizens have more opportunities available to them than they have ever had before."

Rather than sensationalizing myths and rumors which sell papers and stir further violence in such tense situations, the news media could perform a more valuable service by focusing the spotlight on proven police brutality supported by the workable process of justice which is represented by American courts.

As I mentioned a moment ago, the female reporter in Washington cited as one of their reasons for rioting the failure of the Harlem group to have their demand granted that a civilian review board be established to inquire into alleged acts of brutality by police.

Strangely enough, however, the riots in Harlem were shortly echoed in Rochester with even more ferocity and viciousness against the police. I say strangely enough because *Rochester has now and has had for some time a civilian review board of the type advocated by the Harlem element!*

The charge of "act upon act of police brutality" is aired in the newspaper, on the radio and on television when this country has the most efficient machinery of any in the world for the discovery of deprivation of civil rights under the color of law. It is a violation of Federal statute to maltreat anyone under the color of law. If such rampant police brutality exists, the U. S. Department of Justice should have been notified of each and every incident. The FBI, the investigative arm of the Department of Justice, is in Harlem, and it has the responsibility of inquiring into such charges. It will be interesting indeed to see how many authentic cases of police brutality emerge as a result of FBI investigation.

Where such brutality exists, the administrators of the New York City Police Department and indeed the police of the entire Nation would want to see the perpetrators punished because there is no place in professional law enforcement for brutality. But, at the same time, unless the charges are substantiated by convictions in our impartial courts of law then it would seem that the false criers of police brutality are doing a disservice to their fellow man, to their Nation's police and to their country. But perhaps this is their aim.

In 1963, there were 2,692 allegations of civil rights violations of all kinds handled by the U. S. Department of Justice. Following appropriate investigation of these matters, less than 25 resulted in indictments of police officers. This is less than 1% of the total civil rights matters investigated.

Rumor which is viciously detrimental to the police establishment has no place in our society, and opportunism which singles out the police officer as the villain in society's failures is reprehensible. The dedicated and honorable police executives of the country have traditionally condemned and taken severe action against officers guilty of brutality. They are willing and desirous of being governed by the law; it is high time that other segments of our society also seek to accomplish their goals through the courts rather than through insurrection and baseless character assassination.

Where police brutality actually exists, may it be deterred and stamped out by stern retribution in the courts; where public brutality against the police exists, may it also be deterred and stamped out by equally stern retribution in the courts.

To endure, this Republic must be governed by law; no proponents of any cause can achieve their goals through the commission of serious crimes against their fellow men.

The police are obviously the symbol of the law, and a breakdown in public respect for the law is apparent in the senseless assaults upon our policemen. When public respect for the law is regained, then human dignity will be restored in New York City, in Rochester and in other areas of our country which are being blighted by hoodlums who cover their excesses by falsely flying the banner of civil rights.

20. Diagnosis and Solution

It would of course be impossible to choose a single contemporary analysis of the police which would be accepted by all who read it as impartial. But Burton Levy's discussion, based upon his experience as director of the Community Relations Division of the Michigan Civil Rights Commission and as consultant in the same field to the federal Department of Justice, carries unusual weight. For one thing, Levy confesses that he honestly changed his mind about the police during the course of his contact with them. For another, he musters impressive evidence with which to support his line of argument. Again, his evaluation of the police ethos corroborates what Hopkins had discovered in 1931, while duly taking into account the genuine changes in it since that time. Altogether, he is a man whose judgment one is strongly tempted to trust.

But Levy's suggested remedies turn out to be extremely disheartening in their implications. His diagnosis of what needs to be done may well lead to a pessimistic conclusion about the overall state of American society, simply because his matter-of-fact goals are apt to seem totally impossible to achieve. When pragmatic realism becomes utopian, a society is in real trouble.

Perhaps this conclusion may seem too melodramatic. A large reservoir of sentiment for bringing about the changes Levy calls for within legal channels still exists. But the trend of the times seems to be expressed by the popular bumper sticker: "The American Flag—Love It or Leave It." Majoritarian sentiment has lost the expansive generosity it often possessed in the nineteenth century; its tone has hardened. Bancroft had happily declared the Hottentot his equal. The abolition of slavery seemed for a time to confirm that tendency in American thought. But the tensions of rapid industrialization and then of global struggle perhaps were proving too great to overcome the deeply entrenched contrary tradition of racism.

Even recently the outcome had still seemed uncertain. For

something like twenty years, from 1945 to 1965, many had hoped that a majority of Americans were slowly being converted to a new system of values which defined egalitarianism in psychological as well as in legal terms. Those hopes now seem illusory. They have produced instead only a tragic stalemate within our society, where before a consensus tolerant of racism had more freely reigned. The oddity was that in the McCarthy era, when middle-class fear of the unfamiliar should logically have been at its height, the civil rights movement began its greatest advances. But the appearance in the 1960's of a segment of the younger generation which frankly espoused an entirely new morality—including completely casual interracial contact—made the majority suddenly aware of its unwillingness to grant certain crucial kinds of changes in the American way of life.

Thus in San Francisco a widely applauded community relations unit in the police department, established in 1962, was treated with hostility by an estimated ninety per cent of the police force. Fellow policemen taunted its staff for working in the "commie relations department" and called them "nigger-lovers." Though the entire department was invited to the unit's Christmas party, no one came; a drive to recruit police basketball teams to play against ghetto neighborhood teams produced exactly one white police volunteer. As police opposition to the community relations program took clear form, San Francisco's police chief conspicuously avoided giving the unit further open support. Two mayors similarly backed away from the program. And a drive to enlist the cooperation of businessmen in finding more jobs for black youth produced no jobs but a good deal of hate mail.[1] This was the net result of an effort, extending over several years, to bridge the gap between the police and the ghetto in what is widely regarded as one of America's most cosmopolitan cities.

Burton Levy no doubt did not intend that his soberly concrete piece on police racism should be taken to confirm a broadly pessimistic evaluation of the American scene. But its simple, honest statement of the necessary remedy leads one's thoughts to turn in these directions, especially in the context of the long-range history of American attitudes toward law and authority. The twentieth-century record showed that the values of individual respect, wide latitude for experiment, and skepticism toward men

1. Eleanore Carruth, "Our War Was with the Police Department," *Fortune*, LXXVII (January 1968), 195–197; the final stages of this process could also be observed over KQED's "Newsroom" program.

in power had gained considerable strength—but not decisively. And now these values were apparently in retreat before a renewed rise of majoritarian orthodoxy. Qualitatively, though not in terms of physical muscle, American civilization seemed to be in grave danger.

Burton Levy, "Cops in the Ghetto: A Problem of the Police System"

During the past five years, millions of dollars have been spent by police departments, much of it federally funded, for police-community relations programs (really "police-Negro relations"). The summer of 1967, with the destruction in Newark and Detroit, and the actual and threatened civil disorder in some thirty-five other urban communities, provides good reason to question the premises and assumptions on which these programs are based.

I have been a principal contributor to the notion that the gulf between the black community and the police in urban communities could be breached with lots of money spent for police recruitment and in-service training in human relations; for precinct police-citizen programs; and for generally upgrading and professionalizing the police service by raising salaries to retain current employees and to attract college-educated recruits. A short article I wrote two years ago brought requests for thousands of reprints. I suppose I said what everybody wanted to hear: that is, that 96% of the Negro community are completely law-abiding; that 98% of the patrolmen never have complaints of brutality lodged against them; that whatever negative images now exist on both sides are a result of a history of brutal Southern police and the general stereotypes and prejudices that exist in America today. Therefore, I said, what is needed is a new dialogue based on fact, not myth, and a significant program of training for policemen.

My position is now completely reversed. Two more years of

This essay first appeared in Louis H. Masotti and Don R. Bowen, eds., *Riots and Rebellion: Civil Violence in the Urban Community* (Beverly Hills, Calif.: Sage Publications, Inc., 1968), pp. 347–357. Reprinted by permission of the publisher.

intensive experience with police in all parts of the nation, combined with results of other studies and statements by police officers themselves, have convinced me that the problem of police-Negro relations in the urban centers is one of patterns of values and practice within the *police system*. The new assumption is that the problem is not one of a few "bad eggs" in a police department of 1,000 or 10,000 men, but rather of a police system that recruits a significant number of bigots, reinforces the bigotry through the department's value system and socialization with older officers, and then takes the worst of the officers and puts them on duty in the ghetto, where the opportunity to act out the prejudice is always available. . . .

Every poll and survey of black-white attitudes toward the police produces the same results: Negroes believe that policemen are physically brutal, harsh, discourteous to them because they are black; that police do not respond to calls, enforce the law, or protect people who live in the ghetto because they are black. White people simply do not or are unwilling to believe that such racial discrimination by police officers actually happens. Louis Harris' national survey reported in August, 1967, that Negroes feel "two to one that police brutality is a major cause [of the civil disorder]—a proposition whites reject by eight to one. Only 16% of whites believe that there is any police brutality to Negroes."

These attitudes in the Negro community are neither post-riot excuses to explain the disorder, nor new ideas planted by black power advocates Stokely Carmichael or Rap Brown. In 1957, a poll of Detroiters showed that less than one white person in ten rated the police service as "not good"; while over four out of ten Negroes rated the police as "not good" or "definitely bad." Two-thirds of the Negro respondents referred to anti-Negro discrimination and mistreatment by police officers. A 1965 poll in Detroit found 58% of the Negro community believing that law enforcement was not fair and equitable. Similar results occur in other urban areas in the nation, North and South.

Black hostility toward police is not confined to the poor or to those engaged in illicit activity in the Negro community. Black doctors, lawyers, and even police officers share the beliefs. For example, the Guardians, the New York City organization of Negro police officers, endorsed the establishment of a Civilian Review

Board in opposition to the organizations of white officers. The Guardian president publicly stated that he had witnessed incidents of police brutality.

Finally, it is factually correct to note that virtually every incident of threatened or actual civil disorder in the urban ghetto began with an encounter between a police officer and a Negro citizen. Whatever the factual reality is—as contrasted to the belief systems—clearly the cops serve as the "flash point" for black anger, mob formation, and civil disorder.

To what extent does police brutality actually exist—i.e., the verbal insults and harassment, the negative selective enforcement and non-enforcement, the physical brutality? The problem here is that systematic evidence outlining patterns of behavior is difficult to obtain. It is equally difficult to gain evidence on individual cases.

The U. S. Civil Rights Commission's 1961 Report *Justice* noted that the U. S. Department of Justice received 1,328 complaints alleging police brutality in the two-and-a-half-year period from January, 1958, to June, 1960. One-third of the complaints were from the South, and somewhat less than one-half of the complainants were Negro. Police officials note that few, if any, of these cases investigated by the F.B.I. have resulted in prosecution and certainly not conviction of any police officer. Still, the Civil Rights Commission concluded that "police brutality in the United States is a serious and continuing problem. . . ."

The Michigan Civil Rights Commission, established by the new State Constitution of 1963, has the legal authority to accept, investigate, and settle complaints of discrimination by police because of race, religion, or national origin. From January 1, 1964, to December, 1965, 103 complaints were filed against the Detroit Police Department. By December 30, 1965, the Commission found probable cause to credit the allegations in 31 cases, and the new Detroit Police Commissioner, in separate investigations by a newly established Citizen Complaint Bureau, had made similar findings. Citizens received apologies and medical expenses; officers were reprimanded and transferred.

Contrast the 1964–65 results of citizen complaints, when an independent review apparatus was available to Detroit citizens, with the departmental grievance procedure before the establishment of the Civil Rights Commission. The Detroit NAACP filed 51 complaints with the Detroit Police Commissioner from 1957 to 1960, and not one case was upheld. The police "investigated" 121 incidents involving Negro citizens during the first nine months of 1960, and according to the then Police Commissioner's sworn testimony to the U. S. Civil Rights Commission, in only one case was the officer "definitely at fault."

The Detroit statistics cited above, both in terms of charges or findings of police brutality and the polls of attitudes, are not meant to make a special case for or against the Detroit Police Department. Today, Detroit is better in terms of police-Negro relations than some other comparable departments; it is worse than others. What is generally true of Detroit is also true of Boston, New York, Chicago, Los Angeles, and other urban communities. That is, the black community, from top to bottom, is angry about what they call mistreatment by police, from verbal abuse to physical brutality; further, that such mistreatment does occur—perhaps not to the high degree perceived by the Negro community, but certainly to a much greater degree than the police and municipal administrators have been willing to admit or correct. And when this relationship overlies the social and economic despair of the urban ghetto, it is little wonder that the cop on the beat (theoretically, the "foot soldier" of the Constitution) becomes the "flash point" of urban disorder.

Efforts to improve the relationship and increase attitudes of trust between the black community and the urban police move in three major directions: (1) professionalizing police by increasing education, training, and salaries; (2) establishing formal police-community relations programs for police dialogue with the Negro community; and (3) recruiting more Negro police officers.

The first program assumes that education and training—recruit, in-service, and off-duty—will produce policemen better able to cope with the general complexities in law enforcement and also be more understanding of their own conscious and unintended actions toward citizens. Higher salaries will enable departments to recruit more highly educated and talented men. . . .

The problem with the education and salary approach to changing police attitudes and behavior is that there is no evidence that these kinds of efforts, while having other effects, do actually change attitudes and behavior. For example, public school teachers in urban communities, all with college degrees, have not shown any particularly positive attitudes or actions in their work with Negro children.

The second approach used to improve police-Negro relations is the organization of programs to facilitate communication, education, and understanding between the police and the citizenry. These programs usually involve face-to-face meetings between police and citizens. Some departments organize precinct meetings with adults and youths, or seek out local citizen programs where they may participate. Some police departments have regularly scheduled meetings with civil rights leaders; other departments have tried large and small community forums. Others concentrate on the youths—particularly in the inner city.

No valid measurement of the precise effectiveness of programs of this sort has been undertaken anywhere in the nation. At best, it would be difficult to measure effectiveness over a short period of time. It is clear that police-community relations efforts in and of themselves are not sufficient to change police behavior. There are usually ten times more citizens than officers present at each meeting. Over the long run, it is difficult to sell a bad product— or to sell the product to people who are severely depressed socially and economically.

The recruitment of Negro officers assumes that the presence of a fairly representative number of Negro officers, at all levels within a police department, will serve to show the Negro community that the police department is not a white "occupation army," and that within the department the Negro officers will affect the attitudes and actions of their white counterparts.

The problem here is that the theory has not been tested because, with one or two minor exceptions, Negroes simply are not employed in any number in any department. Detroit has had between 200–250 Negro officers of a total force of 4,700 for the past decade, and significantly less before that. Officers who entered the Detroit department following World War II openly testify to the difficulties involved in getting a position at that time. Other cities are in similar situations. There are less than 60 Negro officers in all of the State Police departments in the nation.

My challenge to the traditional programs to improve police-

Negro relations is based upon analysis of the police department as a system, not the actions of individual officers—or, as they are sometimes referred to, as the few "bad eggs" in the department.

The systemic approach to the police has been undertaken by few social scientists. However, a recent study by Arthur Niederhoffer provides a record of trained, long-term observation and empirical evidence which strongly supports my own observation and limited research.

Niederhoffer is not an anti-police radical; he retired after 21 years in the New York City Police Department, earned a Ph.D. in Sociology at New York University, and now teaches police at the John Jay College of Criminal Justice. In Niederhoffer's introduction to *Behind The Shield,* he writes: "The great majority of policemen are men of integrity and good will. Yet it is a fact that a 'minority' goes wrong! Why this should occur even to the extent that it does among a body of men so carefully selected, is a mystery, but one that will, I hope, be less of an enigma by the time the reader comes to the last page of this book." In fact, Niederhoffer's conclusions are a devastating indictment of the police system, particularly as it relates to police-Negro relations.

The police system, as described by Niederhoffer, comes out looking something like this: First, the police departments recruit from a population (the working class) whose numbers are more likely than the average population to hold anti-Negro attitudes; second, the recruits are given a basic classroom training program that is unlikely to change the anti-Negro sentiments; third, the recruit goes out on the street as a patrolman and is more likely than not to have his anti-Negro attitudes reinforced and hardened by the older officer; fourth, in the best departments, the most able officers are soon transferred to specialized administrative duties in training, recruitment, juvenile work, etc., or are promoted after three to five years to supervisory positions; fifth, after five years the patrolman on street duty significantly increases in levels of cynicism, authoritarianism, and generalized hostility to the non-police world. Finally, it is highly likely that the worse of the patrolmen will wind up patrolling the ghetto, because that tends to be the least-wanted assignment.

To put it more bluntly, the police system can be seen as one that is a closed society with its own values, mores, and standards.

In urban communities, anti-black is likely to be one of a half-dozen primary and important values. The department recruits a sizeable number of people with racist attitudes, socializes them into a system with a strong racist element, and takes the officer who cannot advance and puts him in the ghetto where he has day-to-day contact with the black citizens. If this is an accurate description of the urban police system (and my personal observations over the past five years tell me this is so), then the reason is clear why every poll of black citizens shows the same high level of distrust and hostility against policemen.

Another nationally known law enforcement practitioner, now also teaching at John Jay College in New York, Donald J. Mac-Namara, said recently that "the police community is a closed society and it has its own customs, morals and taboos—and those who are not conforming to the police society, to its attitudes, to its customs and traditions, taboos and mores, are ostracized and then excluded . . whatever prejudices and discrimination, whatever anti-minority attitudes he [the recruit] brought in with him, have been tremendously reinforced because they are part of the community attitudes of this police group of which he becomes a member." . . .

Police tend to be secretive and defensive, the good professional advocates as well as the old tough cops. The professional policemen—there are many, and particularly on the highest levels within the departments—seek education, training, and strict standards of professionalism within their departments. The professionals do not decry Supreme Court decisions or believe that local courts, newspapers or citizens are "out to get them," as the old-line tough non-professional "unleash the police" cop believes. The old cop clearly doesn't want interference or review because "only an officer knows how to handle the situation." The good professional doesn't want interference or outside review because the hallmark of a profession, they believe, is the ability to self-regulate the activities of those within the profession, as do doctors, lawyers, etc. Thus, while the professional and the old-line cop will split on most other issues, they do stand together on outside review or criticism.

Government officials and community leaders have another "hang-up" about confronting the harsh reality of the police system and its ability to withstand the minor effects of traditional "remedial" programs. That is, there are good, well-intentioned and intelligent law enforcement officials who recognize a serious problem and themselves are willing to say and often do say the "right" thing. And, in spite of the system, there are good cops actually working in the ghetto. . . .

The problem, then, for government officials (like me) is to retain a working and friendly relationship with the law enforcement professionals who sincerely seek change—and at the same time tell them, and the community, that a basic, long-entrenched part of the police system must be destroyed.

We must say that money alone—whether spent for higher police salaries or more police training—will do little to stop the pattern of police discrimination and brutality against Negroes and other minorities in America's urban ghettoes. Police dialogues with Puerto Ricans in Spanish Harlem, Negroes in Detroit, or Mexican-Americans in Texas, will not significantly reduce the instances of police officers' abuse of their power in those communities. The problem is one of a set of values and attitudes and a pattern of anti-black behavior, socialized within and reinforced by the police system. . . .

What is required are specific objectives by a mayor and police chief, committed to and strong enough to battle and prevail over the police system in their community—a Wilson or McNamara type. It will also require a political base, and sensitive power structure, and, if the white community is politically dominant, a change in the belief system of a large number of white citizens. The program of change will require internal and external controls over the behavior of cops in the ghetto. A program and process must occur that will restructure the police system to exclude—or at least significantly minimize—the racism of cops in the ghetto.

Revised January, 1970

hARPER ✸ CORChBOOKS

† The New American Nation Series, edited by Henry Steele Commager and Richard B. Morris.
‡ American Perspectives series, edited by Bernard Wishy and William E. Leuchtenburg.
a History of Europe series, edited by J. H. Plumb.
§ The Library of Religion and Culture, edited by Benjamin Nelson.
∥ Researches in the Social, Cultural, and Behavioral Sciences, edited by Benjamin Nelson.
Σ Harper Modern Science Series, edited by James A. Newman.
° Not for sale in Canada.
+ Documentary History of the United States series, edited by Richard B. Morris.
# Documentary History of Western Civilization series, edited by Eugene C. Black and Leonard W. Levy.
Λ The Economic History of the United States series, edited by Henry David et al.
¶ European Perspectives series, edited by Eugene C. Black.
** Contemporary Essays series, edited by Leonard W. Levy.
* The Stratum Series, edited by John Hale.

EDMUND S. MORGAN: The Puritan Family: *Religion and Domestic Relations in Seventeenth Century New England* TB/1227
RICHARD B. MORRIS: Government and Labor in Early America TB/1244
WALLACE NOTESTEIN: The English People on the Eve of Colonization: 1603-1630. † *Illus.* TB/3006
FRANCIS PARKMAN: The Seven Years War: *A Narrative Taken from Montcalm and Wolfe, The Conspiracy of Pontiac, and A Half-Century of Conflict. Edited by John H. McCallum* TB/3083
LOUIS B. WRIGHT: The Cultural Life of the American Colonies: 1607-1763. † *Illus.* TB/3005
YVES F. ZOLTVANY, Ed.: The French Tradition in America + HR/1425

American Studies: The Revolution to 1860

JOHN R. ALDEN: The American Revolution: 1775-1783. † *Illus.* TB/3011
MAX BELOFF, Ed.: The Debate on the American Revolution, 1761-1783: *A Sourcebook* TB/1225
RAY A. BILLINGTON: The Far Western Frontier: 1830-1860. † *Illus.* TB/3012
STUART BRUCHEY: The Roots of American Economic Growth, 1607-1861: *An Essay in Social Causation. New Introduction by the Author.* TB/1350
WHITNEY R. CROSS: The Burned-Over District: *The Social and Intellectual History of Enthusiastic Religion in Western New York, 1800-1850* TB/1242
NOBLE E. CUNNINGHAM, JR., Ed.: The Early Republic, 1789-1828 + HR/1394
GEORGE DANGERFIELD: The Awakening of American Nationalism, 1815-1828. † *Illus.* TB/3061
CLEMENT EATON: The Freedom-of-Thought Struggle in the Old South. *Revised and Enlarged. Illus.* TB/1150
CLEMENT EATON: The Growth of Southern Civilization, 1790-1860. † *Illus.* TB/3040
ROBERT H. FERRELL, Ed.: Foundations of American Diplomacy, 1775-1872 HR/1393
LOUIS FILLER: The Crusade against Slavery: 1830-1860. † *Illus.* TB/3029
DAVID H. FISCHER: The Revolution of American Conservatism: *The Federalist Party in the Era of Jeffersonian Democracy* TB/1449
WILLIAM W. FREEHLING, Ed.: The Nullification Era: *A Documentary Record* ‡ TB/3079
WILLIM W. FREEHLING: Prelude to Civil War: *The Nullification Controversy in South Carolina, 1816-1836* TB/1359
PAUL W. GATES: The Farmer's Age: *Agriculture, 1815-1860* Δ TB/1398
FELIX GILBERT: The Beginnings of American Foreign Policy: *To the Farewell Address* TB/1200
ALEXANDER HAMILTON: The Reports of Alexander Hamilton. ‡ *Edited by Jacob E. Cooke* TB/3060
THOMAS JEFFERSON: Notes on the State of Virginia. ‡ *Edited by Thomas P. Abernethy* TB/3052
FORREST MCDONALD, Ed.: Confederation and Constitution, 1781-1789 + HR/1396
BERNARD MAYO: Myths and Men: *Patrick Henry, George Washington, Thomas Jefferson* TB/1108
JOHN C. MILLER: Alexander Hamilton and the Growth of the New Nation TB/3057
JOHN C. MILLER: The Federalist Era: 1789-1801. † *Illus.* TB/3027

RICHARD B. MORRIS, Ed.: Alexander Hamilton and the Founding of the Nation. *New Introduction by the Editor* TB/1448
RICHARD B. MORRIS: The American Revolution Reconsidered TB/1363
CURTIS P. NETTELS: The Emergence of a National Economy, 1775-1815 Δ TB/1438
DOUGLASS C. NORTH & ROBERT PAUL THOMAS, Eds.: *The Growth of the American Economy to 1860* + HR/1352
R. B. NYE: The Cultural Life of the New Nation: 1776-1830. † *Illus.* TB/3026
GILBERT OSOFSKY, Ed.: Puttin' On Ole Massa: *The Slave Narratives of Henry Bibb, William Wells Brown, and Solomon Northup* ‡ TB/1432
JAMES PARTON: The Presidency of Andrew Jackson. *From Volume III of the Life of Andrew Jackson. Ed. with Intro. by Robert V. Remini* TB/3080
FRANCIS S. PHILBRICK: The Rise of the West, 1754-1830. † *Illus.* TB/3067
MARSHALL SMELSER: The Democratic Republic, 1801-1815 + TB/1406
TIMOTHY L. SMITH: Revivalism and Social Reform: *American Protestantism on the Eve of the Civil War* TB/1229
JACK M. SOSIN, Ed.: The Opening of the West + HR/1424
GEORGE ROGERS TAYLOR: The Transportation Revolution, 1815-1860 Δ TB/1347
A. F. TYLER: Freedom's Ferment: *Phases of American Social History from the Revolution to the Outbreak of the Civil War. Illus.* TB/1074
GLYNDON G. VAN DEUSEN: The Jacksonian Era: 1828-1848. † *Illus.* TB/3028
LOUIS B. WRIGHT: Culture on the Moving Frontier TB/1053

American Studies: The Civil War to 1900

W. R. BROCK: An American Crisis: *Congress and Reconstruction, 1865-67* ° TB/1283
T. C. COCHRAN & WILLIAM MILLER: The Age of Enterprise: *A Social History of Industrial America* TB/1054
W. A. DUNNING: Reconstruction, Political and Economic: 1865-1877 TB/1073
HAROLD U. FAULKNER: Politics, Reform and Expansion: 1890-1900. † *Illus.* TB/3020
GEORGE M. FREDRICKSON: The Inner Civil War: *Northern Intellectuals and the Crisis of the Union* TB/1358
JOHN A. GARRATY: The New Commonwealth, 1877-1890 † TB/1410
JOHN A. GARRATY, Ed.: The Transformation of American Society, 1870-1890 + HR/1395
HELEN HUNT JACKSON: A Century of Dishonor: *The Early Crusade for Indian Reform.* † *Edited by Andrew F. Rolle* TB/3063
ALBERT D. KIRWAN: Revolt of the Rednecks: *Mississippi Politics, 1876-1925* TB/1199
ARTHUR MANN: Yankee Reforms in the Urban Age: *Social Reform in Boston, 1800-1900* TB/1247
ARNOLD M. PAUL: Conservative Crisis and the Rule of Law: *Attitudes of Bar and Bench, 1887-1895. New Introduction by Author* TB/1415
JAMES S. PIKE: The Prostrate State: *South Carolina under Negro Government.* ‡ *Intro. by Robert F. Durden* TB/3085
WHITELAW REID: After the War: *A Tour of the Southern States, 1865-1866.* ‡ *Edited by C. Vann Woodward* TB/3066
FRED A. SHANNON: The Farmer's Last Frontier: *Agriculture, 1860-1897* TB/1348

2

VERNON LANE WHARTON: The Negro in Mississippi, 1865-1890   TB/1178

American Studies: The Twentieth Century

RICHARD M. ABRAMS, Ed.: The Issues of the Populist and Progressive Eras, 1892-1912 + HR/1428

RAY STANNARD BAKER: Following the Color Line: American Negro Citizenship in Progressive Era. ‡ Edited by Dewey W. Grantham, Jr. Illus.   TB/3053

RANDOLPH S. BOURNE: War and the Intellectuals: Collected Essays, 1915-1919. ‡ Edited by Carl Resek   TB/3043

A. RUSSELL BUCHANAN: The United States and World War II. † Illus.
Vol. I TB/3044; Vol. II TB/3045

THOMAS C. COCHRAN: The American Business System: A Historical Perspective, 1900-1955   TB/1080

FOSTER RHEA DULLES: America's Rise to World Power: 1898-1954. † Illus.   TB/3021

JEAN-BAPTISTE DUROSELLE: From Wilson to Roosevelt: Foreign Policy of the United States, 1913-1945. Trans. by Nancy Lyman Roelker   TB/1370

HAROLD U. FAULKNER: The Decline of Laissez Faire, 1897-1917   TB/1397

JOHN D. HICKS: Republican Ascendancy: 1921-1933. † Illus.   TB/3041

ROBERT HUNTER: Poverty: Social Conscience in the Progressive Era. ‡ Edited by Peter d'A. Jones   TB/3065

WILLIAM E. LEUCHTENBURG: Franklin D. Roosevelt and the New Deal: 1932-1940. † Illus.   TB/3025

WILLIAM E. LEUCHTENBURG, Ed.: The New Deal: A Documentary History +   HR/1354

ARTHUR S. LINK: Woodrow Wilson and the Progressive Era: 1910-1917. † Illus. TB/3023

BROADUS MITCHELL: Depression Decade: From New Era through New Deal, 1929-1941 ^   TB/1439

GEORGE E. MOWRY: The Era of Theodore Roosevelt and the Birth of Modern America: 1900-1912. † Illus.   TB/3022

WILLIAM PRESTON, JR.: Aliens and Dissenters: Federal Suppression of Radicals, 1903-1933   TB/1287

WALTER RAUSCHENBUSCH: Christianity and the Social Crisis. ‡ Edited by Robert D. Cross   TB/3059

GEORGE SOULE: Prosperity Decade: From War to Depression, 1917-1929 ^   TB/1349

GEORGE B. TINDALL, Ed.: A Populist Reader: Selections from the Works of American Populist Leaders   TB/3069

TWELVE SOUTHERNERS: I'll Take My Stand: The South and the Agrarian Tradition. Intro. by Louis D. Rubin, Jr.; Biographical Essays by Virginia Rock   TB/1072

Art, Art History, Aesthetics

CREIGHTON GILBERT, Ed.: Renaissance Art ** Illus.   TB/1465

EMILE MALE: The Gothic Image: Religious Art in France of the Thirteenth Century. § 190 illus.   TB/344

MILLARD MEISS: Painting in Florence and Siena After the Black Death: The Arts, Religion and Society in the Mid-Fourteenth Century. 169 illus.   TB/1148

ERWIN PANOFSKY: Renaissance and Renascences in Western Art. Illus.   TB/1447

ERWIN PANOFSKY: Studies in Iconology: Humanistic Themes in the Art of the Renaissance. 180 illus.   TB/1077

JEAN SEZNEC: The Survival of the Pagan Gods: The Mythological Tradition and Its Place in Renaissance Humanism and Art. 108 illus.   TB/2004

OTTO VON SIMSON: The Gothic Cathedral: Origins of Gothic Architecture and the Medieval Concept of Order. 58 illus.   TB/2018

HEINRICH ZIMMER: Myths and Symbols in Indian Art and Civilization. 70 illus.   TB/2005

Asian Studies

WOLFGANG FRANKE: China and the West: The Cultural Encounter, 13th to 20th Centuries. Trans. by R. A. Wilson   TB/1326

L. CARRINGTON GOODRICH: A Short History of the Chinese People. Illus.   TB/3015

DAN N. JACOBS, Ed.: The New Communist Manifesto and Related Documents. 3rd revised edn.   TB/1078

DAN N. JACOBS & HANS H. BAERWALD, Eds.: Chinese Communism: Selected Documents   TB/3031

BENJAMIN I. SCHWARTZ: Chinese Communism and the Rise of Mao   TB/1308

BENJAMIN I. SCHWARTZ: In Search of Wealth and Power: Yen Fu and the West   TB/1422

Economics & Economic History

C. E. BLACK: The Dynamics of Modernization: A Study in Comparative History TB/1321

STUART BRUCHEY: The Roots of American Economic Growth, 1607-1861: An Essay in Social Causation. New Introduction by the Author.   TB/1350

GILBERT BURCK & EDITORS OF Fortune: The Computer Age: And its Potential for Management   TB/1179

JOHN ELLIOTT CAIRNES: The Slave Power. ‡ Edited with Introduction by Harold D. Woodman   TB/1433

SHEPARD B. CLOUGH, THOMAS MOODIE & CAROL MOODIE, Eds.: Economic History of Europe: Twentieth Century #   HR/1388

THOMAS C. COCHRAN: The American Business System: A Historical Perspective, 1900-1955   TB/1180

ROBERT A. DAHL & CHARLES E. LINDBLOM: Politics, Economics, and Welfare: Planning and Politico-Economic Systems Resolved into Basic Social Processes   TB/3037

PETER F. DRUCKER: The New Society: The Anatomy of Industrial Order   TB/1082

HAROLD U. FAULKNER: The Decline of Laissez Faire, 1897-1917 ^   TB/1397

PAUL W. GATES: The Farmer's Age: Agriculture, 1815-1860 ^   TB/1398

WILLIAM GREENLEAF, Ed.: American Economic Development Since 1860 +   HR/1353

J. L. & BARBARA HAMMOND: The Rise of Modern Industry. || Introduction by R. M. Hartwell   TB/1417

ROBERT L. HEILBRONER: The Future as History: The Historic Currents of Our Time and the Direction in Which They Are Taking America   TB/1386

ROBERT L. HEILBRONER: The Great Ascent: The Struggle for Economic Development in Our Time   TB/3030

FRANK H. KNIGHT: The Economic Organization   TB/1214

DAVID S. LANDES: Bankers and Pashas: International Finance and Economic Imperialism in Egypt. New Preface by the Author TB/1412

ROBERT LATOUCHE: The Birth of Western Economy: Economic Aspects of the Dark Ages   TB/1290

W. ARTHUR LEWIS: Economic Survey, 1919-1939
TB/1446
W. ARTHUR LEWIS: The Principles of Economic Planning. *New Introduction by the Author*°
TB/1436
ROBERT GREEN MC CLOSKEY: American Conservatism in the Age of Enterprise   TB/1137
PAUL MANTOUX: The Industrial Revolution in the Eighteenth Century: *An Outline of the Beginnings of the Modern Factory System in England*°   TB/1079
WILLIAM MILLER, Ed.: Men in Business: *Essays on the Historical Role of the Entrepreneur*
TB/1081
GUNNAR MYRDAL: An International Economy. *New Introduction by the Author*   TB/1445
RICHARD S. WECKSTEIN, Ed.: Expansion of World Trade and the Growth of National Economies **   TB/1373

Historiography and History of Ideas

HERSCHEL BAKER: The Image of Man: *A Study of the Idea of Human Dignity in Classical Antiquity, the Middle Ages, and the Renaissance*   TB/1047
J. BRONOWSKI & BRUCE MAZLISH: The Western Intellectual Tradition: *From Leonardo to Hegel*   TB/3001
EDMUND BURKE: On Revolution. Ed. by Robert A. Smith   TB/1401
WILHELM DILTHEY: Pattern and Meaning in History: *Thoughts on History and Society.*° *Edited with an Intro. by H. P. Rickman.*
TB/1075
ALEXANDER GRAY: The Socialist Tradition: *Moses to Lenin* °   TB/1375
J. H. HEXTER: More's Utopia: *The Biography of an Idea. Epilogue by the Author*   TB/1195
H. STUART HUGHES: History as Art and as Science: *Twin Vistas on the Past*   TB/1207
ARTHUR O. LOVEJOY: The Great Chain of Being: *A Study of the History of an Idea* TB/1009
JOSE ORTEGA Y GASSET: The Modern Theme. *Introduction by Jose Ferrater Mora* TB/1038
RICHARD H. POPKIN: The History of Scepticism from Erasmus to Descartes. *Revised Edition*
TB/1391
G. J. RENIER: History: *Its Purpose and Method*
TB/1209
MASSIMO SALVADORI, Ed.: Modern Socialism #
HR/1374
BRUNO SNELL: The Discovery of the Mind: *The Greek Origins of European Thought* TB/1018
W. WARREN WAGER, ed.: European Intellectual History Since Darwin and Marx   TB/1297
W. H. WALSH: Philosophy of History: *In Introduction*   TB/1020

History: General

HANS KOHN: The Age of Nationalism: *The First Era of Global History*   TB/1380
BERNARD LEWIS: The Arabs in History TB/1029
BERNARD LEWIS: The Middle East and the West °   TB/1274

History: Ancient

A. ANDREWS: The Greek Tyrants   TB/1103
ERNST LUDWIG EHRLICH: A Concise History of Israel: *From the Earliest Times to the Destruction of the Temple in A.D. 70*°   TB/128

THEODOR H. GASTER: Thespis: *Ritual Myth and Drama in the Ancient Near East*   TB/1281
MICHAEL GRANT: Ancient History °   TB/1190
A. H. M. JONES, Ed.: A History of Rome through the Fifgth Century # *Vol. I: The Republic*   HR/1364
Vol. II The Empire: HR/1460
SAMUEL NOAH KRAMER: Sumerian Mythology
TB/1055
NAPHTALI LEWIS & MEYER REINHOLD, Eds.: Roman Civilization *Vol. I: The Republic*
TB/1231
Vol. II: The Empire   TB/1232

History: Medieval

MARSHALL W. BALDWIN, Ed.: Christianity Through the 13th Century #   HR/1468
MARC BLOCH: Land and Work in Medieval Europe. *Translated by J. E. Anderson*
TB/1452
HELEN CAM: England Before Elizabeth TB/1026
NORMAN COHN: The Pursuit of the Millennium: *Revolutionary Messianism in Medieval and Reformation Europe*   TB/1037
G. G. COULTON: Medieval Village, Manor, and Monastery   HR/1022
HEINRICH FICHTENAU: The Carolingian Empire: *The Age of Charlemagne. Translated with an Introduction by Peter Munz*   TB/1142
GALBERT OF BRUGES: The Murder of Charles the Good: *A Contemporary Record of Revolutionary Change in 12th Century Flanders. Translated with an Introduction by James Bruce Ross*   TB/1311
F. L. GANSHOF: Feudalism   TB/1058
F. L. GANSHOF: The Middle Ages: *A History of International Relations. Translated by Rémy Hall*   TB/1411
DENYS HAY: The Medieval Centuries °   TB/1192
DAVID HERLIHY, Ed.: Medieval Culture and Society #   HR/1340
J. M. HUSSEY: The Byzantine World   TB/1057
ROBERT LATOUCHE: The Birth of Western Economy: *Economic Aspects of the Dark Ages* °
TB/1290
HENRY CHARLES LEA: The Inquisition of the Middle Ages. || *Introduction by Walter Ullmann*   TB/1456
FERDINARD LOT: The End of the Ancient World and the Beginnings of the Middle Ages. *Introduction by Glanville Downey*   TB/1044
H. R. LOYN: The Norman Conquest   TB/1457
GUIBERT DE NOGENT: Self and Society in Medieval France: *The Memoirs of Guilbert de Nogent.* || *Edited by John F. Benton* TB/1471
MARSILIUS OF PADUA: The Defender of Peace. *The* Defensor Pacis. *Translated with an Introduction by Alan Gewirth*   TB/1310
CHARLES PETIT-DUTAILLIS: The Feudal Monarchy in France and England: *From the Tenth to the Thirteenth Century* °   TB/1165
STEVEN RUNCIMAN: A History of the Crusades Vol. I: *The First Crusade and the Foundation of the Kingdom of Jerusalem. Illus.*
TB/1143
Vol. II: *The Kingdom of Jerusalem and the Frankish East 1100-1187. Illus.*   TB/1243
Vol. III: *The Kingdom of Acre and the Later Crusades. Illus.*   TB/1298
J. M. WALLACE-HADRILL: The Barbarian West: *The Early Middle Ages, A.D. 400-1000*
TB/1061

JACOB BURCKHARDT: The Civilization of the Renaissance in Italy. *Introduction by Benjamin Nelson and Charles Trinkaus. Illus.* Vol. I TB/40; Vol. II TB/41

JOHN CALVIN & JACOPO SADOLETO: A Reformation Debate. *Edited by John C. Olin* TB/1239

FEDERICO CHABOD: Machiavelli and the Renaissance TB/1193

THOMAS CROMWELL: Thomas Cromwell. *Selected Letters on Church and Commonwealth, 1523-1540. ¶ Ed. with an Intro. by Arthur J. Slavin* TB/1462

R. TREVOR DAVIES: The Golden Century of Spain, 1501-1621 ° TB/1194

J. H. ELLIOTT: Europe Divided, 1559-1598 *a* °

G. R. ELTON: Reformation Europe, 1517-1559 ° *a* TB/1270

DESIDERIUS ERASMUS: Christian Humanism and the Reformation: *Selected Writings. Edited and Translated by John C. Olin* TB/1166

DESIDERIUS ERASMUS: Erasmus and His Age: *Selected Letters. Edited with an Introduction by Hans J. Hillerbrand. Translated by Marcus A. Haworth* TB/1461

WALLACE K. FERGUSON et al.: Facets of the Renaissance TB/1098

WALLACE K. FERGUSON et al.: The Renaissance: *Six Essays. Illus.* TB/1084

FRANCESCO GUICCIARDINI: History of Florence. *Translated with an Introduction and Notes by Mario Domandi* TB/1470

WERNER L. GUNDERSHEIMER, Ed.: French Humanism, 1470-1600. * *Illus.* TB/1473

MARIE BOAS HALL, Ed.: Nature and Nature's Laws: *Documents of the Scientific Revolution #* HR/1420

HANS J. HILLERBRAND, Ed., The Protestant Reformation HR/1342

JOHAN HUIZINGA: Erasmus and the Age of Reformation. *Illus.* TB/19

JOEL HURSTFIELD: The Elizabethan Nation TB/1312

JOEL HURSTFIELD, Ed.: The Reformation Crisis TB/1267

PAUL OSKAR KRISTELLER: Renaissance Thought: *The Classic, Scholastic, and Humanist Strains* TB/1048

PAUL OSKAR KRISTELLER: Renaissance Thought II: *Papers on Humanism and the Arts* TB/1163

PAUL O. KRISTELLER & PHILIP P. WIENER, Eds.: Renaissance Essays TB/1392

DAVID LITTLE: Religion, Order and Law: *A Study in Pre-Revolutionary England. § Preface by R. Bellah* TB/1418

NICCOLO MACHIAVELLI: History of Florence and of the Affairs of Italy: *From the Earliest Times to the Death of Lorenzo the Magnificent. Introduction by Felix Gilbert* TB/1027

ALFRED VON MARTIN: Sociology of the Renaissance. ° *Introduction by W. K. Ferguson* TB/1099

GARRETT MATTINGLY et al.: Renaissance Profiles. *Edited by J. H. Plumb* TB/1162

J. E. NEALE: The Age of Catherine de Medici ° TB/1085

J. H. PARRY: The Establishment of the European Hegemony: 1415-1715: *Trade and Exploration in the Age of the Renaissance* TB/1045

J. H. PARRY, Ed.: The European Reconnaissance: *Selected Documents #* HR/1345

BUONACCORSO PITTI & GREGORIO DATI: Two Memoirs of Renaissance Florence: *The Diaries of Buonaccorso Pitti and Gregorio Dati. Edited with an Intro. by Gene Brucker. Trans. by Julia Martines* TB/1333

J. H. PLUMB: The Italian Renaissance: *A Concise Survey of Its History and Culture* TB/1161

A. F. POLLARD: Henry VIII. *Introduction by A. G. Dickens.* ° TB/1249

RICHARD H. POPKIN: The History of Scepticism from Erasmus to Descartes TB/1391

PAOLO ROSSI: Philosophy, Technology, and the Arts, in the Early Modern Era 1400-1700. ‖ *Edited by Benjamin Nelson. Translated by Salvator Attanasio* TB/1458

FERDINAND SCHEVILL: The Medici. *Illus.* TB/1010

FERDINAND SCHEVILL: Medieval and Renaissance Florence. *Illus. Vol. I: Medieval Florence* TB/1090

Vol. II: The Coming of Humanism and the Age of the Medici TB/1091

R. H. TAWNEY: The Agrarian Problem in the Sixteenth Century. *Intro. by Lawrence Stone* TB/1315

H. R. TREVOR-ROPER: The European Witch-craze of the Sixteenth and Seventeenth Centuries and Other Essays ° TB/1416

VESPASIANO: Rennaissance Princes, Popes, and XVth Century: *The Vespasiano Memoirs. Introduction by Myron P. Gilmore. Illus.* TB/1111

RENE ALBRECHT-CARRIE, Ed.: The Concert of Europe # HR/1341

MAX BELOFF: The Age of Absolutism, 1660-1815 TB/1062

OTTO VON BISMARCK: Reflections and Reminiscences. *Ed. with Intro. by Theodore S. Hamerow ¶* TB/1357

EUGENE C. BLACK, Ed.: British Politics in the Nineteenth Century # HR/1427

EUGENE C. BLACK, Ed.: European Political History, 1815-1870: *Aspects of Liberalism ¶* TB/1331

ASA BRIGGS: The Making of Modern England, 1783-1867: *The Age of Improvement* ° TB/1203

ALAN BULLOCK: Hitler, A Study in Tyranny. ° *Revised Edition. Illus.* TB/1123

EDMUND BURKE: On Revolution. *Ed. by Robert A. Smith* TB/1401

E. R. CARR: International Relations Between the Two World Wars. 1919-1939 ° TB/1279

E. H. CARR: The Twenty Years' Crisis, 1919-1939: *An Introduction to the Study of International Relations* ° TB/1122

GORDON A. CRAIG: From Bismarck to Adenauer: *Aspects of German Statecraft. Revised Edition* TB/1171

LESTER G. CROCKER, Ed.: The Age of Enlightenment # HR/1423

DENIS DIDEROT: The Encyclopedia: *Selections. Edited and Translated with Introduction by Stephen Gendzier* TB/1299

JACQUES DROZ: Europe between Revolutions, 1815-1848. ° *a Trans. by Robert Baldick* TB/1346

JOHANN GOTTLIEB FICHTE: Addresses to the German Nation. *Ed. with Intro. by George A. Kelly ¶* TB/1366

ROBERT & ELBORG FORSTER, Eds.: European Society in the Eighteenth Century # HR/1404

C. C. GILLISPIE: Genesis and Geology: *The Decades before Darwin §* TB/51

ALBERT GOODWIN, Ed.: The European Nobility in the Enghteenth Century TB/1313
ALBERT GOODWIN: The French Revolution TB/1064
ALBERT GUERARD: France in the Classical Age: The Life and Death of an Ideal TB/1183
JOHN B. HALSTED, Ed.: Romanticism # HR/1387
J. H. HEXTER: Reappraisals in History: New Views on History and Society in Early Modern Europe ° TB/1100
STANLEY HOFFMANN et al.: In Search of France: The Economy, Society and Political System In the Twentieth Century TB/1219
H. STUART HUGHES: The Obstructed Path: French Social Thought in the Years of Desperation TB/1451
JOHAN HUIZINGA: Dutch Civilisation in the 17th Century and Other Essays TB/1453
LIONAL KOCHAN: The Struggle for Germany: 1914-45 TB/1304
HANS KOHN: The Mind of Germany: The Education of a Nation TB/1204
HANS KOHN, Ed.: The Mind of Modern Russia: Historical and Political Thought of Russia's Great Age TB/1065
WALTER LAQUEUR & GEORGE L. MOSSE, Eds.: Education and Social Structure in the 20th Century. ° Volume 6 of the Journal of Contemporary History TB/1339
WALTER LAQUEUR & GEORGE L. MOSSE, Ed.: International Fascism, 1920-1945. ° Volume 1 of the Journal of Contemporary History TB/1276
WALTER LAQUEUR & GEORGE L. MOSSE, Eds.: Literature and Politics in the 20th Century. ° Volume 5 of the Journal of Contemporary History. TB/1328
WALTER LAQUEUR & GEORGE L. MOSSE, Eds.: The New History: Trends in Historical Research and Writing Since World War II. ° Volume 4 of the Journal of Contemporary History TB/1327
WALTER LAQUEUR & GEORGE L. MOSSE, Eds.: 1914: The Coming of the First World War. ° Volume3 of the Journal of Contemporary History TB/1306
C. A. MACARTNEY, Ed.: The Habsburg and Hohenzollern Dynasties in the Seventeenth and Eighteenth Centuries # HR/1400
JOHN MCMANNERS: European History, 1789-1914: Men, Machines and Freedom TB/1419
PAUL MANTOUX: The Industrial Revolution in the Eighteenth Century: An Outline of the Beginnings of the Modern Factory System in England TB/1079
FRANK E. MANUEL: The Prophets of Paris: Turgot, Condorcet, Saint-Simon, Fourier, and Comte TB/1218
KINGSLEY MARTIN: French Liberal Thought in the Eighteenth Century: A Study of Political Ideas from Bayle to Condorcet TB/1114
NAPOLEON III: Napoleonic Ideas: Des Idées Napoléoniennes, par le Prince Napoléon-Louis Bonaparte. Ed. by Brison D. Gooch ¶ TB/1336
FRANZ NEUMANN: Behemoth: The Structure and Practice of National Socialism, 1933-1944 TB/1289
DAVID OGG: Europe of the Ancien Régime, 1715-1783 ° a TB/1271
GEORGE RUDE: Revolutionary Europe, 1783-1815 ° a TB/1272
MASSIMO SALVADORI, Ed.: Modern Socialism # TB/1374
HUGH SETON-WATSON: Eastern Europe Between the Wars, 1918-1941 TB/1330

DENIS MACK SMITH, Ed.: The Making of Italy, 1796-1870 # HR/1356
ALBERT SOREL: Europe Under the Old Regime. Translated by Francis H. Herrick TB/1121
ROLAND N. STROMBERG, Ed.: Realism, Naturalism, and Symbolism: Modes of Thought and Expression in Europe, 1848-1914 # HR/1355
A. J. P. TAYLOR: From Napoleon to Lenin: Historical Essays ° TB/1268
A. J. P. TAYLOR: The Habsburg Monarchy, 1809-1918: A History of the Austrian Empire and Austria-Hungary ° TB/1187
J. M. THOMPSON: European History, 1494-1789 TB/1431
DAVID THOMSON, Ed.: France: Empire and Republic, 1850-1940 # HR/1387
ALEXIS DE TOCQUEVILLE & GUSTAVE DE BEAUMONT: Tocqueville and Beaumont on Social Reform. Ed. and trans. with Intro. by Seymour Drescher TB/1343
G. M. TREVELYAN: British History in the Nineteenth Century and After: 1792-1919 ° TB/1251
H. R. TREVOR-ROPER: Historical Essays TB/1269
W. WARREN WAGAR, Ed.: Science, Faith, and MAN: European Thought Since 1914 # HR/1362
MACK WALKER, Ed.: Metternich's Europe, 1813-1848 # HR/1361
ELIZABETH WISKEMANN: Europe of the Dictators, 1919-1945 ° a TB/1273
JOHN B. WOLF: France: 1814-1919: The Rise of a Liberal-Democratic Society TB/3019

Literature & Literary Criticism

JACQUES BARZUN: The House of Intellect TB/1051
W. J. BATE: From Classic to Romantic: Premises of Taste in Eighteenth Century England TB/1036
VAN WYCK BROOKS: Van Wyck Brooks: The Early Years: A Selection from his Works, 1908-1921 Ed. with Intro. by Claire Sprague TB/3082
ERNST R. CURTIUS: European Literature and the Latin Middle Ages. Trans. by Willard Trask TB/2015
RICHMOND LATTIMORE, Translator: The Odyssey of Homer TB/1389
SAMUEL PEPYS: The Diary of Samual Pepys. ° Edited by O. F. Morshead. 60 illus. by Ernest Shepard TB/1007
ROBERT PREYER, Ed.: Victorian Literature ** TB/1302
ALBION W. TOURGEE: A Fool's Errand: A Novel of the South during Reconstruction. Intro. by George Fredrickson TB/3074
BASIL WILEY: Nineteenth Century Studies: Coleridge to Matthew Arnold ° TB/1261

Philosophy

HENRI BERGSON: Time and Free Will: An Essay on the Immediate Data of Consciousness ° TB/1021
LUDWIG BINSWANGER: Being-in-the-World: Selected Papers. Trans. with Intro. by Jacob Needleman TB/1365
H. J. BLACKHAM: Six Existentialist Thinkers: Kierkegaard, Nietzsche, Jaspers, Marcel, Heidegger, Sartre ° TB/1002
J. M. BOCHENSKI: The Methods of Contemporary Thought. Trans. by Peter Caws TB/1377
CRANE BRINTON: Nietzsche. Preface, Bibliography, and Epilogue by the Author TB/1197

ERNST CASSIRER: Rousseau, Kant and Goethe. *Intro. by Peter Gay* TB/1092
FREDERICK COPLESTON, S. J.: Medieval Philosophy TB/376
F. M. CORNFORD: From Religion to Philosophy: *A Study in the Origins of Western Speculation §* TB/20
WILFRID DESAN: The Tragic Finale: *An Essay on the Philosophy of Jean-Paul Sartre* TB/1030
MARVIN FARBER: The Aims of Phenomenology: *The Motives, Methods, and Impact of Husserl's Thought* TB/1291
MARVIN FARBER: Basic Issues of Philosophy: *Experience, Reality, and Human Values* TB/1344
MARVIN FARBERS: Phenomenology and Existence: *Towards a Philosophy within Nature* TB/1295
PAUL FRIEDLANDER: Plato: *An Introduction* TB/2017
MICHAEL GELVEN: A Commentary on Heidegger's "Being and Time" TB/1464
J. GLENN GRAY: Hegel and Greek Thought TB/1409
W. K. C. GUTHRIE: The Greek Philosophers: *From Thales to Aristotle °* TB/1008
G. W. F. HEGEL: On Art, Religion Philosophy: *Introductory Lectures to the Realm of Absolute Spirit. || Edited with an Introduction by J. Glenn Gray* TB/1463
G. W. F. HEGEL: Phenomenology of Mind. ° || *Introduction by George Lichtheim* TB/1303
MARTIN HEIDEGGER: Discourse on Thinking. *Translated with a Preface by John M. Anderson and E. Hans Freund. Introduction by John M. Anderson* TB/1459
F. H. HEINEMANN: Existentialism and the Modern Predicament TB/28
WERER HEISENBERG: Physics and Philosophy: *The Revolution in Modern Science. Intro. by F. S. C. Northrop* TB/549
EDMUND HUSSERL: Phenomenology and the Crisis of Philosophy. *§ Translated with an Introduction by Quentin Lauer* TB/1170
IMMANUEL KANT: Groundwork of the Metaphysic of Morals. *Translated and Analyzed by H. J. Paton* TB/1159
IMMANUEL KANT: Lectures on Ethics. *§ Introduction by Lewis White Beck* TB/105
WALTER KAUFMANN, Ed.: Religion From Tolstoy to Camus: *Basic Writings on Religious Truth and Morals* TB/123
QUENTIN LAUER: Phenomenology: *Its Genesis and Prospect. Preface by Aron Gurwitsch* TB/1169
MAURICE MANDELBAUM: The Problem of Historical Knowledge: *An Answer to Relativism* TB/1198
H. J. PATON: The Categorical Imperative: *A Study in Kant's Moral Philosophy* TB/1325
MICHAEL POLANYI: Personal Knowledge: *Towards a Post-Critical Philosophy* TB/1158
KARL R. POPPER: Conjectures and Refutations: *The Growth of Scientific Knowledge* TB/1376
WILLARD VAN ORMAN QUINE: Elementary Logic *Revised Edition* TB/577
WILLARD VAN ORMAN QUINE: From a Logical Point of View: *Logico-Philosophical Essays* TB/566
JOHN E. SMITH: Themes in American Philosophy: *Purpose, Experience and Community* TB/1466
MORTON WHITE: Foundations of Historical Knowledge TB/1440
WILHELM WINDELBAND: A History of Philosophy *Vol. I: Greek, Roman, Medieval* TB/38 *Vol. II: Renaissance, Enlightenment, Modern* TB/39

LUDWIG WITTGENSTEIN: The Blue and Brown Books ° TB/1211
LUDWIG WITTGENSTEIN: Notebooks, 1914-1916 TB/1441

Political Science & Government

C. E. BLACK: The Dynamics of Modernization: *A Study in Comparative History* TB/1321
DENIS W. BROGAN: Politics in America. *New Introduction by the Author* TB/1469
CRANE BRINTON: English Political Thought in the Nineteenth Century TB/1071
ROBERT CONQUEST: Power and Policy in the USSR: *The Study of Soviet Dynastics °* TB/1307
ROBERT A. DAHL & CHARLES E. LINDBLOM: Politics, Economics, and Welfare: *Planning and Politico-Economic Systems Resolved into Basic Social Processes* TB/1277
HANS KOHN: Political Ideologies of the 20th Century TB/1277
ROY C. MACRIDIS, Ed.: Political Parties: *Contemporary Trends and Ideas ** * TB/1322
ROBERT GREEN MC CLOSKEY: American Conservatism in the Age of Enterprise, 1865-1910 TB/1137
MARSILIUS OF PADUA: The Defender of Peace. *The Defensor Pacis. Translated with an Introduction by Alan Gewirth* TB/1310
KINGSLEY MARTIN: French Liberal Thought in the Eighteenth Century: *A Study of Political Ideas from Bayle to Condorcet* TB/1114
BARRINGTON MOORE, JR.: Political Power and Social Theory: *Seven Studies ||* TB/1221
BARRINGTON MOORE, JR.: Soviet Politics—The Dilemma of Power: *The Role of Ideas in Social Change ||* TB/1222
BARRINGTON MOORE, JR.: Terror and Progress—USSR: *Some Sources of Change and Stability* TB/1266
JOHN B. MORRALL: Political Thought in Medieval Times TB/1076
KARL R. POPPER: The Open Society and Its Enemies *Vol. I: The Spell of Plato* TB/1101 *Vol. II: The High Tide of Prophecy: Hegel, Marx, and the Aftermath* TB/1102
CONYERS READ, Ed.: The Constitution Reconsidered. *Revised Edition, Preface by Richard B. Morris* TB/1384
JOHN P. ROCHE, Ed.: Origins of American Political Thought: *Selected Readings* TB/1301
JOHN P. ROCHE, Ed.: American Political Thought: *From Jefferson to Progressivism* TB/1332
HENRI DE SAINT-SIMON: Social Organization, The Science of Man, and Other Writings. || *Edited and Translated with an Introduction by Felix Markham* TB/1152
CHARLES SCHOTTLAND, Ed.: The Welfare State ** TB/1323
JOSEPH A. SCHUMPETER: Capitalism, Socialism and Democracy TB/3008

Psychology

ALFRED ADLER: The Individual Psychology of Alfred Adler: *A Systematic Presentation in Selections from His Writings. Edited by Heinz L. & Rowena R. Ansbacher* TB/1154
LUDWIG BINSWANGER: Being-in-the-World: *Selected Papers. || Trans. with Intro. by Jacob Needleman* TB/1365
HADLEY CANTRIL: The Invasion from Mars: *A Study in the Psychology of Panic ||* TB/1282
MIRCEA ELIADE: Cosmos and History: *The Myth of the Eternal Return §* TB/2050
MIRCEA ELIADE: Myth and Reality TB/1369

MIRCEA ELIADE: Myths, Dreams and Mysteries: *The Encounter Between Contemporary Faiths and Archaic Realities* § TB/1320
MIRCEA ELIADE: Rites and Symbols of Initiation: *The Mysteries of Birth and Rebirth* § TB/1236
HERBERT FINGARETTE: The Self in Transformation: *Psychoanalysis, Philosophy and the Life of the Spirit* || TB/1177
SIGMUND FREUD: On Creativity and the Unconscious: *Papers on the Psychology of Art, Literature, Love, Religion.* § *Intro. by Benjamin Nelson* TB/45
J. GLENN GRAY: The Warriors: *Reflections on Men in Battle. Introduction by Hannah Arendt* TB/1294
WILLIAM JAMES: Psychology: *The Briefer Course. Edited with an Intro. by Gordon Allport* TB/1034
C. G. JUNG: Psychological Reflections. *Ed. by J. Jacobi* TB/2001
KARL MENNINGER, M.D.: Theory of Psychoanalytic Technique TB/1144
JOHN H. SCHAAR: Escape from Authority: *The Perspectives of Erich Fromm* TB/1155
MUZAFER SHERIF: The Psychology of Social Norms. *Introduction by Gardner Murphy* TB/3072
HELLMUT WILHELM: Change: *Eight Lectures on the I Ching* TB/2019

Religion: Ancient and Classical, Biblical and Judaic Traditions

W. F. ALBRIGHT: The Biblical Period from Abraham to Ezra TB/102
SALO W. BARON: Modern Nationalism and Religion TB/818
C. K. BARRETT, Ed.: The New Testament Background: *Selected Documents* TB/86
MARTIN BUBER: Eclipse of God: *Studies in the Relation Between Religion and Philosophy* TB/12
MARTIN BUBER: Hasidism and Modern Man. *Edited and Translated by Maurice Friedman* TB/839
MARTIN BUBER: The Knowledge of Man. *Edited with an Introduction by Maurice Friedman. Translated by Maurice Friedman and Ronald Gregor Smith* TB/135
MARTIN BUBER: Moses. *The Revelation and the Covenant* TB/837
MARTIN BUBER: The Origin and Meaning of Hasidism. *Edited and Translated by Maurice Friedman* TB/835
MARTIN BUBER: The Prophetic Faith TB/73
MARTIN BUBER: Two Types of Faith: *Interpenetration of Judaism and Christianity* ° TB/75
MALCOLM L. DIAMOND: Martin Buber: *Jewish Existentialist* TB/840
M. S. ENSLIN: Christian Beginnings TB/5
M. S. ENSLIN: The Literature of the Christian Movement TB/6
ERNST LUDWIG EHRLICH: A Concise History of Israel: *From the Earliest Times to the Destruction of the Temple in A.D. 70* ° TB/128
HENRI FRANKFORT: Ancient Egyptian Religion: *An Interpretation* TB/77
ABRAHAM HESCHEL: The Earth Is the Lord's & The Sabbath. *Two Essays* TB/828
ABRAHAM HESCHEL: God in Search of Man: *A Philosophy of Judaism* TB/807
ABRAHAM HESCHEL: Man Is not Alone: *A Philosophy of Religion* TB/838
ABRAHAM HESCHEL: The Prophets: *An Introduction* TB/1421

T. J. MEEK: Hebrew Origins TB/69
JAMES MUILENBURG: The Way of Israel: *Biblical Faith and Ethics* TB/133
H. J. ROSE: Religion in Greece and Rome TB/55
H. H. ROWLEY: The Growth of the Old Testament TB/107
D. WINTON THOMAS, Ed.: Documents from Old Testament Times TB/85

Religion: General Christianity

ROLAND H. BAINTON: Christendom: *A Short History of Christianity and Its Impact on Western Civilization. Illus.* Vol. I TB/131; Vol. II TB/132
JOHN T. MCNEILL: Modern Christian Movements. *Revised Edition* TB/1402
ERNST TROELTSCH: The Social Teaching of the Christian Churches. *Intro. by H. Richard Niebuhr* Vol. TB/71; Vol. II TB/72

Religion: Early Christianity Through Reformation

ANSELM OF CANTERBURY: Truth, Freedom, and Evil: *Three Philosophical Dialogues. Edited and Translated by Jasper Hopkins and Herbert Richardson* TB/317
MARSHALL W. BALDWIN, Ed.: Christianity through the 13th Century # HR/1468
W. D. DAVIES: Paul and Rabbinic Judaism: *Some Rabbinic Elements in Pauline Theology. Revised Edition* ° TB/146
ADOLF DEISSMAN: Paul: *A Study in Social and Religious History* TB/15
JOHANNES ECKHART: Meister Eckhart: *A Modern Translation by R. Blakney* TB/8
EDGAR J. GOODSPEED: A Life of Jesus TB/1
ROBERT M. GRANT: Gnosticism and Early Christianity TB/136
WILLIAM HALLER: The Rise of Puritanism TB/22
GERHART B. LADNER: The Idea of Reform: *Its Impact on the Christian Thought and Action in the Age of the Fathers* TB/149
ARTHUR DARBY NOCK: Early Gentile Christianity and Its Hellenistic Background TB/111
ARTHUR DARBY NOCK: St. Paul ° TR/104
GORDON RUPP: Luther's Progress to the Diet of Worms ° TB/120

Religion: The Protestant Tradition

KARL BARTH: Church Dogmatics: *A Selection. Intro. by H. Gollwitzer. Ed. by G. W. Bromiley* TB/95
KARL BARTH: Dogmatics in Outline TB/56
KARL BARTH: The Word of God and the Word of Man TB/13
HERBERT BRAUN, et al.: God and Christ: *Existence and Province. Volume 5 of Journal for Theology and the Church, edited by Robert W. Funk and Gerhard Ebeling* TB/255
WHITNEY R. CROSS: The Burned-Over District: *The Social and Intellectual History of Enthusiastic Religion in Western New York, 1800-1850* TB/1242
NELS F. S. FERRE: Swedish Contributions to Modern Theology. *New Chapter by William A. Johnson* TB/147
WILLIAM R. HUTCHISON, Ed.: American Protestant Thought: *The Liberal Era* ‡ TB/1385
ERNST KASEMANN, et al.: Distinctive Protestant and Catholic Themes Reconsidered. *Volume 3 of Journal for Theology and the Church,*

8

edited by Robert W. Funk and Gerhard
Ebeling   TB/253
SOREN KIERKEGAARD: On Authority and Revela-
tion: *The Book on Adler, or a Cycle of
Ethico-Religious Essays. Introduction by F.
Sontag*   TB/139
SOREN KIERKEGAARD: Crisis in the Life of an
Actress, *and Other Essays on Drama. Trans-
lated with an Introduction by Stephen Crites*
                                          TB/145
SOREN KIERKEGAARD: Edifying Discourses. *Edited
with an Intro. by Paul Holmer*   TB/32
SOREN KIERKEGAARD: The Journals of Kierke-
gaard. ° *Edited with an Intro. by Alexander
Dru*   TB/52
SOREN KIERKEGAARD: The Point of View for My
Work as an Author: *A Report to History.* §
Preface by Benjamin Nelson   TB/88
SOREN KIERKEGAARD: The Present Age. § *Trans-
lated and edited by Alexander Dru. Intro-
duction by Walter Kaufmann*   TB/94
SOREN KIERKEGAARD: Purity of Heart. *Trans. by
Douglas Steere*   TB/4
SOREN KIERKEGAARD: Repetition: *An Essay in
Experimental Psychology* §   TB/117
SOREN KIERKEGAARD: Works of Love: *Some
Christian Reflections in the Form of Dis-
courses*   TB/122
WILLIAM G. MCLOUGHLIN, Ed.: The American
Evangelicals: 1800-1900: *An Anthology*
                                          TB/1382
WOLFHART PANNENBERG, et al.: History and Her-
meneutic. *Volume 4 of Journal for Theol-
ogy and the Church, edited by Robert W.
Funk and Gerhard Ebeling*   TB/254
JAMES M. ROBINSON, et al.: The Bultmann
School of Biblical Interpretation: New Direc-
tions? *Volume 1 of Journal for Theology
and the Church, edited by Robert W. Funk
and Gerhard Ebeling*   TB/251
F. SCHLEIERMACHER: The Christian Faith. *Intro-
duction by Richard R. Niebuhr.*
                Vol. I TB/108; Vol. II TB/109
F. SCHLEIERMACHER: On Religion: *Speeches to
Its Cultured Despisers. Intro. by Rudolf
Otto*   TB/36
TIMOTHY L. SMITH: Revivalism and Social Re-
form: *American Protestantism on the Eve
of the Civil War*   TB/1229
PAUL TILLICH: Dynamics of Faith   TB/42
PAUL TILLICH: Morality and Beyond   TB/142
EVELYN UNDERHILL: Worship   TB/10

*Religion: The Roman & Eastern Christian
Traditions*

A. ROBERT CAPONIGRI, Ed.: Modern Catholic
Thinkers II: *The Church and the Political
Order*   TB/307
G. P. FEDOTOV: The Russian Religious Mind:
*Kievan Christianity, the tenth to the thir-
teenth Centuries*   TB/370
GABRIEL MARCEL: Being and Having: *An Ex-
istential Diary. Introduction by James Col-
lins*   TB/310
GABRIEL MARCEL: Homo Viator: *Introduction to
a Metaphysic of Hope*   TB/397

Religion: Oriental Religions

TOR ANDRAE: Mohammed: *The Man and His
Faith* §   TB/62

EDWARD CONZE: Buddhism: *Its Essence and De-
velopment.* ° *Foreword by Arthur Waley*
                                          TB/58
EDWARD CONZE: Buddhist Meditation TB/1442
EDWARD CONZE et al, Editors: Buddhist Texts
through the Ages   TB/113
ANANDA COOMARASWAMY: Buddha and the Gos-
pel of Buddhism   TB/119
H. G. CREEL: Confucius and the Chinese Way
                                          TB/63
FRANKLIN EDGERTON, Trans. & Ed.: The Bhaga-
vad Gita   TB/115
SWAMI NIKHILANANDA, Trans. & Ed.: The
Upanishads   TB/114
D. T. SUZUKI: On Indian Mahayana Buddhism.
° *Ed. with Intro. by Edward Conze.* TB/1403

Religion: Philosophy, Culture, and Society

NICOLAS BERDYAEV: The Destiny of Man TB/61
RUDOLF BULTMANN: History and Eschatology:
The Presence of Eternity °   TB/91
RUDOLF BULTMANN AND FIVE CRITICS: Kerygma
and Myth: *A Theological Debate*   TB/80
RUDOLF BULTMANN and KARL KUNDSIN: Form
Criticism: *Two Essays on New Testament Re-
search. Trans. by F. C. Grant*   TB/96
WILLIAM A. CLEBSCH & CHARLES R. JAEKLE: Pas-
toral Care in Historical Perspective: *An
Essay with Exhibits*   TB/148
FREDERICK FERRE: Language, Logic and God.
New Preface by the Author   TB/1407
LUDWIG FEUERBACH: The Essence of Christianity.
§ *Introduction by Karl Barth. Foreword by
H. Richard Niebuhr*   TB/11
ADOLF HARNACK: What Is Christianity? § *Intro-
duction by Rudolf Bultmann*   TB/17
KYLE HASELDEN: The Racial Problem in Chris-
tian Perspective   TB/116
MARTIN HEIDEGGER: Discourse on Thinking.
*Translated with a Preface by John M. Ander-
son and E. Hans Freund. Introduction by
John M. Anderson*   TB/1459
IMMANUEL KANT: Religion Within the Limits of
Reason Alone. § *Introduction by Theodore
M. Greene and John Silber*   TB/FG
WALTER KAUFMANN, Ed.: Religion from Tol-
stoy to Camus: *Basic Writings on Religious
Truth and Morals. Enlarged Edition* TB/123
H. RICHARD NIERUHR: Christ and Culture TB/3
H. RICHARD NIEBUHR: The Kingdom of God in
America   TB/49
ANDERS NYGREN: Agape and Eros. *Translated by
Philip S. Watson* °   TB/1430
JOHN H. RANDALL, JR.: The Meaning of Reli-
gion for Man. *Revised with New Intro. by
the Author*   TB/1379
WALTER RAUSCHENBUSCHS Christianity and the
Social Crisis. ‡ *Edited by Robert D. Cross*
                                          TB/3059

Science and Mathematics

JOHN TYLER BONNER: The Ideas of Biology. Σ
Illus.   TB/570
W. E. LE GROS CLARK: The Antecedents of
Man: *An Introduction to the Evolution of
the Primates.* ° *Illus.*   TB/559
ROBERT E. COKER: Streams, Lakes, Ponds. *Illus.*
                                          TB/586
ROBERT E. COKER: This Great and Wide Sea: *An
Introduction to Oceanography and Marine
Biology. Illus.*   TB/551
W. H. DOWDESWELL: Animal Ecology. *61 illus.*
                                          TB/543

9

C. V. DURELL: Readable Relativity. *Foreword by Freeman J. Dyson* TB/530
GEORGE GAMOW: Biography of Physics. Σ *Illus.* TB/567
F. K. HARE: The Restless Atmosphere TB/560
J. R. PIERCE: Symbols, Signals and Noise: *The Nature and Process of Communication* Σ TB/574
WILLARD VAN ORMAN QUINE: Mathematical Logic TB/558

Science: History

MARIE BOAS: The Scientific Renaissance, 1450-1630 ° TB/583
STEPHEN TOULMIN & JUNE GOODFIELD: The Architecture of Matter: *The Physics, Chemistry and Physiology of Matter, Both Animate and Inanimate, as it has Evolved since the Beginnings of Science* TB/584
STEPHEN TOULMIN & JUNE GOODFIELD: The Discovery TB/576
STEPHEN TOULMIN & JUNE GOODFIELD: The Fabric of the Heavens: *The Development of Astronomy and Dynamics* TB/579

Science: Philosophy

J. M. BOCHENSKI: The Methods of Contemporary Thought. *Tr. by Peter Caws* TB/1377
J. BRONOWSKI: Science and Human Values. *Revised and Enlarged. Illus.* TB/505
WERNER HEISENBERG: Physics and Philosophy: *The Revolution in Modern Science. Introduction by F. S. C. Northrop* TB/549
KARL R. POPPER: Conjectures and Refutations: *The Growth of Scientific Knowledge* TB/1376
KARL R. POPPER: The Logic of Scientific Discovery TB/1376
STEPHEN TOULMIN: Foresight and Understanding: *An Enquiry into the Aims of Science. Foreword by Jacques Barzun* TB/564
STEPHEN TOULMIN: The Philosophy of Science: *An Introduction* TB/513

Sociology and Anthropology

REINHARD BENDIX: Work and Authority in Industry: *Ideologies of Management in the Course of Industrialization* TB/3035
BERNARD BERELSON, Ed.: The Behavioral Sciences Today TB/1127
JOSEPH B. CASAGRANDE, Ed.: In the Company of Man: *Twenty Portraits of Anthropological Informants. Illus.* TB/3047
KENNETH B. CLARK: Dark Ghetto: *Dilemmas of Social Power. Foreword by Gunnar Myrdal* TB/1317
KENNETH CLARK & JEANNETTE HOPKINS: A Relevant War Against Poverty: *A Study of Community Action Programs and Observable Social Change* TB/1480
LEWIS COSER, Ed.: Political Sociology TB/1293
ROSE L. COSER, Ed.: Life Cycle and Achievement in America ** TB/1434
ALLISON DAVIS & JOHN DOLLARD: Children of Bondage: *The Personality Development of Negro Youth in the Urban South* || TB/3049
PETER F. DRUCKER: The New Society: *The Anatomy of Industrial Order* TB/1082
CORA DU BOIS: The People of Alor. *With a Preface by the Author*
　Vol. I *Illus.* TB/1042; Vol. II TB/1043
EMILE DURKHEIM et al.: Essays on Sociology and Philosophy: *with Appraisals of Durkheim's Life and Thought.* || *Edited by Kurt H. Wolff* TB/1151

LEON FESTINGER, HENRY W. RIECKEN, STANLEY SCHACHTER: When Prophecy Fails: *A Social and Psychological Study of a Modern Group that Predicted the Destruction of the World* || TB/1132
CHARLES Y. GLOCK & RODNEY STARK: Christian Beliefs and Anti-Semitism. *Introduction by the Authors* TB/1454
ALVIN W. GOULDNER: The Hellenic World TB/1479
ALVIN W. GOULDNER: Wildcat Strike: *A Study in Worker-Management Relationships* || TB/1176
CESAR GRANA: Modernity and Its Discontents: *French Society and the French Man of Letters in the Nineteenth Century* TB/1318
L. S. B. LEAKEY: Adam's Ancestors: *The Evolution of Man and His Culture. Illus.* TB/1019
KURT LEWIN: Field Theory in Social Science: *Selected Theoretical Papers.* || *Edited by Dorwin Cartwright* TB/1135
RITCHIE P. LOWRY: Who's Running This Town? *Community Leadership and Social Change* TB/1383
R. M. MACIVER: Social Causation TB/1153
GARY T. MARX: Protest and Prejudice: *A Study of Belief in the Black Community* TB/1435
ROBERT K. MERTON, LEONARD BROOM, LEONARD S. COTTRELL, JR., Editors: Sociology Today: *Problems and Prospects* ||
　Vol. I TB/1173; Vol. II TB/1174
GILBERT OSOFSKY, Ed.: The Burden of Race: *A Documentary History of Negro-White Relations in America* TB/1405
GILBERT OSOFSKY: Harlem: The Making of a Ghetto: *Negro New York 1890-1930* TB/1381
TALCOTT PARSONS & EDWARD A. SHILS, Editors: Toward a General Theory of Action: *Theoretical Foundations for the Social Sciences* TB/1083
PHILIP RIEFF: The Triumph of the Therapeutic: *Uses of Faith After Freud* TB/1360
JOHN H. ROHRER & MUNRO S. EDMONSON, Eds.: The Eighth Generation Grows Up: *Cultures and Personalities of New Orleans Negroes* || TB/3050
ARNOLD ROSE: The Negro in America: *The Condensed Version of Gunnar Myrdal's* An American Dilemma. *Second Edition* TB/3048
GEORGE ROSEN: Madness in Society: *Chapters in the Historical Sociology of Mental Illness.* || *Preface by Benjamin Nelson* TB/1337
PHILIP SELZNICK: TVA and the Grass Roots: *A Study in the Sociology of Formal Organization* TB/1230
PITIRIM A. SOROKIN: Contemporary Sociological Theories: *Through the First Quarter of the Twentieth Century* TB/3046
MAURICE R. STEIN: The Eclipse of Community: *An Interpretation of American Studies* TB/1128
EDWARD A. TIRYAKIAN, Ed.: Sociological Theory, Values and Sociocultural Change: *Essays in Honor of Pitirim A. Sorokin* ° TB/1316
FERDINAND TONNIES: Community and Society: *Gemeinschaft und Gesellschaft. Translated and Edited by Charles P. Loomis* TB/1116
SAMUEL E. WALLACE: Skid Row as a Way of Life TB/1367
W. LLOYD WARNER: Social Class in America: *The Evaluation of Status* TB/1013
FLORIAN ZNANIECKI: The Social Role of the Man of Knowledge. *Introduction by Lewis A. Coser* TB/1372